SLOW COAST HOME

A 5000-mile journey around
the shores of England and Wales

JOSIE DEW

Maps and drawings by Peter Wilson

A *Time Warner* Book

First published in Great Britain in 2003
by Time Warner Books

Copyright © Josie Dew 2003
Photographs copyright © Josie Dew 2003
Maps and drawings copyright © Peter Wilson 2003

A CIP catalogue record for this book
is available from the British Library.

ISBN 0 316 85362 3

Typeset in Baskerville by M Rules
Printed and bound in Great Britain by
Mackays of Chatham plc

Time Warner Books UK
Brettenham House
Lancaster Place
London WC2E 7EN

www.TimeWarnerBooks.co.uk
www.josiedew.co.uk

To Fred, Alex and Jake

'One meeting by chance is worth a thousand meetings by appointment.'
Arab saying

'When I see a person on a bicycle I have hope for the future of the human race.'

H.G. Wells

'… human beings are sanest and happiest when they are on the move.'
Bruce Chatwin

'Women have virtually abandoned cycling, travelling only 21 miles a year.'
Ben Webster, Transport Correspondent, *The Times*, March 14th 2003

'If lost I'd rather go around the world than turn back the way I'd come.'
Neil Peart, *The Masked Rider*

'We are a nation so prone to road rage that we see slow cyclists and pedestrians as the enemy.'
Steve Norris, Chairman of the National Cycling Strategy

Acknowledgements

A hefty portion of thanks must go to: my builder, for putting up with a lot (but please can you reroof the bike shed soon); mum and dad, for various rescuings and dry-berthed pamperings; Val Porter for getting me into this fine mess in the first place – and more importantly for endeavouring to get me out of it again by tackling my fat pile of typings; Barbara Boote, who not for the first time was expecting a book about New Zealand, but got one about a completely different place instead; Peter Wilson, for Maya and more mad, mega-doodle maps and drawings; Hilary Foakes for Isabelle; Clare Norris for coming back from New Zealand; Charles and Ben at The Sensible Bicycle Company; Simon Gershon at Orbit; Sam and Brian at Xynergy; Anja Dalton at Sustrans; Gary Boxall at Petersfield Photographic; Keith Byrne and Helen Samson at The Northface; Frank Bennett at Lyon Equipment Ltd; Chris Charlton at Oakley; Don Dennis at The Living Tree; Chas, Andrew and Brian at Rober Cycles; and Dave Pegler for filling up Arundel with five shops full of everything foldable and packable and wickable.

Other people to whom I'm very grateful have the dubious distinction of being mentioned within.

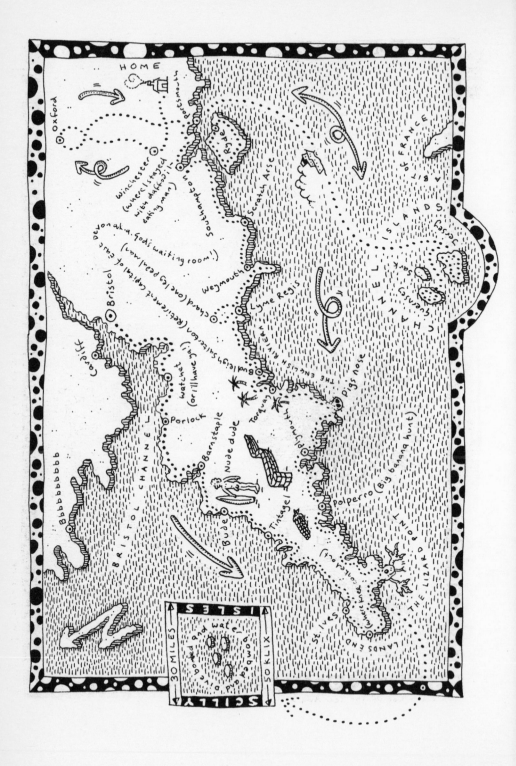

B+B

Big + Bash + Busy + Built-up Beyond Belief But Brain-Bendingly Beautiful

NORTH UPS

N

30 MILES
50 KLIX

THE WASH

BREAST SANDS

King's Lynn

Sandringham
(large royal beach hut)

Great Little } Snoring

California

ZZZZ

NOT AS FLAT
AS IT'S MADE
OUT TO BE?

Southwold
(where I didn't exist)

Ipswich

Orford Ness
(longescut schingle spit in Europe)

manningtree

Harwich

(grave strimmer man) Fobbing

Maldon

Southend

Isle of Sheppey

Margate

B B B B B
B B B B
B B B B

Cooling
(LOTYA)

Faversham
(supermarket tanks)

Deal

Dover

Folkstone

FRANCE *

GARDEN of ENGLAND *

Eastbourne

Dungeness

Hastings
(saved a Cabbage's life !?!)

SOUTH DOWNS

Worthing

Newhaven

Portsmouth
(LOTYA)

Selsey Bill
(mini tornadoes)

(buggered bogs but Pukka Pies)

Beachy Head

* But only a little bit of a tip of it.

* Flowers not drawn to scale.

LOTYA ~ Loo Of The Year Award

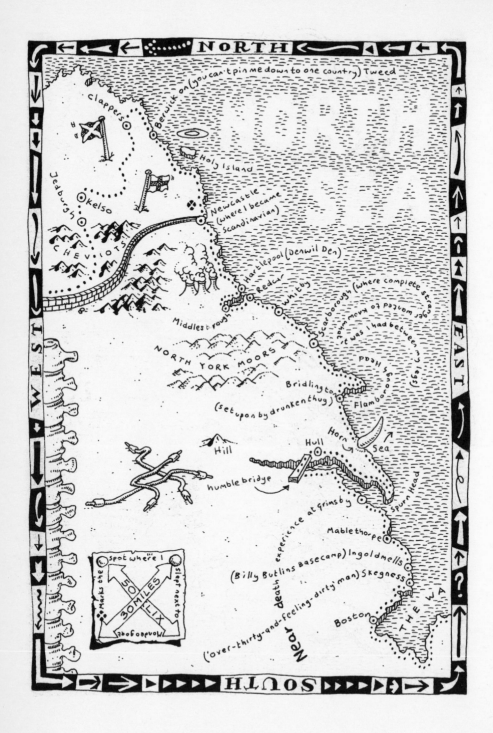

SLOW COAST HOME

CHAPTER 1

 I never planned to cycle around the coast of the British Isles. It just happened that way.

One moment I was fancy-free and poised to go bicycling off alone to New Zealand (via Alaska and Patagonia) and the next I found myself falling for a man in green overalls who had arrived on my doorstep with all tools attached to make a lot of noise and mess in my house.

About two decades later than most of my age group the opportunity had suddenly arisen at last for me to move out of my mum and dad's house into my own. Small, dark and compact, it needed half a wall demolished and a window put in. So along came the builders, one of whom wasted no time in eyeing up my bottom bracket and displaying effusive admiration for all things bicycle. To cut a short story short, one thing led to another and my builder downed his tools and picked up a mean, lean, made-to-measure Chas Roberts touring machine (funny, I seem to have one of those too). And hence to New Zealand we would ride.

But at the eleventh hour the builder had to keep building and as my heart had had a dose of what the Japanese would call *doki doki* (fluttery palpitations), I dropped everything and decided not to go cavorting off alone to the opposite side of the world.

That's one of the nice things about plans. They can come, they can go, and they can turn on their tails and sail straight off up the creek. At least they can for me because when I set off on a cycle nothing ever happens according to plan, but anything else can happen and usually does.

1

Had my original plans gone according to plan I should by now be either fighting off over-inquisitive, cyclist-hungry bears in Alaska or dragging my bike through some piranha-infested Amazonian swamp on my roundabout way to New Zealand. Instead I find myself having just cycled around the Isle of Wight.

Swanning around the Solent-lapping shores of a small piece of land that has slipped its moorings from Hampshire might not have quite the same glamorous ring as transglobally trail-blazing the vast diversity of the hazardous eat-you-alive continents of the Americas, but this southern England island can still be exotic. After all, it does have the award-winning *Days Gone By* ('nostalgic gifts, houseware and toy shop') and a place called Puckpool Point. And it also has something called the Landslip Walk to Luccombe where you can experience the excitement of possibly slipping off the land along an 8000-year-old cliff collapse. What's more, in the nearby Botanic Garden, thanks to the gentle microclimate, one can saunter from the Mediterranean to New Zealand, South Africa to Japan and still have time for a nice cup of tea and a cake. So really, there's no need to go gallivanting around the treacherous world when we have the Isle of Wight lying like a cornucopia of delights on our doorstep.

And not just the Isle of Wight. There's the Channel Islands, the Scillies, Lundy, Ireland, Isle of Man, the Inner and Outer Hebrides, the Orkneys, the Shetlands, Holy Island and the very unholy Canvey Island. For a year I planned – oh all right then, I unswayingly intended – to cycle over 10,000 miles around the coast of the British Isles, including as many estuaries and offshore islands and islets and inlets and outlets as possible. Starting from Portsmouth I chose to cycle in a vaguely clockwise direction because, living in a land of people who drive and cycle (mostly) on the left-hand side of the road, I felt I would be that little bit closer to the sea even if I couldn't see it thanks to the sewage works or power station or savagely barbed-wire fenced Ministry of Defence property. Also, a Shetland granny of a friend of mine told me that if I cycled anti-clockwise I would meet the devil. Whether this devil might be in the shape of the cyclist-crushing wheels of a runaway juggernaut or a life-sucking Midwest tornado blown way off course to Middleton-on-Sea, she did not elaborate. But it was enough to make me cycle down to Portsmouth and turn right.

My support team and back-up crew, if that's the term for such a motley bunch, comprised Gary, my builder, who would intermittently lay aside his chisel and saw and tongue and groove to accompany me in my rotations around this watery and wind-lashed land. As would my mum, who had just acquired her first custom-made mount. (What, not another Roberts? Afraid so.) Not bad for a nigh-on seventy-year-old with a bad back and dodgy knees.

CHAPTER 2

One of the nice things about leaving to cycle around the coast of the British Isles was that it was so easy. Unlike past departures when I had set out on lengthy bicycling jaunts, there were no arm-jarring jabs or visas or communication breakdown phrasebooks or grizzly bear survival rescue remedies to remember. Nor were there any train or ferry tickets to book or buy or mad-house airports to negotiate with large, ungainly, passenger-flattening, check-in-desk-unfriendly boxed bikes.

No. There was none of that last-minute cram-it-all-in mild panicking kerfuffle. All I did was wake up one morning and think: I suppose I might as well leave today. So I did.

It was Wednesday, 25th April. A funny sort of day on which to depart, as I usually like to launch forth on an escapade at the beginning of the week or the month or the year. It just feels a bit more tidy or personally momentous. And it's easier to remember. Specially when you count back to the day of departure to see how long you've been 'on the road' (as we like to call it in the trade), because after a few weeks or months of roughly stuffing your dog-eared belongings into bags day after day and moving on and moving up and moving out, time becomes all a bit blurred at the edges.

But there was nothing special about Wednesday, 25th April. Had I arrived in the country of my original intentions, then yes, it would have been a little more memorable because it was Anzac Day, a public holiday in Australia and New Zealand commemorating the Anzac landing at Gallipoli in 1915.

4

But in England it was just a typical April sunshine and showers nothing-much-happening Wednesday. And in Wigan it was probably wet.

So I spent the morning of this inconsequential Wednesday ambling and bumbling around the house, opening doors and drawers in a happy pottering mood, finding bits of tent to pack and pieces of panniers to fill. I changed the sheets and towels and hoovered and washed the floors and cleaned the toilet and bath (can't leave a ring of limescale when you're off on your bike with the fairies). I also defrosted the freezer and cleared out the fridge. I like to leave a clean sparkling slate in my wake. And then, as time was marching onwards, I thought: I suppose I might as well go now.

So I rang up all the members of my elaborate farewell committee – namely my mum and dad (the builder was too busy building) – and before you could say 'don't forget your flip-flops' they had turned up in force on bikes. Val, my next-door-neighbour, surrogate mother, author of 36 books (it was she who launched me forth into my haphazard writing career), village stalwart, wildlife expert, daily gossip companion and remarkable long-sufferer of my bike-shed hammerings and through-the-wall honky-tonk piano-playing clatterings, augmented my extensive send-off party to the grand total of three.

It was nearly four o'clock. A bit late in the day to embark upon a 10,000-odd mile odyssey but you've got to start somewhere at some time or else you'd get nowhere.

Everyone (well, all three of them) seemed to be most amused by how much heavy clobber I had managed to attach to my bike. Was I not a well-worn worldly travelled transcontinental cyclist highly experienced in all things small and light and foldably packable? Well, I was getting a bit long in the tooth for all that now. I like my home comforts these days and if I'd had the room I would have taken my bed, log fire, hot water and kitchen sink as well.

'Good thing you're strong!' said mum.

That was before I tried to lift my bike off the ground. I couldn't – not without a struggle and hearing several things ping in my back. But then, with a bike weighing some sixty or seventy kilos, who wants to go lifting it off the ground? And anyway, the purpose of a bike is to cycle it, not lift it.

For some reason mum suddenly seemed more concerned not with weight but with whether I'd had a good night's sleep prior to taking off into the unknown (even if the 'unknown' happened to be the very familiar A272). Funnily enough, I had, and I told her how I had dreamt about having elephants in the roof.

'That wasn't elephants,' said dad. 'That was Gary trying to climb back in!'

With a heavenwards look I told him that Gary wouldn't go through the roof when he had a key to the door. Then I said that I'd best be on my way. Big hugs all round. Turning my nose to the wind and face to the sky in weather-assessing mode, I said, 'I'll be lucky if I make it to the end of the lane before that big black cloud gets me.'

And lucky I was, till the end of the lane, when that big black cloud did get me. Mad scramble into waterproofs. Road awash in seconds. Contemplated turning round and heading home to dry out. I was that close. But thought: I can't back out before I've even begun. And anyway, I had said my goodbyes and second goodbyes are never as good as the first ones. So I squelched and dripped onwards waiting for a blue patch to shine on me. It never did though. It was always shining on someone else just over the hill.

It felt strange to be cycling off up the road fully laden with all my touring kit knowing that I wouldn't be sleeping at home tonight or tomorrow night or the night after that or who knows when. Because it didn't feel like I was really going somewhere to cover an unknown (unplanned) distance over an unknown (unscheduled) amount of time. As I don't have a car and because I cycle every day along the same road I was now riding, it just felt like I was going on my regular run, albeit a lot more slowly.

The occasional local passed in their car, waving like they normally waved, probably not noticing that I was carrying half a ton more than usual as I seem to be unable to cycle anywhere for whatever reason without four bulging panniers slung from my steed.

Eight miles down the road I stopped in Petersfield and dived into the doorway of Somerfield to shelter from another violent shower. A man clutching a brolly in one hand and a bag of Tate and Lyle granulated sugar in the other ('All-purpose sugar for drinks and cereals') took one look at me and said, 'You from Sweden?'

'No, Milland.'

'Milan? Ah, *buon giorno, signorina!*'

'No, not Mi*lan*. Mil*land*. I'm not Italian, I'm a local!'

Not a good start. It's not that I mind being mistaken as a foreigner, but please, not outside my local Somerfield on Day 1.

Locking up my bike, I then ran across the road to Woolworths because I needed to buy a mini Pritt Stick (I still haven't grown out of the cutting and pasting process of making my cycle-diary notebook resemble some three-year-old's smorgasbord of a scrapbook). As I was paying, the woman on the till said, 'It's not supposed to rain today. At least that's what they said yesterday. But today it depends which weather forecast you listen to. This morning the TV said rain clearing, then dry all day, while the radio said dry, then rain moving in from the west. So I've brought my brolly just in case the radio's right. Yesterday, coming down the High Street, I got caught in that sudden downpour. Soaked in seconds, I was. I had to sit here all day with a wet seat! I've got a spare pair of trousers with me today – to be on the safe side.'

I went next door to Boots to buy a support for my knee in case it went wobbly like it has in the past. As I was waiting to pay for it, an elderly gent came to get his pictures developed. He was obviously a regular because the Boots woman greeted him by name.

'Hello, Mr Cook. How are we today?'

'Oh, not so bad.'

'Been away again? Where is it this time?'

'Somewhere very adventurous.'

'Where's that then?'

'Tiverton, in Devon.'

The Boots woman laughed. 'That's a bit tame for you isn't it?'

'We've booked Malta for May.'

'Ah, your old stomping ground.'

'Yes, we'll need the sun by then.'

Next stop was Owen's Cycles in Lavant Street because, after completing the grand total of eight miles (only 9992 to go), I decided I needed a new chain even though the one I was using was new. So I changed from a horribly noisy clunky-changing 9-speed Shimano one to a super-smooth 8-speed Sachs. Before I left, Owen attempted to lift my bike to see what sort of silly weight I was carrying. It didn't lift very high. He dropped it back down and emitted a colourful profanity.

'That's as heavy as a mobile home!' he declared.

'It is a mobile home!' I said.

Owen couldn't understand me but then I couldn't understand him. Despite our mutual love for bikes, we both do a very different sort of cycling. I tour, carry a ton of kit, cycle at a pottering pace, and have no end in sight. Owen races, on a bike you can lift with your little finger, at alarming lung-busting speeds and keeps to a tight, well-disciplined schedule. (He rode from Land's End to John O' Groats in seven days. I took five weeks. But then I did it on a bicycle-wheelchair, which felt a bit like riding a back-to-front trike with a wind-catching bath-tub stuck on the front.) Owen's parting words of encouragement were that he thought my bike, loaded up high like an armchair on the back, looked easy to capsize.

Furnished with a new Pritt Stick, knee support and chain, I was at last ready to get going properly.

CHAPTER 3

It was 6 p.m. – about the time when I have usually cycled eighty miles, scaled several mountain passes, set up tent, washed my socks and feasted. Never mind, it was only the first day and it does take a while to get into the swing of things.

With a storm cloud bearing down on my heels I galloped out of Petersfield at a lumbering pace and joined the car-laden A272 to Winchester. Cycling west to Winchester might sound like a funny way to cycle south to Portsmouth but I was setting out on my coastal tour around the British Isles by first cycling to landlocked Oxford. No, I wasn't lost (yet) – I wanted to visit a friend.

Big, squally soak-you-in-seconds showers accompanied me all the way to Winchester, but thankfully the traffic didn't, as I soon turned off the busy, narrow and winding 272 on to the quiet country lanes through Ramsdean and the Meons – villages situated deep in the midst of East Hampshire's Area of Outstanding Natural Beauty. Entering West Meon, I noticed some weather-worn words painted on the side of an old wooden roadside barn:

All Persons Found Begging in this Parish will be Apprehended.

Such welcoming southern souls, I thought, as I carried on my way.

More quiet lanes and more wild skies. As a chill damp darkness fell, I donned my woolly hat and strapped a Petzl miner's light round my head. One last climb elevated me to Cheesefoot Head – a name that refers not to stale feet but to *ches* or *cesil*, meaning gravel or sand, and the foot of the hill – before I dropped off the end of the South Downs and found myself accidentally sucked on to the slip road to the M3.

I had come to Winchester to say hello to King Alfred (who was looking suitably statuesque but nonplussed with a traffic jam slowly circulating around his feet) and Queen Clare, a friend brought up in my village but who has spent the past decade living upside down in New Zealand. Clare was back on her feet in fair green and gridlocked England and staying with Bob and Sue Jarman, friends of her family.

Bob and Sue were both out when I finally arrived at their back door, but Clare was there to welcome me with open arms and a fine-smelling concoction in the oven. It was now nine o'clock and Clare was amazed, if not a little alarmed, at how long it had taken me to cycle just over thirty miles (an impressively slow five hours). Although I had rung Clare from home just as I was setting out to say I was on my way, she had expected to see me about an hour later at 5 o'clock, despite the fact that the drive from Milland to Winchester takes a good forty-five minutes. At six o'clock I had rung Clare from Petersfield station alerting her to my ponderous eight-miles-in-two-hours progress and telling her not to expect me for a while. She still seemed to think that I was cycling a car (or driving a bike) and that, if I put my foot down, I could make it to Winchester by six-thirty. But no: on a bicycle, time-travel lapses into a back-pedalling pace and although you know you're probably going to get to where you want to be, you never really know quite when that will happen because it all depends . . . depends on your legs and the hills and the wind and the weather and the things you find and the people you meet by the wayside. But however long it had taken me to get to Winchester and however long Clare had thought it would take me, we both seemed to find it immensely funny and worked out that if I kept up such an appalling rate of progress it would take me about five years to cycle around the British Isles.

At about 10 p.m. Bob and Sue returned from an archaeological talk and we all sat in the kitchen, dining and quaffing in merry mood. I took to them straight away as they were just the sort of people that you feel you've known for years. Despite having invaded their home with a mountain of dripping pan-niers and an insatiable appetite, there was no standing on ceremony and we all felt wholly at ease insulting each other from the start – which is always a healthy sign. Although their intellect was way above my head they were both warm-hearted, humorous and down-to-earth.

Then I met the cats, a tortoiseshell and a black-and-white fur-ball, who were weathering their advanced years well. Bob said that Susie tended to waltz like Marilyn Monroe while Billy, flopping himself across doorways, acted as a very effective draught excluder.

As Bob was holding a handwriting class in his home the following morning (along with having been a naval officer, journalist, private pilot and yachtsman, he was also a master of calligraphy) I helped set out rows of chairs in their living-room. His audience would be mostly elderly folk.

'The trouble with that,' said Sue, 'is that old people tend to break the chairs because they sway and wobble about in them – they can't sit still. The same thing used to happen at my mother's bridge parties!'

I had always thought the opposite – that it was old people who could sit still because they were either drilled to attentiveness or else fell asleep, while it was fidgety, easily bored youngsters who were bad news for chairs. I remember at school how much more fun it was than paying attention to the blackboard to rock around on your chair trying to balance on the back two legs or pirouette on one before inevitably ending up sprawled in a fit of convulsive laughter beneath the desk behind you. Perhaps that's why I left school as soon as possible at sixteen to cycle to Africa – sitting on saddles was more my style than sitting on seats.

Nearing midnight I retired to my quarters, a small room at the front of the house known as The Pits (the larger spare room was called The Ritz). On a shelf I noticed a book written by Bob – 'a sort of autobiography', as he called it – that he had self-published and written for his family and friends. Before long I was learning how he had arrived in this world in 1934 in a nursing home near Wandsworth. It had been a bit of a rush job, by all accounts, and his father had had to go home on the bus in his pyjamas. Later, as a small boy in his parents' home, part of which was sub-let to another couple, he recalled how a heated argument with the tenants broke out over rent, which resulted in his mother locking them out. Bob remembered coming down to breakfast one morning and seeing an axe coming through the door as the husband chopped his way back into the flat.

Further on in the book he mentioned how he once ate a bunch of daffodils, washed down with Worcester sauce (it's probably best not to know why). More soberly, he also described one of his first-hand experiences of the war: the sound of two aircraft colliding in the sky above his school. Both were British, most likely from the nearby RNAS Yeovilton. He ran to the edge of the playing field to see some wreckage and found the bloody jawbone of one of the pilots lying near a hedge.

The morning dawned beautifully bright and breezy. Clare, mindful of the fact that I exhibited a partiality for porridge, produced an almighty vat of the stuff to which she had, on my *sous*-chef promptings, added apples, pears, bananas, raisins, prunes, dried apricots, yoghurt and honey. It was just the sort of bastardised gloop that I love. Even Clare ate some and declared it tasty. When Bob came down, he looked shocked at both the contents and size of vessel from which I was breakfasting.

'We tend to use that bowl for bathing, not eating!' he said. I told him he was a fine one to make mock of my dining foibles and reminded him of his daffodil-eating past.

Outside, I packed a pile of panniers. With its bags all attached and tent poles and sleeping mats bungeed high on its rear, Clare said my bike was so heavy it felt as if I was carrying a dead cow. (Incidentally, there were plenty of these around as foot-and-mouth disease was rampant throughout the country.)

It was now mid-morning and although I would have liked to have stayed a little longer to rock around on a few chairs in the handwriting class (especially as Bob and Sue had got Fred Fingers on the fiddle coming to warm up the elderly audience), I felt the Ridgeway calling even if it did look as if it was about to rain.

Bob, endeavouring to direct me out of Winchester, told me a tale about how he was once getting directions from a man he knew to a place he didn't. After directing him up this road and round that roundabout, the man said, '. . . then turn right at the rabbit', as supposedly there was always a particular rabbit grazing on that particular corner. I said, please don't give me those sort of directions because if I kept turning right with the amount of rabbits I see grazing on corners I'd be going round in circles and never get anywhere. Which is precisely where I was getting now. Nowhere.

So, in a grand fanfare of waving limbs, I was off. To the bank. I wanted to exchange ten £1 coins for a ten-pound note. The extra clunky weight of my wallet had preyed on my mind the day before, when cycling to Winchester. I know that swapping a few ounces of metal for a banknote was a negligible measure on the grand scale of my weighty cargo, but it made me feel a bit better.

Hovering in Natwest, I watched two old women in headscarves rooting around in their handbags for things they couldn't find.

'I could have sworn I put my cheque book in,' said one headscarfed head in strident country tones.

'Oh, I know, I know,' lamented the other, preoccupied in her own searching. 'Would you believe it, I seem to have left the letter I need at home!'

'The trouble is,' said Headscarf One in a mildly irritated state, 'everything in my bag is back-to-front.'

Drawn to this verbal exchange in a loitering sort of way, my curiosity had been sufficiently aroused to want to know just exactly why Headscarf One's handbag was in such a scene of disarray, because she didn't look the type to be in possession of a chaotic handbag. Her make-up, twinset and pearls were immaculate. Hoping Headscarf Two would indirectly enlighten me by enquiring of Headscarf One how it was that such a disorderly scene had manifested itself in her bag in the first place, I took pains to lend an ear in their direction for that little bit longer.

Instead, evidently wrapped up with her own handbag excavations, Headscarf Two replied in a faintly disinterested tone, 'Sickening, isn't it?'

I have to admit that 'sickening' isn't a word that would spring to my mind to describe the chaotic contents of one's handbag – or in my case, handlebar-bag. It's more apt a word for a distasteful act, maybe, or for a child coming down with chickenpox. As I felt I could linger no longer without arousing the suspicions of the probing eyes of the security cameras, I left the bank a little lighter in pocket but wholly unresolved in meddling mind.

All handbag conundrums were soon forgotten on paying a visit to Winchester Cathedral – the second longest cathedral in Europe. This medieval edifice, which took 300 years to complete and dominates England's first capital city, never fails to impress. There are lots of Norman and Perpendicular style bits, but it was the Gothic 556-foot procession of soaring arches, ribbed vaulting and graceful stained-glass windows that impressed me. Everything was just so big and so intricate and you wondered how on earth anyone in 1079 had started to build such an almighty construction without all the vast machinery and computerised wizardry (not to mention DIY stores) of today. Formidable craftsmanship and size aside, the cathedral was something of a Hall of Fame, seeing as there were a lot of famous dead people wrapped up in the place with coffers containing the bones of the likes of Saxon and Norman and Danish kings such as King Rufus (killed while hunting in the New Forest in 1100) and Canute the not-so-tide-defying Great.

Rufus's dad, William the Conqueror, had something to do with the cathedral as well but by this stage I was suffering from a slight dose of king-and-queen overkill so didn't linger to find out just what that something was. Also I felt the time had come to hit the long winding road to Oxford.

I walked out of the cathedral past the simple tomb of Jane Austen and back to my bike, whereupon it started to rain. So I went back inside again. Oxford would just have to wait a little longer.

It was still raining when I sprinted across The Close, the spacious lawns and grounds in which the cathedral stands, to peer at Pilgrims Hall, where pilgrims used to rest on their journey to Canterbury in the Middle Ages. Over the road lay Winchester College (the oldest public school in the country, founded in 1382) but on this, the cathedral side, stood the college's chapel. Beside the chapel I found a detached building known as 'School', where, inside, the wall bore a faintly saucy-sounding Latin inscription that I translated as 'Learn, leave or be licked'.

Suddenly the sun burst out from behind a heavy wall of wet cloud and I raced back to my bike. As I wheeled it on a footpath through The Close, a man in a suit walking past asked, 'How far you going?'

To say I was cycling around the coast of the British Isles while standing in the non-seaside town of Winchester sounded a bit silly (it also sounded, to my already-tired legs, a bit far), so I said, 'To Oxford.'

The man eyed-up my bulging panniers and towers of bags strapped to the rear. I could see him thinking: that's a hell of a lot of clobber for a day's ride!

'That's a hell of a lot of clobber for a day's ride!' he said.

'Well, I might go a bit further if the fancy takes me.'

He then said he used to do quite a bit of touring himself, End-to-End, that sort of thing, before adding, 'I did some riding in Belgium too, but my tyres kept getting stuck down the gaps in the cobbles. I should have used wider ones!'

Chatting to me for a bit longer he discovered that I spent a hefty proportion of my life cycling around from place to place.

'I'm envious,' he said, 'I'd love to be free like that again but . . . well, I'm stuck with a young family now.'

I had about fifteen minutes of lovely back-warming sunshine before another downpour caught me in Headbourne Worthy, one of four River Itchen-side villages north of Winchester that are called 'Worthy' (Worthy, in this part of the country, usually means a small curtilage or court, enclosed together with the house). I pulled on my brakes in the entrance to a garage, hastily propped my bike against the wall and clambered into my rain gear. By the time I had stuck down Velcro sleeves, zipped up zips and tugged on my waterproof trousers (making sure the bottoms were secured tight round my ankles so as not to catch in the teeth of my chainrings) the rain had stopped and the sun had come out. So I undressed again.

I know that having spent so many years on my bike, I should by now be able to gauge the workings of my internal core temperature in conjunction with certain all-weather garments to a fine degree, but I can't. I'm always stopping at the side of the road to add or remove a layer or layers – a very annoying pastime for anyone with whom I happen to be cycling, which perhaps is one of the reasons I spend most of the time cycling alone.

Anyway, I had noticed that during my whole little roadside clothes-changing rigmarole, I had been observed by a woman behind a window of the garage who looked rather concerned for my mental welfare. As I pulled away wearing exactly the same combination of clothing in which I had stopped, I gave the woman a little don't-worry-I'm-fine-really-I-just-can't-get-my-temperature-right sort of wave. Gamely she returned my wave and I cycled away, quite amused at how stupid I must have looked.

But I didn't get very far before I stopped again, this time because of a village store where I decided to buy a drink. As I was paying, another shower unleashed its load outside. The shopkeeper appeared amazed that it was raining.

'Is that rain I hear?' she said.

'It is indeed,' I confirmed.

'How surprising!' she replied.

'Is it?' I said, unsure whether or not she was being ironic. 'But it's rained practically every day for six months.'

October had had the highest rainfall since 1903, and the autumn had been the wettest since records began. It had been very damp ever since and everywhere there were sandbags and floods and empty houses afloat in moats.

'I try not to look out of the window,' said the woman, 'because the weather never seems to be what I want it to be.'

I fought my way through King's Worthy into the wind and the rain, passing a house called 'Windy Nook'. Arriving in the hamlet of Stoke Charity, I stopped at the small crossroads to sit on a bench on a green grassy island beneath a fingerpost that pointed to Sutton Scotney (which lies just south of Egypt) and Micheldever (which sits on the River Dever – pronounced 'deever' – although the village is confusingly 'mich-el-devver' and, to confuse matters further, some people say 'mitch-el-devver' or 'michael-devver'). Although the wind was cold, the sun had popped out and I wondered if I had time to eat an apple and two bananas before the next downpour. With the vagaries of the British weather being what they are, life outside is always a race against time.

Everything was very quiet. I watched a man pottering in a garden in front of an old thatched cottage, its white walls now dazzling in the sharp sunshine against a dramatic backdrop of threatening black rain clouds. Surprisingly few cars passed by, but the drivers of those that did stared at me as though amazed to see a cyclist semi-reclined on a bench enjoying a banana in the chill breezy sunshine. What's wrong with these people – don't they know how to live?

I was halfway through my second banana when an elderly woman came walking along the side of the road. I smiled at her. She smiled at me. Then, keeping to the true British tradition of talking about the weather, I said, 'I'm just making the most of a nice bit of sun!'

'Good idea!' said the woman, 'I'm doing the same. I thought I must get out now while the sun is shining because it doesn't look like it will last.'

We managed a few more minutes of standard format weather chat before the woman said, 'Going far?'

Despite having covered only a mere pinprick of my intended route, I felt in buoyant spirit and wholly positive of all that lay before me. So I told her about my coastal ride. She appeared suitably impressed.

'How long is it going to take you?' she asked.

'I don't really know,' I said. 'Maybe about a year.'

'A year? My goodness! Is this something you're doing in stages during the school holidays?'

School holidays? I thought, a tad perplexed. I hadn't said anything about being a schoolteacher. Then I realized she thought I looked young enough to be still at school.

'No,' I said, 'I left school a while ago.' (The year of the Falklands War, to be precise.)

'Oh, so you're on your gap year then?'

Gap year? Gap life more like!

'No, I'm nowhere near a gap year. I'm five years off forty!'

The woman looked at me disbelievingly. I suspected she thought I was nothing more than an impudent youth just having her on. Short of showing her my passport as proof of my advancing years, I felt there was probably not a lot I could do to convince her that I was indeed a mere twenty-five years away from my bus pass, so I muttered something about 'suppose I'd best be on my way before the rain comes' and took off up the road for the Popham Beacons.

On the way I passed through the problematical Micheldever and its lovely group of black-and-white cottages before, two miles further north, I came upon Micheldever station – all very Victorian-looking with columns and drainpipes and capacious canopies. It seemed like an inconveniently long way from the actual village of Micheldever but this was because landowners in the first half of the nineteenth century often thought trains scary or vulgar and didn't want them racketting-clacketting close by, so stations were frequently built at a safe distance. To confuse matters further, Micheldever station was called Andover station until 1856, having been built halfway between Winchester and Basingstoke.

Amazingly I managed to cycle about seven miles before feeling hungry again, then I stopped at Overton to replenish energy supplies at St Mary's church. As an angry black cloud raced towards me, I sat speed-eating on a bench in the biting wind before numb extremities and rain forced me to take cover inside the church.

Near the door I browsed through a copy of *The Test*, the parish magazine of Overton and nearby Laverstock, its title referring to the River Test, which flows southwards from its source at Overton into Southampton Water. I used to cook for an elderly woman who, during 'the season', would frequently go fishing on the Test to cast dry flies on the world-renowned river to lure the wily brown trout. Not being a hooks-and-slippery-fish person, it was only later that I discovered the surprising amount of money needed to cast your fly on the Test – between £150 and £200 per day for one rod, and £5000 or more for each of six 'rotating rods' on one 'beat' in the river for one season. Myself, I'd rather have a score of shiny bicycles.

As the rain drummed down upon St Mary's roof, the parish magazine kept me amused with scintillating facets of village life such as how Tulip the Donkey had led the annual procession around the village on Palm Sunday and how a recipe for flapjacks started off the 'Method' with the instruction to:

> Control the children
> Locate accident book
> Wash hands

All very sensible advice: you don't want a child with muddy hands drowning in a pot of golden syrup over a hot flame. Not unless they are being *very* annoying.

Then there was:

THOUGHT FOR THE MONTH
To be perfect is to have changed often.
(Cardinal Newman, 1801–1890)

This made me feel pretty good because I had already changed in and out of my rain gear at least ten times that morning.

In contrast to the Cardinal's words of wisdom, there was a 'Laughline':

PASSENGER: 'I'd like a return ticket, please.'
MAN AT TICKET OFFICE: 'Where to?'
PASSENGER: 'Here of course!'

Which, after momentarily confusing me for a minute, I'm sorry to say I found really quite amusing.

On a nature front, I found in 'Countryside Jottings' how a local resident who gave her name only as Robina (obviously a notable and familiar figure in the Overton circles) posed the question: 'Have you ever wondered what goes on in your house when you're out at work each day?'

Well, no, I hadn't. But come to think of it, maybe at this very minute there were some good-for-nothing neighbourhood moggies dragging decapitated vermin through the cat-flap to be deposited unceremoniously in a gory heap on the bathroom carpet. Or maybe there was a parish whist-drive or Tupperware party in full swing, or even a ne'er-do-well spiking one's pot of Earl Grey tea. There again, heaven forbid, there could well be a wife-swapping orgy taking place in the back room.

Perhaps my imagination was running away with itself, because here's what was happening in Robina's house:

I've been at home recently, well, though fairly incapacitated so observation has become a far more prominent pastime than is usually possible with today's hectic lifestyle.

One or two days have had sunny spells and the warmth brought ladybirds creeping from their snug hibernation spots in the window frames to bask on the inside panes. By the time I would normally have returned from work there was no sign of them, tucked back in their snug nests away from the now cold glass.

Robina went on to disclose that she also happened upon woodlice 'scurrying across the carpet'.

If that is all you've had running amok on your floors Robina, I thought, then you should count yourself lucky. In the short few years I've been a first-foot-on-the-ladder homeowner, I've had a mad-house profusion of nesting bees, wasps, hornets, mice, death-watch beetles, tarantulas (oh, all right then, *huge* galloping hairy spiders), a ghost in heavy boots and a wayward workman. My neighbour, Val, suspects that the last two are one and the same, but I know better because I've felt both.

Robina's 'Countryside Jottings' ended in a grand finale: 'Did you know,' she asked tantalisingly, 'that woodlice are also known as pill bugs not because they roll up but because in earlier times quack doctors used them as pills to treat gullible patients!' Did they really swallow that? I wondered.

As the rain petered out I flicked through the last of *The Test* and read how Fred and Joy Ralph had just celebrated their golden wedding. They had married in this very church in 1951. When she was young, Joy had been ill with polio for a long time and at their wedding the organist, Mrs Titmous, had played 'I'll walk beside you' because 'Fred had always been at Joy's side'.

'We wish them many more happy years together,' bid the beneficent *Test* before exclaiming, 'Well done, Fred and Joy!'

Hear, hear, I agreed, and ate another banana in commemoration of their long and happy marriage.

CHAPTER 4

On a hill over Overton, a car stopped in front of me in the entrance to a field. A man got out and opened the boot to his Peugeot estate to reveal a lot of boxed cages. From a distance I thought at first that they were full of dogs, but as I approached I saw they were full of birds. Homing pigeons. There were dozens of them, and cage by cage the man released the birds into the lowering sky.

I stopped to watch, momentarily mesmerized by the sight of the sudden freedom of the flock as they soared away with the wind.

'Do you always release them from up on this hill?' I asked.

'No, but if I don't let them out here they'll get caught in the rain in Reading.'

I never knew there were such things as fair-weather pigeons.

'Will they all come back to you?'

'I hope so!' said the man.

As I rode away towards Caesar's Belt on the Roman Road of the Portway (I was just a buckle south of his Belt at this point), I thought about the pigeons that a group of Japanese psychologists had, for some unfathomable reason, taught to distinguish between a Picasso and a Monet, although subsequently I had read in the *Independent* that the birds were unable to tell their Cézanne from their Renoir. What is the point anyway of teaching pigeons anything, apart from not to crap on Nelson? Why not simply set them all free? They look so much lovelier that way.

In between Ladle Hill and Watership Down, atop the Hampshire Downs, I stopped in the jacket-flapping wind to take in the view. I could see for miles – 360 degrees of glorious rain-soaked and sun-gleaming shades of countryside stretching across the North Wessex Downs in the four 'shire' counties of Hampshire, Wiltshire, Berkshire and distant Oxfordshire. This small, overpopulated land may be turning more motorised and urbanised by the minute, but luckily it still has its wonderful patches of beauty to enjoy.

My train of view-admiring thought was interrupted by two fluorescent jacketed cyclists on lightweight speed machines. One was a beat-around-no-bushes Yorkshireman in a Barnsley Road Club cap, the other a jocular and lilting-toned Geordie from Tyneside called Tom. Although they had both lived down south for forty years, they had retained their alluring regional dialects.

'There's no fear we'd ever pick up a Reading accent!' said Mr Barnsley very certainly. Pointing into the distance he said, 'See that – over there. That's where the Queen's racehorses are trained, that is.'

I looked along the line of his outstretched arm and saw a sort of splodge in the landscape. It could have been anything really, but it was the location of regal racehorses because Mr Barnsley had said so and if he had said so, then he meant so, because Yorkshiremen give it to you straight. 'Come in, make yourself at home – and I wish you were!' is what a Yorkshireman might say to an unexpected and unwanted visitor at the door. And that's why I like them, because there's no affected namby-pamby politeness. If you know a shovel's a shovel, then you know where you stand with a spade.

'Where you headin' for tonight?' asked Tom.

'I don't know. I'll just see where I get to.'

'Don't you have anywhere booked?'

'No, but it's all right. I've got my tent.'

'I should hope you have among all that load. You've probably got the kitchen sink in there too.'

'I have 'n' all – it doubles up as my porridge pan.'

Mr Barnsley said, 'There's a good hostel up at Streatley, in't there Tom?'

'Aye,' said Tom, 'it's up near the Ridgeway.'

I looked on my map for Streatley and saw the red triangle symbolising a hostel.

'I see it,' I said. 'Maybe I'll head there for tonight.'

'I would,' said Tom, 'it's a bit cold and wet for camping, if you ask me.'

Never mind cold for camping, it was cold now, standing on top of the hill in the fresh squally wind that sent the clouds scudding across the sky like an old speeded-up film.

'Well, thank you for stopping,' I said. 'You've been very useful!'

'Take care, pet!' were the last words I heard as I watched the two fluorescent tops plummeting down the hill to Kingsclere.

In the end I did spend the night in the hostel at Streatley, which lies right at the start (or end) of the Ridgeway. If I had been a cattle-herder in pre-Roman times, this grassy trackway would have been my M4. It crests the downs for forty panorama-packed miles between Avebury and Streatley, with the barrow at Wayland's Smithy an enigmatic highlight.

As the weather was not particularly conducive to hiking or biking, the hostel was lovely and empty and I had a whole bunkroom to myself. A huge window looked out towards the nearby Thames that flowed through Goring. As I didn't have to consider the heating requirements of fellow bunk mates, I could fling open all windows as wide as I liked without fear of remonstrations and accusations of being a fresh-air fiend (I do like to sleep with a Force 10 gale howling across my head).

Although I had stayed in plenty of international hostels, it had been years since I last slept in one in my homeland. As I lay on my bunk in the dark, grim memories of the hostels of my early teenage cycling years came flooding back: sharing sickly hospital-green dormitories with twenty bearded-weirdos; sleepless nights sweating on a crackling plastic undersheet breathing in air that smelt like a fetid cave, thanks to an excess of swirling human gases and beds festooned with wet socks and dripping cagoules; forbidding dictatorial wardens, who forced you to scrub out rows of communal toilets, barked out stern instructions on how to fold your blanket 'whip-end to whip-end' (whatever that meant) instead of, woe betide you, lengthways.

Sleeping in dorms with packs of strangers has never been my idea of fun and I have only tended to take refuge in a hostel as a last resort: stranded in an urban area, say, with nowhere to camp, or in desperate need of a place to shelter from a storm or to wash my body and clothes or to mend or dry my tent. Camping is more my scene – sleep where you want, when you want.

But Streatley was lovely. As well as my room, I had the toilets and showers and kitchen to myself. And no one asked me to scrub or clear out anything – such a welcome unauthoritarian air that automatically made you want to leave everything clean and tidy as a token of thanks.

The brick and flint houses of Goring and Streatley stare at each other over a river crossing that has been in use for at least 5000 years. The ancient Ridgeway and Icknield Way track crossed the Thames at the spot where today's bridge spans the river. North of Goring I passed lots of hazard signs warning road users to be wary of toads crossing at night, while in turn I was passed by far too many stampeding four-wheel-drives, Mercedes, BMWs, Jags and red 'AGA' vans flattening me against hedges – most of whom wouldn't have given a monkey's whether their tyres squashed a toad (let alone a cyclist) or not.

Riding through the village of Berrick Salome I noticed a blackboard sign outside the Chequers Inn which declared:

MARQUEE FOR SALE –
SEE HER INDOORS

As it happened I saw Him Indoors, not because I wanted to see Her Indoors and Her Marquee (after all, I had a tent), but because I asked if I could borrow their toilet.

'Only if you bring it back!' said Him Indoors. I made a mental note to rephrase any future toilet requests.

And then, before I knew it, I was being pulled into the outskirts of Oxford along the horribly fast Cowley Road past endless garages and car showrooms and discount motor centres. Cowley is where the huge British Motor Corporation works were established – a gigantic complex which ironically evolved from a cycle shop opened by William Morris, who later became Lord Nuffield.

At last I surfaced in the centre of Oxford, which proved big and busy and full of buses (urgh!) and bikes (aahh!). Being a country girl at heart, cities have never really been my favourite places in which to linger. In fact, the most enjoyable thing I find about being in a city is cycling through all the traffic. It's not half fun! I don't like breathing in lungfuls of exhaust, mind you, but I love the excitement of travelling faster than cars and nipping through gaps and getting to where I want to be without a jam or bottleneck or care in the world. Speak to anyone who doesn't ride a bike and they will tell you that to cycle in a city is *so* dangerous. But this is a motorist's myth. As long as you're cocksure (but not cocky), or at least pretend to be, and look the drivers in the eye ('You can see me, can't you?') then all will be well. Shooting through a momentary gap between a wall of Routemasters or Toyota Land Cruiser Amazons works wonders for the adrenal gland and helps to keep our cities that little bit cleaner and quieter to boot.

Sometimes I meet people who say, 'You're just a bloody nuisance, you cyclists. You should keep out of our way!' This is odd because if I was to say: 'Oh, I'm terribly sorry – I shall amend my ways to your liking forthwith and sell my fleet of bikes and buy a car instead,' then, by driving around in a large lump of space-wasting metal on the already congested roads (the most congested in Europe), I really would be in their way.

I would also be a far greater hazard in that I could crash into their car and kill them and would only add to the several thousand killed (not to mention tens of thousands injured) on Britain's roads each year. So, in comparison, I don't really think riding two innocuous whirling wheels at the side of the road is being that much of a nuisance. But being seen as a nuisance and a smug, self-righteous sod is something I have to endure because as well as being a smug, self-righteous sod (but a nice one!) I am also in a minority.

And so, with all senses on full alert to car doors flinging open suddenly in my path and all manner of vehicles doing the erratic and haphazard things that vehicles tend to do, I negotiated the busy streets and junctions of Oxford.

CHAPTER 5

Before long, I arrived at Hilary's house – the reason why I had begun my coastal journey by cycling inland to this famous learned city of pinnacled towers and honeystone walls and cloistered college lawns.

I had first met Hils in 1991. It was April and I was on the point of leaving to cycle across Canada to Alaska when I suddenly felt like sending a publisher an idea for a book. Heaven knows what gave wind to such a grandiose idea – after all, I was a chef, not a writer. Maybe I thought I vaguely qualified because I was a reader, and from as early an age as I can remember, I have pondered over atlases and read books about travel and explorers and distant expeditions.

So, with a plane ticket to Nova Scotia in my pocket and with panniers semi-packed, I decided on the spur of the moment to give it a whirl. Holding out precious little hope, I sent off a synopsis for a breezy and blowy book about cycling. It landed on Hilary's desk, she took a fancy to it and that was that; she became my editor and good friend. I have, not unreasonably, liked her ever since.

There was another reason for visiting Hils: to say hello to her freshly born babe, Isabelle – my Godchild No. 5. And very lovely and tiny and baby-like she was too. Hils was happy but exhausted. She said I might have to finish off her sentences for her. So I did.

Something else I finished off for her was a Lebanese takeaway (it's upmarket stuff here in Oxford) – she was too tired to eat. Then John, Hils's husband, came home from work. I was in luck because he too was too tired to eat all of his takeaway. So I finished off his as well. I was rather hoping that a few more exhausted parents with babies and takeaways in tow would come to stay because, not uncharacteristically, I was still hungry.

As I cycled through the city the next morning I saw babies everywhere. Practically every other person I saw was wheeling an offspring in front of them on the pavement. But not in a conventional pushchair. Such buggies had been usurped by style-conscious and expensive all-terrain three-wheelers with their super-gleaming spoked wheels, smooth-rolling bearings, large-looped and strong-grip circular handles, all-weather hoods and off-road tyres. All very handy if you live deep in the craggy Outback, where you might need to jump a few gaping canyons or navigate an alligator-infested swamp to get anywhere. But in a city, with nothing more challenging than a four-inch kerb or discarded Coke can to negotiate, they appear just a little too much like their equally image-conscious four-wheel-drive cousins that so unnecessarily cruise the city streets. Then I remembered that only a month ago I had read in the paper how the sales of Maclaren baby buggies – the standard lightweight fold-away kind on which you could conveniently hook bag after bag of shopping – had plummeted and the company, which made the first front-facing pushchair, had called in the receivers. And I thought: what a shame.

The name Oxford means just that: the ford for oxen. So I escaped the city via Folly Bridge because I wanted to see roughly where it is thought the ford once crossed the Thames. All I could see was murky water diverting past a small island and some boys on the towing path throwing stones at a tin can floating down river past the cricket ground.

Travelling south I kept as close as I could to the Thames through Radley (site of famous boys' college where that very comical man, Peter Cook, and that very poetical man, Andrew Motion, went to school) and on to the nearby market town of Abingdon, which, before being embraced by Oxfordshire, was part of Berkshire. I'm not quite sure how all this exchanging of county boundaries happens (Rutland and Leicestershire, and Dorset and Hampshire, have been playing similar games) – maybe it's just the 'shire'-switching equivalent of wife-swapping: all a bit undercover but good fun to keep you on your toes nevertheless. Whatever the reason, Abingdon, which was the county town of Berkshire until 1867 when the town lost its title to Reading, is now in the Oxfordshire district of the Vale of White Horse.

Anyway, it was up at Abingdon Abbey where Henry VIII brought his court for a long stay to avoid the plague in London. It's amazing how anyone managed to avoid the disease in those days. The principal carrier is the rat flea, which transmits the disease after biting an infected host. And I would have thought there were plenty of rats with fleas that were as at home in sixteenth century Abingdon as there were in London. But at least the outbreak of plague during Henry VIII's reign was nowhere near as bad as the Black Death that arrived in England in 1348. Originating in the Far East, it had eventually entered by way of 'a port called Melcombe in Dorsetshire'. Its symptoms were most unpleasant and Boccaccio, writing of the plague in Florence in the fourteenth century, observed that it struck with such speed that victims often 'ate lunch with their friends and dinner with their ancestors in paradise'. It killed an estimated 25 million Europeans between 1347 and 1352, reducing the population of Europe by a third. During the two years it spread throughout the British Isles, it's thought to have killed up to fifty per cent of the population.

There were a number of imaginative and wishful 'cures', like plucking feathers off the tail of a pigeon; or placing a mastiff puppy on the patient's breast for two to three hours before serving a drink of dill, penny-royal, fennel and aniseed water. A favourite was to lay a live frog with its belly beside the plague sore: if the patient was to escape, the frog would burst and then another live frog was laid upon the sore and so on, until the frogs no longer burst.

Fortunately for Abingdon, the Benedictine Abbey had escaped the Tudor demolition crews when Henry VIII dissolved the monasteries. I was cycling towards the Abbey, with the uncharacteristic intention of giving my head a bit of heavy historical detail, when I noticed a wodge of grubby cloud bearing down on me fast, so I bid a hasty retreat south to Didcot.

The rain caught up with me as I skirted the smoking and hulking bulk of Didcot's monstrously impressive power station. The fact that the rain had caught me at all struck me as most unjust. Not because I got wet, again, but because for twenty miles I had been fighting into the teeth of a headwind all the way from Abingdon. My unmeteorological mind told me that as I was riding into a southerly-blowing gale then the clouds should be rushing northwards. Instead the opposite was true and everything was converging against me – another example of that strange cyclist's weather phenomenon whereby things aren't as you expect, but if they are then they're probably not.

There are some uninspiring towns in England in which I have had the misfortune to cycle that appear to consist entirely of roundabouts – Reading and Basingstoke are two that immediately spring to mind. Now I could add Didcot to my list. I went spinning dizzily round and round and round so many roundabouts that at the Tesco roundabout I pulled over to get a grip on my wavering equilibrium.

As I stood outside the neon-lit store waiting for my world to stabilise, a man rode up on his 'Coyote Extreme' mountain bike ('V-Bar design'). He glanced at me, saw what I was riding and said, 'Ah ha! A Roberts, eh? They're nice bikes. I know Chas. I met him once in a café in London in my courier days. He's a good bloke.'

Chas was my frame builder.

'How long ago was that?' I asked.

'Blimey! Must have been at least fifteen years ago. I only got back into cycling again recently. I'm into jumping and cross-country. But I'm getting married at the end of the year, so I'll have to give up being a big kid.'

'Will you?' I said. 'Can you not be a big kid and be married simultaneously?'

'No way,' he said. 'My other half wouldn't have it!'

I'm glad I'm not marrying her, I thought, as I cycled away.

April's showers became full-blown monsoon rain and gales, resulting in up-to-my-hubs flooded roads. Back on the Thames in the literary country of Pangbourne (where Kenneth Grahame, the author of *The Wind in the Willows*, lived for the last eight years of his life), I gave up all attempts at trying to camp – the land was either too far under water or too private. Everywhere there were big flashy cars, big pretentious houses with blinding security lights, electronic gates and entry phones.

So I started cycling around in the wet and the dark and the cold searching for a bed-and-breakfast. They were all full. My last resort was a pub down near the toll bridge (10p for cars, free for bikes) called The Ferryboat Inn. An owner of one of the booked-up B&Bs told me about it.

'It used to do B&B,' she said, 'but I'm not sure if it still does. It did feature in *Three Men in a Boat*, though.'

Ah, a recipe for disaster, then.

In heavy, waterfalling rain I cycled down to the Ferryboat to investigate. Wet and dispirited, I locked up my bike and trudged through the puddles to the door of the pub. Shoving it open, I entered a hot stuffy room clouded in smoke. Around the bar sat half a dozen locals drinking and smoking. Suddenly all jabber stopped; all eyes turned to stare.

I hate walking into pubs at the best of times, and now, bringing in with me a considerable tributary of the Thames cascading from my saturated rain gear on to the floor, was not a moment to cherish.

All of the turned heads waited for me to open my mouth.

'Do you still do bed and breakfast?' I asked the barman, a northerner with a tough skull-head buzzcut. His arms and face came liberally embellished with various tattoos and multiple piercings. He wore a scowl that said, 'Cross me and I'll kill yer.'

'For 'ow many?' he asked impassively.

Oh, there's only twenty of us, I felt like saying, as I don't really like the feeling of giving away my single travelling status – specially not in front of a whole crowd of beer-swigging strangers.

'Just me,' I said.

'Forty-five quid,' he said.

'Forty-five?' I said, shocked. I had been banking on about £18.

'Includes dinner,' he added.

'How much can you do it for without dinner?'

'Can't do it without dinner.'

'Can't you? Why not?'

He was trying to rip me off, which made me feel cocky as well as cross. He just shrugged and lit a fag. I knew he simply wanted me to go away, but I was going nowhere. I may be small, I may be a young thing on my gap year, but I was going to stand my ground. So I went to the other extreme and, starting off on the silly side of the scale, named my price (I hadn't been to the carpet-bartering school of Morocco for nothing, you know).

'All I want is a bed. I don't need any breakfast or dinner. So . . . could you do the room for . . . a tenner?'

I was banking on the good old haggling method of starting ridiculously low before reaching a reasonable compromise, but I was not in Morocco's Marrakesh. I braced myself for a scoffing.

'Yer wha'? Ten quid? Bloody 'ell! Who are yer?'

I was about to say I was an impoverished student just drifting around on my gap year but, feeling very tired and old in my fourth decade of life, I changed my mind. With Arab-flavoured visions of pushy yet good-natured carpet-sellers, and potfuls of sickly-sweet mint tea, swirling round my head, I upped my haggle price.

'All right, then,' I said. 'Fifteen?'

'Fifteen?' he said. 'No way! Thirty-five.'

Ah! Things were looking up! He had dropped ten pounds. Spurred on by this sudden development I pulled a hopeful face and said, 'Twenty?'

A few guffaws erupted from the audience at the bar, who appeared to be enjoying this Saturday-night haggling match between their hard-man barman and some brazen young hussy in Goretex.

'I ain't going less than thirty,' stated the barman in a drop-fist-to-bar, that's-me-final-price sort of way. But I was in full bargaining flow and not yet finished.

'Twenty-five?' I asked, eyebrows arching beseechingly. I felt I was working my ticket.

'No, thirty.'

'Are you sure?' I asked, knowing only too well that I was sure he was very sure. 'As I'm very wet and cold and tired and it's still raining and I've got nowhere else to go as everywhere is full.' It's always nice to bring out the illogical sob story as a last resort.

'Okay. Twenty-five.'

Although twenty-five pounds was far more than I wanted to pay, thirty had been silly, and forty-five extortionate for a fledgling student of my mere means. The trouble was I hadn't even viewed my sleeping quarters yet, thus breaking in-search-of-accommodation Golden Rule No. 1: never agree a price before seeing the room and checking location and state of toilet.

But it was too late now. The deal was done. I would just have to hold my head high and walk tall (in a short-legged sort of way) and accept whatever lay in wait for me up the pub's decrepit back stairs.

On the other hand, of course, I didn't have to accept anything of the sort. If the room were a total dive with soggy mattress, dirty sheets, filthy carpet (ditto bog), argumentative shower, no tables, no chairs, a tangle of wires hanging out of peeling wall in lieu of TV, a single swinging zilch-watted light bulb and splattered window offering grand panorama over dustbins and empty metal barrels of Bass bitter, then, under the Bloody-Outrageous-Not-Up-To-Standard Act (BONUTS) of 1946, I was at full liberty to walk straight out without paying a peanut.

The room was, but I didn't. In my heyday, I would have most definitely beaten a hasty retreat to more savoury pastures. Now though, I was too old, too cold, too wet, too hungry, too had-too-much-for-one-day doggone tired for that. And where would I go if I did? I only had the lure of a stormy night camping in flood water to tempt me back out. At that moment, anything inside, no matter in what state, seemed preferable to anything outside, even if I was paying through the nose for it.

Then I thought of Streatley hostel. Why didn't I go back there – £11 a night, and only about five miles up the road? I admit I had thought about it earlier in the day, but decided against it: I don't like going back to somewhere that I have already been – not when there's new territory to forge forth into, even if that territory is only a mere few pedal revolutions away down the road.

But now I was in too deep with a will power not willing to do anything other than make the most of what I had. So I flung my groundsheet over the bed (as a preventive 'Say No To Filthy Mattress Livestock' measure), plumped up my sleeping bag, cleaned the hole-in-the-wall toilet and argued with the temperamental showerhead. I then dined on a pannier-full of food (pre-purchased from the local supermarket) and read my book, *Between Extremes*, about Brian Keenan and John McCarthy's travels through Chile – a journey they had first envisaged from the bleak depths of a Lebanese dungeon. (Val had given me the book when she thought, and I thought, I was going to Patagonia.)

At one stage I thought about doing what the soaked and miserable heroes of *Three Men in a Boat* had done: it was at Pangbourne that they had abandoned their craft and caught the train back to London. But as long as I tried to forget about the preposterous price I had paid and tried to ignore the Saturday-night thumping clamour emanating from the bar below, causing the walls and floors of my room to vibrate and windows to rattle (comparable to the din of a campanologists' convention being held inside a printworks) I felt really quite happy.

As I was unlocking my bike from the rickety rails of the staircase the next morning, the barman appeared bleary eyed from the kitchen and we got talking. Now, in the quiet of the Sunday morning, I could clearly detect his strong Yorkshire accent.

'You don't sound like you're from Berkshire!' I said.

'No, Sheffield. I've only been 'ere since January.'

'Did you mean to end up in a pub in Pangbourne?'

'No,' he laughed, 'it's all because of a horrible mess of ex-husbands and ex-wives.'

Propping himself against the doorframe, he went on to explain how he had met Trish, his girlfriend, back home in Sheffield, 'but 'er ex, 'e said that if 'e got 'is 'ands on me, 'e'd slit me throat and dump me in t'canal.'

'Oh, that's friendly!' I said, a trifle shocked. 'In that case I think you're definitely better off in Pangbourne!'

'Aye, that's right,' he said with a wry smile. 'Up there I've always got to watch me back, like, but down 'ere . . . I can relax. It's right nice!'

It was still raining hard as I cycled up a hill out of Pangbourne. A big people carrier came broadside. The driver leant across the passenger seat and, as I prepared myself for an earful of abuse, he shouted through the automatically opening window, 'Josie Dew! I've read all your books! They're great!' He then revved off up the hill. Pleasantly surprised, I thought: I could do with a few more men like that.

Despite the continuous rain, which varied from torrentially vertical to torrentially horizontal depending on the violent bursts of the gusty wind that threw itself at me, and despite the muddy flooded and occasionally washed-away roads, I thoroughly enjoyed my morning navigating along a weaving network of remarkably quiet country lanes, every now and then bursting out of woodland to be rewarded with a smudgy view of the Chiltern hills. The great tits were busy with their 'teacher-teacher-teacher' song, and the silly, strutting ringnecked cock pheasants with their brain-stabbing klaxon horns. What is it about pheasants? They wait until you are almost on top of them before they decide to launch themselves ponderously in a burst of ungainly flight, or flee on foot all over the road, skidding and heel-spinning in their panic?

Now and then I had a taster of the motoring maelstrom that rumbled hectically along the M4 as I soared over its roar – everyone rushing towards Swindon or racing to London – or the A4, a similar scene of cars careering along bound for either Newbury or Reading (two places I was only too happy to avoid).

I stopped to buy a drink and a bunch of bananas in Woolhampton's small village store. The shopkeeper, a friendly and garrulous man with a hearty laugh and East End vowels, said, 'I'm a Londoner, but I've been out 'ere now 26 years. You wouldn't get me movin' back there again in a 'urry.'

He noticed my loaded bike leaning up against the shop front.

'Bloody 'ell! You got enough on there, luv? Looks like you ridin' to Mars!'

When he found out what I was doing he appeared quite taken with the whole idea.

'You're like me son, you are,' he said, 'just can't settle.'

'Does he cycle?' I asked.

'Nah, 'e drives a digger. Lives on a barge. Saves some dosh, then takes off for months travellin' all them canals. Done it for years, 'e has. Can't see 'im doin' nothin' different now – 'e loves the life.'

Before I left, the digger driver's dad asked me if I was going to the Channel Islands. I said I was hoping to be there in about a week's time.

'I know them islands like the back of me 'and. Beautiful place. Used to go there for scrap metal conventions. The wife thought it so smashin' that we was always going back for our 'oliday, like.'

CHAPTER 6

Back into Hampshire again. Its lanes, burgeoning with bluebells and wild garlic, struck me as particularly lovely for a Sunday cycle. Spotted first skylark too, with its soaring song hovering high in the sky above a wide expanse of field.

Being a Sunday, albeit a very wet one, a few cyclists were out. West of Basingstoke I espied a swift-moving tandem, while in Oakley I was passed by an old boy, though a very fit one, who, with his bright yellow cycle-touring cape, Carradice cotton duck saddle bag, and traditional all-leather black lace-up shoes, looked as if he had cycled straight out of the pages of the CTC magazine. He did an about-turn and then looped round again to cycle level with me.

'Rosie Dew! It's a pleasure to meet you!' he said, before disappearing off around the bend, leaving me to think: I'll forgive him!

After passing an abandoned car (POLICE AWARE!), a dumped fridge, a dead computer, two burst bin bags and a mattress and three-piece suite trailing their innards, I came upon various roads around Axford, Preston Candover and Chilton Candover which were closed due to flooding. I managed to squeeze by in places by dragging my bike up the bankside or simply wading on through, and found villages with ineffective fortifications of sandbags, and thatched cottages adrift in lakes. So many homes ruined, lives in turmoil.

Something strange happened to me up on Bugmore Hill. The rain, which had been raining on me all day, suddenly stopped. Heartened by this uncharacteristic development, I rejoiced by tearing off all my clammy rain gear; an impulsive action which was perhaps a little premature, as it was bound to encourage the rain to start again any moment, but sometimes it's nice to act rashly and turn the other cheek to the weather.

More roads were closed as I came into Old Alresford and, this time, like the good citizen that I am, I dutifully followed the DIVERSION signs, as my intended route was completely impassable.

This was a mistake because, in their erratic and peter-out signposting way, they seemed to be leading me astray west towards Winchester when all my weary limbs wanted was to take me a mere half a mile down the road due south into New Alresford, where I was hoping to camp in a caravan site.

It's very frustrating to be within striking distance of your goal (I could see the rooftops of New Alresford) and yet be prevented from reaching it. Two girls on horses tried to direct me on a completely different course altogether, which, taking me northwards, would have led me back towards Basingstoke – a place I most definitely did not want to go.

I thanked the girls warmly and pretended to take their advice by setting off on a new bearing to Basingstoke. Oh, the circuitous lengths we go to so as not to offend! As soon as the girls were out of sight I retraced my wasted tracks back on to the road that lead me nowhere where I wanted to go.

Up on a hill I passed a grand house with sweeping lawns and thought: that looks like a nice bit of well-drained grass on which to camp. So I stopped to reassess the situation. It was the sort of house that looked as if its affluent owner would not readily welcome a mud-splattered and bedraggled cyclist setting up base amid its fastidiously manicured grounds. Never mind, you can never dismiss all your chickens in a basket before your eggs have bolted.

So, on that well-considered premise for life, I was on the point of rolling down the driveway to knock on the front door when I noticed a man walking along the road towards me. As he approached, I could see his moustachioed face more clearly. He looked like a mixture of Basil Fawlty and Charlie Chaplin, with perhaps a touch of Hitler on the side. He was clad in a long green Sprayway jacket. As he drew level I bid him a cheery good afternoon, which he enthusiastically reciprocated. Then he said, 'You all right there?'

'Yes, fine thanks,' I lied, because having nowhere to sleep is not particularly fine. 'I was just going to ask at this house if I could camp in their garden.'

'You won't want to do that,' said Basil Adolf Chaplin.

'Won't I? Why not?' I asked, a little peeved that he was trying to dissuade me from my carefully laid plan.

'It's Lord Wakeham's house!'

'Oh, well, maybe I won't then!'

Although I tend to get Lord This of That and Lord That of This all a bit muddled up, I have a couple of exceptions: Lord Archer, because we all know what *he* did; and Lord Wakeham, whom I remember for being badly injured in the 1984 IRA bomb in Brighton when serving as a member of the Conservative cabinet. Though he once was a minister of Maggie Thatcher's maniacal road-building car-cultured government, I'm sure he is a very nice man. I just didn't feel quite so inclined to sleep between his roses.

As Basil appeared to be well versed in local happenings, I asked him if he could direct me in a direct way into Alresford.

'Of course! Now, what have we here?' he said casting an eye over my trusty steed. 'A ten-speed racer? Should take you twenty minutes tops!'

Actually, it's a twenty-seven-speed tourer, I felt like saying. But I kept my mouth shut.

He then launched into such an incredibly long-winded spiel about following the road down here, turning left, then second right after the third gate (or was that the third left after the second gate?) and taking the right fork after passing a gap in the hedge on the left and to be very careful there because the road is very muddy and rutted where the bank is washed away and to keep going past a field full of cows before turning right at the bottom of the hill where you will see some horses (or was that cows and a field full of horses?) that dusk was falling, along with a fresh and violent burst of freezing rain.

Scrambling to pull on my jacket and waterproof trousers, while simultaneously trying to hold my unwieldy bike and not appear discourteous to the lengthy directions befuddling my brain cells, was not easy. Basil was all right because he was in his knee-length Sprayway. But I really didn't want to get cold and wet before crawling into a cold and wet tent, because that was a recipe for a very bad night indeed.

We stood, two forlorn figures on the empty country lane that mercilessly appeared to be so near and yet so far from Alresford, as the driving rain threw itself at us. Basil seemed quite happy – almost revelling in the wildness of the weather. I was not quite so enthusiastic and felt morale dripping out of me as fast as the drops off my hood. In a sudden wave of despair, I looked up to the darkening and sodden sky and, with a feeble little laugh, said, 'Oh, what am I doing here? I should be cycling in the Mediterranean instead!'

Basil, taking this defeatist comment literally, asked if that was where I was planning to go.

'No,' I said, 'but all this rain is beginning to make me think I should!'

As the rain got harder and the wind more wild, Basil decided to tell me how he had gone to Florida last November on a walking holiday in the Everglades and, oh! what a marvellous place! And with such fantastic weather to match!

Standing astride my bike, trying to balance in the big blasting gusts of wind, I was fast losing contact with my extremities. The rain, cascading in rushing gullies down my trousers, was forming an icy pool in my shoes and turning both feet numb with cold. But there was no stopping Basil. Despite my lack of convivial feedback, he continued to relish his meeting with a fellow outdoor person in the midst of the Great Soaking Wet British Outdoors. Above the racket of the wind, flapping and crackling my hood, I could hear places in Florida being recommended to me for cycling. Any other time I'm sure I would have eagerly absorbed this information, but all I really wanted to do was to find my way into New Alresford with all the roads closed.

Finally, spurring my frozen mouth into action, I thanked Basil for all his help and said that I must be on my way lest I have nowhere to stay.

'I'm racking my brain trying to think if I know of any bed and breakfasts but . . . you know? – I can't think of a single place,' said Basil reassuringly.

Just as I was about to get going it suddenly occurred to him that there might be a slightly quicker way to reach New Alresford. *Oh no! Please Basil, not now. I need to move!*

It was too late. Basil had embarked upon yet more convoluted directions, explaining how if I retraced my tracks back down to the second junction and took the first right (or was that the first junction and the second right?), I could then follow a muddy footpath taking me over the River Alre alongside the weir. The mention of the weir spurred him into giving me a spontaneous history lesson on its construction, '. . . the Bishop of Winchester built it in the thirteenth century . . .' – and so on and so on.

Eventually we parted, going our separate ways into the night. As I didn't fancy falling into a weir in the dark, I kept to the road route until miraculously, making up my own directions, I made it into New Alresford – which, incidentally, dating from about 1200, struck me as looking no older or younger than Old Alresford. Nor did I see any alder trees, from which the town takes its name. But that could be because it was dark.

I found the caravan site. There were no tents and no toilets but just a handful of caravans, most of them still shut up for the winter. As I stood in the rain, flashing my torch around, a woman emerged briefly from one of the caravans to empty her dog.

'It's only caravans here,' she said abruptly when she saw me, before slamming shut the door. Thank you for that, I thought.

I knocked on the door of a house opposite the site to see if the occupants knew any place where I could stay. A man answered. Behind him, hovering in the hallway, stood a woman.

'Now, let me see,' he said stroking his chin. 'There's The Swan – a hotel in West Street. But it's rather pricey.'

He was right: I had stopped to check the rates when I cycled past it.

'I'm afraid I can't think of anywhere else. Can you, Peggy?' he said, turning to look over his shoulder. Suddenly, he was hit by a sudden flash of inspiration.

'Wait a minute, what about Rosie Waring-Green? She does B&B, doesn't she, Peg?'

Peggy agreed and together they endeavoured to direct me in Rosie's direction.

'It's not far,' said Peggy encouragingly. 'Turn left out of here, then at the bottom of the hill take the first right. Go under the railway bridge and then take the first right. Opposite a modern church you'll see a long bungalow. That's Rosie's house.'

So off I went. But before I tried to find Rosie Waring-Green, I cycled back into Alresford to stock up on food supplies in One Stop. Outside the store the newspaper billboard bore a headline from the *Southern Daily Echo*:

WHY I SHOT MY DOG 12 TIMES

Well at least it wasn't thirteen, I thought, because then the dog really would have been unlucky.

I found Rosie's bungalow opposite the modern church and knocked on the door, which immediately set off a yapping dog on the other side. I heard a few shuffles, a light came on, and then the door opened, releasing a swirl of yapping dog around my feet. A woman stood in front of me with a questioning look on her face.

'Sorry to bother you,' I said, 'but are you Rosie Waring-Green?'

'Yes,' she said with a raising intonation.

'Oh, that's good, because I've been told you do bed-and-breakfast.'

Rosie Waring-Green looked slightly taken aback.

'Who told you that?' she asked.

'The people in the house opposite the caravan site,' I admitted, feeling a bit like a guilty informant.

'Oh, that's Charles and Peggy!' she exclaimed bursting into laughter. 'They must be having a brainstorm! I haven't done B&B for seventeen years!'

I laughed as well. The whole evening was turning a bit silly.

'Do you know of anywhere else to stay in Alresford apart from the hotel?'

'I can't think of anywhere off the top of my head, but I'm sure there must be somewhere. Come in anyway.'

So into Rosie Waring-Green's house I went, with the yappy dog snapping at my heels. Rosie led me into the living room, where a man was stretched out half asleep on the sofa. She asked my name. I told her it was Josie.

'Ian? This is Josie,' said Rosie rather loudly to the semi-comatose form. 'I'm going to try and find her somewhere to stay tonight.'

Ian grunted and said nothing more. I felt a bit guilty for disturbing their Sunday evening and said as much to Rosie.

'Oh, it's no trouble at all,' she replied cheerfully. 'I was only trying to fill out a blessed passport application form. Now, I wonder what the best way is of going about trying to find you somewhere. I know, I'll ring the Watercress Line, they're always very helpful.'

The Watercress Line is the shortened form of what was once the Mid-Hants Railway, which used to run between Alton and Winchester. Steam trains now run along a ten-mile steeply graded track between Alresford and Alton. Suddenly, the thought of being able to travel by steam up to Alton and being back with the builder by tonight (he lived in a village not far from the town), struck me as very alluring. It also struck me as rather apt because Gary comes from a family of railwaymen as well as a family of builders. His granddad, Harold, who had lived next door to him in the old railway cottages in East Tisted until he died, had been a 'ganger', a linesman, all his life on the Meon Valley Line. Mending rails and clearing track was a perilous job and it seemed Harold had had a few close shaves in his time. One time he fainted, for some reason or other, just as a train was approaching, and he fell down flat on his back between the rails. As the train passed over him, a piece of metal on the train's undercarriage caught on to him and tore his trousers in half, ripped a slash down his big heavy overcoat and cracked him on the head. Apart from that, he was fine.

Anyhow, the Watercress Line's station, which is run mainly by a band of loyal volunteers, was closed.

'Never mind,' said Rosie, 'I'm sure I've seen an advert somewhere for a thatched pub in Cheriton that does accommodation. Ah, I know, it's in the parish magazine.'

Rosie rifled through a pile of papers on the table.

'Here it is!' she cried triumphantly, holding a pink-covered magazine aloft in her hand.

We looked through the pages together until we found the pub she had mentioned. Rosie dialled the number and handed me the receiver. Finally a woman answered. I asked her if she had any rooms free for tonight.

'I'm sorry,' she said, 'but I'm afraid we're all full.'

'Oh. Do you know of anywhere else?'

'Hold on a minute love, I'll get my handbag . . .'

And I was left hanging on the line wondering what a handbag had to do with finding a bed-and-breakfast. I heard a few doors banging, a lot of shuffling feet, and then the woman was back.

'Here we are,' she said. 'I keep a list of B&Bs in my handbag.'

I thought that the handiest place would have been to keep a list by the phone, but then I didn't have a handbag and I know that people with handbags do seem to hoard all manner of strange things in them. Thanks to my escapade in a Winchester bank, I even knew that the contents of handbags could mysteriously turn all chaotically back-to-front.

The woman gave me the numbers of three or four places to try.

'Are there any you would recommend me to try first?' I asked.

'Well now, let me see . . .' There was a slight pause. I could sense her eyes glancing down the list. 'Ah, yes. I'd try Mrs Margaret Hoskins in Brandy Lea, if I were you. She's a lovely woman. Very grandmotherly.'

Sounded good to me. I tried the number.

'I'm so sorry,' said Mrs Hoskins on hearing my request for a bed, 'I'm afraid I'm full tonight.'

'Are you sure?' I said, not liking what I was hearing and hoping that by questioning her surety she perhaps would not be so sure after all.

'I'm sorry?' said Mrs Hoskins.

'Are you sure that you're sure that you've got no rooms for tonight?' I said, beginning to confuse myself, but then it had been a hard day in the saddle and I was tired and damp and hungry. And I could not believe that all these places could be full on a wet Sunday night in April.

'Yes, I'm afraid so dear . . .' Slight ruffle of paper. '. . . No, no – what *am* I talking about? I beg your pardon. I do have a room. It's Sunday, isn't it? I thought it was Monday!'

I felt like hugging her, and expressed suitable sounds of gratitude.

Then I said, 'How much is the room?'

'Now, you'll be wanting some dinner, won't you?'

'No, I'll be fine, thank you.'

'Well, you'll be wanting breakfast.'

I told her that I wouldn't need any of that either.

'Won't you?' said Mrs Hoskins sounding slightly offended, 'Don't you like my breakfasts?'

'I'm sure I'd love your breakfasts but I was originally going to camp so I've got a bagful of food supplies which I don't want to have to carry over the Downs on my bike tomorrow.'

'Oh my goodness! You're cycling?'

'Yes.'

'How lovely! I could do you a room for £10. How does that sound?'

My relief was palpable. 'It sounds very nice. Thank you.'

I cycled the three or four miles to Cheriton (three-times winner of the prestigious Best Kept Village in Hampshire contest) and found Mrs Hoskins's house, Brandy Lea, next door to the FlowerPots pub. On the way there I had passed a signpost pointing out that Petersfield was only eleven miles away, which meant that home was but a further mere eight miles on from there. It felt strange to think that I could have avoided all this accommodation palaver, and, within two hours, be back in my own bed. But I couldn't do that because . . . well . . . because I was on my coastal jaunt (even though I had yet to find the coast). And besides, Mrs Hoskins was expecting me.

As I stood at the front door, I could see her through the window sitting at a computer in the back conservatory.

'Are you any good with computers?' asked Mrs Hoskins once she had let me in.

I told her I was useless as I had never used one in my life. 'I keep making excuses not to get one because I think it will just annoy me. I'd rather be outside on my bike!'

'How very sensible!' declared Mrs Hoskins, while obviously thinking: what a pity! 'I can't seem to stop mine from suddenly going into capital letters every now and then. It's quite maddening!'

She went on to tell me how she had never really wanted a computer in the first place, but had been encouraged to go along with a friend to a local computer course.

'It was called Computers for the Terrified!' she said, and we both laughed. 'I did manage though to e-mail my granddaughter a few times when she was in Australia. It's marvellous for that!'

As she led me up the open-tread staircase to my room, I told Mrs Hoskins how Rosie Waring-Green had sprung to my rescue.

'That name rings a bell,' she said. 'I believe she put on a superb play for children at the local school.' And I thought: the things you learn about people!

Mrs Hoskins showed me into a small room on the back of the house.

'I hope you like my ladybirds,' she said, by way of some unusual room-peddling patter. 'I'm afraid it's infested with them.'

And it was. There were seven-spot ladybirds everywhere, though most of them were gathered on the window and windowsill for what was obviously a very well attended ladybird convention. Housebound Robina from Overton would have been delighted at such a find. I thought about penning a letter to *The Test* to alert her to such a discovery but decided I had more pressing things on my mind like . . . well, trying to find the coast, for starters.

Mrs Hoskins interrupted my reverie. 'There's supposed to be a shortage of ladybirds, you know, but I think they must all be breeding in here.'

I agreed and said she must be housing the whole of southern England's ladybird population in her back room. I didn't tell her about Robina's personal stash. It seemed a pity to dash Mrs Hoskins's beetle-breeding theory.

Then she said, 'Gracious me! What *am* I doing? I don't know why I'm showing you this room when I've got a much bigger one on the front. I've got a builder booked in later,' (the mention of which sent my heart a-flutter), 'so I don't see why the first arrival shouldn't have the first choice.'

Despite my penchant for all things beetle (I did once choose them for my school scrapbook project), I took the larger room with its quirky furnishings of knitted hot-water-bottle covers and Japanese ink paintings of galloping stallions. It also had a long radiator upon which I could at last dry my clothes. Above the radiator was a window (ladybird-less) through which I saw the builder arrive late and leave early in a car laden with ladders.

In the morning I caught sight of Polly, Mrs Hoskins's feline companion, carelessly losing her sure-footed footing and tumbling down the wooden stairs to land at the bottom in an unceremonious heap of fur.

'She's a Southampton Rescue Cat,' said Mrs Hoskins, as if that excused her for such unsprightly behaviour.

Mrs Hoskins herself was hard at work in the kitchen making Lemon Drizzle cakes for the WI market cake stall. Being a cook, I'm always up for a good bit of recipe-comparison banter, and I conceded that Mrs Hoskins's Lemon Drizzle cakes looked better than mine. This could have something to do with the baking method, for I shove mine in my old Rayburn and time them by going out on a ten-mile bike ride, which, depending on the strength and direction of the wind, results in my catching the cakes in the nick of time. Or not.

Mrs Hoskins was a little more meticulous.

'I give them 53 minutes precisely,' she said. 'If I give them 55 minutes like the recipe says, I find they're just starting to burn. But then I do have a fan oven and I tend to find them hotter than conventional ones.'

Mrs Hoskins appeared most taken with my interest for her baking tendencies, so much so that she encouraged me to copy out her Lemon Drizzle cake recipe.

'What lovely handwriting!' declared Mrs Hoskins when she checked my finished copy to make sure I hadn't omitted any ingredients. As a final flourish of encouragement, she gave me two cake-tin liners (mail order from Lakelands). 'Saves all the mess and fuss of greasing and lining tins,' she said.

So I set out on my final leg to Portsmouth with a recipe for Lemon Drizzle cake and a couple of one-pound cake-tin liners in my panniers – unusual kit for a world traveller but those greaseproof liners could prove life-savers yet by doubling up as emergency water receptacles should rainy England be suddenly struck by drought.

CHAPTER 7

The rain, which had been holding off all morning, arrived exactly five minutes after I left Mrs Hoskin's house. It fell heavily and unremittingly all the way over the Downs to Droxford, where I passed a sign on a five-bar gate announcing:

DOGS CAUGHT SHEEP-WORRYING WILL BE SHOT.

As I climbed the gate to have a pee behind a hedge, I thought: I hope I don't look like a dog.

I skirted Hambledon (birthplace of cricket, as we know it, played on Broadhalfpenny Down in 1774) and the rain eased off for all of five minutes. It returned for a second lease of life and fell biblically – the winds so wild and the roads so flooded that there were waves lapping the banks. By the time I rode through the hamlet of World's End, I felt it was.

So I took shelter in a phone box. As the box had a phone that worked, I took the opportunity of ringing a member of my support crew – namely, my mother – to see if she was still game to accompany me by bike around the Isle of Wight. I held out precious little hope because, back at home, when we had discussed the possibility, mum, although keen to meet me, had added, 'But I'm not coming if it's raining!'

Now though, despite further heavy rain forecast, not seeing her daughter for five long days had obviously softened mum's momentary fine-weather cyclist approach.

'I've been waiting for you to ring,' she said eagerly. 'My panniers are all packed. I can meet you this afternoon.'

I charged back out of the phone box and set off at a keen lick for Portsmouth. After dropping off Portsdown into the north of Portsea Island, I stopped to buy a bunch of bananas in Cosham Market. As I wheeled my bike through the pedestrian precinct, a man pushing his bike in the opposite direction said, 'Blimey! Where're you heading on *that* thing?'

'Portsmouth Harbour.'

'Well, in that case,' he said, 'I'll tell you the best way to get there by bike.'

For the next ten minutes he proceeded to give me the most complex instructions. '. . .go over the railway, take the third exit at the first roundabout . . .' (or was it the first exit at the third roundabout?), '. . . that goes under the motorway – you could take the subway but it's full of broken glass – carry on for about a quarter of a mile then take the right fork and turn right at the pub. Keep going down there, then take the second . . . no, third left and at the end of that road you'll see a footpath that follows the waterfront, so take that until it runs into a cul-de-sac where you'll want to turn left and then, a bit further down that road, you'll come to two mini roundabouts. At the first one take the third exit, and at the second one take the first left . . .' (or was it the second left at the first roundabout and the third exit at the second . . .?) By this time I was certain he had been to the Basil School of Highly Disorientating Directions. I looked at him with a glazed expression and a befuddled brain and, like an automaton, I said, 'Ah, sounds easy! Thank you, for that.'

My tinge of irony clearly washed clean over him.

'No problem,' he replied. 'Good luck and stay safe!'

Using my own navigational means – simply following the A3 all the way down to Portsmouth Harbour – I met mum, complete with my old Karrimor Iberian panniers and cast-off stripy cycling mitts, off the train from Petersfield. Unusually there must have been no leaves or cows or wrong kind of snow on the tracks because the train arrived precisely on time at 14.37.

We hugged, laughed and then scooted off with our bikes and our tickets to Ryde on the Isle of Wight Fastcat catamaran. Amazingly, the moment mum had appeared, the rain stopped and the sun burst out. I told her I thought she ought to join me for the next 10,000 miles around the coast if she could produce such desirable effects on the weather. Mum said that at her age she'd be lucky if she made it to Shanklin.

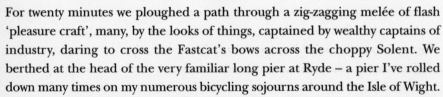

For twenty minutes we ploughed a path through a zig-zagging melée of flash 'pleasure craft', many, by the looks of things, captained by wealthy captains of industry, daring to cross the Fastcat's bows across the choppy Solent. We berthed at the head of the very familiar long pier at Ryde – a pier I've rolled down many times on my numerous bicycling sojourns around the Isle of Wight.

Leaving the majority of our fellow passengers to be either picked up by car or transported across the island by ex-London Transport rolling stock (the electric trains had once run on the Piccadilly Line), we cycled down the long, wet, narrow, tyre-swallowing wooden boards of the pier, which spans a broad sweep of gently shelving sands.

Once in Ryde, we rode along the Esplanade past the flipping and flicking and blipping and blurping amusement arcades and a fish-and-chip shop called The Codfather. The lake at Appley Park was awash with swans of two different varieties: the regal white-feathered mute and the garish plastic-moulded pedalo. The mutes paddled past their berthed brethren without batting a wing, but I couldn't help thinking that it must occasionally lead to the odd spot of confused copulation.

And so to Puckpool Point, where I was disappointed I couldn't see any pucks or any pools, but we did sight a P&O ferry sliding out over Spithead past Horse Sand and No Man's Land sea forts. After sailing through Seaview (favoured holidaying spot of Enid Blyton), we followed the back lanes and tracks and came upon the remains of St Helen's Church. Most of the building had been destroyed by sea erosion, leaving only the landward side of the tower, which would probably have disappeared as well but for Trinity House, who preserved it as a sea-mark. But it was not just the unremitting forces of the sea that had brought about the collapse of St Helen's. Sailors reputedly stole blocks of the sandstone for polishing the decks of their warships and this may be why, until fairly recently, naval men still called deck-cleaning sandstone 'holy stone'.

Offshore ran St Helen's Roads, a strip of sea much favoured by Nelson as a naval mooring due to the shelter it gave against westerly and southwesterly winds. Within the Roads rose another rocky bastion, St Helen's Fort, one of four island-like strongholds built in the 1860s on the order of prime minister Lord Palmerston, to protect the eastern Solent from possible French invasion. The forts were never needed and are known as 'Palmerston's Follies'.

Down we went to the Duver, a broad sandy spit backed by a National Trust area of gorse and open grassland where 260 species of plants have been identified. We rather ignored the botany side of things, as all hands were needed on deck for navigating through a minefield of dog turds.

After teetering across the narrow uneven stones of the walled causeway without ending up in either Bembridge Harbour on one side or the old Mill Ponds on the other, we joined the road that runs around the harbour foreshore, passing a fusty muster of houseboats with a disparate selection of names like *Vanessa*, *Zambezi* and *It's Only Me.*

It was only mum who could laugh at me for calling yet another stop so that I could remove yet another layer of clothing in order to prevent serious overheating, only to put it back on again further down the road. Anyone else would have shot me out of frustration. My long-suffering mother, meanwhile, patiently waited for me to tuck in T-shirts and rearrange a multitude of zips and Velcro fastenings as we stood astride our mounts outside Bembridge Shipwreck Centre.

In the midst of this little clothes-changing quirk, a hiking couple, shod in no-nonsense Zamberlan boots, stopped by for a chat. The man, a bearded birdwatcher, carried a daypack and an ergonomically shaped telescopic trekking pole, with his binoculars dangling at the ready round his neck. They were walking around the island in fits and bursts, they said, using their caravan as a base. This was all the more admirable because the woman was doing it with a frozen shoulder.

There are some words that you first hear mentioned in childhood that stay imprinted in your mind in the way that you initially imagined them all those years ago. A 'frozen shoulder' is one of mine and I still visualise people suffering from such an ailment as walking around with a shoulder of prime Welsh lamb, fresh from the freezer, wedged between their neck and upper arm.

Anyway, Mrs Zamberlan bore her complaint with good humour and proved most observant, remarking upon a label on my jacket displaying the name of a family-run expedition suppliers in Arundel from where I acquired a lot of my equipment.

'Well, fancy that!' she said. 'We know Peglers well too!'

And we spent the next ten minutes enrapt in outdoor equipment boffin-talk comparing variable performances of one product over another and weighing up various so-called 'active comfort layers' for their 'wicking' abilities. We even went so far as to discuss 'high-performance underwear'.

All this talking while standing still after our bout of vigorous exercise made me feel cold again. Hearing the sporting mantra 'retain all body heat' repeating itself in my mind, I removed my jacket to put on my fleece (a North Face 'Expedition Shirt' made of Polartec Series 100M Fleece, to be boffinly precise).

'Oh no!' cried my good mother, raising hand to forehead in an exaggerated show of despair. 'Not again!'

And we all laughed.

Mr and Mrs Zamberlan, having discovered that I was intending to circle the Isle of Wight as well as the British Isles, asked if I was a student and doing the trip in stages during the holidays. (Had I been down this road before?)

'Err, no . . .,' I said.

'Oh! Do you work then?' they asked with surprise, intimating that surely I couldn't be old enough to engage in such an activity.

'Sort of,' I said, keeping my cards close to my chest.

This is when I discovered that travelling with one's mother, when wishing to keep one's past under wraps, is not a good idea.

'She writes books!' piped my suddenly self-appointed southeast sales rep. 'This is *the* Josie Dew – who has cycled round the world!'

Being blushable by nature, I proceeded to blush profusely. With pulse throbbing and face on fire, I had to remove my fleece because I had suddenly overheated again. The Zamberlans appeared a little incredulous.

'Have you *really* written books?'

I don't think they would have believed me, a student of my lowly calibre, had I not been chaperoned by my virtuous-looking mother.

'Can we buy them in bookshops?' they asked.

'Yes, any good bookshops should stock them,' said my forthright sales rep. 'She's written four!'

'Gracious!'

I laughed and gave a heavenly look. 'I knew it would spell disaster going cycling with your mother!' I said.

The Zamberlans, obviously thinking that if I have cycled around the world then I must be in the possession of a very important bike, set about scrutinising its equipment in detail. On spotting my double-legged kickstand lying in its position of rest along my chainstays, Mr Zamberlan declared, 'Goodness, it's even got an exhaust!'

After a little more idle chatter, by which time I was cold again and so had to climb back into my fleece, we all departed in the finest of humours.

But we didn't make it very far as we decided to spend the night in the Windmill Inn. The manageress, presuming that as we were on bicycles we would be travelling light, offered to help us upstairs with our bags. Elephantine loads awaited in the hallway.

'God!' she exclaimed when she saw, and felt, the excessive pile of panniers. 'If I'd known you had all this, I'd have charged you twice as much!'

But she couldn't do that because in these tourist-paucity foot-and-mouth times, she badly needed our custom.

That evening we ate downstairs in the empty dining room. Mum (who, once she has removed her sales-rep hat, is really very lovely at heart) said she would treat me.

'I want you to have a good square meal inside you,' she said, knowing that I never eat out when I travel alone. But she hadn't bargained for just how many squares I would have to my meal.

It all began very normally and very nicely and we both ordered leek and potato soup to start with. For the main course mum branched out, choosing fish cakes, while I went for a plate of grilled sardines. These turned out to be so tasty that I ordered another plate.

In due course my second dose of oily sardines arrived. They didn't last long.

'You look like you're still hungry,' said mum, as I pushed the remaining heads and tails and backbones to the side of my plate.

'I am!' I said.

'You need something more filling – order something else,' she encouraged. This was her downfall, because I did.

'Is this all for you?' asked the waiter disbelievingly.

'I'm afraid so,' I assured him, 'I'm eating for ten!'

The waiter withdrew to the kitchen looking baffled and a trifle alarmed.

Before long I had a baked potato the size of a rugby ball sitting in front of me along with a Greek salad in a bowl as big as a paddling pool. Within twenty minutes the whole lot had clean disappeared. By this stage mum was ready for pudding and ordered chocolate ice cream. Having never been much of a pudding person myself, I ordered another bowl of leek and potato soup.

'Are you sure?' asked the waiter, his eyes popping out of his head.

'Yes, thank you,' I replied nonchalantly, determined not to be made into a laughing stock as the chef peeked around the door of the kitchen with an expression that said: Please no! No more!

Ice cream and soup arrived. Ice cream and soup disappeared. By now mum and I could hardly stop laughing.

'Wait till they see how much you eat for breakfast,' said mum. 'They'll probably ban you!'

In the event I forwent the breakfast. Not because I was suffering the consequences of the previous night's overindulgences – far from it, I felt I could eat a horse – but because they didn't serve porridge. So I left mum sitting downstairs eating breakfast-for-two while I retreated to our room, where I cooked up a big vat of porridge on my camping stove. For Mr and Mrs Zambelan's benefit, should they be reading this (which they better had be after all the motherly PR business they received), the stove is a canister-mounted MSR (Mountain Safety Rescue) Superfly with auto-start. Fortunately I managed to conduct the entire porridge-making operation without either spilling the lot over the carpet, or, more vitally, burning the whole place down.

When mum reappeared we turned on the TV for the May Day weather forecast. It was not good. For a place that claims it reaps 1741 hours of sunshine a year (making it one of Britain's sunniest), something had clearly gone wrong with the Isle of Wight's weather patterns since our arrival in Bembridge. The whole of the south of England was shown covered in black rain clouds as the emergency Floodline number conveyor-belted along the bottom of the screen. Distressingly, the entire north of England and Scotland lay beneath big bright nose-thumbing suns and unseasonably high temperatures. I felt like crying.

'I don't know how you manage it,' said mum, 'always ending up cycling in places while they're having their worst weather on record!'

On cue, the window rattled alarmingly from a violent gust of wind as stair-rodding rain hammered down.

For a mother who had originally said that she didn't fancy cycling with me in inclement conditions, she took the monsoon news in a remarkably buoyant manner.

'Come on,' she said, rallying the forces into action, 'we must do battle with the elements!'

Things didn't start well. While loading up our bikes outside, I was helping to bungee mum's camping mat on to her rear rack when a devilish gust of wind tore off a bit of guttering and emptied its watery contents into my upturned cycling helmet.

Mum, togged up to the nines in copious layers of waterproofs, billowing hood and fluorescent yellow 'I'm-from-the-council-come-to-mend-the-drains' day-glo vulnerable-road-user's top, looked so funny that we were both doubled up in a fit of hysterics and went quite weak, our energy all spent before we had even started.

Eventually, a more sensible air prevailed and we rode out to Foreland before passing through flooded farmland at Longlands and Yaverland. Then, after completing the grand total of 5.4 storm-lashed miles, we collapsed in a dripping heap into the 'Family Restaurant and Coffee House' at Sandown in order to warm our cockles.

'I need my morning coffee and a nice big bun before I go back out there and tackle another stretch!' declared mum. A fat slice of coffee walnut date cake looked like it would do the job nicely.

We sat in the window of the restaurant – a restaurant that served 'A wide range of Simply Scrumptious continental and local dishes' – and watched the teeming rain blowing in sheets across the road. A usually busy shopping street had been virtually washed clean of pedestrians. Occasionally the odd hooded figure, bent over double into the wind and rain, waded past the window. A couple of elderly women in macs and spotted-plastic rain caps shuffled past, battling with their inverted brollies.

Next heaving into view through the spray came the Sandown Express, the tourist toy train, trundling along at walking pace and completely empty save for two bedraggled tourists resolutely determined to 'do the holiday thing' regardless of how wet and miserable they felt. Mum and I found such antics most amusing.

Then I noticed an abandoned bag, sitting on the pavement just up the street at the bus stop.

'Might be a bomb!' I said excitably. 'Shall we alert the police?'

'I doubt anybody would go to the trouble of getting all wet just to bomb Sandown,' replied my unflappable mother. 'Someone must have forgotten their bag when they got on the bus.'

'But there haven't been any buses since we've been sitting here,' I said, 'only the Toy Town Express. And there wasn't a bag there before or else we would have noticed it.'

'Would we?' said mum. 'I've been more intent on ordering another piece of cake and cup of coffee than watching out for bags!'

Suddenly the plot thickened because, a little way down the street from the bus stop, a man in a brown cardigan and sunglasses appeared cowering in the doorway of the Belvedere Hotel (which, incidentally, advertised it had 'Platter Meals Available'). The man stood hunched over, wringing his hands while looking anxiously up and down the street.

'He looks sinister,' I said, smelling a rat. 'Do you think he planted the bag at the bus stop?'

'He's probably just sheltering in the doorway while waiting for the bus. It must be his bag.'

'Yes, but you wouldn't head out into a gale wearing sunglasses instead of a jacket and then stand that far away from your bag, would you? Someone might swipe it.'

'I don't think there's anyone around *to* swipe it,' said mum, 'apart from those elderly women in their spotted rain caps – and they seem to have walked past the bag without even noticing it.'

Mum and I were enjoying this. It was all terribly exciting for a wet Tuesday in Sandown. Then things hotted up.

'Look!' I said. 'The man's moved!'

Looking as miserable as ever, our suspect walked past Platters Café and Restaurant (Sandown likes its platters) in his inappropriate attire to the bus stop. He stopped and glanced at the bag before looking up and down the nigh-deserted street.

'If he's waiting for the bus,' said mum, 'I think he really would have been better off catching the Toy Town Express. It looks like it's got a more regular service!'

Mum may have been making light of such dramatic developments, but I was keeping both feet firmly planted on the ground.

'I don't like the look of this at all,' I said. 'I think he's going to pinch it! Shall I go and stop him?'

'No, stay here Jose! Your pot of tea's coming.'

But tea was the last thing on my mind when, through a rain-streaked window, we were about to witness a dodgy character in a cardigan making off up the street with someone's bag. I was on the point of bursting out of the door to perform an impressive rugby tackle while shouting 'STOP! THIEF!' (or should that be the other way round? – Step 1. Shout; Step 2. Tackle) when the man trudged off up the street past the empty gift shops until he stopped opposite a store called Island Girl. Craning my neck, nose pressed against the steamy glass, I gave mum a running commentary: '. . . He's stopped again . . . he's looking over his shoulder . . . he's still wringing his hands and looking miserable . . . Oh no! . . . He's coming back! . . . He's walking faster . . . he's looking at the bag . . . I think he's going to pinch it . . . he's going to pick it up . . . Oh no! . . . He has picked it up! . . . '

'That's because his bus is coming,' remarked my unperturbed mother, masticating a mouthful of cake.

A big red double-decker bus with 'Route Rouge Southern Vectis' painted on the side ('Vectis' was the Roman name for the island) loomed into view. The man climbed into the bus and his identity became hidden behind the steamed-up windows. After a slight pause, the bus pulled away up the street towards Island Girl. And life for the window-seat occupants of Sandown's 'Family Restaurant and Coffee House' returned to normal.

It was going to be one of those days when it just keeps on raining relentlessly; when no amount of sitting around playing for time over coffee and cake will have any effect on the weather whatsoever.

We carried on aquaplaning through Shanklin until we were directed off our coastal route by mudslides and closed roads. So we headed inland to Godshill, where the chief glory of the village is its church. According to legend, its original builders laid the foundations in a more easily accessible flat site, but every morning the stones were found to have been transferred to the hilltop. The builders gave in and built the church on its commanding knoll.

From Godshill we diverted course through a narrow network of country lanes. Although these were flooded and pot-holed and covered in mud, they seemed like a cycling treat after the annoyance of the incessant overly-close-passing puddle-spraying traffic along the busy A3055 coastal road. I said to mum I felt bad at having to bypass the coast so soon into my seaside voyage. She told me not to worry because, after all, I had cycled around the coast of the Isle of Wight enough times in the past.

'I know,' I said, 'but that doesn't count because I didn't do it on this bike, on this ride.'

'Well, I don't really see that that matters,' said mum, 'but if you're still feeling bad you can always come back and do it later in the year.'

So I did. With my builder. Over Christmas. And the road was still closed. Due to a landslide.

Mum and I took momentary cover from the onslaught of the weather by diving into the sumptuous setting of Chale Green's vandalised and graffiti-riddled bus shelter. Here we kept the nagging hunger pangs at bay by devouring a packet of Ryvita and a bunch of bananas – the best our dripping panniers could come up with at short notice. The only Certificate PG graffiti, daubed in wild aerosol lettering behind mum's head, read: 'SCHOOLS CRAP' and 'VICKY IS A FAT SLAG!' Unfortunately we couldn't stay long enough to read all the more obscene X-rated slogans and decipher all the anatomical diagrams, as we had to get moving. Hypothermia was setting in.

Our chilled state was not helped by a development in the weather: heavy rain turning into heavy hail. Combined with the ferocious winds, it slapped our faces and stung our cheeks.

'What *am* I doing?' shouted mum into the tempestuous gale. 'I'm far too old for this!'

The conditions turned so appalling for what should have been a pleasant potter on a warm May day that we rode along laughing manically at the ridiculousness of it all.

Just before three o'clock we washed up in the village of Shorwell in a sorry state, our mouths so cold we could scarcely speak, our fingers so frozen we couldn't undo the clips on our panniers. All we could do was cackle with laughter.

Mooring our bikes together in the submerged car park of The Crown, we fell through the door of the pub and collapsed in a shivering, teeth-chattering heap at a table next to a radiator pumping out glorious heat. The barman came over to us.

'Sorry ladies,' he said, 'but we're just about to close.'

Crestfallen looks, chattering teeth, numb lips devoid of all life were enough to make him change his mind. *Oh, you lovely, lovely man!* He brought us tea and coffee and biscuits and let us dry our gloves on the radiator. And for that we were truly grateful.

By the time we re-emerged at our bikes, our cheeks and feet were rosy and glowing and we felt we could handle whatever the weather threw at us. Which was just as well because, in the event, it threw a lot of very unpleasant things our way.

CHAPTER 8

The Isle of Wight might not be very big – 23 miles long by 13 miles wide – but it can fit a lot of people on it: the whole of the population of the world, to be precise. At least, that is what the people in the tourist office told me.

Anyway, because this diamond-shaped island is not very big, mum and I found we had cycled to the other side in no time. And it was here, at Totland Bay, that I swapped my mother for my builder. He came complete with bike and roomy Roadrunner II tent. We saw mum off at Yarmouth to catch the Wightlink ferry to Lymington, where dad would meet her and whisk her home in time to play the piano with her local music group, the Linden Singers, that night.

Meanwhile, Gary and I rode out to the chalk cliff-rimmed bay at Freshwater and took big lungfuls of the air that Tennyson described as being worth 'sixpence a pint', before heading off across the north of the island back towards Ryde.

Unlike the dripping and wintery conditions of the day before, the rain stopped and the sun came out and it became so hot that we couldn't shed layers fast enough. Even suncream (factor 25) was called for. This is one of the reasons why I love living among the watery ways of the British Isles. Unlike more continental climes, where it can either be too hot or too cold or too wet for weeks, if not months, on end, these maritime lands of ours can throw every possible season at us, sometimes during the course of only one day. And so did a varied taster of the British weather, for all its endearing foibles, hit us as we stopped to eat bananas and tinned sardines on a bench at Egypt Point. We arrived hot and sweaty, clad in minimum clothing, only to deteriorate within the course of an hour to woolly hats and wearing all our clothes as the sun disappeared and the wind whipped up and the temperature dropped ten degrees. It wasn't until several hills later that a modicum of heat returned to our numbed extremities.

At Ryde we passed a special rope bridge, seventeen metres long, strung above a busy main road and designed to enable red squirrels to cross safely. We booked into The Round House, where 'Bed & Board' for two cost £30, which didn't seem too bad until we discovered just what a ropy old place it was. Gary, being a builder, declared the building to be structurally unsound. Upstairs literally moved. With sinking footings, the walls subsided at an alarming angle, cracks spreading away from the corners of the doorframes. The floor of our room was so uneven, and came with such a concave dip in it, that we dropped downhill on entering before climbing uphill to get to the window. In fact the gradient was so steep that we felt it was negligent of the proprietor, Mrs S.L. Budden, not to issue us with crampons and an ice axe to see us safely up the precipitous slope in order to open the window.

'I really feel we ought to be roped together,' I said, as I attempted an ascent of the North Face of The Round House, determined to summit at the fanlight, 'lest I fall off into the undesirable distant depths of the murky shag-pile carpet.'

Mountaineering requirements aside, we had to feel our way across the room owing to the economic lighting provided: a couple of lamps whose combined wattage would have failed to emit even enough crepuscular illuminations for a child's nightlight. To extricate anything from our panniers necessitated having to strap on our head torches to see what we were doing. The bed gave as much support as a sea of blancmange and creaked and squeaked and twanged and clanked and clinked to such an extent that it seemed more an instrument of torture than a means for sleeping. Stale smoke hung so heavy in the air that our room came decorated in uniform nicotine brown: a wetted finger rubbed against a wall produced a glimpse of its former glossy white glory. Only the corners escaped, pale patches indicating dead areas where the smoke couldn't reach.

The only other occupants of The Round House were a group of what Mrs S.L. Budden described as 'workers'. Heavy-booted, chain-smoking, phlegm-retching ones as it turned out, with whom we shared a bathroom with stained shag-pile bathmat, seat-up splashed toilet and overflowing ashtrays.

Somerfield was open late and we walked up the road to buy bag-loads of cyclists' fodder so that we could graze the night away. On the way Gary stopped to get some money out of the Abbey National cash machine. As I waited for him I was approached by one of Ryde's resident drunks – a garrulous soul called Clive with graveyard teeth.

'Hullo me darlin',' he said, as he lurched and belched and reeled around me. 'Yer know wha'? I think it's me lucky day cos I mettalady on the bus . . . right gorgeous she were . . . big busty sort an' all that . . . said she'd meet me some place later. Phwoar! Now wha' d'yer reckon with that Tony chap an' all that government thing cos I reckon yer can't presume nothin', yer can't!'

'Well, Clive,' I said, building up for a profound philosophical declaration, 'I reckon you just can't presume nothing these days either!'

'Ha, ha! That's right, me darlin' . . . can't presume nothin' these days, can yer? Tell that to Tony, eh?' And for his grand finale, Clive stumbled off the pavement and staggered off down the street shouting, 'Tony me old chap – yer 'ear that? Yer can't presume NOTHIN'! Ha, ha!'

With the General Election merely days away, I felt it might be an idea for President Blair to come to Ryde and lend an ear to Clive.

Around midnight the workers returned to The Round House in an inebriated state. There was a lot of crashing and banging and shouting and prolonged lung-retching, hacking and hawking. The man in the next-door room sounded as if he was coughing up his guts. The walls were so paper-thin that he might just as well have been in our room for all the sound-proofing they provided. I stuck a pillow over my head and tried to forget about life. And I succeeded because eventually I fell asleep.

In the morning Gary informed me that I should have held out for an hour longer because I missed the best bit: next-door's excessive resonations of fornication complete with such extended rhythmic bed-creaking that Gary felt our whole room rock and shake. I was terribly disappointed to have missed such an earth-moving performance and scolded him for not waking me.

Now I know I haven't painted a particularly appealing picture of The Round House, but I would like to give Mrs S.L. Budden credit for one thing: willingly allowing us to park our bikes in her dining room. Such charitable behaviour speaks volumes of a place, no matter how reeking of smoke the rooms, or unsound the structure of the building. Our bikes are our everything and, for that, we can only hold Mrs S.L. Budden in the highest regard.

A bad night's sleep was not followed by a well-deserved lie-in. We were up at 6.25 a.m. and were soon flying downhill to the Esplanade as we had two boats to be catching. The first was the Fastcat that whisked us back to Portsmouth in sparkling sunshine.

The second was Condor's *Commodore Clipper* to the Channel Islands. To reach this ferry we had to slalom through Portsmouth's exhaust-thick morning rush-hour traffic to the continental ferry terminal, where we had to negotiate the measures for foot-and-mouth precautions as issued by the State of Jersey Department of Agriculture and Fisheries. Their form of declaration asked:

1. Have you been on a farm and/or in contact with livestock within the last two weeks? [No]
2. Have you been involved with any country pursuits? (i.e. country walking/horse riding/cycling etc.) [Yes. Cycling on roads]

2a. If yes ... do you have any of the clothing/footwear worn during such country pursuits with you? [Yes]

3. Do you have **any** foodstuffs in your possession? False declaration will lead to prosecution. [Yes. Lots]

Fortunately we were aware of such food restrictions so the only banned produce we had left in our panniers was a yoghurt (me) and a large chunk of cheese (Gary). We had a choice: either eat them, throw them away or pay a £1000 fine if we tried to smuggle them into the Channel Islands. Not a hard decision – we polished them off for breakfast as we sat in the terminal.

We boarded the *Commodore Clipper* along with only three passenger vehicles (the rest was freight) and we were swept across the English Channel to Jersey where, on disembarkation, we had to ride through disinfectant mats before being sprayed with disinfectant jets. Our wheels, panniers, pedals, bottles, legs and shoes smelt like a stale hospital floor for days.

We followed the cars through Customs. The first car was waved through without a hitch. The second, with a young couple and child, was found with one litre of milk and eight flavoured yoghurts in the boot. The woman Customs officer confiscated the goods, looking very pleased with herself. The couple bore different expressions: he looked very sheepish; she very annoyed.

Gary said they should be shot as an example to others. I told him not to get above his station because we still had to get through ourselves and, you never know, we could yet find our panniers had been planted with a large cache of Double Gloucester and half a pig of smoked-back bacon.

The third car, an immaculate open-top red MG with sun-glinting chrome spoked wheels, contained a well-coiffured wife and husband with high clipped voices. They were caught with a carton of milk. This find didn't seem to worry them; they appeared much more concerned at the detrimental effect the disinfectant spray might have on their vehicle's smooth and shiny bodywork because, as they said rather loudly, they were about to partake in Jersey's MG Owners' Club Spring Rally.

When it was our turn, Gary and I handed in our food declaration form and were asked some questions about what we were carrying. We answered 'yes' to foodstuffs but 'no' to dairy and meat. We got waved through without a search. This was a surprise because I had said to Gary as we were waiting in line that being with him, a big bruiser of a builder with a crew cut, we were bound to get hauled over for the Customs officers to go through our panniers, his suspect appearance undoubtedly cancelling out my pure and angelic one.

As soon as we set wheel in St Helier, Jersey's granite-paved capital, the sun was swallowed by a threatening band of cloud. A spitty rain fell. We stopped at Co-op Centrale to restock our depleted dairy department, not to mention a small shipment of biscuits, cakes, buns, pies, pasties, porridge oats, bananas, tinned sardines, wine gums, crisps, honey and jam – most of which, along with several tons of my carrots, apples, cabbages, cucumbers, tomatoes, kiwis, grape-fruits, melons, onions and garlic, I managed to cram into Gary's panniers. Gary, who doesn't like fruit or vegetables apart from bananas or, when very daring, the odd apple or kiwi (he's a bit strange like that), thought this usurping of his bags was most unjust. But I didn't let this worry me.

As we were packing up our panniers, we were set upon by two Jersey born-and-bred road sweeps.

'Polystyrene packaging – you just can't catch the rascals!' complained one as he dived beneath my bike trying to corner a windswept piece. He gave up and lit a half-smoked cigar instead.

'I needs a rest and a puff after that!' he said. He told us he got his cigars brought over cheap from France. 'I smokes about a quarter at a time,' he explained, 'before I puts him back in the tin.'

Spotting a pack of open mints on the pavement, he bent down, picked them up and put them in his pocket.

The other road sweep said, 'Used to cycle meself, I did. Used to go twice as fast.'

'Twice as fast as what?' I asked. 'Lightning?'

'That's it, me luv, I was young and fit in them days. There was no stopping me. All over I went. It was the way we all got around. Used to it, we were.'

During our elongated shopping extravaganza, the spitting rain had decided to call it a day and the early evening sky turned a cloudless watery iris blue. A keen cold wind blew, smelling of fish and France. Gary had never been to France and seemed quite excited at the prospect that the French coastline lay a mere 14 miles away.

'Shall we go there?' I said. 'We could catch a boat tomorrow and then ride down through the middle of France to the Mediterranean for a nice bit of hot sunshine!'

'It's very tempting,' said Gary.

'And then we could cycle across Europe to Turkey and up to China and down to Australia and New Zealand, and then come back through South America and up to Alaska and across Canada to home.'

'What, all by this weekend?'

'Well, maybe a bit longer'

Gary had never been to another country until he was twenty-eight – the year before I met him – when he went to Benidorm for ten days. Apart from the odd trip to the Isle of Wight, his dad, a carpenter for the council earning at the most £100 a week, couldn't afford to take his family of five on holiday. And I don't think Gary really minded at all – he was more than content to spend his time dragging things like old bicycles and broken lawnmowers and televisions and engines and interesting lumps of metal off Hampshire's largest landfill site up the road, which he would either mend or make into something else in his back garden. He told me it was guaranteed that every day among the jetsam of household waste he could find a bicycle that he would be able to ride home – the flat tyres, buckled wheels, broken brakes or stiff rusty chain not preventing the 300-yard haphazard swoop downhill to his workshop-garden. His elder brothers would raid the dump too (until it was closed down and bulldozed to make way for a heap of incongruous and very unvillage-like Berkeley 'executive' homes), but not so enthusiastically as Gary. Paul, the middle brother, preferred birds, while big brother David focused on small engines.

The furthest north in the world Gary had ever been was York, when he acted as my roadie for a cycling talk I had given at the CTC York Rally a few summers ago; the furthest west, Dublin, where, having to do similar bicycle things, I had cajoled him into being my bicycling Sherpa. To reach Dublin from the port of Dun Laoghaire (in theory an easy seven miles along the seafront), we went on a forty-four mile detour as a result of asking the way from an Irishman with a dog called Clogga. Still, like the Chinese say, if you don't change direction you'll end up where you're going. And going to where you are going is never any fun. We ended up getting lost in Sally's Gap, which sounds a bit crude but was actually a lovely wild and empty place in the Wicklow Mountains.

Standing on the sea wall looking out over Jersey's fair shores, it suddenly felt like the world was our lobster pot, that we could dive into the deep end and go with the flow of the wind. But, however tempting the thought of taking off to New Zealand there and then on our bikes, we couldn't really do it because . . . well, Gary had a building to be building and, more vitally, had only one pair of spare underpants about his person. I, on the other hand, had a coast to be coasting around and felt highly enthused to ride to places like Milford-on-Sea rather than Milford Sound. At least for the moment.

So, throwing a leg or two over our crossbars, we cycled off along the Esplanade past Happy Days Fun Club and the site of the Battle of Flowers and on to the grand sweeping cycle path that follows the gorgeous gasp of white crescent beach that curls around St Aubin's Bay. At the small town of St Aubin itself (Jersey's original port) we passed the Abracadabra Craft Centre and Dive Buddies before climbing a narrow winding street so steep that we nearly flipped over backwards. It was a Green Lane, part of Jersey's network of roads which, with a 15 mph speed limit, give pedestrians and cyclists priority over the car. A cyclist's heaven, in other words. Jersey has over fifty miles of Green Lanes and the island's aim is to keep country life at an unspoilt pace and to protect hedgerows and coastal dunes and the wildlife that live among them.

A spectacular flash-gun sunset was followed by a chilly night sleeping outside a noisy toilet block up at Rose Farm Campsite, which was overrun with excitable French schoolchildren. The next-door tent contained a couple of amorous students who, judging from a lot of overly audible panting and moaning, spent the majority of the night in various states of coition. Unfortunately I slept through some of the best bits, Gary once again letting down the side and failing to wake me at the crucial crux of the moment. I ate his banana for breakfast as punishment.

CHAPTER 9

The following morning the builder and I spent so long busying ourselves with inner tent activities – like cooking, eating, reading, writing, snoozing, stretching, scratching, sewing, sorting, sifting, tidying, drinking, flipping, flopping, sighing and a few other things like . . . wood carving (Gary had found a broken wooden tent peg and was fashioning an adaptation for my handlebar bag support) – that it was midday by the time we had packed up and loaded up and taken off up La Route des Genets.

We wound our way along a series of Green Lanes until we briefly joined l'Avenue de la Reine Elizabeth II. Everything smelt and felt very French – a bit like riding through Brittany, though with rather too many Brits.

Despite their close proximity to the French coast (the Gallic novelist Victor Hugo called them a little piece of France dropped into the sea), the Channel Islands have never been owned by France and remain loyal to our very own Queen, even though they are self-governing. To prove how independent they can be, the islanders speak English but they still use a little Norman French patois and many laws and customs remain firmly rooted in the islands' Norman past.

Sitting in the Gulf of St Malo, the islands are supposedly the sunniest in Britain (oh, what about the Isle of Wight?). As if to prove their claim, it was another cold and windy but beautifully bright sparkling day, and I was ready and raring to go for a brisk galloping ride along the wave-slapping shore. But the builder had other ideas. Being something of a historical boffin at heart, he

61

expressed his desire to pay a visit to the German Underground Hospital – now a freshly refurbished museum, which the tourist leaflet described as 'Jersey's most evocative reminder of the five years of enemy occupation during World War II'. Traipsing about underground through miles of tourist-filled tunnels does not really rate as my highest priority on a bright breezy day (or even a wet dismal one, for that matter) when surrounded by a rocky and enticing coast that is just asking to be cycled around at a wild hell-for-leather pace. But I'm ever easy to satisfy (yes, really!) and so we cycled off to the Hospital and ventured from a day of dazzling sunshine into one of chill, artificially lit darkness in a warren of tunnels that were hewn out of solid rock by slaveworkers of many nationalities. The museum proved a surprising eye-opener; until then, I had been only vaguely aware of the German Occupation of the Channel Islands.

As the builder and I wandered out towards the exit, we stopped to peer through the caged-off entrance of an unfinished tunnel (the end of the war had interrupted its completion). The sharp, jagged, hacked-at walls looked black and dripping and menacing and brought back unpleasant memories of blundering through endless unlit road-tunnels on my bike in Norway and Japan. In the shadowy cavernous darkness lay, among the rubble, what looked like the remains of some sort of motor.

'It's a small Lister pump,' declared Gary sounding very certain. 'It'll have "OF DURSLEY, ENGLAND" cast on the side.'

And the trouble was, I knew he would be right. He just knows things like that. Once, when bulleting down a Devon hill on our bikes, we had passed a lay-by in mid-descent in which I caught a glimpse of the remains of a car engine that someone had dumped. When we slowed down I asked Gary if he had seen it and, aware of his affinity for all things mechanical, said, 'I thought you might have stopped to try and resuscitate it.'

This had set him off to enlighten me exactly as to the identification of the engine. Apparently, for those of you who may be interested, it was a Pinto engine out of a Mark 4 or Mark 5 Ford Cortina.

'Could have been a Capri 1800 or 2 litre,' said Gary generously giving a little leeway to its precise identity. 'They made a few 1300s too, but chances are it was an 1800.'

'How can you tell all that from a blur of metal at the side of the road?' I said.

'They've got distinctive cam covers, those engines,' he replied.

'Oh. I see,' I said, with a glazed expression, wondering how on earth I was having a conversation about sizes of car engines and recognisable cam covers while bowling along by bike on a sunny Devon day. What the devil is a cam cover, anyway? I decided it was better not to ask as it would only set him off again and I'd get lost in the mechanical fog of the internal combustion of it all.

By the time we had emerged from the museum we were hungry. So we plunged downhill towards the sea on Le Chemin des Moulins. Never mind windmills – a more apt name would have been Le Chemin des Autos, for the road was full of nose-to-tail vehicles moving at a crawl in a lung-clogging, artery-thickening snarl-up. This was due not to any accident or roadworks, but to the sheer weight of Saturday afternoon traffic. For an island that measures only nine miles by five, Jersey's number of registered vehicles (nearly 100,000) seems absurd. And for an island full of narrow winding roads whose maximum speed limit is 40 mph, you would have thought that the most sensible choice of vehicle – if you *had* to have one – would be a Mini or a Robin Reliant or a bubble car run on electricity or hydrogen or chicken dung or chip fat. In other words, something small and compact and as least polluting as possible.

Unfortunately, thanks to the thousands of multi-millionaires who flock to Jersey to enjoy its sunshine and favourable tax regime, the majority of vehicles we cycled past were gas-guzzling Mercedes, Maseratis, Ferraris, Jaguars, Lamborghinis, Alfa-Romeos, BMWs and fat four-wheel-drives with smoked-glass windows. For these drivers, it was evidently far more important to be seen cruising around in their big shiny weapons of mass consumption than it was to worry about the destruction of the beauty and the peace of the very environment in which they had chosen to live. (Sorry, am I getting all soap-boxy again? I love them all dearly, really.)

Back down at St Aubin's Bay, we wheeled our bikes down Gunsite Slip and, with our backs to its rough stone wall, sat eating a very late lunch in a sunshiny nook out of the chill-zinging wind. The beach was big and empty. Because of the weather's glorious glow of faint radiant warmth, we were able to expose our unappetising white northern European legs to the sun and rolled up our cycling bottoms to the knees. The sight of us looking on the warm side of cold while slumped on the sand set a trend and we were soon joined by several seafront promenaders. Within moments, our little space of solitude had been invaded by two middle-aged couples on holiday from England. They sat down an arm's length away from me and did a fine job at ignoring us both. Above the noise of a wildly flapping kite being flown by another new beach arrival, I caught a few snatches of chat: '. . . ooh, doesn't that bit of sun feel nice . . . shame we've had such parky weather . . . skate wings? . . . Do you? . . . I prefer sticking to a nice piece of cod myself . . . no, he couldn't decide so we bought them all . . . well, if they don't like them, they can take them down the charity shop!'

One of the men (who was absentmindedly stirring up the sand with his toes, spraying a cascade of gritty grains on to my freshly peeled banana) described how at work the other day he had to mend some sort of pump which kept getting jammed. So he wedged a shimmy down it and that didn't work so he got hold of a widget and took it apart again and . . . The other man listened attentively, sporadically injecting his mate's monologue with, 'I get you . . . I hear what you're saying . . . yup, yup, I'm with you . . . yup, I know where you're coming from . . .'

The tide raced in at such a rate of knots that Gary and I were forced to stir ourselves into action. This was a shame because we would have been quite content to continue eating and lolling around in the sun and the sand for several more days yet. We found just enough energy to ride along the seafront cycle track to Stampers supermarket, dodging a torrent of youngsters weaving erratically across our path on a haphazard mixture of unicycles, micro-scooters and rollerblades – the latter adept at skating backwards into on-coming bicycles.

Emerging from the supermarket with bagfuls of Stampers produce, we found an elderly man in a jaunty yachting cap surveying our bikes as he stood astride his sturdy Raleigh.

'That's quite some load you've got on there!' he said.

After asking a few technical questions, like 'Don't front panniers make the bike unsteady?' (answer: no, they steady it), he told us how he had always cycled himself and was over on a day's ride from Guernsey, where he had lived for most of his life.

'But I'm feeling ever more despondent at the ever-growing increase in traffic on the Islands,' he said. 'You find so many roads now stuck in a constant traffic jam.' Ahh, a man taking a ticket after my own high hobby-horsing spiel. I warmed to him immediately.

'I can't see the point of having a car here, specially such expensive status symbols with top speeds of 175 mph,' he said. 'What's the point of driving a vehicle that can go from nought to sixty in about five seconds when we have a maximum speed limit of 40 mph? Makes no sense to me!'

Our behaviour probably didn't make much sense to Danny and Leone, the young couple from Yorkshire who ran Rose Farm campsite – the very site in which we had woken up that morning and checked out from at midday. Seven hours later we had returned to book back in again.

'Do you just like putting up and taking down tents or summat?' asked Leone.

Well, yes, we did – tent erection can be strangely therapeutic as well as satisfying. But we tried to assure Danny and Leone that today's camping behaviour had not been deliberate as we had planned to spend the day cycling around the island before camping on the other side of St Helier, but like all well-laid plans they had come adrift, blah, blah, blah . . . and so . . . here we are now! They both laughed before putting us back by the toilet block, apologising that it was the only space they had left as yet another party of French schoolchildren had invaded the premises.

Having clocked up a grand total of 8.56 miles, we had no qualms about constructing a lavish feast within our torch-lit nylon walls, and dined until the chill of the night forced us to retire to the all-embracing warmth of our sleeping bags.

We awoke the following morning to a cold and persistent drizzle, lightly pattering like a rain of pine needles on the roof of the tent – a lovely sound that makes you want to turn over and go back to sleep. But we couldn't do that because we had to get to the airport. The builder's time was up and he had to fly to Guernsey to pick up a boat to Portsmouth, from where he would pick up a train to Liss from where he would cycle home. Buildings needed building.

I continued riding round the rest of Jersey on my lonesome.

CHAPTER 10

At the barren peninsula jutting out from Jersey's western flank, I ran in the rain across the causeway and stood in the cold frisky wind watching the frothing sea spray the needle-sharp rocks at Corbière Point – site of Britain's first concrete lighthouse.

Down at St Ouen's Bay, I stopped again to stand on the sand of the vast swathe of wind-raked beach. Because Jersey has one of the largest tidal flows in the world – up to forty feet – the water's edge had all but disappeared from view. I knew the tide was on the turn so I waited and was rewarded by the sight of the sea thundering towards me across the beach in great curling arcs of grey-green and frothing white water. No wonder, I thought, that a tide-warning siren is sounded at Corbière's causeway: caught by such a galloping sea it would be all too easy to get stranded.

Onwards I cycled, past the jarring site of the brash Watersplash nightclub. A few miles further north, the roadside was crowded with a flamboyant mixture of wild flowers and small, serve-yourself stalls selling bags of new potatoes and big bunches of parsley.

Diving behind one cliff-hanging hedge for a pee, I came face-to-face with a great mat of fleshy Hottentot fig, a native succulent of South Africa which now thrives in frost-free areas along the coasts of the Channel Islands and southwest England. I like this plant not only because its fruits are edible, but because its former official name, *Mesembryanthemum*, became converted in everyday Cornish speech to Sally-my-handsome, which I find rather dashing.

There was more local nature to be found at Leoville where, in a quiet skinny lane heading down to the wooded valley of Grève de Lecq, I came across a small boy catching a slow-worm with a fishing-net. When he caught it he looped it around his fingers to show me and we both marvelled at its limbless-lizard beauty. Unlike snakes, which have no eyelids, slow-worms, or 'blind worms' (which are neither blind nor worms), look comparatively coquettish as they flirtatiously make eyes at you with their movable lids.

In the little harbour at Rozel Bay, I sat hooded on a bench in a brisk windy drizzle to eat a tin of tuna while gazing at the small fishing boats looking festive with their bundles of balloon-type pink buoys, and names like *Aqua Star* and *Humbug*. By the time I was on my banana course, the wet sheet of cold, grey sky was blowing out to sea to be replaced by a sparkling plate of blue.

The sky was still blue as I cycled down the mile-long breakwater at St Catherine's Bay where, at walking pace, I eased past a man who exclaimed, 'You won't find France that way!' *I won't?*

Further along I rode past another man who called, 'Don't forget to put your brakes on at the end!' Oh dear, I thought. How many more witty wags do I have to endure?

At the end of the breakwater (where I did remember to stop – but it was a close thing), I climbed on to the sea wall and sat for ages in the sun, watching people amble up and down. Huddled around the head stood half a dozen men fishing. One of them was a small rotund Frenchman with a weathered leather face. He was catching fish by the handful. Every time he unhooked a flapping fish from his line, he dropped it in a bucket, which he covered with his jacket. No one else caught anything and whenever the Frenchman wound in his catch, everyone turned to look at him with a mixture of admiration and malice.

Two little girls called Emma and Kirsty were skipping and running around on the quay in their socks. Every so often their irritated father, who was unsuccessfully fishing, shouted at them to put their shoes on in case they stepped on any discarded fish-hooks. They ignored him and kept playing. The older one, Emma, showed Kirsty how to draw a fish with a broken piece of rock on the stone wall.

'Start with a kiss like this . . . ,' she said, 'Then put half a circle at this end for his head . . . and a line the other end for his tail . . . There!' And she gave a little jig of satisfaction. Kirsty latched on to this primitive form of raw art and covered the wall with big kissy fishes.

Dropping down the zig-zag hill into Gorey I met a cyclist on a road bike with tri-bars.

'Josie Wells, isn't it?' he said. 'I read your book a few years back.'

Brian, or even Bryan, told me he was president of the local cycling club.

'I'm a Londoner really. Then I lived up in Yorkshire for a while before I got a job offer as a building surveyor in Jersey. That was in 1963. Been here ever since.'

At the bottom of the hill he said, 'We don't leave the island that often these days. Occasionally we take the car over to France – but the bike has to go too. The wife accepts it – she's got used to it by now!'

That night I rang mum and she told me she had walked round to my house that afternoon (we live four fields away) and picked up and disposed of twenty-eight deathwatch beetles off my bedroom floor. It's nice to know mothers have their uses.

More disinfectant baths awaited me in Guernsey as I rolled off the ramp of the Emeraude Line's MV *Solidor 5* and into the docks of St Peter Port. It was raining again and, as the weather forecasters kept telling me, 'unseasonably cold'; all very different weather compared with the hot May days of my last visit to Guernsey. That was in 1990 when I set off from the Channel Islands to cycle to Romania (just after Ceauşescu was shot) before heading on towards Egypt. But I never made it that far: as I was riding through Turkey, Iraq invaded Kuwait and started firing Scud missiles at Israel. So to spare mum further sleepless nights worrying about my welfare, I did a U-turn and rode home across Greece, Italy, Sardinia, Corsica and France.

I remember Guernsey well because mum had joined me on her old bike and we had a very funny time sleeping in a field in my bivvy bag. It was also the place where I felt my first nephew move: Dave and Mel (my brother and his wife) came over to meet us and one afternoon we were all lying in the sun among the wild flowers of a grassy clifftop when Mel took my hand and placed it on her fast-expanding stomach and I felt the baby kick. Instead of marvelling at the joys of her impending motherhood I said, 'Urgh! Feels like Alien!' Fred turned out very nice, though.

This time there were no moving stomachs to touch and no mothers with whom to crawl into Goretex sacks. But I did find a grandmother to talk to, called Peggy. I spent two nights camping in a field (accompanied by two nocturnally nosy hedgehogs) at her eighteenth century farmhouse. It was the only house on the island with a cellar because, so she said, it was once used to smuggle goods due to its proximity to the sea.

Peggy, an islander from birth, told me how when she was eleven she had been evacuated during the war with her mother and sister, first to Wigan and then to Coventry.

'It's a shame I never kept in contact with any of the friends I went to school with over there,' she said. 'When the war ended we all went our separate ways. My husband, he still sees his school chums as they were islanders.'

It was a lucky thing her husband was here at all because he very nearly might not have been. Peggy described how he was evacuated with a group of children and, once in England, they were all lined up and 'housing-parents' would scrutinise them and say: I'll have that one. Or: you have that one and I'll have this one. He ended up in a house that was bombed during a night raid. The other small boy with whom he shared a bed was killed, as was his temporarily adoptive mother. He had survived unscathed.

As I cycled around Guernsey I found it was an island full of coastal fortifications – strongholds dating from the Iron Age to the Second World War, including castles, watchtowers, batteries, forts and Hitler's Atlantic Wall (over 66,000 mines were laid around Guernsey) – as well as blue postboxes and perfect rocky sandy bays with Gallic-seasoned names like Rocquaine, Petit Bôt, Miellette, Pontenelle and L'Ancresse. Though look a bit deeper and they were maybe not *that* perfect: despite the tourist leaflet bumf extolling the virtues of the island's 'imaginative cuisine highlighted by our seafood, freshly caught in our clean and pure local waters', the blazing headlines of *The Guernsey Press and Star* ('Serving the Islands for 188 years') screamed 'Sewage pollution of our seas must stop'. The president of the Guernsey Hotel and Tourism Association demanded that the pumping of sewage directly into the sea be stopped. 'Visitors to Guernsey see sewage carts running around the island and I'm sure some must think they're in a third world country,' he said.

I can't say that I saw many sewage carts or, as the paper put it, 'sanitary debris' myself. But I did see plenty of completely out-of-proportion-for-a-small-island four-wheel-drives, unfailingly containing one or two infants strapped in like astronauts to their high and haughty child seats, and driven by mothers impatient to squeeze past my bike on the narrow and rocky wall-lined lanes.

The island was also full of flying flags – flapping and fluttering from poles and trees and buildings, or strings of bunting strung out like washing across windows and gardens and hedges and harbours. For Wednesday May 9th was Liberation Day – the day when the intimidating sound of German jackboots was heard no more. Peggy had told me that she thought the islands should no longer celebrate Liberation Day.

'They should still keep the holiday, but I think youngsters now are too distant from all those war happenings,' she said. 'The time's come to leave the past behind us. You can't keep looking back, can you?'

The morning of Liberation Day I awoke to find a glaze of frost sparkling the roof of my tent. The past few nights had been so raw that it felt as if the weather had more winter in its bones than spring. Instead of undressing to go to bed, I had heaved and tugged on every additional piece of clothing I carried, including woolly hat and gloves. I then had to slither my bulky-layered way into my slinky silk sleeping-bag liner before wriggling down into my North Face Blue Igloo sleeping bag (a –7°C temperature rating 600+fill goose down with diamond baffle construction, Pertex Resist ripstop shell and BottomLine taffeta bottom shell – are you still with me, Mr and Mrs Zamberlan?). Then, for my grand finale, I had to twist and turn and squirm and waggle and wiggle and jiggle and writhe down into my bivvy bag. All this thrashing around like a grounded mackerel, grappling for zips while getting thoroughly twisted and tangled in the process, proved a far more exhausting experience than the actual daily exertion of cycling.

Riding into St Peter Port, I found that the town quay of esplanades and piers had become a pedestrian precinct for the Liberation Day celebrations and was crowded with people and stalls and shows and parades and displays and funfairs and steel bands and carnival bands and Belles and Broomsticks and majorettes and markets and robots and dancers and jugglers and clowns and unicycles and something called the Sally Shunter Land Train. I like streets when they revolve around people and not cars. The previous day I'd had to merge with a swirling mass of dense vehicular traffic when negotiating the Weighbridge roundabout at the end of St Julian's Pier. What felt like half a day had passed before a gap opened up and I could finally cross the road on the North Esplanade. Now, instead of frazzled nerves and frustration and pollution and engine domination, there was a scene of happily busy and bustling street civilisation that demonstrated a far more valuable and practical use of space.

While I was on St Julian's Pier I rode down to the Inter Island Quay to buy a ferry ticket to the island of Sark, a prime quirky fragment of feudal England if ever there was one. Under the terms of an Elizabethan constitution that allows the citizens of Sark to do pretty much as they please, they have decided they can live without cars, income tax and political parties. It is Europe's last feudal state, governed by the seigneur – or lord – whose feudal rights date back to the 1560s and whose feudal privileges include being the only person on the island permitted to keep a bitch, along with a flutter of doves (I wonder if they get troubled by rain over Reading too). I also wanted to go to Herm, a tiny island just a mile-and-a-half long by half-a-mile wide but with enough pasture-land to support a hundred Guernsey dairy cattle. But it sounds like the Sarkese and Hermese (is that the right appellation or a shop in Bond Street selling swanky scarves?) are living on borrowed time as they are being buffeted by the winds of change from Brussels.

Anyhow, the apologetic ferry masters told me they didn't have enough room on their boats to take my bike, and suggested I should hire a bike once I got to the islands. That didn't count, though, because I was only going to islands that I could ride around on my own ponderous steed. Wherever I went, it had to come too.

So I aborted the idea of cycling around Sark and Herm, consoling myself that at least I had walked around them with Dave and Mel and mum. Alderney, the northernmost of the Channel Islands and only eight miles from France, was another no-go area because the only way to get there was by the island's own 'national' airline, Aurigny Air Services. And I wasn't going anywhere unless I could go there by boat and bike.

As I freewheeled slowly back down the pier, I was hailed by a Dutchman who told me he had spotted me yesterday cycling around the island. As he was a cit-izen of a country with its head screwed on the right way concerning the practicalities of two-wheeled travel (10 per cent of all journeys in the Netherlands are made by bicycle, compared with a measly 1.8 per cent in Britain), I was not particularly surprised when he told me he regularly cycled back home.

'I am new to pensioning age,' he said rather enchantingly, 'sho I have more time for my bicycling. I have this feeling when cycling of great freedom – more sho than walking, which I alsho enjoy. In a car I always feel *eeargh*! . . . very much aggravated!'

I said I knew that feeling well and that sitting in cars made me all pent up and fidgety and ready to explode.

'Yes, yes!' laughed the man, 'exactly my thoughts!'

'The thing though about Holland,' I said, 'is that most people over here always think that it's a great place for cycling. And it is if you like cycling on cycle paths. But I found motorists aren't so keen on you if you venture on to the roads.'

'Yes, car drivers in Holland are not sho friendly to cyclists. Maybe twice a day I have occasion for my heart to leap!'

He told me he was on a week's holiday with his wife.

'But we are travelling by car. *Eargh*! I miss my bicycle very much.'

As I left he gave me a bicycle-bonded, warm-hearted handshake and, with a twinkle in his eye, said, 'I envy your freedom!' as I cycled away.

CHAPTER 11

The weather continued to be spectacularly bad. It was either too wet or too cold. Or both. I had a problem on the clothes-washing front (specially T-shirts and leggings and fleece) because I couldn't wash them as I was wearing them, and even if I could, I couldn't hang them out to dry as it was raining. I had only finally managed to dry my smalls after dragging them down with me into my elaborate nest of sleeping bags for four nights on the trot. I worked out that I had worn my T-shirt solidly for two weeks and two days. People still seemed to talk to me so I guessed I couldn't smell *that* bad. Besides, I quite enjoy putting the 'Eskimo Effect' to test whereby the longer you wear your clothes, the more a heat-retaining layer of grease and grime builds up which effectively keeps you warmer.

Round in the Parish of Forest I was riding among a criss-crossing lacework of clifftop lanes when, quite by chance, I came across the German Occupation Museum. I locked my bike up outside and entered the small discreet building, feeling rather concerned that Gary's interest in museums was wearing off on me. How shocking to think I was voluntarily taking a dose of German Occupation education all off my own bat.

But very glad I was of it, as it turned out to be an intriguing little museum which I and only five other visitors had all to ourselves. I was also pleasantly surprised to find bicycles and horses featuring almost more than military hardware. The Germans imported 700 horses to the islands and on display was a horse-drawn ambulance, purpose-made in 1944 because of the petrol rationing, and, oddly, a horse's gas mask. Unfortunately, half of the animals ended up being eaten by the time of the Liberation.

As the Germans had forbidden all use of private motor vehicles, the islanders were only permitted to travel around Guernsey by bicycle, horse, bullock-cart or foot. (A newspaper cutting from the time looked on the bright side: 'Walking may be good exercise. That our cars are off the road, and that we now use our legs, may be for our eventual good from a health point of view.') Because of the lack of supplies and materials, many of the cyclists had to substitute hosepipes for bicycle tyres. One machine that caught my eye was 'Percy Ferguson's Bicycle' with its ancient hub gears, ornate rear rack and gear lever situated in an unusual position on the top-tube (cross-bar). Percy used his bike throughout the Occupation for many illicit deliveries, but in his front basket he generally carried only a load of spider crabs. On one occasion an unsuspecting German guard ordered Percy to give him a lift from St Sampson to St Peter Port (about two or three miles).

For those islanders who had cycled, the Germans had forbidden them to ride in anything but single file. A cutting from a newspaper read:

NOTICE

Order is hereby given in the interest of road safety, that cyclists must
ride singly behind one another on public roads. Riding in twos and
threes by the side of one another is prohibited and will be punished.
Feldkommandantur 515
Nebenstelle Guernsey

In a section of the museum called 'Occupation Street' stood a reconstruction of Greens cycle shop with an old metal sign saying 'RALEIGH THE ALL-STEEL BICYCLE – Guaranteed For EVER'. The window display contained boxes of bicycle components such as Phillips 'CREDEX' pedals, Fibrax brake blocks, Ferodo brake blocks, Brampton Standard cycle chains, Raybestos brake lining sets and a LUCAS 'King of the Road' revolving dome bell.

On the wall a poster, in fluctuating upper and lower case lettering, advertised:

THE 'NIPPER CYCLE'
Royal Interest!
The 'Nipper' Cycle that interested H.R.H. The DUKE OF YORK
at the recent OLYMPIA cycle show.
See that you get the REAL ARTICLE!

In the 'Civilian Room' a sepia-tinged newspaper cutting caught my eye. It was written by W.D.M. Lovell (Controller of Clothing and Footwear) and announced:

The public is hereby notified that a limited number of Ladies' and Gents' articles of underwear has been manufactured from imported wool and will be on sale at Clothing Retailers from Friday, April 16th 1943. The undermentioned garments are available at the fixed prices named.

Ladies' Knickers (2 sizes) . . . . 28/9 per pair
Ladies' Vests (2 sizes) . . . . 23/9 each
Gents Underpants (2 sizes). . . . . . 60/- per pair
Gents Vests (3 sizes) . . . . 50/- each

The above are subject to Sales Tax and the surrender of the appropriate coupons and vouchers.

Dated this 13th day of April, 1943.

Being a cook I found myself lingering the longest beside the showcases displaying samples of substitute food: Irish carrageen moss used for making jelly; acorns or grated parsnips, roasted till brown, for coffee; bramble leaves for tea; and potato flour to make bread. There was a recipe for something called 'Masterpiece Pudding', the ingredients of which included a peculiar mixture of haricots beans (soaked overnight before being 'put through mincer next morning'), minced raw potatoes, chocolate powder, jam flavouring, suet and lemon cordial. Other recipes were for Potato and Apple Pudding, Macaroni Blancmange, Macaroni Cake, Sweet Corn Cake, Marrow Pudding and Bran Paste. One woman recommended 'Carrots with Fruit – A few slices of cooked carrot, cut in rounds and mixed with a tin of fruit, makes a tasty combination and enables a larger helping to be served.'

Then there was advice about hay boxes.

Hay Box Cookery – A Useful Timetable.

Hay boxes are now in common use in the Island and are proving invaluable as savers of fuel. Many persons do not get the full value owing to not heating the food on the fire after placing in a hay box, as well as before. This is a very important point.

It then printed a 'Practical Timetable for hay box cookery' taken from the *Jersey*

Evening Post and listed dishes like 'Boiled Meat' and 'Roly Poly Pudding' along-side their appropriate cooking times: 'Time on Fire . . . 20 mins. Time in Box . . . 4 hours or overnight.' The best bit was an added afterthought at the bottom: 'Housewives may wish to cut out this for reference.' Well, thank you! What a generous suggestion! I shall fetch my scissors right now!

One of the most touching things in the museum was the original presentation of a message written by some departing Germans. It was found by Mr and Mrs Barnicoat in their house in St Martins on the day following the liberation of Guernsey to British Forces:

> The Germans wish you all in Guernsey a happy future and
> hope to see you again in more peaceful circumstances.
> Farewell and Cheer-I-oo!
> May 10th 1945

A few did meet again. After spending a couple of years in England as POWs, they were repatriated to Germany where later some of them were reunited with a small number of islanders they had befriended or with whom they had fallen in love during the Occupation. A number ended up marrying, but because of the lingering ill feeling towards the Germans they were unable to move back to the Channel Islands until the 1950s and 1960s.

On my last night on Guernsey something very strange happened. I crawled into my tent, wriggled into my silk sleeping-bag liner and feathered sleeping bag and bivvy bag, dressed as normal for polar exploration, only to wake three hours later in a tropical sweat and desperate to rip off all my clothes. The temperature had leapt that fast into comparatively sultry double figures. But the rain still fell.

Back in St Peter Port I rode past the house where Victor Hugo had lived for fourteen years (it was here that he finalised *Les Miserables*). Before I boarded the *Commodore Clipper* to the mainland, I went to buy some postcards from a twirling pavement stand. As I was whirling the stand while still straddling my bike, a man in a blue bus conductor's cap and a holey-elbowed jumper looked from me to steed and back to me before saying, 'Looks like you could do with a motor on there!' Then, gesticulating towards my wheels, he said, 'I see you're using car tyres – they look like the ones off the old Austin Ruby – you know the one? – the Austin 7. A smashing car.'

'I'm sorry to disappoint you,' I said, wondering what the devil this old duffer was talking about, 'but I can't say I make a habit of putting car tyres on my bike. They're actually cycle-specific Continental Top Touring 26 × 1.75s.'

At this point a woman in a four-wheel-drive mounted the kerb and stopped without warning beside us – her nearside wheels parked at an awkward angle on the pavement. Leaving the engine running to belch black diesel fumes into our faces, she flung open the driver's door and disappeared into a swanky clothes shop. I suddenly found I had a kindred spirit.

'Blessed nuisance they are!' said an irritated Mr Austin Ruby, looking disdainfully towards the big, black, highly elevated Ford Maverick. 'The roads are far too narrow for these beasts! They've usually just got a mother driving one child to school. When I walk along the lanes they push me into the hedge. Don't give a tuppence, they don't!'

As I was mounting up to take off to the port, a very large man from Texas sporting a black stetson said, 'That sure is one helluva load you've got on there, kid. Makes me feel tired just looking at it!' Then, as an afterthought, he added, 'I guess there're times when you bet you wish you had yourself an engine, huh?'

Ooh, yes please! And some Austin Ruby tyres while you're at it!

CHAPTER 12

And so for the third time in two weeks, I washed up in Portsmouth – official START and FINISH point of my coastal jaunt. It felt good to have arrived at the position where I could at last turn my wheels westward, but a bit strange that I had amassed a total of 429 mostly island-dallying miles before I had even reached my proper start. Although 429 miles was but a mere fraction of my estimated 10,000 miles, it was, I consoled myself, still like cycling just over halfway from Land's End to John O' Groats. Suddenly the British Isles, which I had always considered a compact little morsel tucked away on the comparatively limitless face of the world, appeared a rapidly expanding entity as seen from the level of my bicycle wheels.

As Portsmouth Harbour is bordered by motor-heavy highways – the A3, M275, M27, A27 and A32 – and as my map marked not one patch of stress-alleviating green through which to cycle, I left the overnight Channel Island ferry to join the early-morning rush of cycling and suited commuters boarding the *Gosport Queen* passenger ferry (motto: IT'S SHORTER BY WATER), which whisked me across the narrow mouth of Portsmouth Harbour in no time. Pushing my bike off the other side I was hailed by a man who, exhibiting fine taste in bike mags, declared he was a reader of the 'Backpedalling' column I contribute to in *London Cyclist*, the magazine of the London Cycling Campaign, which I found rather touching.

It was 7.30 on a hazy and faintly muggy morning and I sat on Gosport's Millennium Wall eating a breakfast of apples, bananas, energy bars and rice cakes. While I ate I watched the dodgem-like *Gosport Queen*, with her rounded bulbous body, bumbling back and forth across the water to Portsea. She was a friendly-looking plodder in contrast to the evil-eyed Solent-flying Fastcats with their yellow-and-white go-fast stripes. But both boats were mere teenage grunge dressers in their Adidas trainers compared with the funereal sombre-suited naval ships – big no-messing aircraft carriers and guided-missile destroyers. I was halfway down my third banana when the massive bulk of the P&O continent-bound *Pride of Le Havre* slid slowly out of the harbour. The *Gosport Queen* meekly trod water in accordance with the Might is Right convention, and resembled a mere toy-like fairground attraction in the face of the *Pride*'s towering white cliffs.

A white terrier interrupted my harbour observations by running up to me and yapping excitedly at my feet.

'Sophie! *Come* here! Sophie! SOPHIE!'

Sophie wasn't the most obedient dog in the world and continued yelping at me in a very yappy way. Sophie's owner wandered over.

'You can't get much more of a perfect setting than this!' he said, above the imperfect racket of a mutt's ear-jarring bark. 'Touring are you?'

I said that yes, I was.

'I'm a Moulton man myself,' he replied, referring to the small-wheeled bikes fitted with suspension designed by Dr Alex Moulton (who was also responsible for the rubber suspension of the BMC Mini car).

And without further cause for discussion, Moulton Man dragged Sophie away and continued strolling down the Millennium Walk, leaving me to listen to the rich and fluty song of a blackbird prominently perched atop a Millennium Tree.

I remained sitting on the wall, ship-watching and bird-listening, and before long a small, squat man the shape of a toilet cistern shuffled over to me with the aid of a hospital crutch. He was dressed in slinky nylon black shorts, thick brown knee-length socks and scuffed black slip-ons. On his head he wore a flat cap and a dark eye-shield shaped like welders' goggles.

Switching on his hearing aid he said, 'How in the devil's name do you make that thing move? Must be a secret only to yourself!'

'I'm not sure,' I said, 'but I do.' Then, commenting on his attire, I said, 'Nice shorts!'

'Ah, yes. I woke up this morning and thought I'd put them on. Feels a lot warmer today, don't you think?'

'It certainly does. And about time too if you ask me!'

Using his crutch to point towards the sea wall of new Millennium rocks above which I was sitting, Goggle Man said, 'See all that gravel there between those rocks – they've only just put it there. Had to because of the rats. It's the public, if you know what I mean. They were throwing food and rubbish down there. Just what rats like. I've seen them, I have. I've seen the rats come out of those holes. There're foxes too. And if you see foxes you know there's going to be rats not far away.'

'You're putting me off my breakfast!' I said.

Goggle Man leant on his crutch and looked at my bike.

'Used to cycle a bit myself when I was a boy,' he said. 'Used to ride to London back then, we did.'

'How old were you?' I asked.

'Must have been fourteen, fifteen. Took us three hours. Of course the roads were different in those days. Couldn't do it now.' With a far-off look and the faint traces of a smile, he added, 'Seeing you there reminded me of it. Funny – hadn't thought of that for a long time.'

He was silent a moment and I could see him momentarily reliving his past. Then, remembering where he was, he said, 'I'd best be on my way now. Take care, luvvy. Enjoy yourself. Ta-ta!'

I crossed over Haslar Bridge and found I was surrounded by MOD property. At Fort Blockhouse I rode past the big submarine training base of HMS *Dolphin*. There was Haslar Hospital and Haslar Prison; there were MOD training camps and MOD sports fields; and everywhere there was impregnable fencing topped with miles of spirals of razor wire.

By the time I surfaced at Stokes Bay, the sun had burnt off the film of haze and I took a momentary breather to gaze out over the Solent to the Isle of Wight. Queen Victoria used to do the same thing, as it was from this point that she would embark for her island retreat of Osborne House or, as she called it, her 'little paradise'. The Solent was as busy as usual, plying with ferries and tankers and yachts and motor-cruisers and armadas of sea-skimming dinghies. Beyond Gilkicker Point I could just make out the ominous form of a frigate. The Romans used to call this whole area between the Isle of Wight and the mainland (including both the Solent and Southampton Water) *Magnus Portus*, the 'great harbour'.

Entering a block of public conveniences at Lee-on-the-Solent I was intercepted by an out-of-breath man on a bike who said, 'You look as if you're going somewhere!'

I am – the toilet! I felt like saying. But I think he was referring more to my loaded panniers than to my loaded bladder. At this very inopportune moment (I had been dying for somewhere to pee since Gosport), the man decided he would like to give me a potted life history.

'I'm from Torquay – well, Newton Abbot actually, though I've lived in Gosport now nine years.'

He told me he worked in a factory that manufactured cups and plates and take-away boxes for places like McDonalds, Burger King, KFC and Wimpy. Crossing my legs, I asked him how he liked living in Gosport compared with Devon.

'It's all right,' he said. 'There's a lot more going on than in Devizes. That's where I originally come from. I still go there. It's a pretty town all right but the whole place closes down after the shops shut. There's a bus once a week – well, once a day actually, but it feels like once a week!'

As the morning progressed, getting hotter and hotter, I carried on past the site of the HMS *Daedalus* Fleet Air Arm base, which briefly put me in mind of Greek mythology and wax wings (not the most auspicious legend, I would have thought, after which to name your helicopter base – though calling it *Icarus* would have been a lot more dicey), and on to the small clifftop village of Hill Head, which in the eighteenth century was a centre of the smuggling trade.

In the shopping precinct at Titchfield I stopped at the post office to send home my Channel Island maps and a wodge of tourist leaflets. As I was cramming everything into an A5 envelope at the side of the counter, a woman in her early sixties walked somewhat lethargically up to the counter window.

'Gawd struth!' she said to the face behind the glass. 'This warm weather catches you unawares, it does!'

'It's not a nice heat,' replied the postmistress.

'We shouldn't grumble, mind you. It's just that it's come on so sudden, like.'

'Feels like it's going to storm,' the postmistress said.

'Did last night.'

'That's right – but not a drop!'

'Well, at least we should be thankful we're leaving the dark evenings behind. I'm all right in the morning I am, getting up when it's dark and all that. But it's when it gets dark at four in the afternoon – that's not for me. Gets to me, it does. I feel it more the older I get. It's all right when you're young – you're too busy rushing around with the kids and all that. Now that I'm semi-retired, I feel it in the old bones!'

Outside the post office I was clipping up a pannier when an elderly man walked past and exclaimed, 'Whoa! That's some load! Got an engine on there? Must be quite something to ride!' His monologue continued, 'On holiday from school are you? Just travelling around? Got your tent there? Yes? Good!' And then he walked off.

I had just thrown a leg over my top tube when another man sauntering by paused and, directing his gaze towards my cycling helmet strapped to my rear load (I like to protect my panniers), said, 'Glad to see you've got a spare wheel on there!'

'It's not a wheel,' I said, 'It's my fancy hat!'

'Ah. I've not got my glasses on,' he said. 'Mind how you go now.' And he stepped into the post office.

Things then got a bit more confusing because my map wasn't detailed enough to lead me to Locks Heath avoiding the busy A27. As I was perusing my map at the side of the road, a taxi drew up and the driver leaned through the open passenger window.

'Where you trying to get to, luv?'

'Southampton,' I said.

'Blimey! You got a way to go, you know.'

I didn't tell him that ten miles was but a blip on the face of my intended 10,000.

Happily, I made it through the back streets of Locks Heath and Sarisbury without getting (too) lost, before I plopped out on to the A27 to cross the Hamble at Swanwick. By now the late morning sun was out in full force and although I had hoicked my leggings up to my knees, I was still too hot. There was nothing else for it but to bare my sun-starved white legs good and proper. So, spotting an Esso garage, I dived into its unfragrant toilet at the back and climbed into my shorts.

Once back on my bike the feeling of warm wind on my legs was sensational! What wasn't so lovely was the air: thick with a toxic cocktail of endless exhausts chundering into my face. I stopped at the Woolston roundabout to buy a 1.5 litre bottle of Highland Spring water from a newsagent. As I was glugging it down thirstily outside, a lollipop woman said, 'Good God! You need an engine on that thing!' In my heated and sweaty traffic-crazed state, I felt like hitting her over the noddle with her big 'STOP' lollipop. Instead I simply smiled at her sweetly and said, 'All I need's another drink!' And went back inside the store to buy one.

I crossed the River Itchen on the Itchen Toll Bridge. As there was no charge for cyclists I was waved on past lines of cars, which pleased me greatly. From the superior elevation of the bridge I was catapulted at speed into the city centre of Southampton. Despite heavy bombing during the Second World War, I was pleasantly surprised to find that the city had managed to retain quite a number of old buildings, including the remains of its fine city walls and their towers. I rode past the tall stone column of the Mayflower Memorial, reminding me that it was from here that the Pilgrim Fathers set sail in the *Mayflower* from West Quay in 1620 on the first stage of their epic journey, calling at Dartmouth and Plymouth before crossing the Atlantic.

Southampton has always been a frontline port, both as a jumping-off point for English armies and as a target for invaders; it was the site of the Roman port Clausentum; it was William the Conqueror's port for his ships coming from Normandy; and it was from Southampton that Richard the Lionheart sailed on his crusades. In the fourteenth century the French had arrived in Southampton to pillage and plunder, and in exchange for such unneighbourly behaviour, the English had returned the compliment when the armies of Edward III embarked from the port for the invasion of France and their victory at Crécy. More recently, during the two World Wars, over ten million troops had left from Southampton for the battlefields of France.

In between, the town had been a fashionable Georgian spa until the Prince Regent 'discovered' Brighton in 1815. Shortly afterwards, Southampton had been confirmed as a port of importance: sail gave way to steam and the mail services were transferred here from Falmouth.

It was its great sprawling docks (begun in the 1830s and now with over six miles of quays) that made Southampton Britain's major passenger port and the home of the Atlantic liners of the Cunard Company when prodigious and stately ships like the *Mauretania, Queen Elizabeth* and *Queen Mary* once towered above the warehouses. In 1939, at the outset of war as part of the evacuation process, my American grandfather, Wayne Vernon Myers, took his wife and my mother (then aged seven) to Southampton to see them off to New York on the *George Washington*, and onwards to their Midwest home in Normal, Illinois. Mum's only memory of her first trip across the Atlantic is sharing a four-berth ladies' cabin with a woman who lay on the top bunk fully clothed with her shoes on. She told my grandmother she didn't want to undress in case they hit a mine and she would have to 'swim for it'. After the war, mum returned to England on the *Queen Elizabeth*, which was furnished very spartanly as it hadn't yet been converted back from a transport ship used during the war to convey GI troops to England. What mum remembers most about that voyage is sleeping in a hammock and finding chewing gum stuck under every table.

No matter how illustrious the port's past, I didn't much enjoy my time in Southampton: cycling in an incessant stream of cars and juggernauts put me off. Others before me hadn't been too impressed either: J.B. Priestley, in his *English Journey* of 1934, could only muster up enough enthusiasm to declare Southampton 'not a bad town, this', while Beryl Bainbridge, in her repetition of the journey some fifty years later, thought the city 'not a bad place to live'. Not bad, but not particularly good. For me, the big ships and the huge clanking docks and cycling over the Itchen Bridge were what made the lengthy urban detour up the vast stretch of Southampton Water all worthwhile.

To escape the road-strangled clutches of the city, I had to continue cycling in a northwesterly direction following the broad course of the River Test along a motoring maelstrom of multiple roundabouts, dual carriageways, motorway junctions, bypasses, overpasses and underpasses, which all together culminated in a thoroughly unpleasant ride on the hottest day of the year so far. I tore through Totton, eager to espy the more breathable heathland enclosures of the New Forest, but all I saw were crawling queues of traffic on the A326 (they were resurfacing the road) which I had to accelerate past and slalom among while being wolf-whistled and commented upon in a generally loud-mouthed 'LUCKY SADDLE!' way by a hot-day, window-down jam of vans and trucks and oil tankers. To cap it all, as I passed through the worst of the roadworks and the traffic sped up in showy accelerations of frustration, the midday sun turned far too tar-poppingly hot for a fair-skinned traffic-pummelled damsel in distress and on a freshly resurfaced but bumpy loose-chipping highway, laden with oil tankers thundering so close to my elbow it was all I could do to fight with my steering to avoid being sucked beneath their monstrous underbellies, a puncture struck – a sharp-edged chipping had embedded itself in my gooey tar-encrusted tyre. My mood was not good. In fact it was bloody awful. My head was screaming in a smog-induced headache and I muttered blue murder at everything in my path while dragging my limping mount as far as the Heath pub ('The Family Welcome') on a busy roundabout at Dibden Purlieu. In my snappy and snarling state of mind, the name of this place just made me all the more tetchy – why should it always be 'Family Welcome'? How about 'Cyclist Welcome' or even 'Bad-tempered and Prickly Spinster Welcome'?

Strangely, for such a sudden mini heatwave, everyone was sitting and eating inside. This suited me fine and I collapsed at a shady table in front of the pub. After drinking two of my squeezy bike bottles of water down in one, I sat for some time staring into space in a state of sweaty nerve-frazzled exhaustion. Finally, deciding I had better eat, I raided my panniers, my every move being observed through the pub windows by Family Welcome diners, and ate a bag of carrots, a pack of biscuits, a tin of sardines, a tube of tomato pâté and two bananas. I felt a bit better after that – almost ready to tackle my puncture.

I was summoning the energy to dismantle my bike when a young man in a goatee beard and a Moto Guzzi T-shirt walked out of the pub. When he saw me he said, 'Josie Dew, isn't it? I saw you on TV – Meridian News, I think it was. Good luck mate – you've got a long way to go!' And he climbed into an orange Morris Minor before being swallowed by Dibden Purlieu's roundabout.

I was just digesting this information when an elderly couple emerged from the pub. They shuffled my way, towards the car park, the woman holding on to her husband's arm.

'Having a bit of a rest are you, love?' said the woman, a dead ringer for Barbara Cartland, only not quite so pink. 'Used to do a bit of cycling meself in me young days. Just to work and back around Lymington. Nothing that special. Still got the bike in me garage. What's that? No, no, it's not the same one! Don't cycle now, you know – it's too much effort!'

As her husband went to fetch the car, she sat down on the table's bench-seat beside me. 'Where you off to, luvvie, with all that?'

'Bournemouth,' I said. I didn't want to tell her I was planning to go the whole hog round the British Isles as I thought the shock of the distance might give her a heart attack.

Taking my hand in hers she gave it a little affectionate pat and said, 'Awww, how luvvly! But not all by yourself? You're such a little thing.'

Her husband drew up in front of us in an old brown Vauxhall Cavalier. With our parting imminent she draped her arm around my shoulders and, in a tender grandmotherly manner, lunged forward to embrace me. My face sank into her crinkled but soft pink-powdered cheeks as if I had nose-dived into one of Barbara Cartland's velvety feathered cushions. She smelt of roses and mothballs.

'Bless you,' she said as I helped her towards the car. And then, with a little wave through the smudged glass of the window, she was gone.

After mending my puncture, I utilised the Family Welcome Ladies to wash off black smears of oil that stained the most unlikely parts of my anatomy. As I walked back through the pub, I paused to read the front page of the *New Forest Post* ('Incorporating: *Forest and Waterside Observer*'). Dibden Purlieu, I discovered, was making headline news: 'Villagers close ranks to oppose Tesco appeal.' In short, 'angry villagers' were vociferously objecting against a proposed Esso petrol station-cum-mini-supermarket. They called themselves RAT – Residents Against Tesco, a group largely made up of the same villagers who formed RAM (Residents Against McDonalds), which made me wonder where we would be without our acronyms and our doggedly combative villagers.

As I took off out of the 'Family Welcome But Cyclist Shunned' pub, I passed the brash yellow sign at the exit that said:

Thank you for
visiting the
**CHARLIE CHALK
PLAY ZONE**

Don't jump to conclusions, I thought, because all I had visited was the toilet.

CHAPTER 13

Standing on the pier at Hythe I could look across Southampton Water to where the rivers Test and Itchen converge to form a broad arrowhead peninsula upon which are grouped Southampton's docks. As I stood there the snub-nosed *Hotspur IV* passenger ferry pulled away from the pier-head on its short crossing to Southampton. Watching it bouncing off into the distance, I thought: that's what I should have done – taken the ferry and saved a horrible cycle up and around Totton. So I decided there and then that, when I came upon future estuaries that were topped with a city or big industrial area or arteries of trunk roads, I would, if there was one, take the ferry across to the other side. It might save a traffic-traumatised headache and a puncture to boot.

Back on the main road, interminable lines of oil tankers continued to crush me into the gutter as they went crashing past heading for the oil refineries at Fawley. The afternoon grew progressively hotter as I turned progressively blacker – I had slapped so much suncream on my skin that it was acting like a fly-paper to all manner of airborne insects and particles of industrial and suburban pollution.

At Holbury I stopped at the post office to buy two big bottles of water. As I was leaning over filling up my bike bottles on the pavement, a builder's truck rumbled by and a workman shouted out of the window, 'NICE ARSE!' I mean, honestly, how coarse!

Continuing to fill my bottles, I wondered whether it was the country's sudden transformation from a cold climate to a hot one that was making the already highly testosterone-filled male so much more impulsive. Lord Byron, a noted lover of warm climates himself, was in no doubt. As he wrote in a succinct and unambiguous rhyme:

What men call gallantry, and
gods adultery,
Is much more common where
the climate's sultry.

But in fact studies have shown sexual activity to be more fruitful during cool or temperate weather. The hotter the temperature gets, the lower is a man's sperm count and the less likely it is that a woman will conceive. My own hypothesis is that the hotter it is, the less people wear and the more men drive around with their windows (and hopefully only their windows) lowered, making it easier for them to shout out their predatory desires on impulse. In my saddle-bound experience of being at the butt end of workmen's wolf whistles and 'phwoars', men are up for it come rain or shine, hail or heatwave. You just hear about it more when it's hot.

By the time I reached Fawley I had such a pounding headache that I needed somewhere to camp soon so I could have a lie-down in the shade. As luck would have it I came across a farmhouse campsite – only it wasn't a campsite, it was a caravan site. I found the owner in the yard who told me that if I wanted to stay I had to be a member of the Caravanning Club. Oh, and I also had to have a caravan.

As I didn't like the sound of what the woman was saying, I thought the best thing to do was to ignore it. I had also spotted a very inviting piece of cropped grass in the shade that looked like it would fit the bill perfectly for my meagre requirements.

'Couldn't I camp in the corner over there?' I asked. 'I won't be any trouble!'

'We haven't got any facilities for camping,' said the woman.

'Facilities? What, toilets? Can't I just go behind a bush?' I said, with a hopeful grin. It was perhaps a little rash, but then I was desperate for a rest.

'No you *can't*!' said the woman, enunciating her words very clearly.

So I left. Further down the road a man walking his dog told me of a place he thought I could camp near Calshot Activities Centre.

I found the Centre on a long pebble-beach spit of land jutting out into Southampton Water. It had once been an RAF base for flying-boats (which, during the 1930s and 1940s, had been designed and built up the road in Hythe) and its huge hangars and residential buildings now formed the large educational, sporting and activity centre. Inside, past the climbing wall, I found an affable woman called Lorraine sitting at reception.

'Can I help you?' she asked.

'I hope so,' I said. 'I've been told I can camp here.'

'Do you have a tent?'

'Yes,' I said hopefully, 'I do.'

'I'm afraid they only allow caravans here.'

I was beginning to hate caravans with a venomous passion. Why did everyone like big, ugly white unwieldy whales and not little discreet green tents? It was time to put on my crestfallen look, so . . . on it went.

Lorraine had a heart. 'Well, I can ask the manager for you. But I don't hold out much hope because he can only issue permits for caravans.'

In due course, an activity centre-looking manager appeared looking very active. He was very nice but he was unable to come up with the goods. When he had gone I asked Lorraine if she thought it would be all right if I cycled back down the beach and camped between some beach huts.

'Well, sometimes I see people camping beside the toilet block down at that small car park at the entrance. But I don't recommend it – especially not on a Friday night. You get a lot of the local lads drinking and driving around down there. There's been a bit of trouble in the past.'

Lorraine then found a list of bed-and-breakfasts and let me use her phone to try the two nearest ones – both about five miles away. They were full.

'Never mind,' I said, 'I'm sure I'll find somewhere to camp.' And I thanked her for all her help.

'Wait a minute,' said Lorraine. 'There's Joan Moverly, a lovely woman we used to live next door to in Fawley. She's a widow, I'm sure she still does bed and breakfast.'

Lorraine looked her up in the book and gave her a ring. There was just an answerphone.

'I'll cycle back up there anyway,' I said. 'She might be home by the time I get there.'

Lorraine gave me the name of the house, Frigate Cottage.

'Look for the house with the front garden full of hanging baskets and flawless flowers,' she said.

As I was cycling back along the beachfront, a man stepped out from behind a beach hut and did a double take.

'Josie Drew! I've read your books. What are you doing in Calshot? Aren't you supposed to be cycling somewhere exotic?'

'I soon will be,' I said. 'I'm heading for a house covered in hanging baskets somewhere near Fawley Power Station!'

The man seemed disappointed. I think I had just shattered his illusion that I was some sort of bicycling superwoman wading through Amazonian swamps with a machete clamped between my teeth, wrestling with anacondas or biting off bears' heads in Russia's distant Kamchatka Peninsula.

'Do you live around here?' I asked, suddenly feeling conversational even though I had hanging baskets to find.

'No, I'm from Henley-on-Thames. I'm down for a day's sailing. I keep a boat here.'

Henley-on-Thames? That's near Pangbourne. Up and down in a day. I thought about telling him how the same distance had taken me several weeks but I decided not to. Finding me on the Solent and not the Serengeti had blown it for him. Somehow, I didn't think he would be buying any more of my books.

Overwatched by the towering smoke-spewing chimney of Fawley Power Station, an obelisk so lofty that its sky-staining form even appears looming across the water from the more north-facing shores of the Isle of Wight, I wearily cycled back up the road that I had come down an hour before.

In Fawley, a village bordered by a vast field of oil flares, I found Frigate Cottage camouflaged beneath a blooming sea of hanging baskets and blossoming herbaceous borders. I rang the bell. No answer. As I was pondering my next move, a car pulled up in the street outside the house. A woman got out.

'Excuse me,' I said in buoyant tone. 'You're not Joan Moverly, are you?'

'Ermm . . . no. Should I be?'

'Well, I'd like it if you were, but I'm sure I'd still like you even if you're not,' I replied getting myself in a twist.

The woman looked at me as if I had hanging baskets growing out of my ears. I thought I had better untwine myself and explain. 'I've been told this house is a bed-and-breakfast owned by Joan Moverly, but there's no reply.'

'Ahh, I see,' said the woman who I wished was Joan Moverly, but wasn't. 'I'm afraid I don't live in Fawley. I've only come here to get my hair done. Why don't you come with me into the hairdressers and we'll ask in there.'

So we walked across the street and into Hair and Beauty. Being Friday afternoon the salon was a buzzing hive of activity with women getting their hair done for the weekend. The atmosphere, thick with hairspray, was one of cheerful busy banter. Everyone knew everyone, but no one knew Joan Moverly. In spite of this everyone wanted to help. A head in a basin said, 'There's a B&B over in Blackfield. I think it's somewhere down near the common.'

'You mean Ted and Margaret's place?' replied another head, this one covered in rollers and pink butterflies, which I think were elaborate plastic hair clips. 'They stopped doing B&B years ago!'

Oh no! I thought, no more Alresford brainstorms, please!

'Have you tried the Falcon Hotel down the road, dear?' said a head in a heated helmet. Although I had cycled past it I hadn't stopped as I didn't like the look of it – all a bit run-down and seedy, and more a pub than a hotel with a group of skullheads drinking by the door. I could well imagine the dubious toilet, stains on the candlewick bedspread and hairs on the shagpile.

'Nah, don'tgodowntheFalcon,' said one of the young hairdressers, talking as fast as her speed-snipping scissors. 'I wentintheretheotherday – smeltabit mingyitdid.'

Another hairdresser searched through the local paper for any adverts of places to stay. As she was flicking through the pages, a head, topped in a turban of towel, said, 'You're bound to find some B&Bs a mile or two up the road in Hythe.'

I knew The Turban was probably right, but I really didn't want to backtrack any further. Also, I knew that her 'one or two miles' was more like four or five in reality. Cars swallow distances, whereas bikes make a meal out of every dip and every curve. And when you've got a pulsating head and wilting legs, five miles can seem like fifty. I thanked everyone heartily and said that I would ride up the road and see what came my way.

What came my way was a small Spar store run by a lovely Indian family called Singh who gave me a big bagful of half-price bananas, apples and tomatoes. In the phone box across the road I gave Joan Moverly one last chance to save my day. After a number of rings her cockney tones entered my earhole and I swooned with relief.

'I've just got in,' she said. 'I've been takin' me friend to the doc's . . . yes, I've got a room. £12 a night.'

Joan Moverly was eighty-two but looked ten years younger. When she opened her Frigate Cottage door to me she appeared to be dressed for a fancy dinner party in a dapper black dress, a string of pearls and a bouffant of immaculate white hair. Tucked up the short sleeve of her party dress nestled a neat square of white handkerchief with which she occasionally dabbed her brow. It was still very humid.

I complimented Mrs Moverly ('Call me Joan, luv') on her splendid attire, saying she looked like she was dressed for a night out on the town.

'Nah!' she laughed, 'It's only an old thing I run around in!'

Being in a complimentary mood, I then complimented her on the blossoming delights of her tiny fly-swatter-sized front garden.

'You put all the other houses on the street to shame!' I said.

'Oh, it was me 'usband who was the gardener,' she said. 'I don't know nothin' 'bout it really.'

Then she told me how over Easter some youngsters had uprooted all her front garden and hurled handfuls of flowers all over the road.

'Found me begonias on the other side of the street,' she said. 'A neighbour helped me plant 'em all back in.'

Then the same thing happened again. So now she kept her big long-spiked Gardeners Club brolly by the front door.

''Cos if I caught 'em at it, I'd give 'em a ruddy good spikin' all right!' she said in a taking-the-law-into-her-own-hands forthright manner. 'The police officer, ever such a nice fella, said I should get a gun and blow 'em teenagers up the backside!'

I said, 'I thought the police's advice to the public was not to have a go!'

Joan laughed. 'I'll tell yer, me luv – I ain't the sort of old lady to sit back! I like to stick up for me rights, I do!'

After a bit more chat I was shown up to my quarters – a tiny room that looked south towards Fawley Power Station. When I was in Joan's bathroom (where on the wall hung a plastic plaque with the words: 'Georgia, always on my mind'), she called up to me to ask if I would like anything to eat. I called back to say I was all right for food as I'd bought a load of stuff in the shop up the road.

'Well, bring it down, me sweet,' she replied, 'and come and join me.'

All I really felt like doing was showering, eating and flopping on my bed. I felt whacked, hot and headachy. It had been a day that felt as a long as a week, starting with the night boat from the Channel Islands. But I liked Joan so I went downstairs to talk to her.

'It's nice to 'ave the company,' she said, 'specially now since me 'usband died.'

In fact Joan had had two husbands die on her, both of exactly the same heart conditions. Her latest husband, Sid, had been an artist and his paintings of ships and rural scenes adorned the walls. Her first husband had been a keen cyclist and, as newly weds, they would go on long rides together on their tandem, which was kitted out with a sidecar for their baby son.

'Once we got a puncture,' said Joan, 'so we lifted the baby out on cushions and put 'im under the 'edge. When me 'usband 'ad mended the wheel, like, we lifted the baby back, still on 'is cushion, and 'e never woke up in all that time!'

Joan, originally a Londoner, had given birth at home to her first son during the Blitz.

'There was bombs falling all over the place,' she said. 'Me mum was on the stairs outside me room with 'er ear to the door waitin' in suspense to 'ear the first cries of the baby. She was more worried she didn't 'ear 'im cry than she was that a bomb be landing on us! He did eventually cry, but 'e didn't 'alf take 'is time 'bout it!'

Joan now had two sons.

'One of me son's ex-wives rang up the other day,' she said, 'moaning 'bout 'ow 'ard 'er life were and she kept telling me 'ow lucky I was compared to 'er. "Me, *lucky*?" I said. "I've 'ad two 'usbands die on me I 'ave!" What she mean I've 'ad it easy? I've worked 'ard all me life – paid me stamps and social.'

Along with paying her social security, Joan had worked hard too, starting off in the ticket office of her local cinema before progressing to be an usherette, a job she had hankered after for a long time. For many years she was manageress of a vegetarian restaurant in Leicester Square. Finally she moved to Whitehall to work for the MOD so she could get a pension.

The next morning I went downstairs to find Joan cutting a dashing figure in another dazzling dress. Again I complimented her and she told me how she liked to 'look all proper' even if she wasn't going to leave the house. In spite of this she became all abashed when I asked to take her photograph in front of the hanging baskets.

'Nah!' she said, 'I'm a right old mess! I 'aven't even done me 'air!'

This seemed to lead her on to the subject of the marriage to her second husband.

'My biggest regret,' she said with a wistful sigh, 'was I didn't wear a proper dress for me weddin'. I chose one so short it kept ridin' up me backside!'

When I was ready to leave I got out my wallet to give her the £12. But she wouldn't accept it. I protested.

'Let's call it a fiver,' she said. 'It's been nice to 'ave the company. Nah, really, me sweet, I don't want no more than a fiver.'

Then, as if to settle the matter, she put a bag of tomatoes in my hand and added, 'I'm a Christian.'

Oh, does that make it all right then?

CHAPTER 14

With temperatures in the eighties and not a cloud to be seen, Saturday 12th May now took the lead as the hottest day of the year so far. It was also a memorable day for another reason: cycling along a leafy lane just north of Lepe I heard the countryside resound with the first-of-the-year calls of a *Cuculus canorus*. A bit late, I thought. Must have been delayed on his flight path from sub-Saharan Africa. Either that or the computers were down again at the Swanwick Air Traffic Control Centre. And he was a 'he' because the distinctive song that betrays the cuckoo's presence is the male's territorial call: the female's bubbling cry is much less distinguishable, sounding more like a curlew. I only know this because, along with beetles, cuckoos were another of my school self-selected scrapbook projects.

The sand and shingle beach at Lepe was packed with great expanses of bared bodies. When I stopped in the car park to use the toilets I was besieged by the standard issue comments: 'You need a motor on that, me darlin''; 'I suppose you've got the kitchen sink in there too!'; 'You're mad!; 'You're a glutton for punishment!'; 'Here, Hazel, come over here. This young girl says she's cycling to Bournemouth with all this gear!' Hazel: 'My word, that's a way!'

The Solent was sparkling. I wanted a swim but there were too many people and I didn't want to leave my bike in such a crowd. So I cycled off along the shore, dodging the car-jams and scantily clad pedestrians flip-flopping along the road. What a different scene it must have been when Henry II landed here in 1154 to take possession of the English throne. I bet he wouldn't have told me I needed a motor on my bike.

There were more queues of cars and coaches waiting to get into the vast woodland gardens of Exbury House. From the road I could see crocodile lines of people ambling along the azalea and camellia and magnolia shaded paths and marvelling at the towering bushes of flaming rhododendrons alight with their big balls of blooms.

The rich sweet smell of flowering gorse, blending with the distinct aroma of horse dung (delivered courtesy of the wild ponies) drifting lazily across the road, greeted my arrival in the New Forest. I found it disheartening that, for such a beautiful place on such a beautiful day, I passed no one out walking or cycling. Instead everyone was trying to drive everywhere but not getting very far: after the stationary lines of traffic at Lepe and Exbury, I found Beaulieu (French for 'beautiful place') to be one big bottleneck of exhaust-choking cars. This struck me as somewhat ironic because here were people coming to visit a beautiful place by ugly means. Because of this I curtailed any plans I might have had to look around the village or to walk up to the sluice gate of the ancient mill. My automatic reaction was to get away from the noise and annoyance of cars and crowds, so, after buying a drink at the post office, that's exactly what I did.

The peaceful lull didn't last long, because I found more cars and crowds congealed into the overspilling car park at Bucklers Hard. Long snaking lines of people were queuing up for a hefty dose of 'Heritage'. They walked down between the village's two rows of mellow red-brick Georgian cottages to the Beaulieu River, where they would be taken back to the eighteenth century when Bucklers Hard was a scene of hectic shipbuilding activity: when sixty men-o'-war wooden-walled ships were built out of several thousand acres of New Forest oak, among which was Nelson's favourite, the sixty-four-gun HMS *Agamemnon*.

Outside the tourist office in Lymington I was locking up my bike when I was spotted by a girl called Catherine. She told me she had been on a hefty expedition herself when she had cycled across South America with various friends. But she had no inclination to do such a journey again – not because she got robbed at knifepoint (which she did), but as a result of becoming tired of the drudgery of the continuous packing up and unpacking and moving on every day. I think she found it wearing in the extreme and was interested to know whether I ever felt the same.

I had to admit that I didn't. Ever since I started cycle touring when I was eleven, I seem to take an absurd satisfaction in pulling everything out of my panniers, only to cram it all back in a few hours later. I like knowing I can fit a silly amount of clobber into a very small space which, in essence, is my home on my bike. With panniers loaded, I can then take off for local or distant lands in the knowledge that I need nothing more apart from water and food and a small stash of cash in my pocket. Suffering from a slightly perverse enjoyment of folding, collapsing and dismantling things also helps. As for being constantly on the move – not a lot grabs my fancy more than spending days or weeks in a continuous whirlwind of uncertainty and unpredictability. Of course there are moments when road-lag strikes and a floppy-limbed demeanour sets in, when you don't feel you can summon enough energy even to crawl out of your hovel of sleeping bags, let alone dismantle another tent in the mud and the rain, but they don't last long. When there's so much of the planet to pedal and see, what could be better than pedalling off slowly to see and be free?

A schoolchildren's photo-montage exhibition that visualised their views on living in Lymington was taking place in the gallery adjoining the tourist office. I had been to Lymington many times before, always on my bike and always arriving from Yarmouth on the WIGHTlink ferry: taking the Isle of Wight route to Lymington was the watery way I went when cycling to the West Country. Lymington to me had always seemed like a pretty riverside town of steep cobbled streets and Georgian shops and bobbing boats. Lymington's schoolchildren gave me another side to the superficial niceties of the place – a side which, although you know it is there, is still quite disquieting to see. Almost all the teenagers' artwork revolved around drugs, alcohol, boredom, roaming the streets and feeling resentful.

Luke Waller, aged fifteen, explained that his contribution was

a picture of a man from a magazine. In Lymington I see a big youth culture and not much for us to do, once you are bored with swimming and pacing up and down the high street. So I see Lymington as boring. I used this particular photograph because the man looks very bored with his head in his hands.

Another fifteen-year-old, Michelle Race, wrote her views beside her picture:

Lymington is a quiet town, a peaceful place for holidaymakers to come and enjoy the quay and the little shops, but to us residents who see what it is really like it is not quite the same. On weekend nights the town comes alive with youths under the influence of drugs and alcohol. My view of Lymington is this; it is deceptive, and the way that in the day it appears a quiet, pretty little town, making its money from the quay and the yachters, but it is not. Maybe if there were better facilities for younger people these night time brawls might not occur.

Fourteen-year-old Amy Clarke titled her work 'Kids Today'. She wrote:

I've drawn this because if you think about it there is loads to do in Lymington. Yet every weekend I think I'm stuck for things to do and end up just going shopping and wasting money.

One year younger than Amy, Naomi Bridges called her picture 'BORED':

Even with the many things in Lymington, teenagers often sit down and say, 'I'm bored, there's nothing to do!' This shows how I feel sometimes living in a small, quiet town rather than a big exciting city.

Tom Puckering, a sixteen-year-old, had produced a brilliantly imaginative black-and-white photo-montage entitled 'Easy Life'. All the photographs showed scenes and things as seen from a cat's perspective: a cushion left indented with the shape of a cat's curled form; a sea of kitchen floor tiles photographed a foot off the ground; a cat flap; a view of bushes and leaves at cat's eye level where a cat is obviously watching intently for signs of rodent activity. Tom explained:

The idea behind 'Easy Life' came from looking at my own perspective of Lymington and of those around me. I decided to twist the theme slightly, into 'A Cat's Perspective of Lymington', using my friend's cat Liquorice as my object. When studying what he did during his day, it showed me the differences between youth's appreciation of Lymington and a cat's life of simple pleasures. For the majority of today's generation of teens, it is a necessity to be popular. Basically this means that if you do not wear the latest trends, or have the most advanced games machine, you feel you do not fit in. In contrast with the life's of the youths today, all a cat needs to be happy is to have food, drink and liberty.

Much like a cycle tourist, really.

Izzy Bielby had produced another creatively poignant one by looking at things from a wider angle.

This canvas represents my thoughts towards Lymington town as a teenager today. I wanted to show how sectioned off Lymington is to the rest of the world surrounding. I tried to explain this by putting Lymington in a bubble, floating past other dramatic images and events that have happened world wide . . . I sometimes feel people who live in Hampshire turn a blind eye to the rest of the world because they are so wrapped up in the luxuries, too ignorant and too absorbed in their own world, to involve themselves or notice the world as a whole.

Across her canvas she had pasted cuttings of newspaper headlines:

INDIAN QUAKE WIDENS RIFT BETWEEN THE CASTES

PALESTINIANS FACE A DAILY STRUGGLE TO SURVIVE
IN THE KHAN YUNIS REFUGEE CAMP

DRUGS SECRET LIES IN ULSTER'S BIBLE

7 DIE AS SERB CONVOY IS BOMBED IN KOSOVO

TEENAGE RAPIST MAY NEVER BE FREED

RUSSIA TESTS MISSILES

BRITISH TORNADOES JOIN US AIR STRIKE ON RADAR BASES

WIFE, 86, DIES IN HAMMER ATTACK

Cycling along the seafront at Keyhaven gave a grand view across the salt marshes to Hurst Castle. The one-and-a-half-mile-long shingle spit that leads out to the castle was crawling with silhouettes of walkers shuffling imperceptibly back and forth to Henry VIII's creation that he built (from the rubble of Beaulieu Abbey when he dissolved the monasteries) to reinforce his south coast defences in face of possible invasion from the continent. Henry VIII appeared to be looming large along my route, traces of him and his large edifices cropping up in Abingdon and the castles at Cowes, Calshot and Hurst.

At Milford-on-Sea an old-timer in a yellow fluorescent top pulled up beside me on his bike. Following a bit of 'Rosie Drew!' and a spot of cycle chat, he drew my attention to his windproof, showerproof, perfectproof Pertex jacket.

'It's marvellous,' he said. 'Never had one before – never thought it could make that much difference. But you know what the wind's like – can cut right through you. What a difference a bit of Pertex makes! And . . .' he paused for dramatic effect, '. . . it packs down into its own pocket!'

Up the road from Barton-on-Sea lay New Milton, home to Fred Moore who, at 109, was Britain's oldest man. Born in 1892, he has seen twenty-one prime ministers come and go and lived through six monarchs. When he appeared in this world, Rudolph Diesel had just invented the internal combustion engine. In the paper it said that he followed no special diet and that he used to smoke. He celebrated his 109th birthday with a beer. 'I often go down to the pub with my friends,' he said, 'but I do need someone to take me now.'

Milford-on-Sea, Barton-on-Sea and now, Highcliffe-on-Sea, which I entered after crossing the Dorset border marked by a stream called Chewton Bunny. More evocative names resounded down the road in Christchurch. In the days of eighteenth-century smuggling, the 'Chief Riding Officer' of Christchurch, the splendidly named Abraham Pike ('Stupid boy!'), spent his life trying to catch the entrepreneurial Bournemouth-based smuggler, Isaac Gulliver, but failing miserably.

Riding through Pike's town, I was overtaken by three swift-moving cyclists dressed in lurid, body-moulded swirly-swiggling Lycra. With heads down on their tri-bars, rears in the air, they looked like pond-diving ducks. The look was accentuated by their aerodynamically pointy helmets. As the last cyclist in line was passing me he called out imperiously, referring to my brain-bucket, usefully attached atop my rear load, 'That helmet should be on your head!' Ooh, aren't some people bossy!

Entering Boscombe was like entering memory lane. When I was eighteen I used to come down here most weekends to stay with my troublesome Scouser boyfriend, Ward, who was working as a reporter on the *Bournemouth Evening Echo*. He rented a room in a house, which he shared with two other weirdos. Ward was tall, dark, witty, arrogant, difficult, cynical, illogical and, at times, very appealing. One of the most disappointing things about him was his chip pan: it looked as if it had been used to knock in gateposts before being dipped in tar, dragged through a gravel pit, then dunked in diesel. When I threatened to throw it away, or, at the very least, soak my oily bicycle chain in it, I might as well have signed my own death certificate. Ward cherished that chip pan but then he did exhibit a peculiar tendency to get attracted to strange things (excluding me, of course – I'm very normal).

In contrast to his chip pan downfall, one of the more alluring things about Ward was that, without too much fuss, he took my suggestion and bought a decent bike built for long-range travel. (It would seem that, to qualify as my boyfriend, men have to have a sturdy touring machine, be able to cycle 100 miles before breakfast without a whimper, and possess the ability to fend off a flasher or grizzly bear or two when out in the bush. Not for me a snappy dresser in chic sartorial garb and an X5 BMW. But arrive at my tent-flap with oil-stained shins, dripping and panting with pulsating pectorals while standing astride a bulging-bagged bike? Ooh, yes please!)

So as I cycled through Boscombe I thought about Ward and our old haunts. From the clifftop I stopped to gaze down upon Bournemouth beach and thought about the time we had dragged our bikes across the sand to practise for the Sahara. (We did eventually cycle the length of Europe to get to said fabled desert, and found that it was, well, nothing like Bournemouth beach, actually. Apart from quite a lot of sand.)

I stood on Boscombe Cliff in my shorts and sleeveless T-shirt. Although the weather had suddenly taken a dramatic turn for the cooler – thanks to the wind swinging round to the northeast – I had shed all layers following a burst of some enthusiastic hill climbing. While I gazed back into yesteryear pondering the familiar beach stretched out far below, a senior citizen walking his dog brought me out of my reverie by remarking, 'Turned a bit fresh, hasn't it, sweetheart?'

I agreed that, yes, it had turned rather fresh.

Then he said, 'My goodness – you're not wearing much! You know what they say: ne'er cast a clout till May be out!'

'I seem to have cast most of my clouts,' I replied.

'Well, I'd put them all back on again if I was you . . . till June!'

So dutifully I pulled on my fleece and zipped up my jacket. But only for as long as I sat feasting in the draughty confines of a pastel green clifftop pavilion shelter watching paragliding lemmings throw themselves off the edge. I had cast all clouts again on the first hill out of Boscombe; I couldn't wait till June.

There was more harking back to bygone years as I dropped down into Bournemouth (where, said a tourist brochure, 'Summer Winters') and remembered the family holidays I had here, my addiction to playing crazy golf (the doll's house was my downfall) in the Winter Gardens, and flying down West Cliff's zigzag path, scattering old age pensioners in our wake, on our elaborate wooden motorless go-cart with pram wheels and rope steerage that my grandfather, Frank, a fireman, had built with me and my brothers. There were only two problems with the go-cart. One was its temperamental steering – the front axle had an alarming tendency to get locked, which resulted in spectacular crashes that regularly sent the larking carting crew describing a high parabola over a precipitous wall or cliff-side having flattened several OAPs out for a quiet stroll. The other slight fault was that it didn't have any brakes. The way we overcame this was, once we had jumped on board (the go-cart's design was such that it could seat one driver, with two co-pilots standing on a platform on the rear), when the need for a slowing of speed was required the two co-pilots would leap recklessly off the stern while still holding on to the handrail (otherwise know as the 'dragrail'). Then, by way of being dragged along, acting in effect as braking ballast, we would eventually come to a standstill. This not particularly graceful operation entailed having to bid farewell to several layers of skin in the process. But for the adrenalin rush of an under-tens' extreme sport, it was unsurpassable.

Judging from roadside placards clinging to lampposts and bus stops, Bournemouth (aka Britain's Baywatch) appeared to be in the middle of a Shark Awareness Week. As I value my toes I avoided a dip off the pier lest a cyclist-hungry Poole Bay Jaws should happen to be patrolling the shores.

Poole Harbour claims to be the second largest natural harbour in the world (after Sydney) with sixty miles of coastline, six bays and eight named islands (including Brownsea, where Baden Powell's Boy Scout crusade was created). A recent letter to Poole's local paper disputed the claim, saying that Halifax, Nova Scotia, took that second place. Be that as it may, Poole Harbour was awash with so many weekend windsurfers and kitesurfers that I stopped to watch the spectacle of multiple collisions and line entanglements followed by feisty arguments. Kitesurfing, an improbable mixture of windsurfing and paragliding, looks as impossible as it is perilous. But for an extreme sport that combines the inherent dangers of speed, water and massive 'big air' jumps, the apparent ease with which beginners find they can get going means that kitesurfing is, in some places, starting to overtake windsurfing in terms of rigs sold and people getting into it. That said, it can play havoc with the more sticking-out bits of anatomy. One of Gary's workmates, a World Champion windsurfer, told me that fingers and ears are not infrequently ripped off by the control lines attached to the immense wind-tearing power of the ten or more square metres of kite. I visualised rather a lot of blood diffusing into Poole Harbour.

By now the wind, tugging at the pines up on the hill, was so strong that one particularly vigorous gust blew a beached kitesurfer's chute up on to the road, causing a stack-up of cars as a cat's cradle of control lines knotted themselves around wheels and acres of blinding pink sail spread across a windscreen like a giant blob of blancmange.

CHAPTER 15

As Poole Harbour is girdled by mainly busy main roads and dual carriageways, I took the easier and far more enjoyable option of reaching Studland by way of the clunky chain ferry from Sandbanks to South Haven Point. Landing on the Isle of Purbeck (which, although feeling like an island, is actually a peninsula) I came upon a two-mile tailback of cars waiting for the ferry back over to the Bournemouth side. The car occupants watched me with various expressions of boredom, resignation and sizzling frustration as I appeared fleetingly in and out of their field of vision. I knew what was coming. And it came.

'Hey, darlin'! You need a motor on that!' called a bald bloke with a large tattooed arm hanging limply out of the window.

A motor? What a lovely idea! But I was doing all right without one – whistling along in the wind, enjoying the surrounding sandy Dorset heath-land of bell heather and western gorse.

Had I veered off to my left across the shell-strewn sand and dunes to Stud-land's long white ribbon of sheltered beach, I could have taken simple delight (like I had in my misspent short-lived naturalist past – I told you Ward was a bad influence on me) in lying in my altogether among the icing-sugar sands. For you stroll this way at the peril of your blushes. Once past Wide Shell Bay and Knoll Beach, a rough wooden sign declares that 'NUDISTS MAY BE SEEN BEYOND THIS POINT' – which sounds more like an invitation than a warning.

Standing naked on heathland a mile inland from Studland rises the massive bulk of Agglestone Rock, a mass of natural ironstone eighty feet in circumfer-ence and weighing 400 tons. In the Chinese whispering manner of Dorset folklore, there are several explanations for its incongruous location. One tells how it was carried from the Isle of Wight by the Devil, who uncharitably planned to drop it on Salisbury Cathedral. Clearly he hadn't been working out down the gym to develop his pecs, triceps and deltoids, because he didn't get very far. A variation on the theme relates how the Agglestone was hurled by the Devil from the Isle of Wight when he was trying to hit Corfe Castle.

Stirring names abound along the east Dorset coast around Swanage, or 'Knollsea', as Thomas Hardy called it, describing the place as 'a seaside village, lying snugly within two headlands as between a finger and a thumb'. There are the isolated shining chalk stacks and pinnacles of Old Harry, wading through the water up to his pearly-white kneecaps, and the Haystack (Old Harry used to have a wife, but a storm in 1896 toppled her to a stump of her former glory), East Man, West Man, Peveril Point (off which the Danish fleet was destroyed in

878 after being chased out of Poole by King Alfred's galleys), Dancing Ledge, Great Globe, Winspit, Rope Lake Head, Houns-tout Cliff and the old smugglers' landing places – shown on few maps – of Ragged Rocks, Half Moon, Chillmark, Conner Cove, Blackers Hole, Smokey Hole, Shit Yattery Hole and Scratch Arse.

Then there's the underground quarry of Tilly Whim Caves (a whim was a type of derrick used to lower the hewn stone blocks into waiting rowing boats beneath the cliffs, each capable of carrying up to nine tons). It was a Tilly Whim quarryman, John Mowlem, who, in 1807, jumped a London-bound brig with ninepence in his pocket, and returned thirty-seven years later as a director of the great street rebuilding firm, Mowlem. Through his patronage, the small-scale resort of Swanage (dubbed Old London by the Sea) was supplied with some of London's cast-off street furniture, including the flying-fish wind-vane from Billingsgate Market, bollards from Bloomsbury, pillars from Nash's Regent Street, and grand old lamp standards from Westminster and Soho usefully bearing London street names. The star prize was the front of Mercers' Hall, Cheapside (originally designed by a student of Sir Christopher Wren in 1670), which now forms the façade of Swanage's Town Hall. Near the pier is the faceless Wellington Clock Tower that once adorned the southern approach to London Bridge in honour of the Duke of Wellington; having been declared an 'unwarrantable obstruction' by the Metropolitan Police, it was moved out of sight and out of mind to Swanage.

Less than a century ago, paddle steamers brought hundreds of daytrippers to Swanage from Bournemouth and Weymouth. Mostly the holidaymakers made it to their destination without incident but it wasn't always such plain sailing. One of the fastest paddlers on the Bournemouth–Swanage run, the 270-ton *Stirling Castle*, had a disastrous record. It was a Red Funnel steamer run by the Southampton Isle of Wight & South of England Royal Mail Steam Packet Company (pity the telephonist for *that* company). In two seasons, 1913 and 1914, the *Stirling* managed to sink three yachts. In one incident, after pulling away from Swanage's Victorian pier, it was paddling at a keen lick when it swamped a yacht off Ballard Down and cut a second in half, drowning four of the occupants. The accident-prone steamer finally ended its days when, on war service in 1916, it was itself sunk off Malta.

A letter-painter-outer had been at work on the Langton Maltravers village sign. By way of some slap-happy brushstrokes, 'PLEASE DRIVE CAREFULLY' had been transmuted into 'PLEASE DIE CAREFULLY'.

Another road sign awaited me at Church Knowle, just south of Cocknowle. Homemade and carefully painted with the words 'SLOW – KITTENS CROSS- ING', it warned me of the only potential hazard I had to contend with as I crossed the long chalk ridge of the glorious Purbeck Hills until I hit the red flag-flying 'DANGER AREA' of Lulworth's Royal Armoured Corps gunnery range, where a line of tanks were enthusiastically firing live shells at moving tar- gets on a distant hillside. The B3070 passed very close to the rear of the tanks and when they thoughtfully started firing just as I was passing, the shockingly explosive burst of detonating blasts gave me such a fright that I leapt several feet off my saddle and swerved into the path of an oncoming vehicle. Definitely not a very careful way to die.

Things were a lot more peaceful down at the natural sea-nibbled amphithe- atre and almost landlocked pool of Lulworth Cove – a famous beauty spot and geology lesson in one. It was still too early in the year for tourists so apart from a small shoal of fishermen and divers I had the place to myself.

I had been to Lulworth many times before, once arriving on a coach as part of a school fact-finding field trip during which I had narrowly avoided falling into the depths of Stair Hole. All other visits had seen me arriving by the gentler and more blendable means of a bicycle. During my stays I had clawed my way up the steep chalk cliffs, clambered around the forest of fossilised tree stumps, slept in the cove, swum in the cove, walked to the great wave-cut limestone-rock arch of Durdle Door (never fails to impress), camped at Durdle Door, dived at Durdle Door and waded across the feet-sinking shingle sweep of Man o' War beach to Bat's Head. All of which I did this time, in splendid isolation.

Along with the Purbeck Hills, one of the strong contenders in my private pantheon of top cycling roads along this stretch of Dorset coast, is from the hill at Daggers Gate behind Durdle Door, with Vine's Down to the east and Bush Barrow to the west, and down and around through the village that can't decide whether it wants to be called Chaldon Herring or East Chaldon and compro- mises by cramming the whole mouthful on the signposts. The road, a whirlingly wonderful quiet country lane, drifts and twists in an undulating fashion at the foot of the green rolling Chaldon Downs before dipping and rising at Lord's Barrow from where, within moments, you are rudely jettisoned on to the jarring A352.

A blurred glimpse was all I caught of the white horse carved into the chalk hillside at White Horse Hill, as I plunged down across the River Jordan into Preston and on to the tourist-trapping delights of Weymouth (or Budmouth Regis, as Hardy called it).

I have always loved Weymouth. It is so haughtily carefree beneath its brazen veneer of sentimental seaside fripperies and trinkets. The town has George III to thank for popularising it as a fashionable health and holiday resort. He became the first monarch to use a bathing machine when, in 1789, he had gone to Weymouth to convalesce from a serious illness. To the strains of *God Save the King* played by a brass band, a horse-drawn bathing machine had carried the king down the sands. Dressed not in his trunks but his birthday suit, he entered the bracing waters of Weymouth Bay.

I cycled, like I had cycled many times before, alongside the broad curve of the promenade that gently arcs around the sweeping crescent of sandy beach to the harbour, all of which is watched over by the lofty Georgian stuccoed and porticoed terraces that front the esplanade. Being out of season there was no seafront soundtrack of blinking kerr-chink-ing amusement arcades, and the beach was lovely and sparse of human activity. There were no sand-castle-building extravaganzas, no sun goddesses in dental-floss bikinis, no sunhatted mums with rockpool-ransacking toddlers (not that Weymouth has many rockpools to ransack, mind), no granddads in string vests, no kazoo-based patter of Punch and Judy shows, no heady wafts of suntan lotion mingling with the frying grease of chips, and virtually every ice-cream kiosk remained shuttered. The only forms of life were the huddles of well wrapped-up old-timers sitting shoulder to shoulder like ranks of pigeons in the prom-front pavilions, staring silently out to sea. Walking my bike past them stirred them into cooing:

'My word! Look at all the gear on that!'

'She needs a motor on that!'

'Gracious me! How can she possibly ride such a heavy thing!'

'Got the kitchen sink on there have you, me petal?'

I was heading very slowly uphill off the Asda roundabout when a man walking along the pavement at the same speed as me asked me what I was doing and where I was going. In between gulping for air, I told him.

'I wish I'd done something like that when I was young,' he said.

'I don't think . . .' (puff-pant) '. . . you have to be . . .' (pant-puff) '. . . young to do it,' I puffed pantily in between strenuous breaths. 'You just have to like travelling slowly . . .' (puff-puff) '. . . and being outside in all weathers.' It was raining again. 'And anyway . . .' (pant, pant) '. . . I'm really quite old!'

The man looked at me as if I had plastic bags on my feet, which I did – Asda ones as it happened, because I wanted to keep my shoes dry. I could see him thinking: Old? When you're in your gap year? Pull the other one!

That night I camped in the torrential rain and raging wind on a hill over-looking Chesil Beach and Portland Bill. The tent flapped and thrashed around like an angry gibing spinnaker. It was most dramatic. I thought I was going to get blown away. I also thought I was going to lose my bananas: a brazen badger stuck his snout into my bell-end and tried to make off with them into the night.

The next day I cycled all around the ancient Isle and Royal Manor of Portland or, in Hardy's lingo, the 'Isle of Slingers' or 'Gibraltar of Wessex'. Moored to the underbelly of England by an umbilical cord of shingle that runs parallel to the southeastern tip of Chesil Beach (the longest shingle bar in Europe), the Isle of Portland, like the Isle of Purbeck, is not an island at all, though when seen from a distance its vast tilted table of limestone sloping from the heights over Fortuneswell (a small town with shops and houses clinging to the hillside, many with front doors level with their neighbours' chimney pots) down to sea level near Portland Bill looks as if it has been left to float alone.

Cycling over the causeway I stopped at the Chesil Beach Nature Reserve, where I overheard a bit of excited twitcher talk: a purple heron had been spotted – blown off course in the strong winds from France. There had been more excitement earlier in the year when a different species of creature had been seen: a pod of dolphins frolicking in Portland Harbour.

The wildlife on Chesil is spectacular. Apart from a number of species of birds that nest on the shingle (the most important being the little tern and the ringed plover), a vast number of other birds visit the area throughout the year, like the gadwell dabbling duck, the red-breasted merganser, shelducks, gold-eneyes, wigeons, shovelers, pintails, pochards, teal, redshank, dunlin, oystercatchers, little egrets, reed warblers, grey herons, peregrine, cormorant and brent geese.

As for plants, the blackboard on the outside wall of the nature centre alerted me to 'WHAT'S ABOUT IN MAY': thrift, common storks-bill, Alexander cox-foot, little mouse-ear, meadow fox-tail, Portland spurge, early forget-me-not, sea campion, field speedwell, hairy bittercress, Oxford ragwort, bulbous buttercup, doves foot, cranes bill and common mouse-ear to name but a few. At other times of year I could have seen sea pea, sea kale and the yellow horned poppy.

I knew brown hares bounded across the invertebrate-rich beach, but hadn't expected to see a bit of beaver – shoulder bones to be exact. Admittedly they were lying on display in the nature centre, but they still came as a surprise. Found by a man from Bridport, these perfectly preserved bones had been discovered among lumps of peat washed up on the beach and had been sent to the British Museum for identification. Beavers once commonly inhabited the swampy ground in Lyme Bay, before it was covered by rising sea water at the end of the Ice Age.

I carried on down the causeway past the not so natural sight of the vast oil tanks of the Comoco and Jet Mere Tank Farm. It was a grim 'farm' if ever I saw one, the oil-stock containers all brooding gloomily in intimidating fashion behind giant fences of concentration-camp barbed wire.

There were more cordoned-off areas up around Castletown where, at the Royal Navy helicopter base, I peered through a wall of chain-link fencing at a Sikorsky S61N – a magnificent-looking helicopter, responsible for assisting people in trouble in an area from Bournemouth Bay in the east to Start Point in south Devon and out to the mid-point of the English Channel. In the space of five-and-a-half years, the helicopter crews had carried out over 2250 emergency missions – searching for people lost overboard from ships, vessels on fire, divers with the 'bends', people stuck on cliffs, evacuating others with various injuries from all types of vessels and transferring critically ill patients to specialist hospitals.

Although the Isle of Portland is a mere four-and-a-half miles long by about two miles wide, it is home to three castles, all built from the world-famous fine, creamy white Jurassic Portland stone. One of these castles was the squat, tough-looking, fourteen-foot-walled harbour-side fortress of Portland Castle, built by our corpulent and ever-present Henry VIII.

After climbing up to the High Angle Battery at the grand height of 500 feet (Portland's 'Roof of the World'), I powered on down through Wakeham, which is named not after any lords or Old English hamlets, but following a watchman's warning shout that went up when the Navy press-gang crept on shore at night.

I then found myself in the Perryfield Quarry Butterfly Reserve. There are some fifty-seven different species of butterfly throughout the British Isles and because Portland, with its chalk and limestone grasslands, still has substantial areas of vegetation rich in the plants and conditions that so many varieties of butterflies need for various stages of their life cycles, over half of them can be seen on Portland. So, with a butterfly identification leaflet in hand, I went wandering round the quarry, hiding in bushes and crouching behind rocks in an alarming David Attenborough manner, hoping to spot them. There was the royal off-chance of seeing the Queen of Spain fritillary making a rare appearance on her migrations from Europe; even monarch butterflies sporadically turn up, blown across the Atlantic during their spectacular migrations from Canada to Mexico.

But sadly, not one butterfly came my way. I blamed the weather – the mid-May cold and severely blustery conditions were obviously not to the butterflies' liking. My hopes of a lepidopterous sighting were momentarily aroused when I thought I had happened upon the large and brightly coloured chamomile shark moth caterpillar with its snazzy 'V' markings. But the flutter of excitement was short-lived: on closer inspection my pupated shark metamorphosed into a small frayed pupa of vivid nylon rope.

On I cycled, down past some old wooden derricks (in the quarrying heyday, stiff-legged derricks once covered the island) to the triple lighthouses at Portland Bill. My arrival at the Bill (so called after its duckbill-like appearance) couldn't have been better. While the mainland lay encapsulated beneath a leaden grey murk, I was bathed in a cold crisp sun, shining from a blue and cloudless sky. The wind blew so strong I could lean into it at an angle more acute than the Tower of Pisa without smacking on to my face. Standing on the tip of the bird's Bill feels like standing on a boat's prow, carving a passage out through the lumpy seas of the Channel. I was at least four miles south of any other part of the Dorset coast – fifteen miles south of Bournemouth and Lyme Regis and six from Weymouth.

Raging over the two-mile-long Shambles Sandbank that lies just below the surface is Portland Race, a treacherous current that boils around the Bill when tide and sea currents collide. It is one of the worst navigational hazards for shipping in the Channel. A few yards to the west lies Pulpit Rock. From here to Chesil Cove stretches a west-facing cliff-face of grey rock. This is Portland's evil coast. In rough seas seething waves crash and scour into the caves, exploding like thunder. Wallsend Cove, Staple Ope, Mutton Cove, Clay Ope and Hallelujah Bay have been the last resting place of many a fine ship, and detestable names to thousands of mariners.

Pulpit Rock is a pillar of stone that wrecked *Reliance*, the boat in which Ann Davison and her husband attempted an Atlantic crossing in the early 1950s. Her husband was drowned but Ann, refusing to accept defeat, avenged the tragedy by sailing a 22-foot Bermudan sloop, *Felicity Ann,* across the Atlantic in

1952 to become the first woman to sail that ocean alone. The French author, Jean Merrien, in his book *Lonely Voyagers,* wrote: 'This success is truly remarkable, for solitary sailing is very hard upon the muscles as well as on feminine nerves. We admire her but hope she will have few imitators. The craze for record breaking ends sooner or later in death.' Surely Jean is a prime candidate for a good feminist slapping if ever there was one.

Portland Bill lighthouse, painted in immaculate white with a dashing belt of pillar-box red, dazzled in the brilliance of the sparkling sun. Like the castles, it too is made from Portland stone – a stone that has been quarried at Portland since Roman times. Many of London's famous landmarks have been built from this fine building material, including Broadcasting House, St Paul's Cathedral, the British Museum, Buckingham Palace, the Cenotaph, the Tower of London, Somerset House, the Bank of England and the V&A Museum. Even the government buildings of Delhi and the United Nations Building in New York have risen from this outcrop of creamy white stone that carves like a dream, weathers well and retains its colour.

What hadn't kept its colour so well was the 150-year-old large triangular Trinity House navigational sea marker rising from the rocks at the tip of the Bill. Its brilliant white paint had been buried beneath bright blue sprawling daubs of graffiti: IMAGINE – FRISKED 2000 – SPOONFED – SUPANOVA – DIG IT. Even the neatly cropped grass had succumbed to a sprayed dose of the aerosol – LIKE A ROLLING STONE.

CHAPTER 16

For the next three weeks my slow-moving coastal voyage was put on hold. I had been summoned by my publishers to give a bout of cycling (book-flogging) talks around the country. Having to try to talk again felt odd and a little scary. It was even more scary when everything went disastrously wrong, as it did at Waterstones in Reading.

All had started well. Despite my dislike of Reading's confusing roundabouts, I had managed to negotiate the car-orientated town on my bike and arrived at the bookshop in good time. I loaded my slides, tested the projector, located the toilet (v. important) up several flights of stairs and through several pin-numbered security system doors (and managed to find my way back out again) and had a long swig of water. Then, just as the doors were flung open to the thronging crowds of bicycle-chanting fans queuing up down the street – oh, all right then, handful of keen enthusiasts plus sporadic dribbles and drabbles of onlookers and passers-by wooed by the prospect of a free glass of wine – the fire alarm went off and everyone was evacuated unceremoniously into the high street. Sirens, flashing lights and fire engines arrived on the scene, and men dressed-to-extinguish vanished through the doors.

Time passed.

Meanwhile, back outside in the high street, something of a street party atmosphere had spontaneously manifested itself (the free wine had miraculously made it out with us) and in a progressively inebriated spirit the milling audience insisted I stand upon a bench to give them a dose of my cycling spiel. This was when I discovered the advantage of having a couple of fire engines parked beside you – they act as a very effective crowd-puller (I recommend it for any public orator). By the time the big, burly extinguishing fire-crew allowed us to pile back into the bookshop (source of fire alarm still unknown) my original audience had swollen tenfold. Capitalising on this development, I steered them all into Waterstones. Two newcomers, I was happy to discover, turned out to be Beverley, my Geordie sister-in-law's sister, and her husband Richard; they happened to be passing on their motor-bike.

But my ordeal was not yet over. Just as a hush had fallen and the lights had been dimmed, the projector exploded. Goodbye, slides. Hello, Panic Talk Part Two. Somehow I got through it but not without thinking that it was one of those days when I should never have got out of bed. The best part of the whole sorry saga was embarking upon a manic, pedal-thrashing twenty-mile cycle through the Berkshire night, slip-streaming Richard and Bev's motorbike all the way back to their home.

Fire alarms and exploding projectors were the least of my worries when galli-vanting around the country to give cycling talks. Without a doubt, the most harrowing aspect of these self-indulgent, self-promoting publicity stunts was travelling by train with a bike.

Although trains and bikes, and bikes on trains, have been a means of con-veyance upon which I have relied to transport myself since my early teens, carting one's bike up and over hernia-inducing railway bridges to stand on a windy station platform for a mind-numbingly lengthy wait for a delayed train and then being given short shrift by an irascible guard was something I found more and more frustrating. So much for all the empty talk of integrated trans-port policies. The facts were plain: to travel by train was a nightmare; to travel by train with a bike was a double-whammy nightmare.

To add to my woes the sun, which with a few feeble exceptions had failed to shine upon me during my 1062-mile coastal trek, shook off its shiver the moment I had to endure being entrapped for three weeks upon trains and burst into a heatwave. And so: cut to a student in her gap year, travelling on a hot May afternoon with a bicycle on a train from Swindon to London. She sits within the awful chemical-cooled, air-conditioned, body-packed environment, staring out of the sealed window (the Nanny State doesn't trust its citizens to open windows any more) upon a gorgeous sun-blazing English countryside – a countryside through which, and around which, she should be cycling.

Although I was travelling on a train capable of attaining a speed of 125 mph, it stopped and started and haltingly plodded along at barely walking pace before finally accelerating to an exhilarating 20 mph. Then it stopped. Completely. Had the seasons spun out of sequence and autumn's 'wrong sort of leaves' fallen prematurely on the tracks, or had winter come early and frozen all the points before receiving a light dusting of the 'wrong sort of snow', then I could have resigned myself to the inevitable delay. Instead, a barely audible voice announced over the muffled tannoy that we had been held up 'because of hot tracks'.

Yes, on this delightfully warm, but not outrageously hot, early summer afternoon, Britain's rail tracks were suffering from a dose of the 'wrong sort of sun'. Apparently this mild heatwave had buckled sections of newly laid track and threatened to warp other stretches.

Only two days before, the railways were supposed to have returned to normal after seven months of closures and speed restrictions as Railtrack carried out a £700 million programme of safety work following the Hatfield rail crash, which had claimed four lives. And now, an hour after we had ground to a standstill, the high-speed line was shut down. More than a hundred trains were delayed and seventeen cancelled. It didn't bear thinking about what might happen in a real heatwave. How India's or Africa's railways managed to run at all struck me as a complete mystery. I decided Britain's detractors did the Third World an injustice when comparing our transport services with those in countries that have to make do on a fraction of our national wealth and with far more extreme climates. Whatever could be the next excuse for a progressively delayed and deteriorating train service? Camels on the line or the wrong sort of rain?

Mid-June: the time had come for me to return to Weymouth to continue my seaside cycle. With a feeling of 'been here, done that', I shut my front door and loaded up my bike on a hot and cloudless Wednesday afternoon the day after my mother's sixty-ninth birthday. But this time she was not here to see me off. Nor was my father. Sensibly they had decided they had better things to be doing than waving farewell (again) to their saddle-bound daughter. Like going on holiday to France.

But if you can't rely on parents, at least you can rely on your neighbours because ever-dependable Val was there to see me off the premises. Though not before I had given her free rein to keep tabs on the nesting hornet that had built its spectacular abode of paper combs on the inner roof of my bike shed. At first I had felt a bit dubious about dissecting my bottom bracket three feet away from the low-flying and potentially lethal undercarriage of a wasp the size of a cocktail sausage that bristled with artillery and whose approaching drone could quite easily be mistaken for a Chinook helicopter homing in for the kill. But over the weeks I had become quite attached to my industrial-sized wasps. I decided that *Vespa crabro* suffered from a bad press. Mention hornets and most people envisage a scary and aggressive enemy whose only intentions are to launch an attack of barbed and inherently deadly stinging air-to-surface missiles into an innocent patch of nice soft human skin. But in reality I discovered hornets are docile and harmless as long as they are treated with the degree of substantial respect they deserve.

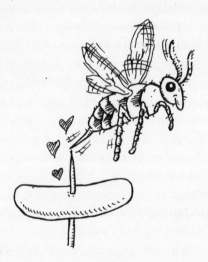

All this dilly-dallying in bike sheds with hornet-sympathetic neighbours paid off because by the time I finally was ready to go, my farewell party had doubled in size to two: Clare had walked across the fields from her mum's house to make sure I really was going. I had planned to follow my tyre tracks of Departure No. 1 and cycle to Winchester where, for the second time, I would spend my first night of Departure No. 2 with Clare and her daffodil-eating friends.

As Clare was going to drive over to Winchester a little later on anyway, she offered to take all my heavy panniers for me.

'I'll take you as well if you want, Jose,' she said. 'After all, you have already cycled to Winchester once with a dead cow in your bags!'

What a splendid idea! There would be no labouring for hours into head-winds or struggling up hills with swaying loads. I could be there in a jiffy, all fresh as a flea and fit as a daisy (or something like that) to resume my journey to Weymouth.

'I can't do that!' I said defiantly. 'That would be cheating!'

My ploy was to try to get around the whole of the British Isles without rely-ing on a car once – unless in an emergency or because of injury.

With Clare gone my farewell party dwindled back down to one and at last I was off. As I cycled down the road I was joined by an entourage of grey and pied wagtails all playfully dipping and diving in front of my bike like porpoises around the bow of a ship. Some would daringly swoop in to land on the road feet from my front wheel before flittering off and dropping like stones over the hedge. At the pond at the bottom of the road, I paused to have one last look at the pair of resident village swans with their cygnets in tow – four little bundles of straggly grey fluff balls. Five miles later I stopped at my builder's workshop to off-load his birthday present – an inflatable camping chair, or (to be Mr and Mrs Zamberlan precise) a Therm-a-Rest Chair Kit Lite 20.

Resumption of my journey on this Wednesday 20th June happened appro-priately to coincide with National Bike to Work Day. *Hallelujah!* I thought to myself. The roads should be as delightfully empty of cars as in the fuel strike! Somewhat misjudging the mood of the moment, I naively imagined I would be whisked along the lanes by furiously pedalling packs of commuting cyclists. Instead, I passed only one cyclist all the way to Winchester – an old woman on a rusty boneshaker with a poodle in her basket.

Apart from surviving a near miss when a woman, slamming along a country lane in her four-wheel-drive, slewed across the road towards me after tearing bull-bars-first into a blind corner, I made it to Winchester without incident. Clare greeted me with a table groaning under the weight of food. Once we had feasted, daffodil-eating Bob ushered me upstairs to his room with the intention of making the earth move for me. And after grappling with various knobs and joysticks he succeeded, in so far as he took me flying, virtually of course, over the Isle of Wight on his computerised flight aviation simulator. Went up to 4000 feet, we did, to enable us to perform a spot of aerobatics above Bembridge. But then we stalled and I felt all giddy and I wanted to get down. So we landed at Southampton airport and I went to bed, leaving Bob to do a virtual jigsaw.

The next morning I rolled down the hill to the station to catch the train to Weymouth. To avoid a mad panicking sprint from one end of the platform to another, I asked the man at the ticket office if he knew which end of the 10.25 to Weymouth I might find the guard's van.

'If it's a nine-car unit it'll be at the front,' he said, 'and if it's a five-car unit it should be in the middle.'

Unit? I thought. Trains don't have units. And they don't have cars either – at least I hoped they didn't because I was trying to get away from the things. Trains have carriages. Kitchens have units. Anyway, the problem was knowing where to wait on the platform. As the ticket office man could enlighten me no further as to whether I should expect a long train or a medium long train, I ended up hovering in a state of suspense somewhere between the Ladies and the Gents.

In the event no train came at all, because it had broken down outside Woking.

Time passed. Seasons changed. New generations were born. Elections came and went. And all the time, cows continued to chew the cud. But no train came down the tracks.

The platform filled with potential passengers (sorry – customers). Some sat on the red curved seats staring glumly at their feet. Others paced angrily up and down the platform with a mobile phone clamped to their ear: 'I'm on the platform . . . what? . . . yes, still waiting for the train . . . what? . . . oh, no idea at all. Could be all bloody day at this rate!' Others simply chose to exit this world by entering another in the form of a fat blockbuster.

Eventually a new century dawned and a train materialized at Winchester station. Its guards' van was neither at the front nor in the middle, but at the rear. Pelted down platform with unwieldy shin-whacking steed. Mad scramble through surging crowds. Located guard's van but no guard. Suffered near hernia single-handedly heaving and hauling and hoisting overloaded bike into overloaded van. Here I discovered that the one and only advantage of waiting a month of blue Sundays for the Weymouth train was that the one that broke down was a 'new' Wessex Electric with capacity to carry a meagre five hanging bikes, whereas the one sent to replace it was a good old sturdy slam-door variety with a caged guard's van capacious enough to carry twenty bikes (with no time-consuming wheel-wrecking hanging hooks), seas of suitcases, a drinks trolley and several stacks of pushchairs and strollers. It was not difficult to tell it was holiday season.

One of the pushchairs belonged to a young mother in big, floppy flared jeans and a black puffa jacket. Her double buggy contained one-year-old Louise and two-year-old Liam – the latter sweetly asleep, the former screaming her little puce head off.

'They always tell you boys are more trouble,' said the puffa mum, 'but Liam's an angel. Goes to bed at 7.30 and doesn't make a sound till about 8.30 or nine the next morning. But Louise – blimey – she's the screamer!'

Liam the sleeper. Louise the screamer. Puffa Mum the revealer-of-all.

'Giving birth to these two was no trouble,' she said unprompted, as I tried to prevent a tottering tower of suitcases from flattening me when the rickety-rackety-clackety train lurched around a corner. 'My problem is being pregnant – I'm ill all the time – hate every bloody minute of it!'

'Sounds horrible!' I said distractedly as the pitching train suddenly tilted in the opposite direction, threatening to crush me beneath a stack of bikes toppling over like a set of dominoes.

'Yeah. But the birth side – gawd it's a laarf! Liam flew out in an ambulance, like. It was that fast and that easy. Louise came out in me mum's house on her bed. It was so quick, like, there was no time to try and get to hospital or any of that!'

'That's the way to have them!' I said, as I helped to lift her double buggy down to the platform at Southampton.

The train was so packed it was standing room only all the way to Bournemouth. I remained in the guard's van, prised into position beside my bike with its oily chain leaving a smeared black imprint upon my shin. A crop-haired man in his late twenties stood in the corridor leaning against the cage of the guard's van. He wore a T-shirt emblazoned with 'IT'S AUSTRALIA' and, pushed up on his head, green-rimmed Oakley Eye Jacket sunglasses. He appeared deeply engrossed in a book open at a chapter boldly entitled 'LIQUIDITY, CASH FLOW AND BORROWING'. Gracious, what scintillating stuff! I made a mental note not to interrupt him lest his talk was of a numerical nature. First babies and birthing and then fluctuating figures and PEP plans and unit trusts: it would all be too much – my head would pop. As Mr Australia read, he simultaneously worked his way through a whole pack of McVitie's digestive biscuits. He was on automatic pilot, never once lifting his eyes from his financial pages, simply dipping his hand into the packet and feeding another wheatmeal biscuit into his mouth.

I wondered if he just liked the taste or whether he suffered from flatulence, because that was for what they were originally devised. In 1839, two Scottish doctors thought up the recipe to help patients suffering from wind: its high baking-soda content was said to aid digestion. But I reckoned Mr Australia probably just liked the taste, as the distinguished Digestive (with a diameter of 73 millimetres and holes to keep the moisture level to a regulation 2–2.4 per cent) remains the most popular and perfectly designed British biscuit. Millions are eaten every day all over the world. Interestingly, if you are interested in this sort of thing – I am, I like food – its size has never varied in all of these 160-odd years. But the number of holes, or 'dockers' as they are called in the biscuit biz (the pins in the mould are called dockers), is coded to signify which of the three McVitie's plants the biscuit is baked at. I thought about asking Mr Australia if he knew he was eating a biscuit whose recipe is a closely guarded secret and never known by more than three people at one time. But then I reminded myself he looked more a man of money markets, not food markets, and I kept my mouth shut.

I don't know where the guard had been hiding all this time but he had now materialised and I was relieved to find he was a chatty chap called Kevin. A bit alternative too – he wore his Bloc shades on his head and his tie on his belt. As I leant over the marooned drinks trolley, a score of bikes and pushchairs and golf clubs, one surfboard, six boogie boards and several thousand suitcases to show him my ticket, I remarked that in the end it was quite a lucky thing the new train broke down because you'd never get this lot in one of those modern hemmed-in no-room-for-nothing guard's vans.

This set him off.

'Blaady right!' he said, 'I'd have had to turn a stack of people away. Them new vans – they're blaady awful!'

Jumping on the moaning bandwagon, I said that I hated those racks that you had to hang your bike up on.

'They're so high I nearly decapitate myself trying to do it,' I said. 'You have to take all your panniers off, and when you finally get the bike up there they ruin your rims! When I've written letters to complain about them I just get standard issue replies about passengers wanting more seats!'

'I know what you mean,' said Kev. 'Management don't want to know that them racks are unpopular. They couldn't care less about no bikes. What's important to them is bums on seats. That's what means money. Not bikes.'

At Bournemouth, Mr Australia, clutching his money-spinning read and trailing digestive biscuit crumbs, alighted on to a platform crowded with holidaying hordes. A tidal wave of suitcases spilled out of the guard's van, only to be replaced by an equal sum bound for Weymouth.

As we rattled onwards across the sun-splashed Dorset countryside, big cauliflower clouds chasing their shadows across the verdant and lush rolling hills, I watched two boys standing in the corridor daring each other to pull the emergency cord. In matronly style, I advised them not to or else this train, already half a day late, would never make it to Weymouth.

'And,' I added a tad theatrically, 'we'll all fry and die in an overheated tin can!' (Well, it was a sizzling summer's day out there.)

'So fuckin' wha'?' said one in charitable style, 'I couldn't give a fuckin' toss!'

And I was left to reflect ruefully over the degenerating conduct of the youth of today. I may look their age but I'm an old maid at heart and would, I like to think, deserve a little respect in my latter years. But I couldn't blame them for goading each other to pull the emergency chain – when I was their age I had done the same thing messing around with my brothers or school friends. It wasn't until I was thirty-two that, unprovoked, I actually got round to pulling it.

It had been during the time that my knee was out of order and so, for the first time in over twenty years of continuous cycle-combined-rail use, I felt what it was like to turn up at a station unencumbered by my mount and free to stand anywhere on the platform. If I fancied boarding the train at the front, I could, ditto the middle and the rear.

No longer did I have to seek out a station supervisor who could and should – but did not always – inform me of the position of the guard's van on the expected train, so that I might be spared a surge of stress as I frantically cantered along with my heavily panniered bike to the other end of the platform than the one he had suggested, scattering a phalanx of peeved passengers in my wake.

No longer did I have to spend the first five minutes of every train journey tethering my steed in the guard's van and removing any easily nickable attachments (computer, lights, bar-bag etc.), before lurching off down the carriage in search of an elusive seat.

But although train travel proved a novel and delightfully straightforward operation without the added stagger up and down an endless succession of steps with a heavily laden bike in order to cross platforms, I felt worrisomely 'naked' without my wheels in tow. What's more, it also felt worrisomely wrong not to have to get up from my seat ten minutes before the train reached my destination in order to sway back to the guard's van, fiddle around replacing the detachable bicycle apparatus and extricate my bike from the entangled mountain of two-wheeled machines, beneath which it would by now invariably be buried. Who really wants an easy life (simply stepping on board a train with a briefcase and newspaper, or even foldable bike tucked under arm) when you can have a fraught and complicated one, attached to a very useful lump of metal?

Anyhow, just once during my months of knee-kaput crutching hither and thither, it proved a happy relief to be travelling by train without my bike. There I was, sitting on the 10.05 Liphook to Waterloo, reading Che Guevara's entertaining *Motorcycle Diaries*, crutches stowed beneath seat (but still doing a fine job of tripping everyone up), when my nose twitched. Smoke. I smelled smoke. Funny, I thought, had I sat in the smoking carriage by mistake? I looked around. No, there were clearly 'NO SMOKING' stickers plastered across the windows.

The carriage was full. I peered at the faces of those seated around me (mostly commuter types) to see whether their noses were detecting similar smoke signals. None twitched. They were either busy in drooling sleep or stuck behind a mask of newspapers.

Thinking that perhaps I had imagined it, I tried to lose myself back in Che's South American travels. Again my nose twitched. Smoke. There was definitely a strong whiff of smoke. But not cigarette smoke. Had the train passed a bonfire? I stood up. The train being one of the nice old slam-door varieties, I slid open the window and, wary not to get myself decapitated by a passing train, gingerly stuck my head out, peering ahead along the length of the train (I was in the rear).

Black smoke was billowing from the underbelly of the guard's van two carriages up from mine. I pulled my head back in through the window and calmly turned to face my fellow travellers.

'Don't panic,' I said, 'but I think the train's on fire.'

No one did anything. Some continued sleeping. Some continued reading. One or two glanced at me with a sheepish expression of mild interest that said: 'Oh no! Not a loony on board!' before deciding I was best ignored and burying themselves back behind their newspapers. Hmm. Not a promising reaction to a potential life-threatening emergency. No one wanted to know. They seemed far more interested in finishing off a dream, or pondering over '12 Across' and '7 Down' of *The Times* crossword or evaluating the latest fluctuations of the Footsie 100, than thinking about grabbing buckets of water or locating fire extinguishers.

Wondering if I had possibly imagined the smoke, I stuck my noddle back out of the window, again first checking the way was clear for passing trains (too bad if the emergency services had to put out a fire *and* pick up a head). With hair flying and eyes streaming in the wind, I saw that, no, my imagination was definitely not running wild. Leaping flames and putrid black smoke were now engulfing the undercarriage of the guard's van.

I wrenched my head back inside. This was no time to contemplate word-arranging anagrams or deliberating the ebb and flow of one's shares. I had to take action – and quick!

'Excuse me, everybody,' I said, swallowing the growing taste of panic rising up out of my throat. 'Please don't worry but there is definitely a fire on this train. I'm going to raise the alarm.'

I then did that something that I had wanted to do all my life. I reached up to the red-chain communication cord, took a firm grip, and pulled long and hard. It felt good. With a jolt, the train ground to a halt. All because of me.

For a stunned few seconds no one said anything. They just stared at me. I thrust my head back out of the window. The smoke was thicker, the flames fiercer. I felt a nauseating knot of fear spasm in the pit of my stomach. My immediate reaction was to want to fling open the door, jump down on to the track and dive across several lines of rails to the safety of the embankment. The thought of being trapped on board and incinerated inside a large tin can was not a pleasant one. But fleeing the train would not be a wise move. Those lines were live and I wanted to live.

The carriage had started to fill with a murmur of voices. A few people were standing up peering out of their windows. Most passengers remained seated, not quite sure what to do next. I poked my head back out of the window to monitor conditions. It looked like the fire was emanating from directly beneath the guard's van, from a motor perhaps. Where was the guard, I wondered? There were no announcements, no signs of life.

Then the lights went out. I had just asked a businessman if he would be so good as to ring 999 on his mobile phone when a young man, who I later discovered was a shop assistant in the High Street Kensington branch of Gap, took off up the train towards the fire. Never one to miss out on the action, I swung myself after him on my crutches. The guard appeared, walking hurriedly down the train. He was still holding a copy of his well-thumbed *Sun.* Although he had been sitting almost directly above the source of the fire, he had been totally unaware of its existence as the smoke was being blown towards the rear of the train.

By now the driver and a group of orange-jacketed men who had been working on the tracks were trying to extinguish the fire. Back in my carriage, the businessman (an archetypal pin-stripe City type with a brolly) was bellowing out of the window, 'Guard! Guard! How long are we likely to be delayed?'

Now on his mobile, the businessman was saying impatiently, 'George, George . . . can you hear me? Good. It looks like I'm going to be late for the meeting. I'm on the train. Apparently there's a fire . . . what? . . . Yes. Bloody nuisance . . .'

A middle-aged woman in a Hermès headscarf and a Burberry raincoat turned to me and said with a sigh, 'Whatever next?'

Then the harassed guard burst into the carriage and instructed everyone to move immediately to the front of the train. Like lemmings, they all started to shuffle forwards – everybody save for me, Gap Man and Mobile Man. The idea of moving back over the fire (still billowing smoke and bilious fumes) before being crammed in a squashed space with all the other train's passengers did not appeal to me. Nor did the train's young and helpful 'revenue protection officer' – who had just appeared on the scene and who seemed to have his head screwed on the right way – think that moving a scrum of people into an already full carriage was a good idea.

A brief argument ensued between the guard and the RP Man. RP Man radioed his colleague, who apparently was caught up in the crush at the front of the train and couldn't move, thanks to the influx of passengers piling through the doors. The guard huffed and puffed and disappeared, jumping down on to the track. He walked for several hundred yards down the line away from the train.

'Where's he going?' I said to RP Man. 'Is he abandoning ship?'

It turned out the guard was heading down to some sort of signal or points-changing box to alert an approaching train that ours had stopped, so that it could automatically pull on its brakes before it rammed us up the rear. That was a relief – I had been a bit concerned about the prospect of another train careering nose-first into our carriage.

Eventually the fire was extinguished. After an hour or so, a diesel came up from Woking to push us to Wimbledon, and the drama was over.

One of the ironic things about this decidedly long-winded tale is that it demonstrates that, sometimes, having a buggered knee is a boon. For the first time in as long as I could remember, I was travelling on a train without my bike. Had I not needed my crutches I would have been on my wheels. And had I been on my wheels my bike would have been in the guard's van. And had my bike been in the guard's van it would have gone up in smoke.

CHAPTER 17

Welcome to Weymouth. Again. This time the sands were seething with beached bodies of all descriptions. Bucket-and-spade brigades, beer bellies, balls, chips, chairs, lilos, radios, pedalos and floats mingled and mixed among the burnt backs and sandcastles. I cycled out to the Stone Pier at Nothe Fort to find a spot of relative calm where I ate two bananas beside a shelter daubed with a swastika. As I headed out of Weymouth into Chickerell I passed a gaggle of long-legged schoolgirls teetering along the pavement in their tight micro-skirts and big clumpy-heeled shoes.

'Are you going to the moon?' shouted one as I rode by.

'No, Piddletrenthide!' I called back.

Actually I wasn't – unless I got very lost. I just had the name of this superbly named Dorset village lodged in my head after seeing it on my map earlier in the day.

I spent that night on a campsite at Bagwell Farm, where I was sighted by Russ, a cyclist who had read my offerings. He had cycled here from Chichester with his mate, Matt, who worked with him at the Environmental Agency. They had planned to do this ride together back in October, but when the monsoons struck they were called on to work full time monitoring the floods. Russ had done some touring before – the previous summer he had ridden from Land's End to John O' Groats with his mum. But Matt was a newcomer to spending any time in the saddle.

'He still wears his underpants under his shorts!' ribbed Russ.

'I did try riding without them,' said Matt, 'but I found it more uncomfortable!'

A little later Russ asked if I got bored of cycling. He admitted that he had had enough after spending three weeks on the road on the End-to-End.

Bored? Err, no.

'I prefer walking,' said Russ. 'Next year I want to do the Southwest Coast Path.'

Dying for a pee, I stopped to use the toilets in the car park at Abbotsbury's swannery and then, before I knew it, I found myself being ushered through the entrance for a closer inspection of the immense swan herd that sits in a marsh at the head of the brackish lagoon of the Fleet, a narrow eight-mile-long inland waterway where Barnes Wallis, who had already made a major contribution to the war effort by designing the RAF's Wellington bomber, tested his bouncing dam-busting bombs. Mute swans, one of the world's heaviest flying birds, have existed at Abbotsbury since at least 1393 and the colony was established to provide the 'birds royal' for the monastery table at Abbotsbury's Benedictine abbey. Some meal that would have been – a mute swan weighs up to forty pounds.

Although I have much respect for the avian equivalent of Concorde (after all, one thrash of their angry wing could break your arm and send you flying) I didn't much enjoy my time at the swannery because I kept thinking I should be cycling and not wandering around swan-crowded pathways with the cygnet-cooing sightseers and excitable schoolchildren. What was I doing being all touristy when there was a home-based pair of village swans camping in the reeds at the end of my road that I could look at in peace and without the added distraction of information boards?

One of the swannery wardens was talking to a gurgle of primary schoolchildren perched on bench seats overlooking the main colony. He explained how two swans from outside the swannery had arrived recently and, rather belatedly for the time of year, had built a nest among the reeds. The parents took turns sitting on the eggs for thirty-five days. Finally the eggs hatched, but the swans abandoned the two cygnets. So a warden put them in a bucket and took them home with him. He mowed the lawn so that he had some grass cuttings to feed the cygnets, which he had living with him, nice and warm, inside his house.

The next day he took them back to work with him and they followed him, and any other warden, around the colony. But they never followed the visitors. It took a week for the wardens to work out that the cygnets only pursued them because they were wearing wellington boots, which the birds associated with their lawn-mowing 'mother'. So they were given their own pair of boots. And from that moment the birds snuggled up quite contentedly to their rubberised parents and no longer gave chase to every wellington boot that passed.

I cycled out of the swannery overlooked by the watchful eye of St Catherine's Chapel which, crowning a 250-foot hillock, is preserved as a landmark for mariners. The monks built it in the fourteenth century and it is dedicated to St Catherine, who, bless her, is patron saint of spinsters (and not Family Welcome 'Charlie Chalk Play Zone' pub-style restaurants). Then I entered the thatched honey-stone, chocolate-box village of Abbotsbury. Stopping at Chapel Lane Stores to buy some food for my lunch, I noticed in the window, among adverts for a cleaner and a baby-sitter and a car for sale, a card announcing in slightly idiosyncratic syntax:

3 FERRETS MISSING
2 B/W Polecats males & cream with brown legs (male) are in this area.
Approach with caution
BUT DON'T LET THEM GET AWAY
We're ANXIOUS to FIND THEM

I hit the first major hill of the trip riding out of Abbotsbury. My bike was so ridiculously heavy that never mind *cycling* 600 feet up the long steep gradient of Wears Hill, I could scarcely *push* it to the top. Even cars were having trouble as the drivers crunched and scraped through their gearbox to engage first gear.

Near the brow of the hill I hauled my bike off the road and climbed a gate to sit in the corner of a field for a spot of lunch. It was a perfect summer's day and my picnicking eyrie offered a grand view out over Abbotsbury and the snowy-looking swannery, the distant hazy horizon-basking alligator head of Portland Bill and the storm bank of Chesil Beach, an eighteen-mile linear ridge of shingle stretching from West Bay to Portland. There is a systematic and gradual size change in Chesil's pebbles from potato-sized 'cobbles', as they are called at Portland, to pea-sized gravel at the western end – graded in size by the strong sweep and suck of tidal currents. This variation in the stones proved useful for smugglers, who used to land on Chesil's long shingle finger at night and could tell exactly where they were on the beach by the size of the pebbles.

Today local fishermen docking during darkness on the shingly ridge, which rises to forty feet in parts, can similarly pinpoint their position from the bigness of the stones.

In heavy seas, Chesil acts like a giant drag-net, catching any foundering ships it can. In the eighteenth century, gangs of marauding ne'er-do-wells roamed the beach when storms blew up, lying in wait as helpless ships were tossed ashore and pounded to pieces on the pebbles. The gangs were such depraved miscreants they would sometimes lure ships ashore with misguiding lights and even murder drowning men as they fought to crawl and clamber up the shingle, robbing them and shoving the bodies back into the sea.

In the great storm of 1824, the only time that the towering bastion of pebbles has been breached by Channel gales, one ship had a luckier escape. The *Ebenezer*, a 95-ton sloop carrying munitions for the army, was thrown by a freak wave on to the crest of the beach. When the storm had blown itself out, it remained standing, stranded on the peak of the beach like the Ark on Mount Ararat. Only two men lost their lives and the *Ebenezer* was hauled down the lagoon side of the beach and refloated.

Refuelled by my food from Chapel Lane Stores and the edible remnants of the contents of my front pannier, I continued bowling along westwards with the sun, the sweeping hilltop road slicing its way between Abbotsbury Fort and Labour in Vain Farm. I love this stretch of road. I first cycled along it when I was twelve on my way to Land's End. I remember it well. I was at the helm of my 5-speed 27¼-inch-wheeled Raleigh Misty – an appropriately named mount for that moment, as the Dorset mists swirled all around. Today, though, the sun was blazing, my spokes spinning on steel wings. With soaring spirits I sped along warbling the words of the Stereophonics' catchy chorusing 'Have A Nice Day' – a song that had been resonating round my head all day after hearing it on every radio I passed.

But it was a mistake to open my mouth. A very large winged insect with a fat thorax and a piercing proboscis propellered into the back of my throat at 30 mph. I coughed, I choked, I spluttered, I sputtered, I spittled, I barked, I hawked and I hacked. Finally I spat out half an armoured abdomen and several antennae. This is the problem with singing when cycling – your protein intake grows alarmingly.

I bulleted on down through Swyre and bounced through the smoky-stoned thatched village of Burton Bradstock, where every house seemed to be wooing fast-congealing jams of passing traffic with signs for cream teas. Descending at full tilt into West Bay, I pulled on my brakes in time to avoid careering head first on to the scaly deck of the *Channel Warrior*, a fishing boat moored in the small square harbour where, through two short piers that cut a canal through the shingle beach, the little River Brit seeks freedom to the sea.

West Bay is where the long, lean Chesil Beach runs aground. It was also where I happened upon a flush-of-face holidaymaker clinging to that endearing ancient tradition once commonly found at the Great British Seaside before the ubiquitous baseball cap invaded our shores: a man with a knotted handkerchief on his head.

A lot of knotting used to take place up the road in Hardy's 'Port Bredy', our Bridport – a knotting not of hankies but of hemp. This ancient Dorset town was once so famous for its rope-making industry that being 'stabbed by a Bridport dagger' was another way of saying that a person had been hanged. The ships that defended the shores against pirates, the ships of the French and Spanish fleets, Nelson's *Victory*, and the great trading square riggers with their masts sweeping arcs across the relentless Southern Ocean skies off Cape Horn – all were lashed together with forests of mostly Bridport rope.

The next part of my ride I didn't enjoy at all, joining the fast car-rushing truck-sucking A35 to Chideock. Hot, tired, thirsty and coated with exhaust fumes, I stopped to buy a drink and bananas from Chideock Hill Stores. The owner, a thickset man with a buoyant air, asked me where I was coming from and where I was going. When I said I hailed from Sussex he said he was originally from Arundel – a town I told him I knew well from frequenting its five Pegler's camping and expedition supplying stores. I asked him how he came to be running Chideock village store.

'For years I used to sell office furniture to West Sussex County Council, but I became so stressed from the job that when I turned forty I said to the wife, "Let's do something completely different." We looked all over the country to buy a small business and found this store. Been here six months now and we love it. True, foot-and-mouth has hit us hard, but money isn't everything.'

He told me how he got up at five every morning to do the paper round. Then he worked in the shop until 6 p.m. He only had Sunday afternoons off a week.

'Those half days are very precious!' he said. 'I've got a five-year-old and eight-year-old so I make a point of spending it with them. But we're all happy here. The locals are so friendly and helpful – much more so than in Sussex.'

That evening I swooped down the hill into Charmouth and cycled along to Seadown Camping and Caravanning Park.

'I'm afraid we're full,' said Roy at reception. 'It's the hot spell. Seems to have brought everyone out. We're not normally this busy at this time of year. Must be foot-and-mouth. They've all had enough of staying inside.'

I was sorry to hear this. Because of foot-and-mouth disease I couldn't go off and camp in any old field as there were 'FOOT & MOUTH PRECAUTION: KEEP OUT' signs everywhere. Ah, foot-and-mouth. It was clearly confusing a few of our friends across the pond. In the rather highbrow *Washington Post*, house journal of America's governing classes, they set the taxing quiz question:

'Great Britain is having great trouble with which disease affecting livestock:

a. Tongue and tail?
b. Foot and mouth?
c. Bubble and squeak?
d. Foot and tail?'

'Why, Chuck, them Brits sure have got one helluva bubble-and-squeak problem!'

Anyway, before I put my foot in mouth, I said to Roy, 'Are you sure you're full?' and put on a hopeful I-only-need-a-small-space face.

Roy looked at me and said, 'All right. One night, then.'

As he led me along driveways lined with vast lengths of static caravans, he told me how he used to live near Portsmouth. When I told him where I was from he said, 'Is that anywhere near Rogate?'

'Yes,' I said, 'It's just down the road.'

'My grandfather used to own the telephone exchange there – behind the primary school. He had a farm too. I remember when I was a boy he took me with him to look at some potatoes on a farm near a pub in Trotton and we bumped into Gary Glitter. He used to live round there in the seventies.'

'I know,' I said, 'in that big white house near Nyewood. I used to ride past there most days on my way to the Downs when I first started cycling. But I never saw him.'

'Probably just as well,' said Roy, 'because now look at him, a disgraced Rock Star.'

Roy had moved to the Southwest in 'seventy-five'.

'I had a pig farm for years,' he said, 'but it was a hard life. I prefer it here on the caravan park. The money's more certain.'

I asked him how much the caravans cost.

'About sixteen to twenty-two thousand. We change them every twelve years or else they begin to look tatty.'

I expressed suitable sounds of amazement at the cost of them.

'And,' said Roy, 'the owners have to pay an annual site rent on top of the initial purchase which amounts to thousands. But folk love them. Those who've retired spend a lot of time in them. Most of the owners are from the Southeast or Salisbury area and can be down here in a couple of hours.'

Roy showed me where to pitch my tent. It was out of sight of the caravans and in a dip beside a playground, which seemed to serve as a dogs' toilet. There were only two other tents and they belonged to a small gang of motorcyclists.

'They're not typical bikers,' Roy said. 'They won't cause you any trouble. We know them well, they come every year.' Not that I was worried, mind. I feel more at home among bikers than I do caravans.

My living near to his grandfather's roots obviously caused Roy to have a change of heart because, as he was walking away, he said, 'You can stay two nights if you want.'

So I did, as I wanted to spend a day cycling inland to Chard to visit Paul and Caroline Butterworth. A few years back when my knee went wonky, Paul, an engineer who manages Unicam Therapeutic Pedal Systems, made me an ingenious invention that enabled me to cycle with one leg. Paul's assortment of pedal systems helps people who are disabled or injured to enjoy the benefits of cycling, whether as part of a rehabilitation programme or as a means of recreational exercise.

It was good to meet Paul again, this time with both my knees in operational order. He and Caroline lived with their two teenage sons, Jason and Daniel, at

1 Bampton Avenue, which, since my first visit, had undergone a name change and was now 'Les Avanchers'. Why this slide into *français*, I wondered?

'It's a place in the French Alps that we like going to on holiday,' explained Paul.

Ah, I see.

Caroline, a nurse at Yeovil hospital, made us all a cup of tea and we sat around the table chatting and laughing mostly about injuries and accidents. When Caroline first met Paul he was one of those long-haired bikers that Roy thought might have frightened me. When Paul gave her a lift home on the pillion she hated it and found it horribly scary. The first time she put on a full-face helmet she wore it perched on the top of her head like a cap – protecting, if anything, only the crown of her skull.

'I thought, what's so good about these full-face helmets? They don't even keep the insects out of your eyes!' she told me in her soft, West Country burr. 'I suppose I was just a bit stupid. All my friends thought it was hilarious though!'

But Caroline didn't have to put up with motorbikes for too long because one day Paul crashed into a car and flew off, narrowly missing a lamppost before nearly ending up as dead meat when he landed in the doorway of a butcher's shop. He hasn't ridden a motorbike since, though he now fancied getting a Harley. Caroline didn't like that idea.

'I don't want you ending up in a black bag,' she said.

Probably good advice, because Paul did seem a little accident prone – in the past he had broken his leg three times. The last occasion had been during a Sunday morning football match. He was playing against a team who, Paul said, were all vicious pub thugs. One of them, a certain Mr Bealey, went for him with such a violent tackle that he both broke and dislocated Paul's ankle and broke his leg as well. When Paul was carried off the pitch by stretcher and transferred to an ambulance, the Pub Thug Club all cheered and took commemorative photographs. To them, victory was putting as many of the opposing team out of action as possible. Paul was off work for nine months. On his final check-up at the hospital he saw Bealey in the waiting room with a few broken bones of his own – a result of his own goalkeeper running into him. Paul gave him a wry smile and walked past.

After three cups of tea I needed a pee so padded off to the downstairs toilet where I found a notice saying:

Please put the seat down
BUFFY IS USING TOILET AS A LARGE DRINKING BOWL

Buffy was one of the Butterworths' three cats: one was a mog, the other two Burmese.

'They're all housecats,' Caroline said, 'but I put them outside for two or three hours a day for some fresh air.'

Their 'outside' turned out to be a large and elaborate caged cat play area in the back garden bursting with cat toys and jumps and ramps and sleeping platforms and scratch poles.

'I don't let them roam around the streets, because they disappear or get hit by cars,' explained Caroline. 'We've lost a few that way.'

Bang outside the cat den stood a bird table patronised by a large assortment of garden birds that were all very blasé and unconcerned by three lip-licking whiskered faces and pulsating cats' claws a mere wing-tip away.

'I call the bird table the cats' television,' said Caroline. 'They sit watching it for hours, totally besotted!'

On the way out of Chard I stopped at Tesco's to replenish food supplies. As I was packing it away in my panniers outside the store, two teenage girls in big floor-flopping flares and skimpy halter-tops revealing pierced belly-buttons collapsed on a nearby bench for a fag and a bottle of Fanta.

'Did yer shag Sean last night?' said one, as she took a perfunctory slurp from her bottle of fizz.

'Yeah. Fuckin' 'ell! Talk about wicked! I ain't going back to Dave after that!'

It was a lovely ride to Chard and back: climbing and falling through narrow, car-free lanes bordered by overgrown banks of high hedges that rose like towering tunnels above my head. No white lines around here – just a thick tufty swathe of grass growing down the middle. I passed through rich haymaking smells swirling on the warm wind, green rolling hills and, up at Fishpond Bottom – which lies just north of Wootton Fitzpaine and south of School House and Saddle Street – was rewarded with a grand view overlooking the broad green patchwork span of Marshwood Vale. But there were also signs that the countryside was feeling battered and bruised following a tough few months: countless disinfectant-reeking foot-and-mouth mats passed beneath my wheels and everywhere the lanes bore the evidence of the past winter's floods with a

131

surplus of collapsed banks and partially washed-away roads which, in several places, were still impassable due to mud slides and dirty thick brown water that had yet to drain away all these weeks later. Despite this, you could tell the country was enjoying a weekend of rare summery sun: every lawn of every house and cottage I passed had a whirring and jarring and rasping and grunting lawn mower interfering with the chattering birdsong. All these mowers made me think of hapless Sally Southard, who had recently made a brief appearance in the papers because, after entering 1200 competitions hoping for prizes to furnish her first-floor flat in Blackburn, she had won a lawn mower.

CHAPTER 18

Back in Charmouth I stopped to ring the builder from a phone box at the entrance of the campsite. He was in the middle of telling me how he was making a six-metre, 4.1-tonne octagonal oak tower with a Serlio floor for part of a house in Chiddingfold that belonged to (just to drop a name) Tony Smith, the manager of Genesis (didn't give him any tea and biscuits though), before adding that he might later make a few counter tongued and grooved tabled under-squinted abutments, when I noticed some people walking by who seemed to be taking great interest in my bike propped outside. Then they stopped and gazed rather too intently at me. In a state of under-squinted befuddlement, I interrupted Gary, who was still in full flow telling me he would need a forty-tonne crane to lift his herculean construction up to the tower's six-metre brick base (such riveting conversations we have), by telling him that though I would love to hear more about the phenomenal size of his abutment, I had better go because I thought some people were trying to stare me out of the phone box. Being a mobile phoneless person, I knew how impatient you could get hanging around a phone box for someone to finish their lengthy hobnobbing. But Gary was eager to tell me more about his six-metre erection and so I said, 'Hold it right there – I'll just ask if they're admiring my bike or waiting to use the phone box.'

As soon as I stuck my head out of the door, I was being blamed by one of the men for sending him on a recent cycle up to the Arctic.

'I saw the picture of you in your book standing beside the Arctic Circle sign and I decided I wanted to go there too!'

Jim Bettley was not only now a keen cyclist but also Traffic Chief Inspector of Hampshire Police. As well as a bicycle he rode a motorcycle the size of a small family car. Anyhow, the fact that I indirectly sent him packing off to the Arctic apparently qualified me for being invited into his lengthy static caravan to meet his family. Or maybe it was because my name began with a 'J', as I met Jim and Jean and Jim and Jill and Julie. Whatever the reason, we all seemed to find it very funny with all these 'J's flying around – and that was before we had even had a drink. But normal conversation did manage to prevail in that we started talking about 'food miles' and bemoaning the vast increase of motor traffic generated unnecessarily by transporting produce from one end of the country to the other, only to bring it all back and sell it near to where it was first grown (the other Jim used to be a fruit farmer so had some forthright opinions on the matter). The subject was prompted when Chief Inspector Jim told me how he had gone on holiday to the Highlands and bought some Scottish shortbread to take back to Julie, his mother-in-law. When he looked on the packet he saw that it was made in Eastleigh, a town just a few miles down the road from his home in Fareham.

'I decided Scotland was a long way to go to buy some shortbread when it was being made on my doorstep!' said Jim.

We also got on to the topics of policing (Jim explained how joining the police thirty years ago had been his 'vocation' but now he felt much disillusioned at how piles of paperwork had taken over from actually policing the streets); cycling (Jim had raised a lot of money for charity through various money-raising rides); bike bits (he was pleased to see I was still using my antiquated cantilever brake system because, in his opinion, 'V' brakes were 'crap'); car crashes and road deaths. He had recently attended a horrific crash where a couple had been driving with their seven-year-old grandson when their car had been hit from behind by a lorry, crushing the car from fifteen feet to less than seven feet. The car then caught fire and all three died, burnt so badly that they could only be identified from dental records, and a few remaining oddments of jewellery. The magistrates fined the lorry driver £90. The little boy's devastated mother, who was in the court, said, 'That's what it costs here, does it – £30 a body?'

Lastly, we talked about road planning. Jim had recently taken the council to task over plans for installing a roundabout. 'Where are the cyclists going to go?' he had asked. 'Cyclists? Oh, we haven't thought about them,' they admitted. It was an all too common occurrence, said Jim.

When he was out cycling, Jim told me, he preferred it if mindless drivers performing dangerous manoeuvres had open-top cars because then he could catch up with them at the lights and 'discuss it with them' – something that is not so easy to do when the driver is sitting behind sealed glass, staring straight ahead, refusing to acknowledge the tap on the window.

Early the next day I rose with the sun to walk along the empty beach at Charmouth. It was a glorious morning, the eastern sky a fluctuating ribbon of wispy reds and pinks and mauves and purples. The uplifting scenery is top-notch round here, with beaches set against dramatic cliffhanger backdrops. To the east, Golden Cap, a flat-topped band of cinnamon-orange sandstone, rose theatrically from a filigree of loose lacy mist. At 626 feet high, Golden Cap crowns the highest cliff on the Channel coast. Shouldering alongside, there inclines a princely procession of varied headlands and forelands, promontories and peaks, capes, points and spurs, all pitching their summits to the sea.

This stretch of shoreline where fossil hunting first began has recently been recognised internationally as one of the richest prehistoric sights in the world, by becoming a UNESCO World Heritage Site – putting it rather grandly on a par with the likes of the Grand Canyon and the Great Barrier Reef. Because the rocks, originally stacked horizontally (the oldest at the bottom, the new stuff at the top), were tilted to the east by some violent fluke of ancient subterranean disruption, these rocky shores slope downwards. So by walking along the beach horizontally I could walk through time for 160 million or more years. Jumping on to the 'geotourism' bandwagon and to keep abreast with the modern need to theme everything, the local councils have rebranded the area the 'Jurassic Coast'. So now it's official: this 95-mile stretch of Dorset and East Devon coast, from the oldest Triassic rocks near Exmouth in the west, through to the Jurassic material in the middle and on to the young fledgling Cretaceous chalky offerings comprising the corpses of minute forms of marine life that are seen mostly in the east as far as Swanage, is one of the best places on earth to find a dinosaur. It is a prehistoric graveyard.

Back at the caravan site, Chief Inspector Jim and family saw me off with cheery picture-snapping. I rode away up the hill through Charmouth. Opposite the Queen Armes Hotel I decided it was already so hot I needed to stop to slap on some more suncream. As I stood smearing my skin I noticed I was being informed by words on the front of the hotel that Catherine of Aragon stayed there in 1501 and King Charles II slept there in 1651. I wondered what had brought them this way. It couldn't have been the excitement of fossil hunting on the Jurassic Coast, because Dorset council had yet to redub it. Besides, serious 'fossiling' had not taken off until the early nineteenth century, after twelve-year-old Mary Anning found the first specimen of an ichthyosaurus, a twenty-one-foot-long fish-like lizard. She later discovered the first nearly complete skeleton of a plesiosaurus – same model as the Loch Ness Monster – and the first British pterodactyl, the early proto-bird.

After a bit of delving and digging around, I learnt that Catherine of Aragon had walked through the doorway of the hotel to rest on her way to meet her future husband, Henry VIII ('Henry, old boy, you don't half get around'). Charles II, on the other hand, had passed a fretful night in the same building during his flight from Cromwell after the defeat at the Battle of Worcester. His plan, to charter a boat and escape by sea to France from Charmouth Beach, was thwarted by the boatman's wife, who had been led to believe that Charlie was the servant of a young woman eloping in the same boat with her lover. Her suspicion of her husband's passengers was aroused when she heard in the town that death was the penalty for helping the King to escape. So she hid her husband's trousers and locked him in a bedroom. When he ranted and raved she threatened to get the neighbours and make him look a laughing stock in his trouser-less predicament. Within hours, Charlie's whereabouts were known. The hunt was on, forcing him to beat a hasty retreat and flee the town on horseback instead. Charlie, a witty, intelligent and popular man, did eventually escape, and later in life he took much enjoyment in regaling his dinner-party guests with tales of his foiled attempt to flee to France.

I could have done with a horse myself to drag me up the long steep incline of Fern Hill to Penn Cross. All a bit too much like hard work for a Sunday morning with temperatures peaking into the eighties, I thought. But I was duly rewarded for my efforts when, on the other side, I plunged at breakneck speed down Dragon's Hill into the Georgian resort of Lyme Regis, where I jammed on my brakes to avoid slamming into a jam of cars. The high street, Broad Street, which snakes downhill to the sea, was crawling with tourists either sitting motionless in their sun-trapped vehicles or slipping and slopping in and out of such worthy establishments as the Cobb Gate Fish Bar, Sweet Thursday or Ye Olde Tobbacco Shoppe. Any thoughts of doing a Mary Anning and coming up trumps with a monster find of fossil, or even doing a Meryl Streep in *French Lieutenant* style on the massive curling breakwater of The Cobb, were hastily abandoned when, dropping down to Marine Parade, I caught sight of a beach packed solid with fossilised sun-worshipping dinosaurs clad in inappropriate swimwear and a crawling Cobb seething with sightseers.

And so to Devon, England's third biggest county, which, with 300 miles of coast-line, dips a craggy-shored northern foot into the Bristol Channel while its southern sibling, a spool of exquisite beaches, bathes in the sun of the English one.

At Axmouth I stopped for lunch under the shade of a tree in the graveyard of St Michael's Church. Feeling a bit hill-wilted and heat-lagged, I lay back on the grass looking up through a swaying fan of lime green leaves to dappled pockets of deep blue sky and dreamily reflected on all the people who must have been married and buried here. This led me drifting along the lines of a death-theme train of thought which reminded me of that Yiddish story about the tale of Mrs Schwartz, who popped down to the offices of the *Jewish Chronicle* one day to announce the demise of her husband, Mori. 'Please print this: "Schwartz dead",' she told the secretary in the Death Notices office, who replied, 'Isn't that a bit terse? You can have more words for the same price.' So Mrs Schwartz thought and then said, 'Okay, how about "Mori Schwartz dead"?' The secretary responded, 'Forgive me if I'm being personal, but that still seems a little cold. Remember you may have *six* words for the same fee, you know.' So Mrs Schwartz thought a little longer, then scribbled the following message: 'Mori Schwartz dead. Volvo for sale.'

Inside the shivery shade of the church, I leafed through a copy of *Axmouth Parish News* until I came to an enlightening section entitled: 'HANDY HINTS'. 'Even gardening gloves don't seem to protect your hands from being stung by nasty nettles,' I read, 'so try putting your hands in a couple of plastic carrier bags when pulling up these garden weeds.' Nettles nasty? What could this Axmouth parishioner possibly mean? They're not weeds, they're tasty fodder, especially when crammed in a pan with potatoes, leeks, carrots and garlic. And butterflies like them too. So I say: keep those nettles where they are and save those carrier bags for enwrapping your feet when cycling in the stinging rain.

Energised with second wind after my ecumenical stop, I charged up and down the rolling waves of Devon hills as unstoppable as a full-rigged galleon under sail and swept through Beer, Vicarage, Branscombe, Street, Berry Barton and Salcombe Regis until, hitting the bicyclist's bonk, I ran out of steam at Sidmouth. But the nearest campsite was up and over Peak Hill, whose gradient was so steep it was marked with a leg-wobbling triple-whammy arrow on my map. As I stood swaying with fatigue on Sidmouth's esplanade, speed-eating bananas and wishing I was momentarily cycling in flat fenland and not alpine Devon, a woman came dashing across the road, shook my hand with a hearty shake and effused about my Japanese scribblings. Her name was Frances and she lived in Marchwood, which was just down the road from Dibden Purlieu with its population of RATs and RAMs (remember them?).

'I was looking out of the window of my hotel and I saw you arrive on your Roberts and I said to my husband "That must be Josie Dew!" and tore out of the door! Ooh, I'm so pleased to meet you!'

Such head-swelling praise was all very nice but a bit too much to take on board, preoccupied as I was with feverishly cramming bananas and energy-boosting bars into my mouth with unseemly haste in a desperate attempt to keep my bonk at bay.

'Well, I mustn't keep you,' said Frances, 'it really has been lovely to meet you!'

And then she was gone, trotting back across the road to rejoin her abandoned husband.

Sidmouth's Peak Hill is both very steep and very long. I was about a sixteenth of the way up when a car passed me, did a U-turn and then paused as it came alongside. A large American woman was at the helm, her identikit large offspring in the passenger seat.

'Say, hon,' she said, 'can I help take your bags? It's a long way to the top and you sure look loaded!'

'Yes please!' I said. 'And while you're at it, could you take me and my bike as well and then drop us off at Land's End?'

Actually I didn't say that at all. Instead I adhered to Cycle-Touring Golden Rule No. 2: never wave goodbye to your panniers lest you never set eyes upon them ever again.

An eighth of the way up Sidmouth's Picos de Europa, I was struck by a wave of *déjà vu* as I recognised the precise location where a minor event had occurred in 1978. I was twelve and an infuriatingly keen cycling sibling to the younger of my elder brothers, a guitarist and ornithologist but no cyclist. After much cajoling, I had managed to rope him into cycling with me to Land's End (I was under strict parental orders not to do the ride alone). As we were riding up Sidmouth's Peak Pass, a blind man cautiously tapping his way up the hill on the opposite side of the road suddenly veered off course into the path of an oncoming vehicle. To avert an unpleasant happening, my brother, who was in front of me, shouted, 'To the right sir!' The man immediately responded by swerving back to the bank and acknowledging his thanks by a wave of his stick. The phrase 'To the right sir!', which still occasionally pops up in various permutations of our speech, has mindlessly amused us ever since.

CHAPTER 19

Carting sixty kilos of kit up Sidmouth's monumental mountain range took its toll on my energy-spent body. To aid recovery I had a day off after setting up base in Ladram Bay.

This June-day Monday turned into the hottest of the year so far. It was astonishingly hot – even hotter than the Med, so bragged the papers. Feeling as if I was cycling on hot air without my leaden panniers, I went soaring alongside the River Otter before emerging at Budleigh Salterton, the retirement capital of East Devon, known locally as 'God's Waiting Room'.

As if to reinforce the fact that the Southwest has the highest number of pensioners in England (at just over one in five of the population), there were old people everywhere; sitting on the seafront staring out to sea or shuffling up and down the High Street past zimmer-frame shops like Budleigh Mobility ('Shop for Independent Travel'). Even Plymco, Budleigh's local supermarket, was known in local jargon as 'Norman's'.

I watched one old biddie slalom at speed among a forest of legs a-board her nippy Shoprider electric wheelchair as she adroitly scaled the steep zig-zag slope on the seafront. Every now and then she would stop and purposefully scan the horizon with a pair of large, antiquated field-glasses dangling from her neck. What was she looking for? Some rare lesser-spotted feathered creature blown off its migrating course? The Spanish Armada charging up the Channel? Maybe she was searching the horizon for a lost lover last seen heading off for the Great War. Or maybe all this binocular business was just a nervous habit and something she did involuntarily, being of a puggle-headed disposition.

Loaded up with food supplies from Norman's, I started back towards Ladram Bay. But it was such a broiling afternoon, pipping the nineties, that by the time I reached East Budleigh all I felt fit for was collapsing in the church-yard under the solid shade of a yew tree. When I came to, a state of comatose sun-druggedness had hit my heat-fuzzed head and it was all I could do to drag myself into the sobering cool of the church. This turned out to be quite inter-esting, because on one of the sixteenth-century oak pews I found a carved family crest of Sir Walter Raleigh. After further churchy dabblings I discovered that he had been born over yonder nearby hilltop in a manor, now a farm, called Hayes Barton. So on my way to Yettington I rode past the birthplace of the man who introduced the potato to these shores some four centuries ago.

I then rode up to Newton Poppleford, a village on the Otter, which I fancied visiting purely on account of its name as it sounded like a well-to-do country gent with an apple on his head. But in reality Newton Poppleford stemmed from nothing more exciting than a 'new town' having been built on a pebbly ford – 'popple' being the local term for pebble. Popple – what a nice word! I much prefer to think of Chesil Beach full of popples than pebbles. And if the BBC's Birmingham moved to Devon we could have Popple Mill at One.

By the time I pedalled into Poppleford I wished I hadn't bothered; I found a town carved in two by the horrendously horrible A3052, full of swooshing cars and caravans and buses and lorries all hurtling to Exeter. In between fighting for my space on the road, all I had time to notice was an Orange mobile phone shop (how lovely! how rural!), the Southern Cross Tea Rooms and a restaurant called Jolly's which sounded as if it would be more at home in Sloane Square.

The best thing about pebbly Poppleford was leaving it, which I did as soon as possible by turning off near Northmostown (even though it is a very south-most hamlet) on to a single-track country lane that led to North Star along the River Otter. North Star? What with those Southern Cross Tea Rooms, things were getting all a bit astronomical. But it was a beautifully quiet and scenic ride, made even more memorable by a young farmer who did a wheelie for me on his tractor at Burnthouse Farm.

Although my aching hill-climbing muscles still felt sore and over-used when I awoke the next morning, I packed up my tent and hit the road back to the salty seaside at Budleigh. Feeling old and slow, I sat on a seat alongside benches full of pensioners and, like them, stared out to sea. I sat there so long that the weather underwent several transmutations. The burning blue sky of my arrival disappeared beneath a film of blurry haze that slowly rolled in to blot out completely the 250-million-year-old red sandstone cliffs of the Floors that stretched to Straight Point. It was so pre-storm humid that even without moving I felt little drops of perspiration trickle with a tickling from temple to cheek. From somewhere in the distance, an ominous rumble of thunder and a sudden wind flapped my map from lap to ground. Shortly a few fat raindrops sploshed with watery explosion upon the prom, each one big enough to form a mini puddle. As pensionable promenaders made for cover, I stood my ground, daring the storm to soak me. But the storm never came. It slipped off north to Tipton St John.

The sun reappeared along with all the elderly bench-sitters. I watched one old creaky and cadaverous man, eyes sunken in a skeletal face, slowly pushing his well-padded wheelchair-bound wife along the seafront until they came to rest beside a neighbouring bench. A packed lunch appeared and they both sat silently, gazing out to France as they each worked their way through two ham-stuffed white buns, a hard-boiled egg and a packet of crisps. After a while, the whip-thin man creaked along the prom, his clothes hanging off him like bunting, to buy a couple of ice creams topped with an antenna of chocolate flake.

As I was getting up to leave, a woman in her late forties looked at my bike and asked me how on earth I managed to balance with so many bags.

'Ohh,' she said, 'I would *so* love to ride a bike! I've tried and I've tried but I just can't balance.'

She told me she had never learnt to cycle as a child because she had a cerebral cyst that affected her ability to balance.

'And although I've had it removed I still can't cycle. I keep trying to learn, but now that I'm an adult it hurts when you fall off! I've asked around various cycle shops trying to find some stabilisers, but it seems they only make them for children.'

I said maybe she should try a trike or a tandem or a recumbent or to contact the London School of Cycling that teaches anyone, children or adults, how to balance and cycle safely. As I was pushing away the woman sighed, 'Ohh! I just want to feel the wind on my face so bad!'

Further along the prom an elderly couple asked where I was heading. When I told them, the woman, who had a cake-like mouth, said with concerned expression, 'By yourself? Watch out!'

Another white-haired pair sauntering along asked me exactly the same question, but instead of saying 'watch out!' the woman said, 'Ahh, bless you! We'll be thinking about you, we will, won't we, Bert?'

It was just as well I didn't have a plane to catch because yet another passer-by paused to pass comment. This one was a big, swag-bellied woman in late middle age who spoke with a Yorkshire-toughened accent.

'Weather's been kind t'yer, in't it pet?'

Along from the toilets I came upon a small 'Romahome' camper van parked up on the side. In the window a sticker professed that the owners were on a permanent 'Ski' holiday:

RETIRED AND HAPPY
SPENDING OUR KIDS' INHERITANCE

I found the retired and happy couple on a seafront bench that they had just sat down on having spent some of their kids' inheritance on two very whippy ice creams.

'We've worked hard all our lives,' they told me, 'and we don't mind saying we want to enjoy what's left of them!'

I asked them, like people asked me, where they were going.

'We don't know,' said Mrs Romahome. 'We never plan our route, we just see what happens.'

Ahh, a Romahome roaming after my own heart.

'We usually park up in a lay-by or on a clifftop and only go to a campsite when we get a bit smelly,' said Mr Romahome. 'Yup, we don't mind saying we're enjoying life to the full!'

Heading down along Sandy Bay and into the mouth of the Exe, I stopped in a driveway to turn over the map that I keep on my handlebar bag for ease of mid-flight navigation.

'You lost, darlin'?' came a voice from atop some nearby scaffolding.

It belonged to a square-shouldered brickie with a tough-man fuzz-cut. He moved closer to the edge and I could see he had the chiselled-from-granite build and stiff-legged gait of a former squaddie.

' 'Ere, I'll tell yer what, sweetheart,' he said, 'put me on that saddle and I'll give yer the ride of yer life!'

Cheeky bastard, I thought, and went on my way.

Within about four miles I had passed from Budleigh and its enclave of pensioners to Exmouth and its swarms of students and clusters of marines – the latter emanating from 45 Commando, Royal Marines HQ which I found

High seas. Chesil Beach, Dorset

The Angel of Freshwater Bay, Isle of Wight

Mum sheltering in our sumptuous lunch-stop setting. Chale Green, Isle of Wight

Meeting up with the builder before we hit the heady heights of Bognor.
Chichester marina, West Sussex

Bikes, kites and lounging builders. St Aubin's Bay, Jersey, Channel Islands

Life in the fast lane. Near Fishpond Bottom, Dorset

Riding home from Sheffield after a windswept mid-tour talk. Near Vale of Belvoir, Nottinghamshire/Leicestershire border

Wishing I left the kitchen sink at home

Top: Near Collapit Bridge, South Devon
Bottom: Between Penare and Boswinger, Cornwall

Sunset over the Serpentine – cycling through Hyde Park on my way to King's Cross

Flying high, sailing low. The Liver Birds as seen from the Mersey ferry

Stripes, lights and low-lying land. Happisburgh, Norfolk

Colours, castles and fo'c's'les. Gorey Harbour, Jersey, Channel Islands

In Devon's lanes of highrise hedgerows, some things fit easier than others.

Top: Near Dartmouth, South Devon
Bottom: Near Thurlestone, South Devon

straddling the traffic-laden A376 at Lympstone. At the first opportunity I turned off this unpleasantly fast stretch of road and dived down across a weir into Topsham.

Topsham was lovely, at least the old part was, all very narrow and Amsterdam-like with its rows of tall houses with curved Dutch gables; in the town's heyday as a port, these had all been merchants' homes and sail lofts and storehouses that kept the shipyards supplied. The Dutch-style buildings were built with Dutch bricks brought back as ballast after merchantmen had sailed cargoes of wool and Devon serge to Holland.

In Exeter I spent the night at the Heavitree home of head-in-the-clouds-high Peter Tansley and his same-size-as-me wife, Gethyn. I had first met Peter, an engineer, silversmith, bike-builder, solar car constructor, paratrike and tandem recumbent maker, electric fiddle inventor, Dalek fixer, paraglider, teacher of autistic children and handyman superior, in 1989 when I rode that wheelchair-bicycle contraption up to John O' Groats. He looked just as large as the last time I saw him and appeared just as amazed at my four-bowl porridge-eating capabilities.

But the day I arrived was not Peter and Gethyn's happiest; that afternoon their vet had rung to confirm that Ghandi, their big, fluffy ginger cat, had FIV (feline immunodeficiency virus).

'He used to be such a lively tigger,' said Peter in his lingering Shetland dialect, 'always playing with his toys. But now all he does is sleep.'

Peter's woeful state was not improved by being unable to cycle more than ten minutes at a time any more because of shooting pains in the palm of his hand. This pain had come about as a result of a paragliding accident several months previously. Peter wasn't actually paragliding at the time: he had decided it was too windy to go jumping off the cliff, so was packing up his 'chute when, out of the blue, another paraglider crash-landed on top of him, knocking him heavily to the ground. There was a 'crack' as his wrist broke and it has never been the same since.

Gethyn, a prize quilter, allotment lover and ex-optometrist who now worked for Oxfam, told me how her mother had recently died aged eighty-four.

'She was busy and active right up to the end,' said Gethyn, 'then one morning she went along to the surgery to pick up the results from some tests. She was sitting in the waiting room when she suddenly said, "I don't feel very well", and dropped dead from a heart attack.'

Over a supper of cashew roast, potato salad, carrot and apple and olive salad and a big fruit bowl (they were both vegetarians), I had a brief history of how Peter and Gethyn had met (in Plymouth) and how long they had lived in Exeter (twenty-eight years) and learnt that all their previous cats had had dogs' names (Rover, Spot, Bonzo, Fido – that sort of thing). When my circumnavigation of the Isle of Wight cropped up in conversation it prompted the Tansley Two to tell me how the Isle of Wight had been the location for their 'honeymoon' (seven years after they got married) and had been the first cycling trip when they could afford the luxury of a B&B. On the first day of this belated honeymoon, Gethyn fell off a five-bar gate (on the way to answering the call of nature) and split her head open. She spent the rest of the day in hospital getting stitched up.

'That's as close as we ever came to the exoticism of the Isle of Wight,' said Peter.

Peter told me about his family, all of whom still lived way up north as north can be on the Shetland Islands. He said that when I finally got up there I had to go and visit them all. There was his dad and mum (workshop and the world's best traditional Shetland oatcakes); his only sister Annette (horses, jam sessions and an extensive local knowledge of all eccentricities on the mobile library van round of the five northern isles); brother-in-law (snowplough driver); cousin Angela (civil servant and international musician); and Aunty Gretta (eighty going on seventeen, line dancer and great storyteller, whose war effort had included data analysis on seasick pill experiments before D-day – wouldn't have been any good, said Peter, had the troops felt decidedly green around the gills on their arrival in France).

During my third helping of nut roast, Peter told me how Annette had remarried the previous year following an unhappy marriage to an alcoholic who beat her and had finally left her over Christmas. There was a big wrangle over money and divorce and then he suddenly dropped dead of a heart attack. Annette's second husband was a man with whom Peter had gone to school. He had never married himself because, since their young days, he'd always had the hots for Annette and had, so Peter said, 'been waiting for her'. Because he was a road maintenance digger driver, he had proposed to Annette by way of tarmacking her rutted driveway by cover of night and leaving a bouquet of roses at her door. Seeing as they both shared a love of Land Rovers, they went on their honeymoon to Land Rover 2000 – a big Millennium meet in Essex.

In nearly thirty years Peter's parents, Vic and Mary, had only once come down south to visit him and Gethyn. That was three years before my visit. They had taken some persuading, too, because they were nervous of the unknown. They didn't like the sound of England – a country they imagined to be covered with motorways and full of crime. But they found that their fears were unfounded. One evening, back at Peter's and Gethyn's after another day of sightseeing, Mary had rung her family in Shetland to tell them about England and the English. 'And they even chat to you in the post office like back home!' she said.

The next morning Peter left early to cycle off to the state school in Topsham where he worked as a supply teacher for an autistic boy and a group of 'Pupils at Risk of Exclusion', which Peter said was a euphemism for fifteen-year-old fruitcakes and dingbat psychopaths incapable of joined-up writing. But then I think his patience had been severely tested. Over breakfast he had said, 'It's quite an easy job really because most of the pupils aren't there as they're bunking off school!' Peter had got quite attached to the autistic boy, a young teenager called Joe, who was fascinated by people's eyes.

'He's got a fantastic memory,' said Peter. 'He remembers the eye colour of everyone he meets – even if he's only met them once.'

Sometimes Joe would burst into howls of laughter by himself. 'Joe, don't *do* that,' Peter would say. 'Why not?' Joe would reply. 'I just thought of something funny that happened in May last year.' 'Because people will think you odd,' said Peter.

Riding into the centre of Exeter I stopped at Holland and Barrett to buy a bumper bag of porridge. As I was cramming it into my panniers a man walking past stopped to say hello. He was a janitor at a local school and had recognised me through some pieces I'd written for the CTC magazine.

'I'm a Londoner really,' he said, 'but it all got too expensive so I moved to Exeter three years ago. Down here I can afford to buy my own flat.'

He told me how at first he had found the Devon pace of life so slow that he'd had to keep going back on regular visits to London for a 'faster fix'.

'But now I love it,' he said. 'You wouldn't catch me living in London again even if I had all the money in the world!'

In Sainsbury's I met a woman over the banana counter who got all flummoxed and thoroughly flurried with excitement because apparently she was in the middle of reading my book.

'I'm in Iceland at the moment!' she said, and a neighbouring woman bagging bananas gave her a strange look that said: oh no you're not, love, you're in Sainsbury's.

CHAPTER 20

Down on the River Exe I bounced over the cobbles of the Historic Quayside. A tourist leaflet to Exeter ('It's a Capital City') said: 'The vastly revitalised quayside holds a special magic – it's easy to imagine wool-trading vessels of yesteryear drawing alongside . . .' Whoever wrote this 'Experience Exeter – City in the country near the sea' blurb must have a thing for the 'yesteryears' because a few sentences later the city's 'quaint lanes' were described as being 'redolent with the history of yesteryear'. Perhaps, if you're lucky, you might even find a Ye Olde Tea Shoppe to transport you back to yesteryear too.

Myself, I prefer to live in today-year while looking forward to tomorrow-year. So I escaped the city by way of a cycletrack alongside the sixteenth-century Exeter canal, which, having been built in yesteryear, is now the oldest poundlock waterway in the country.

I powered on through Powderham (site of a powdery-looking castle that has doubled up as a family home to the Earls of Devon for over 600 years) and Dawlish Warren (warren of caravans). It was among these caravans that I put up my tent under the pine trees in a gaudily named place called Peppermint Park. 'Only 680 metres from the beach!' said its glossy tourist brochure. Got to get these things exact, you know: 700 metres could just be that much too far for the punters to traipse with their buckets and spades.

My tent-dwelling neighbour was a lovely singsong Welshman from Swansea, camping with his svelte young daughter. Like me, they weren't at Peppermint Park for a holiday.

'My mum and dad moved to Teignmouth a few years ago,' he said, 'and I've decided to do the same. There's nothing for me back home any more. We're camping here while I look for a job and a place to live.'

The next day he had found some work as a cleaner in a local hotel.

Walking down through 'Dawlish Warren Beach Resort', I passed clamorous dodgems and go-carts and clattering amusement arcades and bustling beach shops selling T-shirts featuring such tasteful inscriptions as:

MY BOSS IS LIKE A NAPPY – FULL OF SHIT
AND ALWAYS ON MY ARSE

or

BEER IS LIFE – THE REST IS JUST DETAILS

or, in recognition of that particular problem:

MY WIFE HAS A DRINKING PROBLEM – ME.

And I thought: do people really buy these things? But then I saw this monumental man. Twenty stone, at a guess. Bull-necked, thighs so massive he had to walk spread-legged, his shorts straining to retain the prodigious beer-gut lolling out from beneath a T-shirt that read:

DREAM MY PANTS OFF.

So I concluded that sadly, yes they did.

And then of course there were the ranks of saucy postcards. One pictured a blonde bimbo with ballooning breasts standing at a bar in a tight, arse-hugging micro dress. She had removed her knickers and was holding them seductively in her hand while introducing herself to a man in a suit evidently swooning with lust. 'So you're Nicholas,' she was saying. 'What a coincidence!'

Another pictured a voluptuous nurse in a tight white coat, leaning over a patient in blue-and-white stripy pyjamas. He was flat on his back in bed beneath a sheet, and, owing to a rather large tent effect, it looked as if he was lying there with his knees up. 'Put your knees down, Mr Jones,' the nurse was saying. 'They are down nurse!' he replied.

I was about to buy it to send to mum, but then I thought she probably would think it *was* his knees sticking up under the sheet. She's rather lovely like that. Not so long ago I went with her to the local cinema (a cavernous town hall where they still show the film split in two to allow an intermission for ice creams preceded by an advert showing a photograph – circa 1974 – of a woman in the High Street holding a carrier bag advertising the name of the local jeweller) to see *The Full Monty*. At one point during the film mum leant over to me in the packed-out hall and said, a little too loudly, 'Jose, what's a "*hard on*"?' 'It's one of those hard hats you have to wear on building sites,' I said, as a man in the row in front turned round and gave us a strange look. With mum looking more flummoxed than ever, I added, in motherly tones, 'I'll explain later!' Fortunately I never had to as by the time the film had finished, mum had forgotten all about it.

Leaving the saucy postcards behind me, I walked out to Dawlish Warren Nature Reserve, which sticks its neck so far out across the mouth of the River Exe that I was almost back in Exmouth. As I sauntered back through the marram grass and the big, wind-ruffled blooms of the evening primroses that swathed the dunes in yellow, I stumbled upon some RSPB men in a state of high ornithological excitement. It seemed they had spotted two pomarine skuas blown off course on their way to Africa. One of the men invited me to have a look through his fat-barrelled telescope, planted strategically in the sand. But all I could see was rather a lot of sea and rather a lot of seagulls. Oh, and a very large piece of driftwood. It looked good though. Bit like a lesser-spotted alligator.

Overcome by a sudden surge of energy, I decided to run to Dawlish and back along the coastal path that extends right alongside a section of Isambard Kingdom Brunel's Great Western Railway. The track had been laid so close to the sea that the waves were practically breaking on the rails. In Dawlish I paused to buy a drink in Poppadums and then, walking back down the Strand, I passed an osteopathic practice, which, so a plaque outside the door told me, was run by a Mr P. Hands. Sometimes I wonder if certain people are predisposed to a profession because of their names. I was once tied in agonising knots by a chiropractor called Dr Payne, whereas my plumber is called Mr Bucket. I think Mr Bucket's parents were having a laugh when they named their son, giving him no option as to what his profession should be: in full he is Mr Adrian (a drain) John (bog) Bucket. How much more watery can you get?

That night, lying in my tent, one of the 'talk topics' on Radio Devon was about a recent survey which had revealed that children watch on average five hours of TV a day. This led on to a discussion about how children's playground areas were going to be made more dangerous because at the moment they were too safe. The new spongy black safety matting, constructed to ROSPA (Royal Society for the Prevention of Accidents) requirements, is apparently so soft that children never get a sense of real danger. All this nannyingly unnecessary expenditure could surely be solved simply by planting some natural hurt-if-you-fall-out trees to climb instead. That way, the money saved from all this needless overcoddling could be put towards making roads safer for children to walk and cycle to school rather than pampering and ferrying them everywhere by car. Which really is dangerous: these days, one in ten children under four is obese.

The stretch of road from Dawlish to Teignmouth that passes the aptly named Shag Rock and the Parson and Clerk Headland brought back more memories of early pre-teen touring days when cycling towards Land's End down this way with my brother. By this stage of our trek he'd had quite enough of this hilly cycling lark. He'd also had enough of lying in wet tents and fighting into headwinds. And, not to put too fine a point on it, he had had quite enough of me.

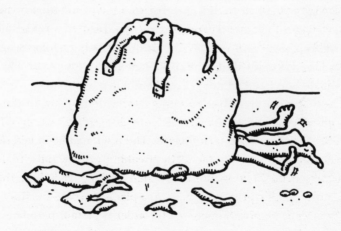

So near Shag Rock he announced, in imperious tone, that we would continue riding down the road to Teignmouth from where we would catch the train home. Naturally, being a difficult sibling, I wasn't having any of this. My sights were set on Land's End and I was going to get there come what may, even if it meant cycling there by myself, which of course I knew I couldn't do as we were under strict father-issued orders that we could go cycling anywhere in the West Country as long as we went together. I tried to reason with Ant along the lines that having got this far we couldn't give up now and so on and so forth. But he adamant. So in bolshie mood I retaliated by flagrantly flouting his commands and taking off up the road at a rate of knots. I wanted to get to Land's End. Badly.

Apart from returning home to my parents without me, Ant had little option but to give chase. What happened next was like the modern equivalent of some wild, gun-slinging Western. Ant, surged on with anger, finally caught up with me on his ten-speed racer (only, I hasten to add, because I had run out of gears – I couldn't pedal my Misty five-speed any faster). Where all the traffic was I have no idea, but he pulled broadside and then, like a couple of galloping warring cowboys, we thumped and we fought as we tried to whack each other off our respective steeds, slewing at speed across the road. Then, espying my slip-road escape route, I charged up a ramp on to an elevated pavement and was momentarily spared from a barrage of sparring punches. But Ant, exerting a sudden spurt, cut off my getaway exit by braking violently across my path like a police-chasing squad car. Inevitably, I crashed into him and, amid a great show of colliding metal and scraping skin, we both went for a burton.

The next stage of combat was like a comic-strip Bash Street Kid brawl. Amid a great battling scrum-ball of dirt and dust and cries of Oomph! Oww! Pow! Zow! we boxed and we brawled and we clashed and we grappled and we struggled and we squabbled and we tussled and we scuffled and we . . . collapsed. Utterly exhausted. I never thought I could hate my brother so much.

But we made it to Land's End. I'm a bit stubborn like that.

CHAPTER 21

I carried on. Teignmouth ('The Gem of South Devon', said the road-side sign) to Torbay ('The English Riviera') would have been a fine plunging up and down sea-view hair-pinned ride, had it not been ruined by impatient drivers displaying a hazardous tendency to overtake me at the very stupidest moments on uphill blind corners with an inch to spare. I felt the target of their frustration. Each bend was approached with my heart in my mouth and the hope of an escape route in mind. Would there be a dent in the bank to dive into, a hole in a hedge to plough through, a ditch to fall in? But there never was. Cars of every shape and size continued to sweep and snarl past as though oblivious to the possibility that they would meet something of similar size and colour on the bend. Which they inevitably did. Erratic swerve. Squeal of brakes. Flattened into the bankside. Oh, to rotten-tomato machine-gun the lot of them!

Past Kent's Cavern (where 40,000 years ago Stone Age Man fought bears and sabre-toothed tigers), I rode up Walls Hill before heading out to Hope's Nose and down around Daddyhole Cove ('Daddy' is old Devon-speak for Devil) until I came to a halt on Torquay's fancy harbourside. Here I lounged in a striped deckchair eating my lunch while being stared at and talked about by a lot of old people lounging in identical chairs around a small fountain. The wind whisked snippets of these passing comments to land in my ears: *Look at the gear she's got on there! – All on her own! – Such a little thing! – Must be dangerous! – Must get lonely! – Must get scared!*

151

Attention was momentarily diverted from me to a group of glowering boys scuffling along in untied trainers and flappy combat trousers jangling with keyrings and penknives and industrial chains. One of them was sporting pierced-lip hardware in the shape of a unicorn horn protuberance. They all wore hoodies and baseball caps on backwards. Surrounded by serried ranks of senior citizens, I looked different and stood out a mile – ripe for rich teenage pickings.

'So where yer been then?' said one scowling boy accusingly as he gobbed a globule a foot from my feet.

'To Dibden Purlieu,' I replied, for no other reason than I had the name on the brain.

'Yeah, right. Must be some shite life,' he replied before spitting out another phlegm-bomb and joining his baggy trousered mates in attempted sabotage of the fountain.

The best thing about Torquay was picking up a copy of the *Western Morning News* ('The Voice of the Westcountry') and reading about a chef from the town who almost had his head torn off when a dead shark he was transporting back to his restaurant shot out of an icebox in the back of his car when he braked sharply.

Round Torbay I rode, passing through Paignton, once famed for its very large and sweet 'flatpole' cabbages, as well as its part-time resident – the American sewing machine millionaire, Isaac Singer. Outside Somerfield in Brixham, I packed a bagful of bananas into my panniers beside a bench on which slouched a man with such a vast lard-cake of a belly that it looked like he was smuggling a Space Hopper down his shirt. Beside him slumped his wife, who was verging on equal heft. The man was in the middle of glugging down a whole 1.5 litre bottle of Diet Coke when his very fat son waddled up.

'Dad,' he said, 'I just saw this wicked watch I want to get.'

'What d'yer want with another watch?' said his mum.

Then, coming up for air from his Coke, his dad said, 'Now yer workin' son, yer got'er learn to save yer dough. I ain't keepin' yer now, yer know.'

'Aww, dad!' whined the fat son, 'I hate yer!'

And off he stomped.

Down the road in Drew Street, I stayed in the 400-year-old haunted house of the great cyclist, Ian Hibell, which he shared with Dot, his 97-year-old mother. I had first met Dot several years before – a small, round, lovable white-haired woman full of fun and laughter. But she wasn't here now because her doctor had finally persuaded her to go into a nursing home for a while to give Ian a break from the demanding, round-the-clock care that was making him ill with depression and exhaustion.

At the age of twenty-eight, Ian had given up his job to cycle around the world. He thought he would be gone about a year, but in the event he was gone for ten. Part of the journey saw him completing the first recorded overland crossing from Patagonia to Alaska. With two other men, both Kiwis, he somehow managed to machete his way across Panama's impenetrable Darien Gap, dragging bikes and belongings through the python-inhabited Altrato Swamp, even beating the British Army, led by Major Blashford-Snell, who were attempting it from the north.

'I thought we would never do it,' said Ian. 'We were young, wanting a bit of an adventure, so had planned just to give it a try before retracing our tracks. But we got in so far it was impossible to return. We simply couldn't face the awfulness of going back. It would have killed us.'

They very nearly died anyway, living as they were on starvation rations of one handful of dried oats in the morning, and another in the evening. Drinking directly from the swamp, they all caught severe bacterial stomach infections. Ian was also suffering from a horrific wound as a result of accidentally hacking into his shin with his machete. It was one of the only times in his life he had fainted and he thought he was dead.

'By that stage,' said Ian, 'it was every man for himself and the others just kept going.'

He became so wasted that when one of the trees he had tied his hammock to gave way during the night, leaving him submerged in the evil murky waters of the swamp, he was too weak to get up to do anything about it.

Apart from his huge achievements on the cycle-touring front, Ian, a small, quiet, unassuming man, bore a great shadow of sadness about him. This is mainly down to Laura, a woman he met when she was twenty-four, who went along to a travel lecture he was giving on his Norway-to-Africa trip. She was so taken with Ian's future plans to cycle across the breadth of South America that she persuaded him to take her too.

All apparently went very well. They fell in love and had some wonderful cycling adventures. But then she caught hepatitis and had to fly home. Shortly after her return she wrote to Ian to tell him she was pregnant. When Ian arrived home, he moved in to live with her on a commune where one of the men fell madly in love with her. The situation became intolerable for Ian, so after a few months he left to go back to Devon. Laura and her new man moved to live on another commune in Yugoslavia and she gave birth to a boy, Jamie, who, now in his twenties, seems to want nothing to do with his Brixham-based dad. To add to Ian's pain, Laura had died the previous year, aged forty-four, of breast cancer. Ian is nearly seventy now, but the ever-burning desire for further two-wheeled explorations still simmers within.

I spent the morning dallying around Brixham, once England's leading fishing port crowded with brigs and schooners and smacks. Now all that was left was a mere fraction of this fleet moored around a full-size replica of Sir Francis Drake's *Golden Hind*, the surprisingly small ship in which he sailed round the world at the end of the sixteenth century. Its decks were teeming with tourists so I wandered off and came across the disconcerting sight of a Roman Catholic church with a car park located on its roof.

Up on Berry Head, a promontory 190 feet above sea level that has a long history of fortification going back to the Iron Age, a small obelisk informed me that forty-two miles to the east lay Portland Bill, which could be seen on a clear day. Forty-two miles? Was that all? How depressing! It didn't sound very far for all the effort it had taken me to get here: ten days and 276 very hilly miles to be precise. Suddenly the idea of travelling by boat struck me as very appealing.

As I peered into the distance, straining to make out the snout of Portland, all I could see was a man from Manchester in a string vest and a pair of tight office trousers who stepped into my line of vision with a neck bristling with various strap-hanging cameras and monoculars.

'Sun always seems to be shining somewhere else, don't it, love?' he said, obviously disappointed that Berry Head was buried beneath the shadow of a big, dark, slow-moving cloud, while, across the bay, East Shag, Thatcher Rock and Hope's Nose could be seen shimmering in sunshine.

With over a thousand birds, the guillemot colony on Berry Head is the biggest on the south coast. At one time, it was a local sport to bring a boat in under the cliffs and fire off a gun for the fun of seeing a thousand guillemots in flight at the same time. How gullible can a guillemot be? Anyway, Devon Bird Watching and Preservation Society knocked that idea on the head by campaigning to have the birds protected. Now all sight-seeing shooting activity is strictly banned.

I had planned to follow the River Dart up around Pigeon Point to Totnes and then down and round the other side through Tuckenhay and Bozomzeal. But the previous year, after giving a cycling talk at Dartington Hall, I had cycled this route with the builder and, although it had been a wonderfully scenic ride, it had been hellishly hilly, especially around Dittisham and Corkscrew Hill. This time I decided to preserve my knees and give it a miss. So after walking out to Sharkham Point, from where I could look across to Cod and Mussel Rocks, I left Brixham by way of struggling up Guzzle Down before gunning down Boohay and Waterhead Brake into Kingswear – the southern terminus of the Paignton and Dartmouth Steam Railway. I then caught the very sedate Lower Ferry, which whisked me across the Dart to Dartmouth.

After all that, I ended up cycling up river to Dittisham anyway – not because I masochistically wanted to kill myself on the hills again, but just because it had turned into such a gorgeous day for such a gorgeous cycle. Well, gorgeous if you ignore the hills. The air smelt warm and buttery one moment, and deliciously stickily muddy the next as I rose and fell through deep grassy fields and waterside lanes. The tiny village of Dittisham clings to the hills of the estuary and on the opposite shore stands Greenway House, one of the family homes of Humphrey Gilbert, Sir Walter Raleigh's half brother, who searched for the North West Passage and claimed Newfoundland for England. Greenway House is supposedly the famed location where Raleigh, having just introduced tobacco to England from the Americas, sat smoking a pipe and was doused by a servant who thought he was on fire.

Back in Dartmouth, I filled up my water bottles at The Singing Kettle Tea Shoppe, took a loop up and around Jawbones Hill and was pursued by a retired police officer from Scotland Yard called Tony Pill who found me guilty of having written some cycling books that he had read.

From Dartmouth I contemplated cycling inland to Blackawton, venue for the International Worm Charming Contest, but having decided I charmed enough worms (and slugs) of my own in my tent, I continued on down the coast.

Diving downhill among evergreens and pines to the golden crescent of Blackpool Sands ('Relax or play, it's South Devon's most picturesque beach any day!'), I stopped only to use the toilets and to notice that in the Venus Café they served sun-dried tomato ciabatta 'brushed liberally with extra virgin olive oil'. How very Islington.

The cycle from Strete to Torcross has long rated as one of my favourites of the south coast along with Dorset's Purbeck Hills. I shot out of Strete, peered down to Pilchard Cove, sped round the hairpin at Strete Gate and sailed along the straight of Slapton Sands, which is actually something of a misnomer as the 'sand' is fine shingle and mini pebbly 'popples' where D-day forces practised for their assault on Normandy in 'Operation Overlord'. I stopped to pick a few handfuls of fennel, which was towering six feet high or more beside the roadside – I thought the aniseed-tasting fronds and seeds might spice up my supper of sardines, rice, peas and bananas. In Anglo-Saxon times, the seeds were prized as a cure for flatulence:

> In fennel seed this vertue shall you find
> Fourth of your lower parts to drive the winds.

Of course, I was fine on that front. I just liked the taste.

That night I camped near Stokenham on a small, family-run site at Old Cotmore Farm, which their leaflet advertised as being 'situated in an area 'twixt Dartmouth and Salcombe'. I was half expecting to find an Olde Tea Shoppe of yesteryear on site but all I found were dogs. Everywhere. One woman in a caravan had seven horrible yapping mutts. Every time I walked past they lunged at me wildly against their leashes. Most of the other dog owners blatantly ignored a sign that read: 'PLEASE: DOGS ON LEADS, CLEAN UP DEEDS'.

Lyn and Graham Bowsher owned the farm, but had only done so since November. They had moved from Guildford, the commuting capital of Surrey. Lyn had been a receptionist, travelling back and forth to Leatherhead every day. Graham had worked as a site construction manager, driving all over the country.

'We never saw each other,' he told me, 'so we decided to do something completely different with our lives.'

Urbanites, downshifting to live in the country. But it was touch and go at first.

'We arrived in the floods of last winter,' said Lyn. 'It was awful. Mud and wet everywhere. I was miserable for months. I stood in the courtyard and screamed "I WANT TO GO HOME!"' But now the sun was shining and they couldn't be happier.

'We certainly did the right thing!' said Lyn, her downshifted tantrum now well in the past.

On waking up the next morning I tuned in to South Hams Radio and heard, '*Ahhhhhhhhweeeeeargh!*' Then the presenter said, 'That's better. First stretch of the day!' I liked that. You don't get John Humphrys doing that sort of thing on the *Today* programme. The next issue of great intellect on South Hams Radio was being asked to guess what caused one in five car accidents in Sweden. Listeners rang in with their ideas: 'Alcohol!' 'Fallen trees!' 'Buxom blondes!' 'Suicidal tendencies!' *No. No. No. And no.* The answer? Moose. Which I could well believe. When I was cycling in Sweden, a very clumsy-hoofed moose went crashing through my tent. I think they like running into things. The only trouble is: if you're in your tent at the time, it hurts.

Cycling around this part of the South Hams coast, which stops at Start and Prawle Points, proved preposterously hilly but scenically spiffing in spite of a pervasive mist that cloaked the area for most of the morning. It was just a shame about those supercilious Shogun Supertrooper four-wheel-drives that ruined my hard-earned downhills by pressing impatiently past before jamming on their brakes mid-descent when, lo! – they met another shiny Shogun supertrooping up. And if they weren't Shoguns (which of course had nothing to do with hereditary commander-in-chiefs in feudal Japan and everything to do with young upwardly-mobile down-shifting townie mothers with matching labradors) they were Land Rover Discoveries or Freelanders or Grand Cherokee Jeeps or Toyota Land Cruiser Amazons.

Talking of which, I was huffing my way up a hill along one of a multitude of single-tracked, high-hedged lanes somewhere around Loo Cross when a Land Rover Discovery roared up behind me, impatiently engine-revving, drowning the birdsong and my breathing. Why all this hasty irritability I really don't know. Had there been any space to let it pass, I would have pulled over, as it's not in my nature to annoy intentionally. *No, really, it's not!* But the lane was so narrow that the only way for the snarling Discovery to get by was to drive straight over me. Which it very nearly did. Under pressure, with a bumper up my bum, I pushed hard on the pedals to whip up my speed. With bursting lungs, I arrived at the brow of the hill where I ever so generously paused in a bramble-riddled nettle-stinging field gateway to let it pass and Mrs Discovery, *sans* acknowledgement, swooshed on her way.

I followed in hot pursuit, muttering uncharitable thoughts under my breath. The pursuit didn't last long because as I swooped round a corner I came up against a pair of lane-blocking brake lights. Mrs Discovery had met Mrs Shogun. And both were standing their ground. Fortunately for me, there was a dent in one bank (result of an earlier Land Cruiser collision perhaps?), which pleasingly was just sufficiently deep enough to let me pass.

The hill was a long one and I continued falling . . . until . . . whoa! I hauled on my brakes. For belting uphill towards me was a Cherokee Jeep – a jeep which of course had nothing to do with being a member of a North American Indian people formerly living in the Appalachian Mountains and everything to do with a young, upwardly-mobile down-shifting urbanite (with matching labrador) recently in possession of a large country pile. I ground to a halt. She skidded to a standstill. I stared at her. She glared at me. A panicky blackbird clattered out of the overgrown sunken-lane shrubbery and dived over a high-rise hedgerow. I turned from looking at it to look back at Mrs Cherokee, who was still looking daggers at me. Her dirty glower said, *Go on you pesty pedalist – get out of my way! For I am bigger and I am grander!*

But trying to get out of her way was pointless. For one thing, I had just descended a gradient so steep and so severe on a bike so weighty and laden that to try to turn round now and push my leaden load back up the precipitous hill would have been about as easy as hauling an elephant over the Eiger. The other thing was that I knew that, any moment now, Mrs Discovery would come haring round the corner. So, to alert Mrs Cherokee to the impending scenario, I gesticulated, in enthusiastic manner, back up the hill to indicate in a pantomimical '*she's be-HIND yoooou!*' charade that there was a vehicle fast approaching from my rear. So to speak.

Right on cue, springing from the wings, loomed Mrs Discovery who, amid much burning of rubber, just managed to slam on her brakes in time before I became entangled in her bull-bars. I was now pig in the middle of two very fat and shiny elevated bonnets, polished up like cut glass with an Aga-type metallic-enamelled finish, behind which sat two irritated women staring down their noses at the low-life in their way. But I wasn't really in their way. *They* were in *my* way while being in the way of each other. Such are the consequences when one chooses to drive tanks down narrow country lanes.

Finally, there was nothing else for it other than for Mrs Cherokee to relent and reverse. Unfortunately, I don't think Mrs Cherokee had ever relented in all her Cherokee-helmed life, for it became evident she could not find reverse. I watched her, and Mrs Discovery watched her, as she sat strapped into her all-terrain flight deck grappling unsuccessfully with her controls while turning the air blue as she did so. At last, more by luck than anything else, the Cherokee shuddered, then violently lurched backwards before stopping abruptly. A painful symphony of crunching and grating reverberations and clatterings then erupted from the vicinity of the engine, which sounded as if some ferocious creature was trying to escape from the gearbox. Several light years later, the Cherokee began inching backwards.

But oh! – what reversing! With diabolical technique, Mrs Cherokee edged her way in reverse down the hill by way of rear-view mirror navigation. I mean, honestly! Even I, as a non-motorist, know that in order to conduct such a backward manoeuvre successfully, one must look over one's shoulder while simultaneously grabbing a hold of the rear of the passenger seat. At least, that's what my mum does and it always makes me laugh. Especially her expression of sincere concentration. But it never seems to fail and she has triumphantly got us out of some tight squeezes in the past.

Anyway, Mrs Cherokee's reversing technique was definitely not one to emulate. She ground up against the bank on one side before mounting it on the other, removing whole clumpfuls of delicate wild flowers in the process. Black clouds of diesel-flavoured exhaust shrouded the lane, cloaking me with fine carcinogenic carbon particles in her wake. Eventually, having grubbed out several hedgerows and obliterated great chunks of rare bankside flora, Mrs Cherokee reached the mouth of a track. The ether cleared and the dust settled and we each went on our own respective ways.

CHAPTER 22

At Prawle Point, the most southerly headland in Devon, everything sounded very porcine. After walking along the coast path from Gammon Head to Pig's Nose and Ham Stone, I stopped to fill my water bottles at the Pig's Nose Inn before buying a bunch of bananas from Piglet Stores, which tailed on to Grunters Café from where emanated the wafts of frying bacon.

Down to Gara Rock I tumbled, along Kingsbridge Estuary to East Portlemouth and Goodshelter and up and round and down a tangled skein of steep lanes (some so narrow that the only sounds were the complaining gulls and the clatter-smash of colliding wing mirrors) to South Pool, whose small cluster of thatched colour-washed houses huddled around the head of a winding tidal creek. 'Best Kept Village 1999 CPRE' proudly announced the village sign on which were also the paint-daubed words 'Snooty Pool'. Well, there did seem to be more four-wheel-drives than houses.

At Chillington I passed a sign to the Health Centre, so, on the spur of the moment, I went to see if I could get anyone to shed light on a sore gash that I'd had for several days between my toes. It had appeared all on its own and I thought maybe I should make sure it wasn't going to get infected in my sweaty-socked trainers.

The receptionist was very friendly and said that there was an appointment free in an hour to see Dr Christopher Trounce. Dr Trounce turned out to be also very friendly. He drew up his chair around the side of his desk and told me to put my bare foot in his lap, which I thought was a little brazen of him. Obediently I perched said foot precariously upon his knee.

'Sorry it's a bit sweaty!' I said.

'I'd be surprised if it wasn't!' replied Dr Trounce. 'It's hot out there!'

'It certainly is,' I said, before adding, 'I just want to check it's not athlete's foot or anything horrible like that.'

'Have you had athlete's foot before?' he asked.

'No,' I replied, 'so I'm not quite sure what it looks like.'

'Well, the good news is you haven't got athlete's foot.'

'Oh. That's good,' I said, cautiously waiting for the bad news. But the bad news never came. Dr Trounce said I had nothing more than a bit of a gash between my toes.

'Have you got any antiseptic cream with you?' he asked.

'I've got tea-tree oil,' I said. 'I'll slap some more of that on.'

'Ahh, tea-tree,' said Dr Trounce contemplatively. 'I've got some patients who swear by the stuff but I'm afraid I don't know anything about it myself.'

And that was that. For the remainder of my ten-minute consultation, Dr Trounce appeared far more interested in where I was cycling and where I was camping than in my foot. So I removed it off his knee and put it back in my shoe.

At Chillington Post Office, I stopped to buy and send Jake, my three-year-old nephew, his birthday present of felt-tip pens and colouring books. At the till an old West-Country biddie was passing time of day with the postmistress.

'Turned out noice now,' she said, her voice a soft Devon burr, warm and buttery. 'Never thought it would, whart with all thart mist thart blew in.'

'Oi know,' said the postmistress, 'Oi was saying to Betty it was even a little cold at dinner toime.'

'Sounds loike we're in for a stormy week, though. I reckon we've 'ad enough o' thart sort o' caper for one summer! Oh, did Sid say thart we got new people moving in next door?'

'You 'ave? Where they be coming from?'

'Only Frogmore.'

'Thart's noice thart they be local, then.'

Outside a farmer pulled up on his tractor. When he saw me he said, 'Oither you need a bigger boike or a smaller load!' Which made a welcome change from telling me I needed a motor.

Cycling into West Charlton I passed a pub with a menu board outside exhorting passers-by to:

BE KIND: WHAT GOES AROUND COMES AROUND.

But what came around for me was an overly close encounter with Mondeo Man who swished past an inch from my elbow before cutting me up. A trifle riled, I stomped on my pedals and, pleasingly, caught up with him at the lights in Kingsbridge. Taking this opportunity to have a 'little discussion' with him, I drew alongside and tapped on his window. Mondeo Man was in late middle age and sat beside a grey perm-haired woman whom I took to be Mrs Mondeo. Surprised by the tapping, they both cast a fleeting glance in my direction before pointedly turning away and staring po-faced straight ahead. I gave another tap. Mondeo Man looked worried. The window remained firmly closed. What did he think? That I was going to proposition him or something? That I was going to adopt seductive tones and say, 'Well, hell-*o* there . . .' while, with a come-hither pout, slowly undoing the Velcro on my low-necked I'm-from-the-council-come-to-mend-the-drains fluorescent yellow vest? Was he worried that I would scoldingly say, 'You're a very naughty boy. And would you like to know what I do with very naughty boys? Well, I flash my red LED – oh, I'm sorry – Light Emitting Diode rear cycle lamp right in your face (or any-where else if you prefer). Then, following a little inflation, I might insert my smooth, schraeder-ended pump into the valve head of your presta-topped ori-fice . . .' Sadly though, before I could put my provocative enticements into practice, the red-light district of the traffic lights turned to green and that naughty Mondeo Man was beside me no more.

To calm myself down, I bought a cooling cucumber from Alan's Apple greengrocer in Kingsbridge. This ancient market town is the 'capital' of the South Hams, an area of South Devon that is full of sheltered coves and estuar-ies, hills and second homes and which lies between the rivers Dart and Tamar.

I half expired on some of those hills along high-banked lanes, some with the roots of the trees peering down at me – the steepest greenest tunnels I had yet encountered – when following the back way to Salcombe through Blanksmill and Batson. My route jigged around the Kingsbridge Estuary (which actually isn't an estuary at all, but a ria, or flooded valley) and was only marred by a bar-rage of Shogun Warriors and Grand Cherokees on away-day lane-blocking missions from their second homes.

As I was entering Salcombe by way of one of the tiny arteries of the town, a gleaming late-model, flash-twat Range Rover impatiently squeezed past me before immediately slamming on its brakes when it met another infernal com-bustion engine of similar dimensions coming the other way. It was another scene of motorist deadlock: neither could reverse without the bedlam of vehicles up their rears reversing first. For me, life was a little less complex; I had ample space to weave through a gap between the two stalemate bonnets. As I passed the stationary top-of-the-crop-but-bottom-of-the-environmental-food-chain Range Rover, the driver, a fat toff in a yachting cap and striped Breton shirt, thrust his ugly geezer head out of the window and shouted with a death-wish snarl, 'CRAZY WAY TO DIE!'

'Crazy place to drive!' I retorted, continuing calmly on my way.

I didn't enjoy Salcombe. The jumbled streets were all very twee and all very lovely, especially the steep stepped alleyways or 'back doubles' overlooked by the church. But there were just too many yachting sorts and wealthy young la-di-da hoorahs cruising around in their oversized vehicles or guffawing loudly into their mobile phones as they swaggered up and down Fore Street. What's more, a tin of tuna I bought cost nearly twice as much as normal village store prices, which I found quite scandalous.

I left Salcombe along Cliff Road, which afforded grand views of the sun-spangled sweep of the harbour with its swanning yachts, heeling in the fresh breeze with their sails of white wings. Elsewhere, tenantless sailing boats and motor-cruisers rode to their mooring buoys. The Salcombe yawl, once a crabbing boat, is no longer tethered to some of the 4500 moorings found in the estuary. It has been usurped by a different class of vessel: the pleasure-seeking 'pleasure craft'.

To the accompanying soundtrack of forlorn and mewing gulls, shouted sailing commands and distant rumblings of thunder, I dipped and dived and sweated and shinned along the roller-coaster road as far as Splat Point where, heading inland, I camped along the sharp contours on a farm at Rew. No sooner were my panniers opened and tent half up than the stormy heavens opened, soaking belongings and body in one.

Over near the toilet block I found that the showers were communal ones. In order to activate them, a 20p piece had to be fed into a box fixed on a wall outside the cubicle. This method was all very fine if you happened to be a couplet, as you could work as a team – one showering within, one money-feeding out-with – but it was not so easy for a singlet like me. To avoid wasting your strictly limited two-minute supply of tepid water, you had to undress before stepping out of the cubicle in your altogether to grapple with the easy-to-jam 20p-eating machine, then dive back in to hair-wash and body-scrub feverishly before the shower abruptly shut off, leaving you shivering with soapy lather in your eyes. Then, if you could see through the stinging shampoo suds to find another 20p, you had to go back out to turn it back on, then run back in. Not easy if there is a man waiting outside, as there was in my case. I tried my best to conceal my bits with a desperate splayed hand and an ill-positioned flannel, but I still think he got more buttock and breast than he bargained for.

All this stressful showering was made up for when I collapsed back in my tent and tuned in to South Hams Radio and heard how a mob of sheep and a pandemonium of ducklings had broken loose from a farm near Frogmore and were making their getaway up the A379 to Kingsbridge. I also learnt how a man in Florida had sued a lap-dancing nightclub for whiplash injuries sustained from being biffed in the face by a pair of prodigious pendulous breasts.

Suddenly I went through a spate of being spotted. Some lads driving past in a black Fiesta tooted and honked and shouted my name and, hanging out of the window, handed me a banana. I wasn't quite sure how to take that, but I took it anyway. An elderly woman, with a helmet of white curls and a local West Country burr, wanted to clutch my hand and feel the legs that had taken me over the Himalayas. And a whiskery chap in his fifties and knife-creased trousers told me he had sold his car all because of me.

'Sorry!' I said.

'No, don't be,' he replied. 'I've bought a bike and now I feel happier and healthier – and richer – than ever!'

And he gave my hand such a vigorous shake, I felt my knuckles crumple.

Then there were caravanning John and Rita, originally from Birmingham, but now living in retirement in a bungalow with a sea view in Exmouth. They both loved cycling too, though they were getting sick of the ever-increasing amount of cars on the roads.

'The mentality of motorists in this country,' said John, an ex-engineer, 'is all wrong. Most have no patience. They think cyclists have no right on the roads!'

John was right. The one thing that was spoiling my ride around England was the traffic. The amount of it, the speed of it, the impatience of it. From the seat of a bicycle you see and smell and feel how motor traffic ruins everything; from villages to towns, from lanes to roads, from hills to cities, from flora to fauna, from people's health to people's lives. Nothing is spared. Cars and trucks and buses and lorries take their destruction to almost every corner of the land.

And the strange thing is, people seem to love them. Private motoring is seen as a personal freedom beyond all others. The love for cars is reflected in our tolerance of an annual massacre on the roads that would be utterly unacceptable in other spheres: 3600 deaths, 38,000 serious injuries and 279,000 minor injuries in 2000 alone.

And so through Hope Barton to Hope Cove, passing through Inner Hope to Outer Hope to almost no hope on the steep hill out. Further on I stopped at the Thurlestone Hotel to wash my socks in the downstairs Ladies. The car park of this family-run establishment resembled a BMW and Mercedes show-room in Mayfair, with a nice line of 4 × 4 and open-topped sports cars on the side. The strident-toned guests sashayed around in checked golfer's uniforms, dripping with heavy gold jewellery inlaid with dazzling gems. As I walked out through reception, I bid good day to an expensive-looking couple who refused to acknowledge my presence. I think they mistook me as the sock-washer.

In the post office across the road I bought a bottle of locally pressed apple juice and a book about the history of hedgerows. (I love hedges. I sleep behind them, I shelter behind them, I picnic behind them, I widdle behind them. And I cycle alongside them. In short, I stare at them. A lot.) As I was waiting to pay, two Etonesque boys with floppy forelocks sauntered in.

'Have you got any change for a pound? We need some 10ps,' one of them said to the unsmiling postmistress.

'No,' she said, 'I told you yesterday we don't do tens.'

'Oh, sorry,' said the boy, 'I thought you meant you didn't have any in the till at the time.'

Then the postmistress sneezed.

'Bless you!' I said, trying to liven things up.

But all I got in return was a scowl. So I left. I decided I didn't like Thurlestone.

To reach the thatched and whitewashed village of Bantham, which was but a mere popple's throw from Thurlestone, seemed to involve expending an inordinate amount of energy on a short-sharp and very long-winded hill at Buckland. By the time I staggered into Bantham, I was tired and hungry so I sat on a bench eating bananas on the edge of a small car park overlooking the River Avon – pronounced 'Awn' in local tongue. As I ate, a lot of wealthy young men arrived in a cavalcade of a BMW, a Jag and a Toyota Land Cruiser Amazon (the latter of course having nothing to do with a 4150-mile-long river that drains two-fifths of the South American continent and everything to do with a cyclist-crushing tank). They had sun-bleached hair, loud haughty voices, wetsuits and surfboards.

Then the dog walkers arrived – dog walkers in checked slacks and shorts who I suspected weren't really dog walkers at all, but golfers with canine fashion accessories. Whatever they were, they did a fine job of ignoring a sign that pointed out 'ONLY RESPONSIBLE DOG WALKERS WITH POOP SCOOPS ARE WELCOME' and allowed their dogs free rein to poop-mine the path.

One man did turn up with a dog on lead in one hand and something that looked like a wooden meat tenderiser in the other. As his dog dragged him past my bench I said, 'Is that what you call a poop scooper?'

'You could say that,' he replied, a trifle tersely, without breaking step. After witnessing his dog's steaming offering being sent airborne, I decided it was more a poop flicker than a scooper. By this stage, my appetite had been quashed, so I mounted up and cycled off.

But I didn't get very far. About 100 yards, in fact: I stopped at the Sloop Inn to use the toilets. When I emerged from the pub, I found a man and his wife – local sorts – contemplating my bike.

'That's not the way to travel,' said the man very certainly.

'It is,' I replied in defensive mode. 'It's lovely!'

'I've got a bad back,' the man said, 'and you're making it worse just looking at all that gear you're carrying!'

Later, they drove past me on a hill and gave a cheery tonk and wave.

In the small village of Churchstow, I stopped at the post office to buy some supper and breakfast supplies. But it was closed.

'It's early closing Wednesdays,' said a local woman walking past. 'You won't be foinding nothing open round 'ere now, pet. Not unless you 'ead all the way loike into Kingsbridge.'

But I couldn't do that! It would mean going back on myself and I couldn't spend time and energy going backwards when I had enough forwards to be getting on with. So with a mild panic rising within at the fretful prospect of being potentially provisionless, I dropped down through Venn, crossed the Avon and arrived in Aveton Gifford. I located the village store where, although I was prepared for the worst, I still stood bewildered in utter disbelief on finding the CLOSED sign hanging on the door. Sometimes when people have a shock, all sense of time goes flying out of the window. I have no idea how long I stood staring at the CLOSED sign in Aveton Gifford's store in a state of village post-office traumatic stress. If someone was watching me through net curtains on the opposite side of the street, then they would have been right to have expressed deep concern for my mental wellbeing.

Time marched on as time stood as still as I stood still. Then a car pulled up behind me and I was back in the land of the living. A woman got out, followed by a dog. They made towards Marsh Cottage, a house next door to the store. The woman was fortyish with lustrous long blonde hair.

'Hello,' she said.

'Hello,' I replied. And then, because I thought I had better explain what I was doing loitering suspiciously in a quiet village street, added, 'I'm just suffering from shock at having found this shop shut even though I was quite prepared to find it shut.'

That didn't come out quite as I hoped, but then solo cycling does tend to give your tongue mental blockages.

The woman kindly took my malformed syntax in her stride and said, 'Yes, early closing. You get used to that sort of thing when you live round here.'

The next thing I knew I was downstairs in the basement kitchen of Marsh Cottage and the contents of Mrs Schroeter's fruit bowl were being emptied into a bag together with a few frozen offerings from the freezer.

'Here you are,' said Mrs Schroeter. 'It's probably not quite up to shop standards, but it should fill a few gaps!'

Then she told me to put my money away because she didn't want anything for it.

'I'm glad to be of some help,' she said.

But I foisted some money on her anyway. She had single-handedly spared me from a hungry night.

Mrs Schroeter was a Kiwi. Her husband Neil, from Wales, now worked on the river as he was the new boatman on the tiny passenger ferry between Bantham and Cockleridge Ham. For years he had hankered after the job and when the old ferryman had retired after thirty-odd years on the job, Mr Schroeter left the RAF and took over the service.

'Now that he's dabbling about with boats all day, he couldn't be happier,' said Mrs Schroeter, who told me she also couldn't be happier with her job as a music teacher. There was a lot of job-satisfaction floating around because the framed words suspended on the kitchen wall declared:

IF YOU DO A JOB THAT YOU LOVE
THEN YOU NEVER DO A DAY OF WORK IN YOUR LIFE.

CHAPTER 23

Things then got quite exciting because from Aveton Gifford I followed a tidal road along the western foreshore of the River Avon with the waves and seaweed lapping at my wheels. The sides of the wet slippery road were lined with big wooden piles demarcating the edges, but even so I felt it was easy enough to slide off the slime and be swallowed by the oozing bubbling mudflats.

Then in St Ann's Chapel what should I find but a village store. Open. On Wednesday afternoon.

'Shouldn't you be closed?' I said to the big friendly bloke behind the till.

'Can't afford to close, me luv,' he replied, 'and if I were, you'd be having no tinned tuna for your tea.'

This was true. He then told me about Farmer Tucker who lived up the road at Folly Hill Farm on Mount Folly.

'He's a good sort,' said the store man. 'He'll let you camp on his land.'

Sheep Farmer Tucker was only too happy to help me out. In fact, he was so accommodating he invited me to camp in his front garden, which enjoyed what estate agents might call an advantageous position. High up on a cliff, it overlooked the sandy-bayed splendours of Bantham beach where, further out, surfers bobbed on their boards on the ocean swell. But along with the exposed tent-flattening wind, his frisky collies appeared more intent on rounding up me than his sheep, so I said the field was fine.

I erected my home among an interesting assortment of old farm machinery, a battered horsebox holding three blocked toilets on the tilt, a few mouldy remnants of caravans and lots of sheep cack. A little later a Range Rover arrived on the scene, towing a caravan. Steve and Ann, from Waterlooville, were friends of Farmer Tucker and invited me over to lounge in a deck chair as they plied me with mugfuls of tea. Shaven-headed Steve, who wore a goatee and a JURAS-SIC PARK T-shirt, had taken early retirement.

'I used to be a service engineer,' he said, 'working on cars at Wadham Stringers. But I got fed up with the job so I did a stockbroking course and made LOADSA money! Now I just bum around!'

Steve told me he used to cycle himself.

'Mostly racing,' he said. 'I once rode from Portsmouth to Land's End and back in five days.'

Only five days? How depressing!

That night the weather turned on its head and threw an almighty storm. I was camping behind Farmer Tucker's hedge at the time, but for all the protection it gave I might as well have been lying in a wind tunnel while under fire from ballistic water cannon attack. The next morning, when Radio Devon reported there had been 310,000 lightning 'hits' overnight, I reckoned I was lucky to be alive, if not a little wet, and I counted and recounted my lucky blessings that I hadn't been struck by a fork or a bolt.

But my luck though was nothing compared to the most remarkable lightning story I know concerning a certain Roy Sullivan of Waynesboro, Virginia. During his thirty-six years as a park ranger he was struck seven times. In 1942 he lost a big toenail to lightning. In 1969, his eyebrows were blown off. His left shoulder was seared in 1970 and his hair set on fire in 1972. In August 1973, a bolt hit him on the head through his hat, set his hair on fire again, threw him ten feet out of his car and knocked his left shoe off. Sullivan died on September 28th, 1983, aged seventy-one, but not from lightning. He shot himself.

I finished breakfast and it was still raining hard. The forecast was diabolical. However, to brighten things up, South Hams Radio asked its listeners to phone in if they knew the difference between 'simple' and 'aggravated' assault in the state of Louisiana. Callers came up with some hilariously outlandish ideas but no one hit the button. Apparently, the law in Louisiana states that 'simple assault' equates to being bitten by someone with natural teeth; 'aggravated assault' is being bitten with false teeth. Easy really.

As the weather was so wild and wet and windy, I decided to walk along the coast path back to Thurlestone to buy some more food supplies from the post office. I descended Mount Folly to Cockleridge Ham where, on the beach, walking his rotund old labrador Dillon, I met a local man, originally from Plymouth. Like me, he was planning to take the passenger ferry across to Bantham.

It was an unusual ferry because the method adopted to catch it was to stand at the water's edge and flap your arms around while shouting out across the Avon to attract the attention of the boatman, Neil Schroeter, who was busy at work on the other side in the thatched boathouse at Bantham. Eventually, after much wild semaphoring and enthusiastic shouting, we received a distant shout and wave of limb in return. Before long, the little wooden ferry, the size of a rowing boat, was chugging towards us and, with shoes and socks removed, we waded out to clamber in over the side.

I wanted to tell Neil that I was the guilty party who had raided his fruit bowl the previous day and what a nice compassionate wife he had, but it was impossible to make myself heard above the loud buzzing drone of the growling engine and the slapping wind and the slopping slosh and wash of the waves. Once the other side he quickly disappeared back into the boathouse where he was restoring a hull.

I walked up the steep slip with Dillon's master, who told me he was a flight engineer working on C130 transport planes at a base in Saudi Arabia. 'I've been living out there too long,' he said. 'At last I'm retiring next year. It'll be good to be home. I'm going to walk Dillon out here every day and then sit in the pub. That's what retired life's all about, eh? Doing what you want with not a care in the world.'

He was off to the pub now and invited me to join him. But I told him I couldn't as I was off on a mission to find some bananas.

I walked past the surfers and up along the coast path where, over Butter Cove, the rain fizzled to a grizzle. Then I hit Thurlestone Golf Course. I watched a woman in checked shorts and matching waistcoat and sun visor, preparing herself for a shot by doing a few peculiar little jumps before placing golf club to rear of ball, wiggling her substantial posterior with such preliminary showy build-up that I felt certain I was about to witness a bonanza of a ball-flight of which Tiger Woods would be proud. Following much fanfare, she at last launched into a grand finale of a flamboyant golf swing and . . . WHAAACK! The ball sliced off at a severely unintended angle and landed all of twelve feet away in the middle of the brush.

I emitted an impulsive yelp of delight.

'Ohh . . . NO-ah!' cried the woman in nasal-toned self-disgust.

Amazingly none of her companions, similarly clad in a busy medley of checks and tartans, saw the funny side. Then another woman took up batting position (or whatever it's called) with a lot of ostentatious swinging, wiggling, jiggling and jumping. But this time, when club hit ball, it was sent flying so far into oblivion that it must have landed in Cornwall.

'SU-per shot, Caroline!' came the tartanesque appraisals.

I don't understand people who enjoy golf. The ones I've seen tend to potter about the manicured green swathes and sand bunkers thinking they are communing with nature (all that grass and fresh air), apparently unaware that nature has been destroyed to create this illusion. Golf seems about as far removed from a sport as you can get. It lacks the crucial element of physical exertion, of pushing the body to the limits, of endurance, power, allurement, vigour and sweat that surely 'real' sport is all about. Mark Twain once said that golf is a good walk spoiled. And John Peel recently said, 'Whenever friends say they've taken up golf, I tend to cross them off. It just seems like an antechamber to death.'

The rain came on heavy again so I sat in the sheltered entrance of Thurlestone's twelfth-century church (on top of which a fire pan once served as a lighthouse) munching my way through some of my freshly purchased post office provisions. As I ate, a golfing couple dressed in golfing civvies sauntered up to the big oak door. I bid them a cheery greeting, which they chose to ignore. But I did have my mouth full at the time, so I let them off.

The man tried the door and said, 'Blast it! It's locked!'

'Oh, what a frightful shame!' came the woman's clipped reply.

And without looking at me, they walked off down the path, protected from the elements beneath a golfing brolly the size of a bunker.

I was surprised the church was locked. It wasn't as if Thurlestone was situated in some roughy-toughy inner city enclave or anything. When I finished eating I lifted the latch and shouldered the door. And it opened. There, what was I saying? No muscles these golfing types!

CHAPTER 24

The fourth of July may be a big celebratory day for Americans, but for us Brits the date marked a more momentous 'National Kissing Day'. Kissing, according to South Hams Radio, is said to be good for keeping tooth decay at bay. To add to the excitement, National Kissing Day coincided with National Bad Trousers Day. The idea of this was to wear the most hideous pair of trousers you possessed and, by way of compensation for all the public scoffing, you could raise 'dare money' for local hospitals.

Back in St Ann's Chapel, I rode past a house called Le Petit Pain and stopped opposite The Pickwick Inn ('A Dickens of a good pub') to buy a drink from the village store. As I stepped back outside I was intercepted by White Van Man, a young, dark, unshaven lad who worked for Compton Cleaning Services.

He was obviously a bicycle man of fine taste because he said, 'That your Roberts? Haven't seen one of those beauts for a while!'

He then led me round to the back of his big, white van to show me his prize offering – a Giant mountain bike.

'I try and fit a ride in every dinner break!' he told me enthusiastically.

In misty dripping weather, I plummeted down and laboured up a series of outrageously steep hills, traversing six severe gradient arrows on my map in the space of half a mile around Oldaport Fort. No wonder my legs felt like wilted celery stalks.

And on I went, pitching up and down the switchbacks through damp green sopping tunnels of sunken lanes until I burst out on a richly wooded creek of the Yealm estuary at Noss Mayo. I barrelled down the hill, leant round the hairpin at Newton Ferrers and then stopped at TREBLES – SHOP AT THE GREEN, which turned out to sell a strange mixture of women's clothing and essential groceries. When the elderly gent behind the counter asked me where I was going he exclaimed, 'You daring little thing, you!' And he presumed I was travelling in my gap year. I had hoped that all the stress of the hills, the 310,000 lightning 'hits', not to mention the endless worry over the early-closing hours of village stores, would have aged me considerably by now, but apparently not.

Then, before I knew it, I was being sucked into Plymouth across the Laira Bridge in driving rain and bow-wave swishing traffic. Apart from The Hoe and the sea and the boats and the friendly corner shop where they gave me a half-price bunch of bananas, I wasn't much smitten with Plymouth. After weeks of thatched villages and dainty hamlets it was a big, scary, car-clogged and architecturally uninspiring wide-road city (after all, it had been bombed to bits in the war). But I liked the people. Especially the couple who came up to me outside Holland and Barrett (more porridge bulk-buying) and told me they had seven bikes between them. I also liked the excitable woman who excitedly said that she cycled eight miles to work every day from her home in Wembury and seemed to spend half her life ringing up the local council to rant about the appalling design of the city's cycle paths.

'There are two cycling officers on the council,' she told me with an exasperated air, 'and neither of them cycle. So how can they have any idea of what is needed if they don't ride the streets themselves?'

I knew what she meant. Entering the city earlier along the A379, I had joined a strip of cycle track that turned into a shattered glass-covered pavement before leading me straight into the path of a row of parked cars. Personally I suspect that these sporadic cycle routes are a conspiracy thought up by the council just to kill us cyclists off. That way they don't get rung up by excitable two-wheeled oddities ranting and raving to them down the blower and can concentrate on the important issues in life, like how to kill cities with cars.

I thought about cycling up and down and all around the estuaries of the rivers Tary and Tamar. But that's all I did – think about it. And it was a thought that didn't last long, thanks to the rain-shrouded mist and dirty-grey skies that had dropped so low they had blotted out all signs of Brunel's Royal Albert railway bridge stretching out its girders to Cornwall.

So I boarded the Cremyll passenger ferry, propped my bike in the *Northern Belle*'s bows and, six minutes later, me and the five other passengers had chugged across the Devil's Point mouth of The Sound and stepped into Cornwall.

It was drizzling and I was hungry. Again. But I found a prize position to picnic, sheltering in a folly of Mount Edgcumbe country park – an 800-acre expanse of lawns and gardens and woodlands and follies and temples and arches and terraces and deer herds that enveloped a very large red-stoned crenellated and turreted Tudor house – the walls of which survived a direct hit by bombs in 1941.

Playing outside in the garden entrance of the house a group of young teenagers sat enthusiastically clashing and banging and blowing and horning and tromboning as part of their brass band school concert. Despite the cold damp wind, the dismal mist, the perpetually gusty drizzle and, save for a handful of proud parents, the non-existent audience, the band continued playing in a very 'the-show-must-go-on' Titanic-sinking way. Any other nationality would have given up long ago and waited for the sun to come out.

I inched onwards to Cawsand Bay, which, in the eighteenth century, was a popular centre for smuggling when bladders of brandy, concealed beneath women's skirts, were taken to Plymouth. I rounded Rame Head, jiggled past Wiggle, and then, catching sight of dozens of small wooden chalets and cabins clinging like limpets to the Cliffside over Whitsand Bay, raced with the wind towards the former pilchard-fishing harbour of Portwrinkle. From there it was down to the long cliff and sea-squeezed strip of Downderry – wedged in by beach and steep slopes with its Downcliff and Stormcrest and Sea-Fever sea-flavoured house names. There was no room for any fancy alternatives round here. It was all sea or all nothing.

Overlooking Seaton's beach of coarse grey sand and popples, I rang the builder and he told me how, cycling to the wood yard that morning, he had come up against the Charge of the Light Brigade in the form of a legion of rabbits, running flat out down the sunken lane towards him. Oddly, they didn't alter course when they saw him, just kept stampeding past. The explanation for this bizarre behaviour came seconds later when a fox, going like the clappers, rounded the corner in hot pursuit.

On my way to No Man's Land, I passed the Monkey Sanctuary (full of the Amazon woolly variety) before a hard-earned descent down into Looe past Great Tree and Sunrising was ruined by a black, tinted-window Mercedes four-wheel-drive that lurched out to overtake me into oncoming traffic and then braked on every corner hindering my spinning wheels from smoothly swooping and falling. Another deserved recipient for a rotten-tomato machine-gun job.

Wheeling carefully among the throngs of tourists, I entered the narrow cobbled streets and twisting alleys of East Looe (HQ of the Shark-sighting Club of Great Britain – formerly the Shark Fishing Club of Great Britain) and went down to the end of Banjo Pier where an old, cider-swilling Polperro man with ruined teeth and drink-shiny eyes told me he used to ride a fixed-wheel every day round this area when he was a boy. I was impressed. Riding a one-geared bike up and down these monster hills was no mean feat. I had twenty-seven gears and that still wasn't enough. But then I am only a little thing in my gap year. Or so I've been told.

Across the seven-arched stone bridge and not far from the sixteenth-century Jolly Sailor Inn, I sat on the quayside in a sudden ray of sunshine eating my lunch. As I ate I stared at boats and barnacles. It was the barnacles that really grabbed my attention. A busy bevy of these marine crustaceans were locked on to the harbour wall beside my dangling legs and I became totally preoccupied with trying to knock a few off. But they were very nicely settled, thank you very much, and had no intention of being budged. Barnacles owe such stubbornness to a cement-like substance secreted by their antennae. More fascinating than their renowned rock- and hull-fixed intractabilities is the lesser-known fact that a barnacle is equipped with a penis twenty times the length of its body. I'll say no more. Actually I'll say a little bit more. If I may. Because these barnacles got me thinking about penises, which may not be a common link for a train of thought to take, but, well, that's the way it works for me. The phenomenal size of a barnacle's penis made me think about female hyenas (which have a penis) and reptiles (many of which have two penises to maximise their mating opportunites) and male seahorses (which give birth). And this led me on to thinking about the mating rituals of the *Pseudoceros bifurcus* flatworm, which lives off Australia's Great Barrier Reef. When it wants sex it stabs its mate with its penis. But as the species is a hermaphrodite, its partner also has a penis, and it jabs its penis in return. This ritual is known as 'penis fencing'. Apparently, only one out of six strikes leads to successful copulation, but the stabs that miss leave several flatworms badly injured. Isn't this just an elaborate form of what young, hormone-busting lads have been doing for years with their so-called trouser snakes?

Anyway, all I really wanted to say was that there's more to a barnacle than meets the eye. So I let them be on the wall.

While I was struggling up the long steep lane of West Looe Hill to Portooe, another woman stopped her car and offered to take my bags to the top. Dear me, I thought, I must really look in a bad way. There was a time when I could cycle over an Alp before breakfast and now I couldn't even get up a West Country hillock without people running to my aid. In spite of the temptation, I adhered to my rule that it was better to half die on a hill than to wave good-bye to bagfuls of mouldy tents and dirty washing.

I spent a couple of nights camping on top of a hill just outside Barcelona. My reason for spending two nights in this one location was because, unlike its namesake, it rained. Endlessly. The first night, squalls roared in overnight, throwing dirty weather and drenching rain upon my tent. This very wet form of rain remained with me all the next day, though gradually slackening into an all-pervasive Cornish sea mist. To prevent myself from getting 'tent rot' I decided to walk from Talland Bay to Polperro – an admirable two miles of the 630-mile South West Coast Path (the longest walking trail in Britain). And then I walked back again.

I would like to be able to say what splendidly craggy cliffs and spume-splashed scenery I looked down upon but, thanks to thick mist, I only heard the heaving seas crashing and frothing on the rocks far below, and smelt the brine and felt the salt spray lash my face with its intoxicating verve. Apart from my feet and the slippy muddy trail, I couldn't see a thing. Saying that, I did see some words on the back of the door in the cold, gusty and dripping public toilets on Talland Beach: 'Bored Housewife. Anything goes. Ring Sarah . . .'

I was about to give her a ring but I had better things to be doing with myself. Like buying bananas. This in fact was my sole purpose for slogging through the undesirable elements to Polperro. When I finally arrived, as sopping and stiff as a frozen cod fillet, I found that the only greengrocers in town had shut at 2 p.m. And it wasn't even Wednesday, for heaven's sake! It was Monday! Although there were other food shops open, not one of these stores sold a single banana. No, the only hope was the greengrocers and they were closed. Shut up shop. Dark. Gone home. Pressing my dripping, bleak-featured face up against the window, I could see in the dimness a whole row of sunny yellow bananas happily hanging from their sturdy steel S-hooks. Oh, the agony of it all!

By this stage I was so traumatised that I went to wander round a museum, which goes to prove what a very mentally unstable state I was in. As it happened, this was quite a fortuitous move as Polperro's 'Heritage Museum of Smuggling and Fishing' momentarily took my mind off my fruitless state.

The museum was the old pilchard factory. Pilchards were once a staple food of Cornwall because of the prolific shoals that swam around the coast. Special pilchard spotters looked out for the immense shadow of a mass of fish in the water and alerted the fishermen for huge landings. Cornwall's celebrated stargazey pie, with its pilchard heads poking out of a sea of pastry, originated at this time of fishy surplus. But not all pilchards were eaten locally – each year, from the 1850s to the beginning of the twentieth century, some 12,000 tons of pilchards would be exported, mostly to Italy.

On the walls of the museum hung old, time-tinged photographs of men hauling in 1000 stone of pilchards on a wooden vessel called *Our Daddy*. The pilchard fishermen appeared to have a great affinity for specialised pullovers. Several pictures (circa 1910) showed them clothed in Polperro 'knitfrocks' – the thick Guernsey sweaters knitted in one of the traditional patterns used by Polperro fishermen's wives. One fisherman, Tim Curtis, was even wearing a pair of very fetching knitted braces.

The fishermen looked like a fine, strapping bunch of strong sea-weathered men, with a fine selection of monikers to match: Jack 'Spanish' Langmaid; Dick 'Dingle' Curtis; Bill 'Butcher' Curtis; Charlie 'Pudden' Hicks; Samuel 'Shot' Puckey; Jack 'Jack 1' Jolliff; Dick 'Lalley' Jolliff; Thomas 'Boy Doy' Jolliff; Alfie 'No father, no mother' Jolliff. Only Dicky Searle had no nickname. But they did all have hats; either flat caps or peaked caps or berets or, in one case, a semi-bowler.

Then there was the smuggling, which was so rife in the eighteenth century that the trade with Polperro, organised by Zephaniah Job (known as the Smugglers' Banker), involved almost all the village's inhabitants from the Rev. Sir Harry Trelawny to the local innkeeper. Life for the locals seemed to revolve around shipping, storing or transporting contraband goods. There was, as they say, 'baccy for the preacher and brandy for the squire'. To combat the problem, Polperro was the first place in England to have its own 'Revenue Men', who were as unpopular with the general public then as they are now. No villagers would billet them so the taxmen had to sleep on board their ship. In a picture of them taken around 1860 they all looked miserable, as they stood shouldering their bayonet rifles with glum expressions.

More storms and unseasonable gales battered me for the next few days. At times the dips of the narrow lanes became so flooded I had to forge through deep lakes of china-clay muddy waters. At night, I lay within my tent listening to the drumming of the saturated sky waterfalling upon my flimsy dwelling while watching with alarm the mud and floods rising fast around me.

The weather was so bad that even the newly opened Eden Project, the £86 million development at St Austell that recreates Earth's climates under giant bubble-like domes or 'biomes' (forming the world's biggest greenhouse) in a former china-clay gravel pit, was urging people to stay away on wet days because it couldn't cope with the thousands of visitors flocking to see it. On one rainy morning alone, 9000 people in 3000 cars tried to get in to see what the people in the know say is arguably the biggest tourism success story of the new century. And judging from the streams of traffic, clogged roads and thicket of fumes, I think I saw and smelt and felt them all. Banishing cars to boost the project's green credentials is now a priority for Eden.

The sun did momentarily burst out of a cloud-hole further down the mountainous coast in the fishing village of Mevagissey. This was quite an appropriate place to be lit up in a beam of sudden sunlight as Mevagissey was the first place to have electric street lighting – powered by pilchard oil.

After filling up my water bottles in the Sharksfin Hotel, I sat on the harbour wall outside the Shark Angling Centre. As I ate my lunch I was stared at solidly by a worrying man sitting on the opposite wall who was so bald and so bearded it looked as if he had his head on upside down. I put on my sunglasses and angled myself to make it look as if I was watching the water when really I was monitoring his movements. At one point he made an obscene gesture with his tongue and finger so I packed up and left.

But not very fast. Look at an Ordnance Survey map of the small and compact village of Mevagissey and you can count up a leg-trembling total of nine arrows indicating killer hills. On top of that, most of the street names seem to indicate inclines of one kind or another, what with School Hill, Tregoney Hill, Polkirt Hill, Cliff Road and Cliff Street. I think it might act as a caveat to cyclists if Mevagissey reverted to its name in the Middle Ages: a back-to-basics Porthilly.

For the next few days, Cornwall was a wall of hills. My life revolved around an endless exhaustive switchback of climbing and falling, climbing and falling. It was impossible to get into any kind of riding rhythm because, compared with spending a whole day or more crossing a mountain range when muscles relax into a same and certain pace, the incessant short sharp corrugations of Cornish hills cruelly send your confused and screaming legs all over the place. Your muscles are in complete disarray. They don't know what's happening. The reward for straining and struggling up gradients that forever went much further up than down was a split-second free-fall drop of feverish speed until I was upon the apparently compulsory ingredient of every hill in Cornwall – an ancient stone-humped narrow bridge and a hairpin bend. And then it was there. That wall. To start all over again. To hurt all over again. But that's what makes cycling fun – the intensity of the pleasure and pain.

Near Portholland, I pulled into St Michael Caerhays church for a rest and a food stop. With strength replenished I had a look inside the 700-year-old church and found a parish magazine in which I read that: 'A local farmer has stated how pleasant it has been not to have dog excrement on his land during the foot-and-mouth ban. Also the farm animals have been free of parasite diseases that are transmitted through dog excrement. Dog owners please note and please "pick up" after your dogs on the footpaths as well as other areas. Thank you.'

Elsewhere in the magazine I found a statement by Robert Frost which suggested he had never tried cycling in Cornwall:

> Happiness makes up in height
> for what it lacks in length.

On a campsite near Veryan, I met a mother and daughter camping together. The mother drove a white VW Polo and slept in a big blue inflatable tent shaped like an igloo, while her daughter rode a red 650cc BMW motorcycle and slept in a small and lightweight Vaude one-man tent. After hailing me up by the telephone box to ask me if I was who I was, to which I said I think I am, she told me her name was Carol and that she too had once cycled alone in Norway. But she had found it all too big.

'Everything was on such a large scale,' she said, 'I felt so small and insignificant. I also found it all a bit like hard work! I had to do a lot of pushing! I could have done with an engine!'

Oh no! Not an engine!

On her return home, Carol found an engine in the form of a motorbike, which she bought off a friend on the spur of the moment. She took her test and now loves motorcycling.

'I still cycle though,' she added, 'but my friends can't understand it when I do because they're all petrol-heads.'

Originally from Nottingham, she now lived in London.

'And I always vowed I would never live in the Southeast!'

She told me she managed an ecology centre in south London.

'I said I would do it for three years and then travel round the world. But I'm still doing it. I do still want to travel round the world, but I probably never will. It's just a dream.'

CHAPTER 25

At three minutes to seven on Radio 4, Everton Fox launched with time-squeezed gusto into the morning forecast: '. . . heavy rain is making for some tricky driving conditions . . . so take care out there.' But Everton, I thought, it's not really that tricky because if you're driving you're not 'out there', you're 'in there' – in your vehicle, sealed from the elements, warm and dry in your comfy armchairs with music, mobile, food and fags. Also, Everton, if you're telling motorists to 'take care' re rain, could you also ask them to 'take care' with lesser mortals than they on the roads? Because yesterday I was cut up on my bike by a car. I managed to 'discuss' the matter with the driver, a man in his sixties, who apologised and said he didn't see me because he was 'watching the traffic'.

'But I *am* the traffic!' I told him. 'Just a self-propelled version!'

I finished off my breakfast, eaten to the accompaniment of rain hammering down on my tent, and set out to ride to the end and back of the mellifluous-sounding Roseland Peninsula, which has nothing to do with roses and everything to do with long sticking-out bits because, in Cornish, *ros* means peninsula.

On the edge of Portscatho, I stopped in Gerrans village store to buy some provisions. The shopkeeper, a large and fleshy northerner who wore a voluminous singlet revealing a wayward bra strap that had slipped to her elbow, was on the phone when I entered. It was a long-winded call. Eventually, she plonked down the receiver and, turning to me, said, 'Don't you *hate* pushy salesmen?'

'I can't say I'm too keen,' I replied.

'Soon as I get one on the line I just want to throw the phone down!' she said forcefully, wiping several beads of sweat from her brow; she was obviously quite het up.

'I know,' I replied, 'I've thrown a few phones down in my time!'

That night I listened to 'Crossing Continents', a programme on Radio 4 presented by Julian Pettifer. He was travelling around the United States in a small seventy-miles-to-the-gallon car, trying to understand America's refusal to cut fossil fuel emissions (with 4% of the world's population, the US is responsible for 25% of greenhouse emissions). At one point he talked to an SUV salesman (Sport Utility Vehicle – America's version of the four-wheel-drive) who explained to him that these vehicles have now become so essential because 'there are some crazy drivers out there who drive at crazy speeds, so you need more metal around you for protection'. Later Pettifer interviewed an SUV owner who described his ozone-eating vehicle, which did fourteen miles to the gallon, as 'real pretty'. When asked if he would consider driving a smaller vehicle if fuel prices were equal to those in the UK, he said, 'Hell, no. I like my comfort. I'll pay whatever it takes to have a comfy ride.'

Crossing over the River Fal on the King Harry Ferry (motto: More Fun – Less Stress – Less Pollution) I met a man called Norman in a red camper van. Not the Norman from Norman's supermarket in Budleigh Salterton, but the Norman Nokes married to Hazel. Or so I learnt. Leaning out of his window, Norman was interested to know the weight of my bike. I told him roughly sixty kilos, depending on how much food and water I had on board. Then Norman wanted to know if I was on a sabbatical. This gladdened me greatly because I had obviously aged significantly in the last few days. No longer was I presumed to be of a gap year age, but now looked old enough and sophisticated enough to be a university professor. Or something like that.

Suddenly it seemed the tide had turned away from people telling me I needed a motor to one where they wanted to know the weight of my bike. Not long after my encounter with Norman, I was cycling up a hill somewhere near Goonpiper, which is just south of Come-to-Good (which in itself is just south of Playing Place), when a man in deck shoes, immaculately pressed shorts and a Henley boater said in a clean-cut voice, 'My God! How much weight are you carrying on there?' Dutifully, I told him.

His little flaxen-haired daughter stared at me uncomprehendingly.

Then he wanted to know whether I had come across on the King Harry Ferry. I told him that I had and he told me that he owned it. Had done for two years, no less. I found this hard to believe. I imagined people who owned ferries to look like Captain Birdseye. But Regatta-hatted Man looked more the sort you'd find in a striped blazer punting down the Thames with an ice-bucketed bottle of champagne at his feet.

I asked him how he had come to own a ferry.

'I saw it advertised for sale in the local paper,' he said.

I laughed. The thought of seeing a ferry for sale tucked in among the ads for old bedsteads and Thomas the Tank Engine duvet covers ('As new. Unwanted gift.') struck me as rather funny. 'So was buying this ferry a spur of the moment thing, rather than a life-long ambition?'

'Well, I had been in the army for twenty years when I felt the time had come to lead a more peaceful life,' he said.

So in a devil-may-care sort of way, he answered the ad, bought the King Harry and downshifted to Cornwall.

'Come *on*, Daddy!' called his daughter impatiently as she kicked stones across the road.

'I'm coming, dear,' he replied rather grandly as if responding to a great aunt demanding attention rather than his own four-year-old infant.

As he was being dragged off down the road by his daughter's hand, Regatta-hatted Man glanced back over his shoulder and called, 'All the best of British luck!' And I laughed, because I didn't think people really said that any more.

At Mylor Bridge I filled up my water bottles in Cornwall's oldest inn, The Pandora, which dates from the thirteenth century. It was given its present name by the commander of HMS *Pandora* who sailed to the South Seas to capture the *Bounty* mutineers after they set their commander, Lt William Bligh, adrift in an open boat in 1789.

The sun came out so I sat in its fleeting warmth on a wall over Mylor Creek. A small boy was playing alone in the shallow waters. He was happy and humming away. Then a voice cried out from a house whose garden backed on to the creek. It was his mum, and she was calling the boy in to lunch.

'What is it?' he shouted back.

'Pasty,' came the reply.

Ah, the great Cornish pasty. That plump, traditional tin-miner's mainstay that was once described by the American food critic, William Grimes, as 'only good for being used as a doorstop'. Pasty makers responded with a ceremonial burning of the Stars and Stripes. Though William Grimes might not have been too taken with the pasty, many people are: Cornwall produces three million pasties a week, and exports 90% across the Tamar.

After several minutes of under-rock investigations, the boy splashed back up the creek towards his house.

'MUM!' he yelled. 'Can you hear me splashing?'

Of course mum couldn't hear him splashing because she was busy deep in the kitchen serving up hot pasties.

The boy climbed up the rock wall and over some raggled sheep-netting before jumping down into his garden. He then stood in dripping shoes and shouted, 'MUM! I saw two eels. A big eel this big . . .' (demonstration of wide crucified arms) '. . . and a baby eel this big . . .' which, with arms remaining at full splayed stretch, appeared just as big as the big eel. Definitely a fine fisherman in the making.

In Falmouth High Street, I bumped into Norman and Hazel from the King Harry Ferry. Norman still had a raft of questions up his sleeve to fire at me so he gave me his address in Whitley Bay.

'If you ever make it north of the Tyne,' he said, 'come and say hello.'

I told him that if I did, I would.

Henry VIII reared his head again at Pendennis Point. The castle he completed here in 1545 was yet another of his chain of defences along England's south coast. Riding up around Castle Drive I looked out over and into the mighty Falmouth Docks that included the very imperial King's Wharf, Queen's Wharf, Empire Wharf, Duchy Wharf and County Wharf. On the other side of the headland in Falmouth Bay sat a stack of parked cars containing a fine selection of the Great British Public eating sandwiches wrapped in tinfoil and drinking tea out of thermoses while staring silently out upon a horizontal greyness of brooding sea through their insect-splattered windscreens.

That night I spent camping up at Pennance Mill Farm. Early the next morning, a fieldful of lowing dairy cattle plodded in line along a well-trodden path, an elongated udder-length away from my tent. They mooed and chewed and stopped and slopped on their way to the milking shed. Rounding them up from the rear the local ruddy-cheeked cowman chivvied and chided them along with calls and commands and the random hind-whack hit with his stick.

'Had a few showers in the noight,' he said to me as he trundled by.

Two hours later the cows, looking lesser of udder, were back. Along with the cowman.

'It's looking noice now,' he said, a man of many words.

He was right. It was looking nice now as I packed up my tent in a warming patch of sun. Cramming the last of my clobber into a fit-to-bursting pannier, I was intercepted by Frank Parker, who told me he had been at a fire-free cycling talk I had given in Stafford in May. He and his wife Val were down this way to visit their son, Chris, who built the Trice range of recumbent tricycles over at the Tregoniggie Industrial Estate in Falmouth. Frank and Val told me they had a Trice tandem, an amazing-looking machine with its two wheels up front sandwiching a sunlounger-type seat, while stretching several furlongs behind on a similar seat sat the stoker, Val.

'It's revolutionised my cycling,' she said. 'Now I can lie back in style and never get left behind!'

More hills saw me to Mawnan Smith, where I stopped at the village Spar for food supplies. The woman behind the counter was a boisterous local who wore her light auburn hair in tight St Trinian bunches.

'What are you looking tired for?' she demanded. 'There're no hills in Cornwall. It's just a myth!'

It didn't quite ring true. Specially not when, a few over-undulating miles later along the densely wooded Helford River, I hit the hills of Nancenoy that my map marked as a crumpled collection of dips and arrows and double arrows. Two of these hills were so steep and so over-shaded and drippingly green and slippery (it was drizzling again) that I kept getting wheelspin. I tried pushing but even my feet kept spinning out of control. I struggled and battled and scuffled and wrestled and almost gave up, thinking I would either have to lose some ballast in my bags or take an alternative route inland through Comfort and Constantine. In the end, in a last-ditch state of near-zonked despair, I grabbed hold of my handlebars while simultaneously mounting the bank with my feet like a starting block. Only by adopting a sort of Superman-in-flight stance, pushing at such an acute skew-whiff full-stretch horizontal, feet practically level with my head, could I combat the North Face of Nancenoy.

Everything was so exquisitely iridescently green. I passed through dripping jungles of palm trees and Australian tree ferns and vast rhododendrons, giant rhubarb and cala lilies. And then, after a mad rushing gush downward, I was up against yet another hill, creaking painfully slowly towards the tree tops in my lowest of granny gears – all traces of speed and energy diminishing by the milli-second – when I came upon an elderly couple walking down the lane towards me.

Referring to the even steeper incline ahead, the woman said, 'You're not going to cycle up *that*, are you?'

'Certainly not!' I replied and promptly got off to push.

But instead of pushing I chatted (any excuse for a rest). The woman was Swedish and told me she had come to England in her early twenties to learn English. Here she had met her husband, a film animation man, and lured him back to Sweden.

'Because the weather is better in Sweden,' she said. 'At least the summers are. In England it rains *all* the time!'

Not all the time – it's nice between the end of July and the start of August.

Mr Swede looked at my bike and muttered something about needing a motor. I didn't tell him he was the 127th person to say that to me. Then Mrs Swede presumed I couldn't even yet be twenty, could I? *Oh no! Just when I thought I had aged, my hopes are dashed.* To save argument, not to mention energy (I still had that prodigious vertiginous hill at my feet), I gamely went along with her teenager presumptions. But then I immediately became unstuck when Mrs Swede asked me if I had ever been to Sweden.

'Yes,' I said, 'I cycled across Sweden in 1987 on my way to Iceland.'

That's when I put my foot in it because, if I wasn't yet twenty, then I would have been about six when I rode across her motherland with those accident-prone moose tripping over my tent.

The mid-July weather remained wet, wild and wintry while the hills continued to veer more up than down. Nights were spent lying congealed with cold in my tent. I battled onwards through the undesirable elements past the deadly ship-wrecking rocks of the Mannacles before heading over the bleak moorland of the Goonhilly Downs, with their faintly disturbing extra-terrestrial satellite-dished 'Earth Station', until I hit upon a rarity: a long straight hill-free road on the way to Lizard Point – the most southerly tip of mainland Britain (only three more points to go, plus a few thousand islands and Ireland). All over the Lizard Peninsula I kept reading and hearing how it was the warmest and one of the sunniest places in Britain, with a difference of only 8°C between average daily temperatures in summer and winter. But as a rattlingly cold, salt-laden westerly gale swept in off the Atlantic I felt as if I was standing more on one of the wettest and windiest places in the world. The only advantage of being blessed with such appalling weather was that, despite being at the heady heights of holiday season, I had the extremity of this remote peninsula to myself. As the high heaped seas sent lofty plumes of white water spuming over the Man of War Rocks, I stood getting spectacularly wind-slapped and wave-splashed. It felt fittingly lovely.

Camping up on the hills at Trelowarren, I became friendly with Angie and Ginger, gipsy-souled sorts who, when not running the campsite, seemed to be constantly on the move, roaming around the country in their caravan. Angie, a small buxom blonde, had five children, while Ginger, a big strapping chap with a ponytail, pacemaker, piratical bandanna and large looped bull-nose ear-ring, had two. Together they had ten grandchildren, whom they only managed to see about once a year because of their itinerant lifestyle. As a result, their grandchildren called them Faraway Granny and Granddad.

Angie was quite unusual because she said she was actually frightened of houses. They had bought one once, in Mousehole, but in twenty years they only lived there for seven weeks. She hated the feeling of such solidity. Their current idea was to design a narrowboat, which would serve as their mobile home for the next decade or two.

Strangely, for such a portable lifestyle, Ginger had a collection of the most untransportable objects: milk bottles. He had over a thousand. They were all British Unigate bottles but each of them was different and all of them were rare. Some cost £100, some cost £1000 or more. I had never met a milk bottle collector before. Whereas to me Ginger's collection looked nothing more than shelf after shelf of old bottles (many were pre-war), to him they represented mini works of art. This was not just because of their shape and size: they also had aluminium adverts stamped on their sides. For health and safety reasons, this practice has been banned for the past thirty or so years because the aluminium prevents some of the bacteria from being destroyed when the bottles go through the pasteurisation process.

A lot of the bottles carried straightforward adverts but the majority were, as Ginger put it, 'quite beautifully done'.

Pointing to one species of bottle, he said, 'Look at these, me lovely . . .' (he was always calling me his 'lovely') '. . . they're hand-etched, rare and worth a bob or two. While these ones here are quite comical with Walt Disney characters. They're rare too and much sought after.'

Ginger had the full fifteen different Cornflakes, Weetabix, and Humphrey collections.

'Most collectors will have maybe seven or eight of a kind,' he said with evident satisfaction, 'but to get the complete collection takes time and patience.'

I had to keep reminding myself that we were talking about milk bottles and not an anthology of fossilised bone fragments from a Tyrannosaurus rex.

Advert-style bottles aside, Ginger also had some of the very first milk bottles that had ever hit the streets – large heavy bottles with an inverted lip, which contained a cardboard insert to stop birds from drinking the milk. He also had two eighteen-sided pint bottles in mint condition that he said were 'very rare'. Another had a solid silver spout brazed on to the bottle ('the only one of its kind'). Then there were the quart bottles (2 pints), ⅓ pints, ½ pints and ¼ pints. The ⅓ pint bottles were the same size we used to have at school, given out, so the governmental propaganda went, 'FREE – to build strong teeth and bones'. (Didn't make me grow, though.)

What, I wondered, makes someone suddenly start collecting milk bottles?

'Well, me lovely,' said Ginger, 'I was just struck by the art and beauty of some of them. And away I went. Searching hedgerows, dumps, boot sales, auctions and chasing after milk floats all over the country from John of Groats [*sic*] to Land's End. I have always got me weather eye open for new bottles.'

He offered to show me some pages off the internet entitled MILK BOTTLE NEWS, but by then I was feeling in serious need of some alternative entertainment.

CHAPTER 26

So I got back on my bike and continued west to Porthleven where, opposite an ice-cream shop called 'NAUTI BUT ICE', I spotted a memorial stone set in the harbour wall:

TO COMMEMORATE
POLICE CONSTABLES
JOE CHILDS AND MARTIN REID
Who drowned on the night of the
13th December 1978
when their police car was swept in this harbour
during a violent storm.

Although it was still five months till December, it was not hard to visualise such turbulent conditions: another unseasonable storm was raging as I raced round Mount's Bay to Penzance, where I camped in the waterlogged grounds of the hostel. Better to be a damp squid alone with myself in the Great Outdoors, than all fugged and fidgety within the crowded bunkhouse.

The next morning dawned big, bright and sparkling and I bombed off back down the hill through Penzance to land on the decks of the *Scillonian III*, the rampant-with-schoolchildren ferry that delivered me and crated steed twenty-eight miles southwest of Land's End to the Scilly Isles – where it was cold and grey and raining.

Legend has it that the Isles of Scilly are all that remain of Lyonnesse, a magical land ruled over by King Arthur before it vanished beneath the Atlantic. (The previous day I had cycled past The Loe, a lake of brackish water near Porthleven, the lake into which King Arthur is said to have thrown his sword, Excalibur.) Of the hundred or more islands, only five are inhabited and on all of these wild camping is prohibited. So, along with the straggling school parties and squadrons of scouts, I camped up at Garrison Farm on St Mary's – the largest of the islands, where all but about 350 of Scilly's population of 2000 live.

After cramming myself in a corner behind the remnants of the eighteenth-century stone ramparts, I found myself caught up in a water-bomb attack when innocently walking to the toilet block through the besieged area of the scouts' battalion. Once undercover in the Ladies, I soon became caught up in a battle of a different nature. As I was washing my socks a schoolgirl came rushing in, her arms full of lettuces which she proceeded to rinse in a drain-clogged basin two up from me. Moments later a clatter of feet announced the arrival of further school-girls. They screeched to a halt and stared slack-jawed at the lettuce-washer.

'Oh my god!' they exclaimed, in disgusted tones. 'What do you think you're doing? That's *so* unhygienic! You can't wash lettuces in here – the basins are *dis-gusting*!'

Miss Lettuce Washer retorted, 'Well, it's a lot more hygienic than the sinks in the washing-up area!'

And up to a point she was right; the washing-up sinks were clogged with filthy bacteria-breeding cloths and the tangled remnants of the scouts' spaghetti.

'If you don't want to eat it,' continued Miss Lettuce Washer, a beleaguered prawn in a sea of belligerent piranha, 'then that's your problem!'

Although I was doing a very good job at pretending to be totally unaware of the vitriolic world of words being batted about around me, concentrating only on removing a stubborn ingrained oil stain from my socks, Miss Lettuce Washer suddenly turned on me and said, almost accusingly, 'So! What do *you* think?'

Oh no! Don't ask me! I'm only a sock-washer! Everyone's faces turned in my direction, watching and awaiting a response. As a tomboy during my misspent youth, I was never very good at girly matters. Whenever a female altercation arose, I either thumped my opponent or went running back to my brothers to release my frustration in a brotherly brawl. So now, finding myself drawn into a schoolgirl squabble, I had no idea how to react. Not wanting to incite fervour on either side, I decided the best thing for it was to adopt peace-making mode.

'Well, seeing as you've asked me,' I said as the bickering bevy held their breath, 'I would say that in their own different ways the sinks are probably all as unhygienic as each other. But washing food in them will probably contribute to giving you a healthier constitution in the long run as your large intestines will undoubtedly build up a robust resistance to fight further infection.' (I was thinking friendly flora here.)

Judging from the expressions on their faces, I don't think that my audience was bargaining on an impromptu biology lesson on the gastrointestinal tract and the lower duodenum.

Thankfully I was spared further involvement because another anti-Lettuce Washer girl came charging round the corner. She took one look at the leaves of said lettuces floating forlornly among a mat of long black hairs in the basin and cried, 'Urgh! How *vile* can you get?'

For Miss Lettuce Washer, this was the final straw that broke the little gem's heart – she exploded in a screaming tirade of expletives before running off in floods of tears. The remaining gaggle of girls erupted in cruel cackles and howls of delighted laughter. And I was left to slink back to my tent feeling bad that I had solved nothing. But at least I had clean socks.

The following morning it wasn't so much raining as drizzling. My waking to this drizzle had coincided with hearing Peter Cockroft on Radio 4's five-past-six weather forecast talking about plenty of drizzle around in southwest England. As I lay cocooned in my mummified sleeping bag summoning up enthusiasm to tackle the drizzle, I thought about what a strange word 'drizzle' was. When applied to weather, it conjures up visions of darkness and dullness and greyness, whereas when applied in culinary terms it suggests Mediterranean sunshine pouring forth from a TV chef's bottle of extra virgin olive oil. Rick Stein, Nick Nairn, Gary Rhodes and the saintly Delia and Nigella drizzle all the time. Even Jamie Oliver, who likes to come over all nakedly rough and ready ('Do yerself a favour!') can 'scatter with torn basil leaves and drizzle with balsamic vinegar'. In nineteenth-century meteorological use, drizzle was strictly something between a 'mizzle' (this often kept ladies indoors, tied to their needlework, in Jane Austen novels) and a 'shower'. But now it can be sprinkled over food just as much as it can be lightly sprayed from the sky.

Two hours later the drizzle had fizzled out and made way for the sun. The green ground steamed. Suddenly it was hot.

After a leisurely few hours cycling around every cyclable road (there aren't a lot of roads to be found on the Scillies), I turned to foot and spent the week walking round the islands of St Martin's, St Agnes, Tresco, Bryher and uninhabited Samson with its glamorous curl of ivory sand. Any postcards round here, if you could find them, would be more Bora Bora than Benny Hill. I spotted dolphins (dead and alive – a lot get washed up on Cornwall's beaches after getting entangled in the furlongs of fishermen's trawling nets slung across the North Atlantic) and survived vicious aerial attacks from a shrieking squabble of dive-bombing seagulls.

With eyeballs still intact I made it back to Penzance, where once again I camped up at the youth hostel. This time, though, because the sun was still out, I was surrounded by an overflow of hostellers in hired tents. On one side of me I had a small, dumpy man with an Ayatollah Khomeini beard and a single forehead-spanning eyebrow who sat stiff and unsmiling. Later on he did a lot of very disconcerting grunting in his tent. On the other side of me I had two young Korean girls who seemed very timid and uncertain of everything, including the toilets. Further away, but sadly not out of earshot, congregated a pack of rumbustious teenage lads, who looked like escapees from a juvenile detention centre – their prison-pale faces, pinched and sun-starved, their hair cropped to a fuzz. They all appeared intent on making as much skull-splitting noise as possible while getting legless on litres of cheap cider swilled from dirty-brown plastic bottles. Fortunately, around eight in the evening, they all went trooping off to town in a serious boozed-up state and all silence-activated thought cells had a chance to regroup.

The peace was shattered about midnight when the escapees returned to their tents in ever more clamorous style. There followed an excruciating hour of mind-scraping sounds of beer cans being crunched and stamped and kicked, snorting howls of drunken laughter and incessant zingings of tent zips zapping up and down. Just as my patience was verging on the point of insanity, pushing me to shed my shield of English reserve and yell something very unpleasant at the cacophonous throng, someone else did it for me.

'WILL YOU SHUT THE FUCK UP!' hollered my hirsute neighbour, with such explosive resonance that I felt my eardrums rattle and my spine vibrate.

But such body-shaking moments were a small price to pay. The ayatollah's outburst did the trick. I heard not another sound.

It was even hotter the next morning when I set out for the final assault to Land's End. But rather than arriving fighting fit in flourishing style at this westernmost theme park, I limped in lame and in pain. Though spirit was willing, the starboard knee was weak. It had given up the ghost.

I was not happy. In fact I was thoroughly unhappy. I hated my knee for letting me down despite knowing that a destructive mentality does nothing to aid recovery. Several years earlier when the same knee had broken down on me (yes, that old onion) I had been told by a touchy-feely practitioner to 'love' my knee back to a full bill of health. But I'm not very good at things like this.

There are certain things in my life I can love very easily, and a malfunctioning joint that prevents me from cycling is not one of them. No, that hot July day I felt I hated my knee just as much as I suddenly hated Land's End.

I have arrived at Land's End several times by bicycle, but it had never been as bad as this. Maybe it was my knee, maybe it was my mood, maybe it was the heat of my skull-splintering headache. Or maybe it was the noise of the cars and the coaches and the crowds and the endless array of garish 'themes'. 'Land's End is a priceless part of Britain's heritage, we take our conservation responsibilities very seriously,' said the *Make a day of it! – Legendary Land's End* leaflet. In that case, why make such a stunningly wild and rocky place into a gaudy and tacky Disneyworld with such delights as the 'Air and Sea Rescue Motion Theatre', 'Wreckreation Adventure Playzone' and 'Smugglers Burger Bar'? (Surely no one in their right mind would want to smuggle-a-burger.) What is so wrong with standing at the end of an exposed bony finger of land that points out into the tempestuous Atlantic and appreciating it simply for its stark rugged beauty?

Instead, if you want to visit Land's End you are forced to walk past a building advertising its 'hands-on' exhibition of 'The Relentless Sea', while in the 'award-winning multimedia show' of 'The Last Labyrinth' you can 'descend into the dark depths of Land's End itself and prepare to have your senses dazzled!' Well, thanks all the same but the rocks and the waves and the sea and the sky are good enough for me.

I limped past the Land's End Signpost, whose arms indicated the distances to the Scillies, Wolf Rock, the Longships, John O' Groats (874 miles) and New York (3147). Another was in the process of being lettered with the city and distance to the home of a family of holidaymakers from 'BLACKPOOL 405'.

The direct route from Portsmouth to Land's End is 241 miles. When I was twelve I had stretched this distance out to 360 miles and ridden it on my oversized five-speed Raleigh Misty in seven days. This time, a couple of decades later, I had managed to stretch it out even further to a meandering 1590 miles, which I had ridden on a made-to-measure twenty-seven-speed bike in fifty-seven days. The Land's End Signpost alerted me to the fact that by cycling from Portsmouth to Land's End in my own curvaceously long-winded and winding way, I had cycled the equivalent of riding halfway across the Atlantic. Do the same thing again and I could be in New York by the end of September. That rather splendid thought aside, I realised that at this fine plodding rate I was on track for cycling the equivalent of four times around the world just to get to Scotland. But that's one of the nice things about travelling by bicycle – it makes the ground beneath your wheels bigger and better and infinitely more interesting than anything seen in a motorised flash. And besides, why travel somewhere speedily when you can go slowly, or directly when you can go circuitously?

Since my last visit to Land's End, another feature of supreme tackiness had been installed: the Millennium Beacon. To mark the year 2000, people must have paid 'good money' to have plaques inscribed with their hopes and ambitions for such a 'monumental' year (which turned out to feel just like any other). Here is a taster of the public's resolutions for the Year 2000:

VIDA DRAYTON
I will become computer literate during the Year 2000

RIO JADE MAIN
I will donate all my old toys to charity

RICHARD CURTIS
I will give one hundred pints of blood –
I have given forty-one already

THE CAREY FAMILY
We will carry donor cards

MICHELLE COATES
I will donate blood twice a year

THE YOUNG FAMILY
We will recycle more of our rubbish and read more books

DALE PRISK
I will swim in the sea every day

GILES FORD
I will put the footwork in

THE FOGG FAMILY
We will do more for charity and smile at a stranger every day

KINGSLEY AND NAOMI WRIGHT
We will be faithful, true, respect, trust, cherish and keep our love alive

THELMA BATTERSBY
I will make craft items to raise funds for the Sidmouth Donkey Sanctuary

And on and on it went in a similar theme of recycling or learning a language (notably French or Cornish), donating one's blood or one's organs, giving to charity or talking to God every day. I wondered if I was too late to add my own contribution for all and sundry to contemplate as they ambled towards the Dollar Cove Suspension Bridge and the First and Last House:

JOSIE DEW
Please God smile on my knee and I will smile at a stranger every day
(I might even make a few craft items too)

But God wasn't yet smiling because by now I could scarcely walk. So I hobbled across to the front of the Longships Family Restaurant (which I presume bars entrance unless one is in possession of a family – not that I've got a discriminatory chip on my shoulder or anything, of course) and sat on a rock in desultory mood pondering my next move.

I was getting nowhere with my thoughts when I was approached by a tanned and muscular lad with a head of hair cropped to stubble. He was pushing a Scott mountain bike.

'Have you just finished or about to start?' he asked me.

I stared at him a moment before the penny-farthing dropped. He had mistaken me for a potential 'End-to-Ender'.

'I'm not doing either,' I told him, 'I'm riding round the coast.'

He wasn't quite sure what to say to that, so instead chose to ignore it and told me about how he had just ridden from John O' Groats in fifteen days (main road route all the way) and how crap the weather had been the first week and how he had sent a heavy parcel home because he realised as soon as he started that he was carrying too much crap and that he'd begun the ride with a crap tyre because he'd had a blow-out before he'd even left Scotland and how hostelling was so much better than camping because you didn't have to carry the amount of crap I was carrying and that he had met about forty people doing the End-to-End, most of them cyclists but one man was pushing himself along on a microscooter and because he hadn't swapped legs his left leg looked like a tree trunk while his right looked like a twig.

Mr Scott Rider then paused momentarily to catch his breath before asking me what charity I was riding for.

'I'm not,' I said, 'I'm just doing it because I like riding my bike.'

He looked at me slightly askance. I was obviously not shaping up well in his eyes. Then the bulging pocket on his shorts burst into a commotion and he pulled out his mobile phone. It was his dad, who was driving down to pick him up. He was calling to say he was stuck in traffic on the A30. Mr Scott Rider did not look happy at having to hang around here any longer. I asked him what had motivated him to do the ride in the first place.

'Like you probably, I was bored.'

IF YOU CAN SEE THE SCILLIES IT'S
GOING TO RAIN.
IF YOU CAN'T SEE THEM, IT'S RAINING

So said the 'Local Weather Forecast' on one of Land's End's outdoor flip-up information boards (ooh, how rustic!) that was sprouting from the rocks overlooking Longships Lighthouse. Well, I could see the Scillies, but it didn't rain so they'll have to rethink that one.

I couldn't stay at Land's End all day (nor did I want to) and so, in ungainly one-legged pedalling style, I made it a few miles up the road where I put up my tent in a farm campsite overlooking Whitsand Bay. Standing in a sauna-hot red phone box, I got on the knee-kaput helpline and tried ringing the builder who was mid-big-building construction so I couldn't get through. But I had more success with mum who, after expressing suitable motherly sympathy (made me feel better immediately), threw her bike and the capacious Roadrunner II tent into the back of her Fiesta and six-and-a-half hours later was with me (a six-and-a-half hours that had taken me two months to ride).

For two weeks we camped together on Trevedra Farm, which was run by three generations of the same family. Jean Nicholas (the no-messing gran) ruled the roost, helped along by her daughter and grandchildren. Jean's mother-in-law, who still lived in the house at the bottom of the field, started up the campsite at the beginning of the Second World War when one tent, no matter how many people, cost 1s 6d (today it was a shocking £3 per person). If I had to be immobile it was a lovely place to be rooted to the spot and I sat in the field and the shade, knee-resting, while mum cycled off on hunter-gatherer food assignments.

Apart from the moments when I got thoroughly fidgety and unpleasant while woefully thinking I was missing the best of the short-lived summer sun for cycling, it was all very enjoyable. Mum was a laugh a minute, specially on our nocturnal toilet missions when we had to clamber out of our sleeping bags, crawl over each other in the dark to evacuate our nylon premises before tripping over guy lines and falling into cow pats. Still, I assured mum that she was miraculously agile for a gran.

By the end of the fortnight I felt a lot fatter and my knee a bit better, but not enough to carry on toiling up and down the vertiginous Cornish coastal hills. Big head-crunching quandary. I didn't want to give up but I didn't want to ruin knee for life (it's got to get me to New Zealand and across China yet). I hemmed and I hawed before I grudgingly relented to mother's-always-right insistence that she should ferry me home where I could get writing and give the wayward knee a proper tonic-boosting rest before venturing forth again.

So, on the seventy-fifth anniversary of the first set of traffic lights going into operation (in 1926 at Piccadilly Circus), we crammed two bikes, two tents, two camping mats, two sleeping bags, two rugs, nine bulging panniers, a deckchair, sun-umbrella, cold-box, small library of books and half the contents of the neighbouring farm shop into the back of the groaning Fiesta and set out for home. Sometimes cars have their uses.

CHAPTER 27

August – such a sizzling month – slipped through my fingers. I should have been in Ireland or Scotland. Instead, I cycled up and down the same stretch of road six times a day on knee-testing pursuits. Towards the end of the month I gradually added a few hills and a few concrete slabs to my panniers. By the first week of September I decided the wonked knee had turned up its toes for quite long enough. So, ignoring its niggling protests, I revved it into action, with my Roberts-riding mother in tow. She had gamely volunteered to accompany me on Day 1 (of Departure No. 3) about twenty miles down the road to Rowland's Castle.

That's funny (do I hear you say?) – I didn't think Rowland's Castle was in Cornwall. Well, you're right. It's not. It's near Cowplain on the Sussex and Hampshire border. But instead of resuming my haphazard coastal quest where I had left off among Cornwall's leg-conking hills, my flimsy limb had felt more inclined to go to Portsmouth where it would hang a left (even if it meant cycling into the face of the devil) and lead me across the comparative flatlands of the southeast.

The big question was: would I even make it to Portsmouth? Things didn't look too good as I struggled to keep up with my septuagenarian mother (well, 69¼ actually, but I like to remind her what a spring chicken she is at heart) over the eight-and-a-half miles to South Harting – site of famous church spire faced with copper shingles, creating a bright verdigris hue which can be seen for miles. We cycled past the ancient set of parish stocks and the whipping post complete with three pairs of wrist irons (into which I once found myself shack-led, but I think it's best if I don't go into that now – we all do things we regret). By this stage, my out-of-breath knee demanded a rest and so we called a halt and sat on the village playing field, trying to shelter out of the whistling wind as we consumed a hearty packed lunch. If in doubt, eat, and then eat a bit more, is my motto. It might not mend knees or get you any closer to Portsmouth but it tastes nice all the same.

Anyway, when all was said and done (or not done) and eaten, it was so late it was almost time for tea, and Rowland's Castle – let alone Portsmouth – felt about as far away as Vladivostock.

'I could do with a nice cup of tea and bun,' said mum.

Everything then became very funny, specially when dotty mother spotted Stonehenge on top of the South Downs (but that's another story and we only had an overdose of bananas to blame). When I remarked to mum that this wasn't much good, that I used to be able to cycle to Africa and back no trouble and now I couldn't even make it down the road to Rowland's bloody Castle, we guffawed even more. By the time our stomach muscles had recovered and we had decided Stonehenge was perhaps the Vandalian Tower up at Uppark House after all, it was so late that the only sensible solution to a highly unsensible day was to pay heed to my mother's advice (and not oft can I say I've done that).

'Why not cycle home with me now,' she said, 'have a good night's sleep, and then try again tomorrow?'

'I can't do that! I can't give up before I've hardly even started!' I said, before quickly adding, 'Actually, sounds like a very good idea!'

So we did an about-turn and headed back into Harting, where we stopped at the village store for mum to buy a nice resuscitating chocolate and caramel slice. I bought a jar of Sussex honey and a bottle of Radox liquid soap. Not for me, but for Val, my neighbour. Presents to bring back to her from my half-day holiday to Harting. Also presents to make up for turning up at home again so shockingly unexpectedly (and just when she thought she had got me out of her hair at last). While walking out of the shop I bumped into my chimney sweep, who was walking in. He had seen my loaded bike propped up outside.

'Aren't you getting too old for all this cycling?' he asked.

'Yes,' I said. 'That's why I'm giving up and going home.'

And home we went, where my false-start day came to a close with me sleeping in my tent in the front room. Made me feel I had gone somewhere even if I hadn't.

CHAPTER 28

'WELCOME TO PORTSMOUTH,' declared the sign, 'FLAGSHIP OF MARITIME ENGLAND'. Yes, following my wobbly-kneed faltering-at-the-first-hurdle downfall the day before, I had set out again with determined and renewed vigour. And miraculously made it – but alas, with no support cycling-crew mother in my wake. I think she was still suffering from the bout of Sussex Downs Syndrome that she had contracted the previous day.

A large yellow sign planted in the pavement on the approach to Southsea's King's Road roundabout announced an 'EXPERIMENTAL SCHEME AHEAD – BEWARE OF CYCLISTS', which made us two-wheeling souls sound like dangerous creatures from the Alaskan outback: *WARNING – STAY IN YOUR VEHICLE, CYCLISTS CAN BE DANGEROUS*. And anyway, I wasn't so sure I liked the idea of being used as a roundabout's 'experimental scheme'. What if the experiment went wrong and I ended up being blown up by the Bunsen burner?

A little light relief was to be found in an immaculate Public Convenience situated on the seafront. A wall plaque graciously informed me that it had won the much-coveted 'LOO OF THE YEAR AWARD 2001'. What an honour to use such a cleanly convenience! Made one almost proud to sit upon such sparkling thrones.

I was back on the Henry VIII trail again: Southsea, the residential and holiday district of Portsmouth, derives its name for the 'goodlie and warlyk castill' that the king had planned to be a 'south sea castle' at the entrance to Portsmouth.

As the strong gusty wind blew me at a lickety-split past Eastney Marina, I caught the name of several boats swaying from side to side beneath a complaining whorl of wheeling seagulls: *Fitz, Wooden Shoe, Drywind, Freedom* and *Here we go Again.*

And here I went again, into a public toilet, to change into my shorts. The morning's rash of fierce squally showers had taken a different tack and sailed off across the Channel to France, leaving a brilliant sun raining down upon me. Back outside I found a man, stripped to the waist, sitting on the wall beside my bike. He had short bristly hair, a guitar and a bottle of Becks from which he took a couple of large glugs before launching into *There ain't no sun-shine when you're gawn*. He opened his mouth so wide I had a full sighting of his adenoids. Moments later a nubile blonde in a halter top emerged from the ladies, walked over to guitar man and cut short his chorusing sun-shining song by sticking her tongue down his throat. He didn't seem to mind though.

Hail, Hayling Island, which came and went in a mire of traffic and chips, funfairs, and holiday homes intermingled with big, ostentatious houses with electronic gates topped with stone lions. I also came upon an inordinate amount of wheel-trims, surgical gloves and left-footed shoes lying forlornly at the roadside. Oh, and 10 mm spanners, which I added to my tool-bag. I can never say no to a spanner. But the trims, shoes and gloves I left to someone with a peculiar fetish.

The best thing about Hayling Island (apart from its spanners) was its bounteous bushfuls of blackberries, from which I readily grazed. Thorney Island was equally well-endowed with its black bushes of berries, but it let me down on the tool front. All I found was a self-tapping screw. I salvaged it anyway because . . . well, you never know who you might meet on the road who needs a good self-tapping screw. And it's best to be prepared.

Now the thing about Thorney Island is that it is actually not an island at all;

it is joined to the mainland by a road bridge and two narrow strips of land that act like braces holding up its breeches. What a confusing country! There I am, cycling around islands that aren't islands and estuaries that aren't estuaries and Lizards that aren't lizards. How am I expected to know where I am, when where I am is not what it is?

I had reached the not-really-an-island Island of Thorney from Hermitage (which was not really a hermitage but a busy little place on the A259) where two angst-ridden adolescents, riffling their buzzcuts for scurf, asked me for a self-tapping screw. Actually, they didn't; they asked me for the time. They made a bad choice of humanoid to ask because when I'm off on my bike with the flibbertigibbets I tend to do away with all chronometers of time. I know when it gets light. I know when it gets dark. I know when the banana shops shut (apart from in early-closing Devon). That's all I need to know. I have no meetings to attend, or trains to catch, or programmes to watch, or children to feed, or deadlines to reach, or baths to run. Like Neanderthal man, I simply eat when I'm hungry and sleep when I'm tired.

'Sorry,' I said to the two anguished pubescents, 'I haven't got the time to hand.'

'Where you from?' said one of the boys recriminatingly. 'The moon?'

As I cycled away, I wondered what it was about teenagers that made them think I was either heading for, or arriving from, the extra-terrestrial world.

Though I had ascertained that Thorney Island is not actually an island, I did discover that, paradoxically, its title is partly correct in so far as it is a prickly place. For 'Thorney' in effect makes the 'island' part redundant, as it translates as 'island overgrown by thorn bushes', from the Old English *thorn* (thorn bush) and *eg* (island). As I pondered this, I thought how disappointing then that The Lizard couldn't be overgrown with lizards (its name is thought to be derived from the old Cornish word *Lisart*, meaning 'palace on a high place'), though it did have lots of three-cornered leeks and Hottentot figs to make up for it.

So there I was, on a very thorny sort of island, going great guns when I was suddenly brought to a standstill by an obstruction across my path. At first I thought it was some type of toll booth and was about to sail clean on through in a 'bikes-no-charge' superior-than-thou toll-bridge fashion when I was apprehended by a sallow youth in army fatigues.

'May I see your ID?' he asked.

ID? I thought, how very tiresome! There's Thorney Island not even an island, and now it's getting all above its station and pretending to be another land. But you don't argue with men in battledress. So I've been told. Dutifully, I handed over my passport for his perusal.

'Where are you wanting to go on camp?' he asked.

Camp? I thought. Is there a campsite here? How very convenient. My knee was aching and I could do with calling it a day.

'Camp?' I replied, looking all angelically innocent. 'I was actually only thinking of cycling down to West Thorney church and back.'

(Incidentally, West Thorney, which was recorded as simply *Tornei* in the Domesday Book, is situated on the extreme eastern edge of the 'island' and only acquired its 'West' later on in life to distinguish it from Thorney Farm at East Wittering – which really is 'east' and not 'west' across the entrance to Chichester Harbour. But maybe you didn't want to know that.)

'I'm afraid that's forbidden!' said the khaki-clad lad.

Suddenly the befuddled brain-fog cleared.

'Oh,' I said, 'is that because it's all MOD land?'

'Yes,' came the stern reply.

'Well, if I can't cycle through your camp, can I follow the track around the island on the Sussex Border Path?'

'Yes, but you can't take your bike.'

'Oh. Well, that's the end of that idea then!'

He then handed me back my passport and I retraced my tracks, noticing, as I did so, a very large sign saying:

47th REGIMENT ROYAL ARTILLERY

BAKER BARRACKS

Funny how sometimes the most obvious things can slip your notice.

I was busy minding my own business in Bosham (pronounced 'Bozzum'), contemplating the scene of King Canute's legendary attempt to prove to hero-worshippers that, no, he could not defy the incoming tide, when a man in a tweed jacket and flannels walking along the harbour front exclaimed, 'Gee whizz! You must be fit!' And I laughed, because that was yet another one of those expressions that I didn't think people really used any more.

Cool, blustery weather that pushed me along one minute before slapping me back down the next continued to accompany me as I rode beneath piled-high cauliflower clouds skimming across a patchy blue sky. Bosham Hoe, Fishbourne, Apuldram, Dell Quay, Crouchers, Manhood End Farm, Birdham, Itchenor Reach and the Witterings whistled by beneath my wheels until I rolled up at another Bill, this one Selsey.

Selsey may look like a beak but it has more affinity for seals than bills. For Selsey, in Old English, means Seal (*seolh*) Island (*eg*). Though of course it's not really an island, it's a peninsula. The name Seal Island was recorded in about 710 when seals could be seen on Selsey's beaches. Today you're lucky if you see much of a beach at all, never mind a seal, because Selsey stands in the front line of Britain's battle against wild weather and accelerating coastal erosion. With its headland shaped like a ship's bow, Selsey has become almost a byword for meteorological wrath, having recently been struck by two tornadoes in as many years. With 100 mph winds pelting hundreds of homes with damaging golfball-sized hailstones, and monster 30-foot waves crashing over sea defences, Selsey does not sound like the somnolent West Sussex town that (according to a plaque) inspired the composer Eric Coates to write *Sleepy Lagoon*, the theme tune to *Desert Island Discs*, when he lived there. On the other hand, he also wrote the music for *The Dam Busters*.

While I was in Selsey I heard a report on Radio Solent about a school in Havant trying to recreate an earthquake by getting all the children to jump up and down. Dear me! First we have tornadoes in Selsey and now we have earthquakes in Havant. Whatever next?

Meteorological extremes aside, what came next was Chichester where I met up with the bicycling builder. Together we got lost in Bognor, muddled in Middleton and camped in Littlehampton. Worthing's WCs proved a far cry from the splendours of prize-winning Portsmouth's. 'DUE TO VANDALISM THIS CONVENIENCE IS CLOSED' read the inconvenient notice pinned to the padlocked doors of countless conveniences spread along the five miles of seafront. The builder, who by this stage was in need of a convenience just as much as me, consoled himself by tucking into a take-away from MACARI'S FISH & CHIPS, where, so a notice in the window declared, they also sold 'PUKKA PIES'. We sat eating with crossed legs on a bench on the pier in a bright shaft of draughty sunshine.

Aided by a blustery westerly, we shot out of Worthing at a rate of knots and belted through Lancing, past the notable landmark of Lancing College with its Gothic high-rise chapel, and on to Shoreham where everything was dominated by the twin chimneys of Brighton Power Station. The populated and traffic-congested coast road that stretches from Littlehampton to Brighton, with its excess of cars and oil tankers and dumper trucks and gravel heaps and scrap metal mountains and prefab steel companies and power stations, is not the most uplifting for scenic cycling. But for fast, kamikaze cycling, it's grand.

The eyesight of the large population of retired motorists leaves a lot to be desired too. A recent report in the *Financial Times* had revealed how one in twenty motorists has defective eyesight. And I think Gary and I met more than our fair share of them, judging from the number of close calls we had as we negotiated the highways and byways with the aged citizenry of the south coast.

Added to that, the Conservative leaders of Sussex county councils showed little sign of supporting cycling. Worthing has a nice wide prom along which cycling once used to be permitted. Now the only traces of ever having been allowed to do so are the scrubbed-out remnants of the pavement-painted bicycles. Cyclists are now forced on to a seafront road running amok with senior citizens who possess an alarming tendency to plough straight across mini roundabouts or shoot out of side turnings inches from your wheel. With such erratic motoring skills as these, it was easy to catch up with the elderly offender and, following a tap on the window, have a 'quiet word' in their ear about their muppetry behaviour. They were always very nice. 'Sorry, love. I didn't see you there!'

And, worryingly, you knew that to be true.

Before Dr Richard Russell of Lewes published his famous *Dissertation on 'the Use Of Sea Water In Diseases Of The Glands* in 1753, Brighton was an obscure fishing village known as Brighthelmstone. But by trumpeting the medical virtues of the sea air, sea bathing and even drinking sea water, judiciously mixed with milk, Dr Russell's ideas gradually gained favour among the rich and influential until the reputation of the resort was affirmed when the Prince Regent, later King George IV, chose to sample them himself.

Every year bar one, from the ages of eleven to seventeen, I took a bracing dose of Brighton's sea air and waters myself when, like a pedalling pilgrim, I would join the masses and cycle from London to Brighton – or, as it's now been reborn, Brighton and Hove City. Having taken the air and the sea, I would then take to the saddle and ride back up to London again. Alone.

So as Gary and I pushed our bikes along the prom past the battered and faded hulk of West Pier (where in the Who's modfest, *Quadrophenia,* the mods slept next to the rockers), which looked ever more shaky on its spindly black legs (soon after our visit a storm turned it into a ruinous pile of flotsam), and into Madeira Drive, I thought about those early morning mass departures from Clapham Common, multiple pile-ups on Ditchling Beacon, and devouring a phenomenally large packed lunch (for one so small) on the pebbly beach.

I like the town formerly known as Brighton. I like its rakish sprightliness and its fantastical Oriental pleasure dome, the Royal Pavilion (once described as 'a large Norfolk turnip with four onions'), and I like its slot machines outside the Olde Brighton Rock and Candy Shoppe that promise things like: 'Knickers for a nicker, pouches for a pound'. I like the fact that Brighton is the epitome of 'Sussex-by-the-Sea', the acknowledged queen of British seaside resorts with its touch of the naughty but nice on the side. Its buildings are either flashy and bold or seedy and jaded while its beaches are hard and pebbly. And as it is the South of England's archetypal seaside resort, I also like the fact that even in winter you will usually find a few hardy souls, knees covered in rugs, sitting on benches or lolling in striped deckchairs, lapping up the bracing air, their faces turned to a chill milky sun and a forty-knot wind, looking for all the world as if they are warming themselves on the Costa del Sol rather than an English holiday haunt on the lumpy, grey Channel that shares a similar latitude with southern Siberia.

The other thing about Brighton is that it always seems to come up with the unexpected. The week of our arrival, a lifeboat crew, called out to rescue a woman who had been swept out to sea, found it was a blow-up doll wearing stockings and suspenders.

On the eastern outskirts of Brighton, the South Downs reach the sea, and for the next twenty-five miles or so the coast road veers up and down as it heads towards the vertical cliffs of the Seven Sisters before plunging off into the Channel. With the builder in tow, I passed through Rottingdean, dominated on a hill above the road by the massive buildings of two schools – St Dunstan's Training Centre for the Blind, and Roedean, which has seen the likes of Princess Anne pass through its portals.

Then came the sprawling residential estates and bungalow developments of Saltdean and Peacehaven, most of which were built on the Downs between the wars – the dark age of coastal management. Peacehaven arose during the First World War as a 'plotland' development and in 1916 a competition was announced to find a name for the new resort. The winning choice was a down-under name for a country on top, New Anzac-on-Sea, chosen as a tribute to the Australian and New Zealand Army Corps (ANZAC) who were stationed locally. But after some dispute about the legality of the competition, the original planner of the plotland, Charles Neville, a wealthy businessman, declared the name to be Peacehaven, denoting not merely a 'peaceful haven', but a desire for peace to end the war.

Gary and I continued over the Greenwich Meridian (a monument on the cliff marks where it leaves England). Not long after that my coastal ride came a bit adrift at Newhaven where, on overshooting the seafront, we ended up in France. For a week. By the time we had found our way back to England's famous, immortalised-in-song, chalk-cliffed coast, the builder had to get back to building, so once again I was left to eat bananas on my lonesome.

CHAPTER 29

Up at the 530-foot crown of Beachy Head I was in the middle of reading a plaque commemorating 'the epic Dieppe Raid in 1942 which was partly controlled from the radar station on this headland', when a middle-aged couple from Newark, Notts, started chatting to me.

'I'm actually originally from Surrey,' said the woman, dressed in a skirt and sensible shoes and a sky-blue cardi zipped up tight over an ample midriff, 'so I know this area well. We used to come down here a lot.'

They also knew France well as both of their sons lived there – one in Brittany, the other in Alsace.

'If you ever go to France,' said Mrs Newark, 'you must stay in the Formule 1 hotels. We swear by them, don't we, love? They're very comfortable and very reasonable.'

Another place they knew well was the Norfolk coast and here Mrs Newark (obviously the driving force) recommended I turn off down all the little dead-end roads to the sea, which apparently, in local tongue, were called 'chitties'. Closer to home, or more like closer to where we were standing, Mrs Newark advised that when I cycled through Hastings I should keep to the east of the town as the west was 'very shabby'. As for Brighton (and Hove City), well! friends had told them not to get out of their car or else they would get mugged!

'In my day it was safe to walk anywhere,' lamented Mrs Newark. 'We're staying in Eastbourne at the moment and it's a very different place by night. The streets are teeming with noisy young people all heading off to clubs and bars.

Mind you, you're only a young thing yourself so you'll probably join in! But we worry that they might mug old wrinklies like us!'

When Mrs Newark had run out of places she could either advise or warn me about, she wandered off with her husband. I sat down on the grass to eat an apple near a sign that said 'Samaritans: Always There Day and Night' (Beachy Head, the highest chalk sea cliff in Britain, is a much favoured location for suicides) and stared at the sky and the ships and the sea. Two men came ambling along slowly behind me and I heard them talking about the attacks on America on September 11th that had so shocked the world only a few days earlier.

I had been in France at the time. After arriving by boat in Dieppe at two o'clock in the morning, Gary and I cycled through the dark and the dense freezing fog until we had escaped the city's clutches and found a village churchyard. In the biting bitter chill of the silent still pre-dawn, we lay down on the gravel between some marble tombstones to try to get an hour or two's sleep. Annoyingly, the builder succeeded while I, in a semi-hypothermic state, failed miserably. An early opening *boulangerie* with its oven-warm interior and its melt-in-mouth bread went some way to help restore benumbed circulation. Later on we found moustachioed Jacques, a farmer who let us camp in his thick grassy field, which we discovered, a little too late, was overrun with rats. Whole migrations of these horribly fat French rodents would dash and dart past the door of the tent as they ran like the clappers from one hedge to another. It made toilet missions quite exciting for fear of being caught in an uncompromising position in the line of stampede.

That evening we were in the tent making steady progress by torchlight through several bagfuls of tasty provisions purchased from the small village *supermarché*, when Gary managed to find a very static Radio Five Live on my little radio. At first I thought I was listening to an advert for some Hollywood blockbuster extravaganza because in between all the hissing and interference all I could hear was a lot of dramatic talk about hijacked planes flying into the Pentagon and the World Trade Center, followed by shocked commentaries of explosive fires and the total collapse of the Twin Towers. By then I had realised this was no big movie commercial. It was real-life drama and horror. While millions of people all over the world sat glued to their television sets in disbelief, Gary and I lay in a field in France staring into the darkness.

CHAPTER 30

In Eastbourne I went through a mini spate of being spotted again. One such spotter was a man who stopped me in my urgent tracks as I made haste to enter the threshold of the Ladies near the bus station. After a bit of book and travel chatter, he said, 'Where are you off to for your next trip?'

I told him that I was on it – riding round the British Isles.

'Oh,' he said sounding a little surprised. 'Is this a break you're taking before you head off on a proper trip again?'

'I think this *is* a "proper" trip,' I replied. 'At least, it feels pretty proper to me!' Although, to be honest, I wasn't quite sure what a 'proper' trip was supposed to feel like.

The man looked at me with one of those looks that told me that any cycling status I might have held in his eyes was slipping away fast. I could tell that he would have preferred to hear how I was about to drag my steed in a state of reckless dehydration across the Nubian desert to Djibouti. Instead he heard how I was heading off down Marine Parade to Bexhill. Oh well, it seemed exciting enough to me.

Over in South Street outside Sunny Foods Health Store, I was restocking my food panniers with honey and raisins and oats when Mrs Sunny Food Owner came hurrying out of the shop to give me a big bagful of organic apples for no other reason than she had once gone on a cycling holiday herself. How touching, I thought. After thanking her, I rode off down the street.

But I didn't get very far because as I passed Sunflowers Café I was hailed by a man sitting with a coffee and another man at a table outside on the pavement. He turned out to be a local cab driver called Tim.

'Having read your books, I feel I know you!' he said.

Coming from a man whom I had never set eyes upon in my life, my inbuilt self-preservation mechanisms found this comment a touch disconcerting: he may feel he knows me but I knew him not from Adam. Anyway, he must have felt he knew me so well because a couple of sentences later he asked if I would like to come and stay with him as he only lived just round the corner.

I don't make a habit of spending the night with men with whom I've spoken little more than ten words. When I declined his offer by saying that I wanted to keep riding as I had a few miles to get under my belt, he said that as he had the day off he could go and fetch his bike and come riding with me. Bit insistent, I thought. Bit forward, too. Although I was sure Tim the Taxi was a very nice man, I don't like being pushed into doing something with someone I don't know. Travelling alone as a small young thing in my gap year, I know only too well that some people see me as a vulnerable and easy target. How was I to know that Tim didn't have ulterior motives like bludgeoning me with a blunt instrument on the Pevensey Levels? I didn't. So I made my excuses and left.

Back on the seafront I passed the 152-room, five-star Grand Hotel that sits on King Edward's Parade like a gorgeous wedding cake. Amazingly it was built as a private house, albeit for a man with thirteen children. Anyone who was (or is) anyone has stayed here. There was Debussy, in 1905, who wrote *La Mer*. Then there was Churchill, Haile Selassie, Edward VIII, Prince Naseem, Liam Gallagher, Anna Kournikova (who brought 'only-the-balls-should-bounce' sex appeal a-plenty), Martina Navratilova (who brought her two chihuahuas) and the late Oliver Reed, who ordered a hard-boiled egg for breakfast with a bottle of champagne.

As I was pausing on the seafront to take in this grandiose edifice, a little old lady shuffled up to me and said, 'You're not all alone, are you?'

'I am,' I said.

The woman emitted a small groan.

'Ohh, take care dearie,' she said, clasping my hand tight between hers. 'It's such a dangerous world.'

I was reminded of this 'dangerous world' as I sat with my back against a wooden groyne eating my lunch on the beach. Greg, an American holidaying in England with his young family, crunched across the pebbles to come and talk to me. He was interested to know where I was going and told me how several years back he had cycled around Normandy, which he had found

211

'mindblowingly beautiful'. Then we started talking about September 11th because he told me he was waiting to fly home. But as there were still no transatlantic flights he had no idea when that might be. Ironically, Greg worked for a weekly aviation magazine.

'It's a good week for business!' he remarked wryly.

More poignantly he had once worked in one of the Twin Towers himself.

'I can't believe they're gone,' he said with a slightly far-off look in his eyes, 'I just can't believe they're gone.'

I once spent Christmas Eve in Eastbourne, alone in a seedy B&B. It was the only one I could find open on a last-minute Christmas Eve phone-around and my room was full of shagpile and unemptied ashtrays. The window looked out over a fenced-in backyard strewn with rubbish and bottles and car tyres and cracked crates and plastic bags whirling around in the swirling winter wind. The B&B was something of a misnomer because it provided no breakfast, only a bed. Anyhow, I had arrived at the B&(no)B on my bike in the dark and the place had looked closed. After fifteen minutes spent banging on the door, there was the sound of extended foreplay with locks and bolts and it was finally opened by a woman with big, picture-perfect purple hair. But she spoke no English. A cigarette drooped from her lips, while another one, waiting in the wings, hung from her fingers. After she had shown me to my room, I never saw her again. I never saw anyone else either. But I didn't mind. I hadn't come away to be all festively social. I had come away to cycle along the length of the swooping series of rounded curves of the 'majestic mountains' (as Gilbert White called them) of the South Downs Way.

On the edge of town I caused a slight altercation in Tesco. I had stopped to use the toilets and was walking out via the fruit and veg department when I passed a lone Savoy cabbage. It caught my eye because it was sitting there all by itself in the organic section. I decided I would buy it and make a soupy gloop for my in-tent tea. When I picked it up I noticed it was one day past its sell-by date, so I asked a young and rangy acne-dappled shop assistant if I could have my cabbage at a reduced price.

'Can't do that,' he said with a sluggish, I-hate-life troubled teenage scowl.

'Why not?' I asked.

'Cos we ain't allowed to sell stuff if it's past its sell-by date.'

'But this is a cabbage. It's not like listeria-filled cheese or salmonella-stuffed chicken.'

'Yeah, but if it makes you ill you might sue Tesco.'

'I'm not going to sue anyone,' I said. 'All I want is this cabbage, which will probably still be fine to eat in two months' time.'

'Yeah, but basically we ain't allowed to sell it.'

'So what will you do with it?' I asked.

'Bin it out the back with all the other stuff that gets chucked away.'

'You can't do that!' I said, in a sudden fit of despair with this stupidly wasteful supermarket world. 'This cabbage is completely fine!'

'Yeah, but there still ain't nothing I can do abou' it.'

'Well, if you're going to throw it away, can I just have it?'

'Can't do that cos we have to take it out the back.'

'Oh. So if I walk round to the back,' I said, pulling a light-heartedly hopeful face, 'can you give it to me then?'

I didn't mean to be this much of a difficult customer but by this stage I had become quite attached to my cabbage and had set my sights on saving it. Surely brassicas have rights; everything else seems to these days. I could tell the boy had had quite enough of me and I didn't blame him. I would have had quite enough of me as well. But for the moment I had had quite enough of these perniciously dictatorial hare-brained supermarkets. I asked the boy if I could see a senior supervisor. And off we went, wandering up and down the packed Saturday aisles in search of a senior supervisor – or its nearest equivalent.

As I followed the boy, clutching my cabbage to my bosom like a cherished child, I thought: what *am* I doing spending so long trying to save the life of a cabbage when I've got coasts to be cycling around? But once I start something, be it cycling to Land's End with difficult brothers or fussing about the fate of supermarket cabbages, I like to see it through.

At last we found the more senior supermarket man doing something more senior beside a shelf of 'moist towelettes' (surely these have got to be two of the most unattractive words in the whole of the English language?). I put my cabbage case to Mr Tesco Senior while Mr Tesco Junior continued to glower with furrowed brow (somehow I didn't think I had made his day). Mr Tesco Senior said what I expected him to say about suing and so forth. I laughed. The whole situation seemed so absurd.

'I'd like to think I've got better things to be doing than suing Tesco on account of a cabbage! And by the time I've eaten all my cabbage I'll probably be in Ramsgate or Gravesend so I'm not going to cycle all the way back down here again to file a lawsuit against Tesco just because I've eaten a slightly dodgy cabbage leaf.'

Mr Tesco Senior was a nice man, a northerner, and he laughed. He could see the ridiculous side of it.

'Have you got a rabbit?' he asked with a twinkle in his eye.

I looked at him for a moment, absorbing and untangling the inner meaning of what he had just said.

'Of course!' I blurted. 'Don't I look like I do?'

'Well, in that case, madam,' he said, swiping a price-marker gun off a passing shelf-stacker, 'you can have this cabbage for 10p. What's good for a rabbit is good for me!'

He gave me a knowing wink and I gave him a hearty thanks, feeling happy that there were at least little pockets of sanity left to be found in the mad world of massive conglomerating supermarket chains.

CHAPTER 31

According to the road sign, I had now entered, in tourist-luring theme-park speak, '1066 Country'. Onwards I cycled through Pevensey and Norman's Bay, which was the area where Willy the Conqueror's invasion of England began among the sea-flooded marshes. Added to their historical importance, the Pevensey Levels are also an internationally recognised wetland site and Site of Special Scientific Interest (SSSI), because, among other things, the levels provide a haven for winter-visiting lapwing, redshank and snipe as well as providing a home for our largest arachnid, the rare fen raft spider – a wonderful creature that looks like a water-skiing tarantula.

Approaching the Edwardian seaside resort of Bexhill ('birthplace of British motor racing') I was riding past a row of wet-sounding beach huts (White Horses; Pegasus; Seashore; Spindrift; Dog Watch; Wild and Wet) when the thin, mid-September sun was replaced by ravaging storms and floods. I wrapped two Tesco bags round my feet, battened down all Velcro hatches, zipped up all zips and carried on riding through Hastings (home to the largest beach-launched fishing fleet in Europe and Jack-in-the-Green Festival of Morris Dancing), Fairlight and Cliff End. By the time I had reached Winchelsea (site of inspiration for artists like Turner and Millais) I was well and truly weather-logged and too zonked to continue after hours of fighting with the vicious wind gusts that hurled themselves at me between the gaps in the traffic.

I washed up at a few regimented caravan parks, but all of them turned up their noses to tents. Time to select a garden, I thought, so I rang the ding-dong bell of a bungalow. An elderly man appeared at a crack in the door clutching a rolled-up copy of the *Sunday Sport*. I wondered if he was going to take a swiping swat at me like he might a bluebottle. Instead he smiled a sympathetic caught-out-in-bad-weather smile and let me camp in his small garden beside a wind-tossed viburnum bush. The rain continued to hammer down all night long.

The next morning the inside of my tent resembled a venue for a daddy-longlegs convention. I counted over sixty of them. Most were caught between my flysheet and inner tent, many in various states of coition, while others were either flapping and thrashing around excitedly within my legions of plastic bags, or nose-diving on suicidal sorties into the boiling cauldrons of my porridge.

Chalets, caravan parks, Pontin's Holiday Camp, broken beer bottles, smashed phone boxes, supermarket carrier bags bowling across my path like Nebraskan tumbleweeds, and beaten-up Fiestas and GTis, erratically driven by tough-looking crop-skulled teenagers throwing liberal doses of fags and fucks out of the window as they went blasting off up the road in a cloud of burning rubber, were the delights to greet me at Camber. Apart from stopping to use a graffiti-riddled and broken-doored public toilet, in which I carefully side-stepped a hypodermic syringe and two used condoms, I felt little inclination to linger.

A raw, wet wind that held a hint of winter in its bones hit me head on as I crossed from East Sussex into Kent ('The Garden of England'). This was Walland Marsh, which merged with Romney Marsh. With their broad sweeping landscapes dominated by huge Netherlandish skies, the whole area felt more reminiscent of East Anglia than compact, southeast England. When the

Romans landed in Kent, all of this marshland was covered by a shallow sea. Today the grey ruins of Stutfall Castle preside over a hundred square miles of flat, sheep-cropped pastureland. Nineteen hundred years ago, the builders of this castle would have looked out over a bustling port, skeins of sailing ships and a hundred square miles of shining-armour sea.

This was Portus Lemanis, one of the leading harbours of Roman Britain and protector of waterways navigable deep into what is now rural Kent. Tenterden, a pretty town southwest of Ashford that sits on the edge of the Weald, is twelve miles from the sea and once had Roman wharves.

Dropping sea levels and centuries of continued siltation behind a barrier of coastal sandbanks eventually converted the area into rich pastureland that became the home of one of the world's best-known breeds of sheep, the long-woolled Romney Marsh which, with its aquiline nose and supercilious expression, really does look as if it is fully aware of its superior breeding. But during the last two to three decades much of the marshland has been drained and fields of winter cereals have replaced the grazing meadows, destroying the traditional landscape in the process.

Although Romney Marsh looked a lot less marshy than I was expecting, it can still be a pretty damp place; its forty pumping stations had to pump round the clock for the whole of 2001 to clear the floods from the previous winter.

Everything looked very bleak as I fought into a rain-stinging wind. I saw no sheep, but plenty of burnt-out car wrecks, gravel pits, pylons, dumped mattresses and armchairs spilling their guts of soiled foam and rusty springs into the mud. Barriers of barbed-wire and chain-link fencing lined much of the road. On one side I was grazing elbows with MOD property ('FIRING RANGE – KEEP OUT') while the other scraped the fenced-off perimeters of Brett Specialized Aggregates. Apart from the odd Camber-strip boy-racer screaming past along the straight to Lydd, the only vehicles to pass me were either cement lorries or tipper trucks.

Opposite The Two Bob Shop in Lydd, I stopped at the Londis store to buy some food, which I ate behind the church of All Saints while stamping the ground in the vain hope of keeping warm in a knife-cutting wind that whistled between the gravestones off the hedgeless prairies. Known locally as the Cathedral of Romney Marsh, the church is a massive building 200 feet long and 132 feet high – far too big for the village that clusters around its feet, but it stands as a reminder of the medieval importance of Lydd.

By the time I reached the great shingle spit of Dungeness I was teeth-chatteringly cold and had to sit for a while in a corner of the Pilot Inn to restore a semblance of circulation. Jutting out into the Channel, the windswept promontory of Dungeness adjoins Romney Marsh but with its vast size, dryness and lack of vegetation it appeared more like an extraordinary shingle desert. Apart from the fact that it was raining. Hard. This wild desolate place, where the fog can fall thick within minutes and where the ever-shifting banks of coarse brown shingle are inhospitable to all but the hardiest of sea plants, is dominated by two lighthouses (and the remains of a third – there has been a lighthouse on the treacherous expanse of Dungeness Point since 1615, when it was stated that '1000 persons perished there from want of light every year') and the almighty and intimidating hulk of the nuclear power station, out of which marches a perilous army of pylons. The Environment Agency has just embarked upon a £40 million programme of repairing sea defences in the Romney Marsh area. And because the sea is constantly moving the shingle from the west side of Dungeness round to the east, bulldozers and trucks are constantly trundling it – 33,000 cubic metres a year – back again. If they stopped, the nuclear power station would be swept away by the sea.

I followed Lydd-on-Sea's single ribbon of bungalows, houses and holiday homes and huts that lie between the Romney, Hythe and Dymchurch Railway ('The World's Smallest Public Railway', with its scaled-down replicas of powerful steam engines with names like *Samson, Typhoon* and *Hurricane* – all of them just a third full size) and a long shingle beach which was sprouting clumps of dramatic sea kale. Beyond that lay the bumpy waves of the Straits of Dover. Through the murky mist I could just make out a few lumbering forms of tankers and container ships suspended in the gloom outside Folkestone.

As I rode in the pelting rain past the endless row of sea-staring bungalows with ocean-faring names – Sea Haze, Seawitch, Saltaire, Blue Haze – I gazed into their big, view-hungry windows. There were jungles of houseplants and macramé potholders, easels and music stands and veritable observatories of tripod-mounted telescopes all pointing in a Big Brotherly way towards me. There were plenty of binoculars too – pressed to faces and training on grey ships and wet cyclists. Any potential invading force wouldn't stand a chance of stealing past England's nose what with the senior citizenry look-outs and watch-posts of Lydd-on-Sea. Those off duty sipped tea in strategically positioned armchairs and sofas – the men lost behind a defence of newspapers, the women, knees covered with rugs, pouring Tetleys from knitted tea-cosied pots. One old chap stood in a double-glazed window towelling off his upper body. As I battled past, swathed in dripping Goretex, in the raging wind and rain, he looked at me with an expression of disbelief. I flashed a manic smile in his direction and a 'come-on-out-it's-lovely' wave.

And so, still clad in full wet-weather battledress, I arrived drenched and wind-battered in New Romney, one of the five original Cinque Ports. Once New Romney, the 'capital' of Romney Marsh, had stood at the mouth of the Rother and vessels had been able to sail into the bay and anchor alongside St Nicholas' Church. But the great storms at the end of the thirteenth century diverted the river mouth to Rye, about ten miles to the west, and New Romney was cut off from the sea.

Just outside the town, I spent the night in a waterlogged caravan camp park where, in the toilet block, a staff notice advised:

IF IT MOVES – SAY HELLO. IF IT DOES NOT – CLEAN IT.

I made sure to keep moving.

News that night was of George W. Bush colourfully claiming to the world that the United States wanted Osama bin Laden 'dead or alive'. Later, following a bit of argy bargy between various nations, he said, 'I have opinions of my own – strong opinions – but I don't always agree with them.' What reassuring words of contemplative intellect coming from the president of the world's superpower.

CHAPTER 32

'Looks like the weather is closing in for winter,' said a man in a hat with ear flaps as I stood piling on another layer on the seafront at Hythe. He was right. It was late September and it certainly wasn't getting any warmer.

To try to keep numbness at bay, I cycled with scarcely a stop through Folkestone (aptly the birthplace of William Harvey, discoverer of the circulation of the blood), past the mouth of the Channel Tunnel and into Dover (packet port and white cliffs – which are actually quite green). Dover also proved to be a hub of cycle-crushing articulated container trucks bearing exotic registration plates from Germany, France, Holland, Belgium, Bulgaria and the Czech Republic. Then it was on to St Margaret's Bay, which is the closest point to the French coast – twenty-one miles away – and long-favoured spot of cross-Channel swimmers. Incidentally, in January 1999, there were stupendous cliff falls at St Margaret's Bay, as there were at Beachy Head. These events were quite normal: the white cliffs of Kent and Sussex retreat a metre further from France every year.

Deal was lovely but it was too cold to linger longer than to read the plaque in Marine Road proclaiming the spot where Julius Caesar landed in Britain on August 25th, 55 BC. Halfway between Ham and Worth, I stopped at a farm shop to buy a mixed bagful of locally grown apples – Katy's, Coxes, Worcesters and Russets. I was rather hoping they might have the gravity-falling Flower of Kent – the type of apple that conked Newton on the nog. They didn't, but I couldn't complain – the ones they did have were so tasty I couldn't stop eating them as I stood in the shop commiserating with the owner, an old boy who was slicing runner beans by the mountainful, about what a shame it was how supermarkets flew in insipid and tasteless air-freighted boxes of mush from the other side of the world instead of supporting the local growers and saving the centuries-old orchards on their doorstep from being grubbed.

As I was packing an extra bag of apples into my pannier, an elderly couple paused in their car beside me. The man, originally a sarf Landaner from Crystal Palace, wound down his window and said, ' 'Ere luv – yer got enough gears on that thing? Used to ride a 16-sprocket fixed wheel meself, I did. I once cycled from Crystal Palace to Brighton on it and when I got to Godstone 'ill, I collapsed! Ha! The fellas had to put me back on me bike. But I made it to Brighton 'n all!'

He asked me where I was from.

'Near Portsmouth,' I replied.

'Ah, good ol' Pompey! Used to be stationed down there, I did – Lee-on-Solent – in '43.'

I couldn't quite hear what he said next because of a flushing gust of squally wind that sent a tower of cardboard boxes cartwheeling across the car park, but it sounded something like how 'they never matched yer size, they didn't. 'Ad to be 'andcuffed to a wallopin' great German chap who was six foot seven. Gor-blimey! Did the fellas larf!'

His wife, cutting him short, leant across him and asked me where I was going. When I told her she said, 'Not alone?'

'Yes,' I said.

'Aww, bet yer mum worries 'erself sick about yer!'

Then, apropos of nothing, she said, 'I'll tell yer somethin', luv – yer find the cheapest cuppa tea in Sandwich is at the Co-op. Don't go to them tea shops – they're a right rip-off!'

I thanked her for this little tea-tip and as they drove off she called, 'We'll be thinkin' of yer!'

Medieval Sandwich is the northernmost of the Cinque Ports, though now it is situated some two miles from the sea. By this time it was raining so hard I didn't stop for a cheap cup of tea at the Co-op, nor did I stop for any sustenance from Ye Olde Fish and Chip Shoppe. But I did cycle down some rather nice little streets with such beguiling names as Moat Sole and Holy Ghost Alley.

On the road to Ramsgate, things looked up as I cycled past the massive-girthed Pfizer works (manufacturers of Viagra) because the rain stopped and the sun burst out. Then, on the spanking new Viking Coastal Trail cycle path, I met a man on a bike riding towards me. In an excitable fluster, he hailed me by name before letting me know he had just been looking at me in the book-shop in Ramsgate.

Biking-Viking Man was a young social-care worker and lived in Dover. He couldn't understand how I enjoyed cycle-camping alone because he hadn't liked it at all when he had tried it; he found it dull and boring.

'I prefer staying in hostels and chatting to people,' he said. 'Don't you get lonely spending so much time by yourself?'

'No,' I said, 'I like not having to talk to anyone.'

Unfortunately, Biking-Viking Man failed to catch this subtle hint because he not only wanted to talk to me but cycle with me as well.

'Can I ride with you for a bit?' he asked.

'But I'm cycling in the opposite direction from you,' I said.

'That's okay,' he said, 'it's my day off so it doesn't matter which direction I go.'

Oh dear, I thought, another persistent pedallist. Like Tim the Taxi before him, Biking-Viking Man might have felt he already knew me, but in my eyes he was unknown territory. He might have been coming over as a friendly young soul on the outside, but how was I to know that he was not a man with a mur-dering mission suddenly set on strangling me with my bicycling bungee behind a bush or bumping me off in Margate?

No, I would give it to him straight and not let any namby-pamby English reserve of not wanting to offend prevail over my innate life-preserving instincts.

'All right,' I heard myself saying, 'but just for a little way. I'm not very good at cycling and talking at the same time.'

So off we cycled towards Ramsgate, keeping two abreast on the Viking Coastal Trail as Biking-Viking Man asked me how I did this or why I did that. I answered in defensive mode. My guard was up. Chillenden was just down the road where not so long before Lin Russell was murdered with her six-year-old daughter, Megan, in a horrific hammer attack. The other young daughter, Josie, survived, but had to have a titanium plate inserted into her skull. A man had been charged with the murders, but not yet found guilty.

My English reserve did not prevail for long. With my sixth sense feeling uncomfortably jittery, I felt it was high time to put Part One of my Try-To-Shake-Him-Off Ploy into action by grabbing the opportunity to call a halt at a tourist information board. I then took an absurdly long and in-depth interest in looking at and reading about the full-size replica of the Viking Ship *Hugin* which had sailed from Denmark to Thanet in 1949 to celebrate the 1500th anniversary of the invasion of Britain (Thanet is the name of this easternmost peninsula of Kent, which in Roman times was an island, known to the Romans as *Tanatus*). Meanwhile, Biking-Viking Man remained standing astride his bike up on the cycle trail. My tactic to get shot of him was to hope that he would get so bored he'd turn tail and sail off back to Dover.

Unfortunately his staying power was as astounding as his boredom threshold. He waited . . . and he waited . . . and he waited. I now had no doubt about it; he was definitely a cyclopathic serial killer on the loose. There was no other explanation for such determination. He was awaiting his moment – killers are very good at that – and then he would pounce. So, after reading the same Viking information board for the fiftieth time, it was time to flex my gluteus maximus and put all extensive bodily mechanisms to the fore. In a word, I turned politely shirty and shook Biking-Viking Man off my trail, allowing me to continue on my way to Ramsgate in glorious solitude.

Menacing tent-soaking clouds were racing towards me off the North Sea as I plunged into one of London's favourite playgrounds – the busy Kent corner of Ramsgate, Broadstairs and Margate. As I hadn't slept inside since France, I thought I would save another waterlogged night's camping and treat myself to a B&B.

I tried a few places in Ramsgate but they all either smelt of the mingled odours of spilled beer, stale smoke, fried grease and sordid sex, or had nowhere safe to store my bike. Next stop: Broadstairs, 'Kent's Best Kept Secret' and 'The Jewel in Thanet's Crown'. (What's wrong with saying that Broadstairs is simply a bit more upmarket than the larger and louder and brasher Margate and Ramsgate between which Broadstairs is sandwiched?) I rode along the top of the cliffs that spurred the naming of this coastal resort; Broadstairs refers to a 'broad stairway' that was apparently built in the cliffs here to gain access to the sea some time in the fifteenth century.

At one point I came upon a man with edging shears in hand who was doing a spot of last-minute lawn border maintenance before the rains came. Behind him stood a small hotel with slightly ramshackle windows. I asked him if it was his hotel. He said that it was. I asked him if he had a vacancy. He said that he did. I asked him the price of the room. He told me £34. I asked him if I could see the room. He said that I could. By the time we had had a little chat and walked up to the room (which came with four beds, a balcony and a sea view with full wave-crashing-on-beach soundtrack), the price had dropped to £12. Geoff, a Kiwi, then gave me a tall glass of orange juice and two bananas and told me that in the seventies he had left Auckland and travelled overland to England on the hippy trail through Pakistan, Afghanistan and Iran, so he knew what it felt like to travel on a low budget. Geoff was also a long distance runner. His longest run to date was a cross-country one of sixty-two miles, which started at two in the afternoon and went through the night. He completed it in a dizzyingly fast fifteen hours. I had to have a sit down after hearing that.

That night, watching the first bit of television I had seen in weeks, I saw some of the New York Remembrance Service for British victims who died in the September 11th attacks. Later I heard Mayor Giuliani updating his daily index of disaster: 5422 missing; 201 confirmed dead, 37 uniformed officers among them; and 49,553 tons of rubble moved to a Staten Island landfill site by 3788 trucks.

The next morning, in a temporary lull in the rain, I rode past Bleak House (where Charles Dickens wrote *David Copperfield*; it is now the punter-pulling 'Dickens and Smugglers Museum') and North Foreland Lighthouse – the last one in the UK to be fully automated, in 1998. A light of some description has been at this point since 1499, to warn ships away from the treacherous Margate Roads and Goodwin Sands, which used to be an island, seven miles off shore. George Bernard Shaw applied for a post as assistant lighthouse keeper but was turned down.

Then I arrived in Margate. The best thing about Margate in my eyes was the half-a-century-old brass-plated instructions on the back of the doors in the cavernous time-warped toilet block on the seafront: SHOOT THE BOLT TO LOCK DOOR. I liked that – a forthright no-messing shoot-from-the-hip shoot-the-bolt. And very nice bolts they were too for shooting: massive great missiles of metal so robust that I was surprised that undercover arms dealers hadn't smuggled them out of the country and appropriated them as weapons of mass destruction. There's nothing like a good sturdy toilet bolt manufactured for indestructible durability to put the mind at rest.

After such a rank of resorts it was a relief to cycle far from any car along the sea wall following the marshland pasture that in Roman times was The Wantsum (it's all right, I've already got some, thanks) Channel. This waterway, once two miles wide, flowed between the Isle of Thanet and the mainland. Gradually it silted up and narrowed and was first bridged in 1485.

The peace of pedalling and the sounds and sights of the seabirds wheeling and crying overhead ended at Rulculver. Here, sharply etched against the sky, the twin towers of the ruined St Mary's Church stand as the principal landmark of the ten-mile stretch of coast between Herne Bay and Margate. So great is their importance as a navigational safeguard that these twelfth-century towers, nicknamed the Two Sisters, were restored by Trinity House.

There was no one else around apart from a short, bald, bespectacled bloke with a mouth like a tea-towel holder. I presumed he was a birder or a twitcher, or possibly even a Peeping Tom, dressed as he was in camouflage kit and bristling with cameras and tripods and telescopes.

'You look like a glutton for punishment!' were the only words he said to me as he trudged along, labouring under the weight of all that telescopic hardware. *Look who's talking!*

I stopped near Seasalter to eat my lunch between some gravestones at All Saint's Church. The door of the church was locked. A notice said it cost £145 a week to keep it open. A woman with a puffy cloud of white hair appeared, read the notice and, like me, tried the door. When the door failed to open the woman did as I had done and peered through the big, dungeon-sized keyhole.

'What a shame,' she said. 'It's those young vandals, you know. That's why it's locked. I tell you, violence is ignorance by any other name.'

Outside Tesco's in Faversham, I was making light work of a double-decker energy bar while attentively watching an invasion force of young yummy mummies coming and going in their fleet of flashy super-Shogun urban tanks. It was all I could do to stop myself from automatically adopting the defensive warfare fighter's crouch, as I was half expecting to see the Shoguns' support troops fanning out behind them armed to the eyeballs with rocket launchers, bazookas, death rays, spider powers, war dogs and mystical rings. These days, there can be few sights more riveting than watching well-groomed women trying to steer their monster Landcruisers or Outriders or Mavericks or Trailblazers or Nissan Patrols round the chicanes and obstacles of a superstore's car park, displaying all the advanced motoring skills of a toddler forcing a Tonka toy through the playground sandpit. At one point I counted eleven of these unforgivingly immovable brutes all vying for top position on the grid. Anyone unaccustomed to the sight of these aggressive fashion-accessory vehicles could be forgiven for mistaking this troop of young urbanite mothers as either an invading force or formidable, gung-ho, trans-Saharan explorers stocking up on supplies before setting off in convoy for Africa. But they were merely stopping by at Tesco's after dropping little Johnny off at his league-table-topping primary school. These days, one apparently needs a domesticated armoured carrier to pick up a trolley-load of shopping.

I was distracted from my musings by a small but generously built woman in her sixties waddling out of the superstore laden with shopping. She entered the sparse-of-cycles bike park area whereupon she proceeded to load the worn and faded canvas panniers on her old rusty-chained boneshaker. As she placed a box of All Bran (it's not, you know, it's got other things in it) and a pack of toilet rolls in her bicycle basket, she noticed me standing beside my equally well-laden steed.

Straightening her back, her bosom magnificent in white pinafore, she said, 'It's amazing what you can get on a bike!'

'It certainly is!' I replied. 'You always think that you'll never fit it all in, but you always do!'

'My friend says I'm mad!' said the woman, trying to cram a bag of sugar, a jar of beetroot, a loaf of bread and two pork chops into a packed pannier already straining at the seams. 'Says I should take a taxi. But I hate paying for taxis. It costs £2.70 from my house to here and it's not even half a mile. I tell my friend: why would I want to waste all that money on a taxi when I can ride to the supermarket for free? *And* I'm not polluting the air!'

Mrs All Bran obviously felt she had found a soulmate. There was no stopping her now. 'And don't you think one car's enough for one family? On my estate there's a woman next door who's got a car. Her boyfriend's got one too and their three kids have all got one each. That's *five* cars sitting in the street outside my house! So when a friend comes to visit there's nowhere for them to park.'

I watched Mrs All Bran mount her bike unsteadily and ride off through the Shogun car park in a laboriously high gear. No sooner had she been swallowed behind a swirling maelstrom of bull-bar-fronted Mavericks, nudging aside a snaking line of unmanned wayward-wheeling Tesco trolleys making a break for freedom, than her vacated bike park stand was filled by a woman's small-wheeled Kingpin shopper with an appropriated wire-caged supermarket basket strapped to the rear rack. Mrs Kingpin, cloaked in a tatty mac and topped in a headscarf drawn tight around a crinkled grey face, took one look at me and tethered mount and said, 'Oh my word! I thought I carried a load on my bike but I think you beat me to it!'

Purloining Mrs All Bran's words, I said, 'It's amazing what you can get on a bike!'

Mrs Kingpin agreed.

'I cycle in to the shops,' she said, 'but I always push home. At my age I haven't got the confidence to ride it full of shopping. I haven't got the balance.'

'I think you're doing very well that you're coming in on your bike at all,' I said.

'Well, I do my best!' she replied as she extracted two blue string bags from her basket. 'Take care luvvie!' she said, before disappearing through the gaping-hungry doors of the store.

It was all happening in Faversham's Tesco bike park because next on the scene was a very round man on a moped who locked the front wheel on to the leg of the bike stand. He removed his open-face peaked helmet and unzipped his padded Rukka jacket, revealing a body so broad in beam that he resembled a bus with trousers.

'Gor blimey!' he said, 'Yer gotta lotta gear on that bike of yours!'

'I know,' I said. 'It's amazing what you can get on a bike!'

This utterance surprised the man because he said, 'Oh! You English? I thought you was foreign like!' Then he said, 'I toured once on me bike an' it killed me! Never again, I thought, an' I ain't either!'

Ah, that's the spirit!

CHAPTER 33

The Isle of Sheppey conjures up visions of a lovely rural retreat full of grazing sheep and gaily gambolling lambs: in Anglo-Saxon, its name literally means Sheep Island. I had hoped to reach Sheppey on what my map marked as the Harty Ferry, but when I got there I discovered I was about forty years too late. A man laughed and said that since the beginning of the 'sixties, the Kingsferry Bridge has been the way to go. So I went.

Twenty miles later, having passed by industrial parks, housing estates, gated communities and immense warehouse retailers, I found myself being sucked on to the car- and truck-laden A249 to cross over to Sheppey by way of this bridge – a spectacularly ugly edifice with four stained grey concrete towers, which from a distance resembled a giant table floating upside down in the muddy dock-polluted drifting waters of the Swale Channel.

Things didn't improve much from there. Instead of grasslands sprouting sheep, I found hillsides mushrooming with spanking new sterile housing developments under the flapping flags of JONES HOMES and BOVIS HOMES. I also found dockyards and scrapyards and chimneys and ports and pylons and charred roadside wrecks and trailer parks a-plenty. I camped behind a scrub of razor-wire-enclosed wasteland on the edge of Sheerness as depleted energy levels had left me with no leg-power to reach the supposedly quieter eastern reaches of the island. With handbrake-turn teenagers performing doughnuts of burnt rubber on a nearby road competing with the sounds of smashing bottles as a gang of youths beat each other up, I can't say it was the best night's sleep I've ever had. As I lay in this urbanised nightmare of screaming and screeching brakes and wailing police sirens, it was hard to believe that Sheppey is noted for the variety of birds of prey that over-winter on the island. Short-eared owls and hen harriers quarter the fields, while marsh harriers both breed and winter here. Merlin and peregrine can pay flying visits too.

Sheerness, whose name ironically means 'bright headland', was a pretty dismal place to wake up in. My litter-strewn camp spot probably wasn't enhanced by a view of power stations and pylons and concentration-camp fencing. The weather didn't help, either. After a night of scattered showers, the rain had now set in solidly, streaming down with a stubbornness peculiar to areas of grim wretchedness.

The port of Sheerness lies at the point where the River Medway meets the Thames and was once the sight of a naval dockyard laid out in the time of Charles II under the supervision of Samuel Pepys, who described the location as 'a most proper place for the purpose'. It was here, too, that HMS *Victory* docked in 1805, bringing Nelson's body back home after the Battle of Trafalgar. Following a death theme (my spirits were not soaring) I steered off down the side of Sheerness to peer out through the veil of sopping grey cloud to Deadman's Island. This was once the location of a burial ground for sailors who died from deadly diseases while quarantined on board their ship.

After visiting Minster (a highly unlikely spot for one of the oldest sites of Christianity in the country), and passing a bungalow that had obviously got way above its station by calling itself Ben Nevis, I cycled around the rest of Sheppey, enjoying only its more rural offshoot, the Isle of Harty.

Heading west up the Thames Estuary towards the mighty maws of London was not conducive for cycling or camping. It felt as if all the cars and articulated container trucks in the world had descended upon my route, all seemingly intent on crushing me into the gutter. National Car Free Day occurred while I was on this stretch, but I wouldn't have been aware of it if I hadn't already known it, as there seemed to be more cars than ever. And then I got depressed thinking about how cars spoil so much and how they will keep being driven here and there just for the sake of getting there and coming back here – until the oil runs out.

When bicycles were first invented, church attendance in the nineteenth century became affected by the popularity of cycling. This prompted a preacher in Baltimore, Maryland, to deliver his forthright condemnation from the pulpit:

Those bladder-wheeled bicycles are diabolical devices of the demon of darkness. They are contrivances to trap the feet of the unwary and skin the nose of the innocent. They are full of guile and deceit. When you think you have broken one to ride and subdued its wild and Satanic nature, behold it bucketh you off the road and teareth a great hole in your pants. Look not on the bicycle when it bloweth upon its wheels for at least it bucketh like a bronco and hurteth like thunder. Who has skinned legs? Who has a bloody nose? Who has ripped breeches? They that dally along with the bicycle.

If he felt hell hath no fury like bicycles back then, who knows what that preacher would have made of today's 'diabolical devices' swarming over our roads? I think the fact that a bike could teareth a hole in his pants would be the least of his worries.

The evenings were drawing in, the nights turning chilly. And they continued to leave a lot to be desired as I camped among a profusion of power stations, power lines, scrap yards, oil refineries, derelict buildings, landfill sites, building sites, wasteland, scrubland, litter-ridden cemeteries and Channel Tunnel rail links. Every so often I would pass incongruously through fat-cat commuter territory – big money, big houses, big cars, but still little hope for grand panoramic camping.

The highlight of this area was Cooling, a village in the heart of the Hoo Peninsula, which I came across on the way to the Isle of Grain peninsula and its sprawling chimney-flaming oil refinery. The unexpected thing about Cooling was its public convenience, because for one thing I wasn't expecting to find a public toilet in such a small and relatively isolated spot, and the other was discovering that it had received a 'Highly Commended Loo of the Year Award 1996/7'. It wasn't up to Southsea's standards, but it was still pretty dapper. And as I revelled in the functioning door locks (no shooting-bolts here, just gentle sliders) and the abundant supplies of toilet paper, I tried to imagine what type of clip-board-ticking person travels around the country trying and testing these amenities.

Across the way stood St James's, the church of Dickens's childhood wanderings. With its Early Gothic chancel and eerie churchyard, it was here that he found inspiration to write one of the most famous descriptive passages in English literature:

I found out for certain . . . that the dark flat wilderness beyond the churchyard, intersected with dykes and mounds and gates, with scattered cattle feeding on it, was the marshes; and that the low leaden line beyond was the river; and that the distant savage lair from which the wind was rushing, was the sea; and that the small bundle of shivers growing afraid of it all and beginning to cry, was Pip.

'Hold your noise!' cried a terrible voice, as a man started up from among the graves at the side of the church porch. 'Keep still, you little devil, or I'll cut your throat!'

There seems to be no place for Pip and Magwitch in the likes of today's government. The recent *Great Expectations* in the crazy world of runway politics is Her Majesty's Secretary of State for Transport's proposal to build a four- or five-runway airport on these Kent marshes, home to 200,000 migratory birds (Hoo is Heathrow for wildfowl), which is intended to handle 110 million passengers a year by 2030 (about 60 million passengers used Heathrow in 2002). This backward way of looking forward idea is for planes to land and take off over the Thames estuary, allowing the airport to operate twenty-four hours a day in order to appease the voracious appetite of the British for cheap holidays in the sun.

Along with the wintering birds, this area of Cooling and Cliffe is among other hairy and fluttery things home to Britain's largest heronry, five RSPB nature reserves, water voles, emerald damselflies and the rare maid of Kent dung beetle, not to mention 1100 human beings – some of whom may be rare maids in themselves. 'You are now entering government killing fields,' said the signs put up by local residents fiercely opposed to the Cliffe airport strategy – a strategy whose document appears to ooze with corporate panic that London might 'run out' of runways in twenty years. *Oh no! Not run out of runways like we might run out of sugar or the rare maid of Kent dung beetles!* Apparently, there is a 'very real danger' that if we don't go building extra runways all over the southeast (in desperately vulnerable Essex, it is proposed to concrete over 3000 acres of green belt, sixty listed buildings and two ancient monuments just to satisfy flying demand), rival European airports such as Charles de Gaulle will overtake us.

Overtake us in what? Overcrowded skies? Excess aircraft noise. Air traffic controllers' hair-pulling stress levels? Near air collisions? Congested roads? Smelliness? Pollution? Killing off rare maids? It all sounds like some sort of 'Who Can Ruin the World First?' competition. But in my grand capacity as a member of the Cooling Public Toilet Appreciation Society I have a solution: stop right there, slow right down, and go by boat. After all, their runways already cover 70% of the world in a lovely sloppy soup.

CHAPTER 34

'The river sweats oil and tar,' wrote T.S. Eliot of the Thames. Nowhere is this more evident than on the industrialised shores of its lower reaches, where muddy waters, awash with the detritus of an up-river metropolis, ebb and flow and stain and swell between low banks built up with docks, pylons, flaring chimneys and oil refineries.

Gravesend sounds like a death of a place, but instead of 'graves' its name really means 'groves', though no small green leafy wooded areas made themselves apparent to me. Once upon a time, maybe, but not now.

Appropriately enough, it was at Gravesend that my rear inner tube died on me by expiring in sudden spectacular style on a busy main road just as a ferocious bone-rattling storm was breaking. I dragged the stricken steed to the nearest shelter – some builders' scaffolding – and was tending to Puncture No. 2 by changing tubes with oily numb wet hands when a violent gust of wind caused a partial collapse of the scaffold. Fortunately I had my helmet on at the time or else I would have sustained a sizeable dent in my head.

By this stage, feeling in serious need of cycling among green trees and green hills and green lanes instead of London's car-spewing grey urban entrails, I decided Gravesend would be the end of my journey west up the Thames and so jumped on the little passenger ferry that runs between Gravesend and Tilbury. There were only two other passengers on board. I presumed it must be busy during the rush hour.

'Nah, we only take a handful,' said the deckhand man. 'Often we get over to the other side and there's no one to pick up, and then when we get back here, there's still no one.'

The deckhand man had a worn and rugged face like a beaten hull and hands strong and knotted as hawsers.

'Have you worked on boats all your life?' I asked. 'You look as if you have!'

'Do I?' he laughed. 'Must be the stress of it all! I've only been doing it four-and-a-half years!'

'Is that all? I thought you were an old sea dog!'

'Nah! I've done a thousand different jobs in me time.'

'So do you quite like this one if you've managed to do it for four-and-a-half years?'

'It's good in the summer, but in the winter it's hard. This morning the fog was so thick we couldn't see nuffink.'

'Do you have a lot of near misses?'

'We've had a few close calls! We've got a radar but it's not that accurate. A container ship just missed us one morning. When it's bad we ask the Port Authority what's coming.'

What with Tilbury docks and the International Cruise Terminal sitting opposite Gravesend, shipping is busy this stretch of the Thames, with cutters and tugs helping to maintain a steady flow of river traffic. Because of this, Gravesend marks the point at which ships entering the Thames – some half a mile wide at this stage – take on a river pilot for guidance upstream.

I could have done with a pilot myself to lead me to a toilet in Tilbury. Instead, I got very confused amid an industrial sea of dock walls, cranes, containers, construction sites and high fencing before almost getting arrested when I burst through the back doors of a building inconveniently holding a police conference.

'Whoops! Sorry!' I said to a rank of uniformed officers. 'I'm just trying to find a toilet!'

Eventually I ended up gaining a little light relief behind a wall in the salubrious setting of a scrap yard where a darting rat ran out behind me. It's a perilous process, this peeing lark, because then I narrowly missed being garrotted by a car bonnet that suddenly took this highly inopportune moment to slide off a towering heap and land at my feet. I blamed the rat for dislodging it.

I never imagined I would find grazing horses at Tilbury Power Station. They were eating grey, polluted grass scattered with the decaying and indigestible remnants of refrigerators, mangled car doors, ripped mattresses and three-piece suites, but it was still nice to see nature's four-legged power stations standing defiant in the face of the monstrous pipes and wires and spewing chimneys that made their ancestors redundant. I paused in the rain on a railway bridge to take in the arresting sight of the dreary but rather magnificent power station. One of the inside walls of the bridge bore the aerosoled mantra:

GROW IT – ROLL IT – SMOKE IT – GANJA.

Over on the other edge, down beside the track, sprouted an oxymoron: a sign, slowly being submerged by a small patch of dirty dull-leaved foliage, declared that here lieth the 'Tilbury Power Station Nature Reserve'. Which is just another way of saying: *'It's okay! We may be burning 5 zillion tons of fossil fuels and slowly poisoning the world into all oblivion but look here'* (though you have to look hard) *'we have saved this bit of bush at our feet.'*

Henry VIII appeared again in the form of a fort. He was the first one to build a defence to guard the river approaches to London from possible attacks by the French. His fort was adapted by Charles II to deal with the threat of raids by Dutch warships. Any well-aimed cannonballs from the river would probably have sent the whole lot tumbling, but as no shot was ever fired in anger, it was never put to the test. So now it remains a perfect late-seventeenth-century fort with arrowhead bastions marooned in a modern sea of industrialisation. It was strange to look at this scene of giant power stations, dockland cranes, sprawling oil refineries and skeletons of burnt-out vehicles stretched out before me and think that this was where Elizabeth I once reviewed her troops before the onslaught of the Spanish Armada. I don't think she would be much impressed with what she would see today, though she'd probably approve of the horses.

Mucking Landfill Site came and went, as did the optimistic Stanford-le-Hope. It was an uninspiring place on the oil-tanker-laden main road to Coryton – one of the largest oil refineries in the country, sprawling for more than three miles along the north side of the Thames at the unheavenly Thames Haven.

A little later I happened to meet a man who used to work at the Coryton's vast Shell refinery. I was sitting in a graveyard in Fobbing at the time. The rain had stopped and a surprisingly hot sun filled its place so I grabbed the opportunity of soaking up a few stray rays to eat my lunch beside two tilted headstones. The grave-strimmer man had been strimming around the graves at the bottom of the churchyard. After about ten minutes he walked over to me and said, 'If yer 'avin' a break, me darlin', I'm 'avin' one too!'

He flipped open a can of Carlsberg and, uninvited, came and sat next to me. But I didn't mind. He was a nice man, a Londoner.

'Yer know wha'?' he said, swilling a mouthful of beer. 'It would make me job an 'elluva lot easier if they buried them bodies in straight lines. Then I could cut all this grass easy like with me mower!'

He told me he had fallen into this job by chance when his neighbour, who used to cut the grass, had an accident and strimmed off his foot.

'I said I'd fill in for 'im an' I've been doin' it ever since!' he said. 'I like it up here. Feel I do me bit for the local community, if yer know wha' I mean. I don't go to church or nothink like that. Used to come up 'ere when I was working at the refinery.'

He paused to slug down several more mouthfuls of beer and I took the opportunity to finish off my banana. From where we were sitting up here on the hill, we could look down over Coryton's massive reels of storage tanks and flaming chimneys. In the haze of the Haven, supertankers floated like fallen skyscrapers. Beyond them rose Kent's Hoo Peninsula, looking quiet and countrified where Kent's rare maids were busily beetling away in the dung. But for how much longer?

'We used to 'ave 35,000 men down there,' said Grave Strimmer man. 'Now there're only 23,000. It was all them computers coming in, like. They took away the work. I was offered early retirement 'n all 'n' I took it like a flash. Seven years ago now, that was. I'd been there thirty long years, yer know. These days it's an 'ard decision whether I'm goin' to spend me day playin' golf or go fishin'. I go down to them marshes too from time to time cos I like a spot of birdwatchin' on the side, I do!'

His life now was a nice contrast to the dangers of the refinery.

'They 'ave a lot of accidents down there,' he said, 'a lot of explosions. One killed seven men. We was 'avin' a flair to burn off the excess gas at the time. It's a dangerous job all right. Very dangerous. Can't say I'm sorry to be out of it meself.'

We chatted a bit more about this and that and then, after asking me where I was going, he said, 'Blimey! Yer takin' a gap year or summink before yer 'ead off to university?'

'No,' I laughed, thinking, *here we go again*, 'I'm a bit older than that!'

'Yeah?' he said. ' 'Ow much older?'

'Loads older,' I replied.

'Like wha'?'

'Like a decade or two.'

'Nah – yer 'avin' a larf, intcha?'

'I'm not,' I said, 'I'm deadly serious!'

Mr Grave Strimmer looked at me disbelievingly. Then he unbuttoned his shirt and took it off, revealing wheatfields of chest hair. *Hello? What's going on here?* I could smell stale male sweat. But it was okay, he was only using his shirt to mop his clammy damp armpits.

We sat in silence a moment before he said, 'I'll tell yer wha', darlin'. I'll give yer one bit of advice.'

'What's that?' I said. *Do I really want to go down this road?*

'Give Canvey Island a miss. It's blaady awful!'

'But my great granddad used to have a bungalow there between the wars.'

'Yeah? Well it's still blaady awful!'

When I left he helped me push my bike out of the long thick grass he had yet to tackle with his strimmer between the gravestones and said, 'Look after yerself, darlin'. And mind them 'ooligans down S'arf-end!'

CHAPTER 35

Grave Strimmer Man had been right: Canvey Island was bloody awful. But only in parts, even if those parts were majority parts. It's a flat bridge-connected shoe-shaped piece of land full of bungalows, trailer parks, holiday chalets, fun fairs, bingo halls, amusement arcades . . . and cars. That said, I did find a few patches of grassland, a dirt road, a 'popply' beach and lots of fen-like drainage ditches, which though no home for rare maids, are watery palaces for the likes of newts and dragonflies. And up on the massive concrete sea wall there were stirring views of supertankers and container ships sliding past at arm's length in and out of the Yantlet Dredged Channel.

My great granddad, a Londoner, had his own builders business – Lewis Frank Dew & Sons – based in Hammersmith. Most weekends he and his wife Li (Eliza) would take their son Frank (my dad's father) and two daughters, Ethel and Dot, to Fenchurch Street where they would catch a train to Benfleet. There was no bridge connecting Canvey Island to the mainland in those days so instead, at low tide, the whole family piled on to a horse and trap and crossed over the muddy sands of Benfleet Creek to their self-built bungalow. Another great granddad, Fred, would probably have liked to go to Canvey too, had he not dropped dead of a heart attack on a London bus.

If it wasn't for the immensity and relative security of the sea wall, Canvey would be well awash, as most of the island lies below high-water level. The present sea wall was raised and strengthened after the 1953 flood disaster when the full force of the storm-driven tides swept across the island on the night of

237

January 31st, drowning fifty-eight people. This storm surge arose after a day of gale-force winds and high spring tides which effectively sucked up water from the north of the North Sea, pushing it southwards to hit the east coast with devastating effect: 100,000 hectares of eastern England were flooded and 307 people lost their lives that night, making it the largest natural disaster in Britain in modern times. Essex and Suffolk suffered the most. People who had no reason to believe they were at risk of flooding – and in some cases lived two miles inland – found themselves waking in the middle of a swirling sea. The surge was predicted by the Met Office and the Dutch Surge Warning Service in that forecasts of dangerously high water levels were issued hours before they occurred. But because the telephone lines along the east coast had been brought down by the wind, virtually no warnings of the severity of the storm reached the affected counties until it was too late.

I cycled back to Basildon, whose boundaries include the town of Billericay which, with its decidedly exotic appellation, always sounds as if it should be rubbing shoulders with Australia's Toowooba or Africa's Ouagadougou rather than Essex's Basildon.

And so to Southend-on-Sea, which may be all big and brash and noisy, but so it should be, having been a day tripper's delight of fun and frivolity for well over a century – since the first Thames paddle-steamer thrashed down river to land Londoners at the world's longest pleasure pier. I cycled along the seven miles of built-up seafront past acres of pristine parkland sloping down to the road flanked by benches colonised by Southend's senior citizenry lapping up the thin sunlight as they gazed out across the murky sea. It was all really rather pleasant – much better than I expected. I think I was too early in the evening for Grave Strimmer Man's ' 'ooligans', or even Germaine Greer's Essex Girl, whom she once described as 'anarchy on stilts. When she and her mates descend upon Southend for a rave, even the bouncers grow pale'.

That night I camped at the eastern end of Southend in Shoeburyness beside an MOD artillery range and a trailer park in a cheerless chain-fenced cage with high, bolted hooligan-proof gates. I found a red public phone box, which had a sign in it saying 'PLEASE DO NOT USE THIS TELEPHONE BOX AS A TOILET'. And yet it still smelt like a stale urinal. I rang the builder, who told me his perforated inlet manifold gasket was looking good (I think he was talking engines here, but it was best not to express too much interest), and then mum, who said that dad had found a family of rats nesting in the log pile outside the back door.

The next morning I finally escaped the clutches of an industrial mind-jangling area of overpopulation. Suddenly, just north of Southend, I emerged into countryside. Ahh, the outback of Essex! I could take a deep breath once again! It seemed like a rural backwater in comparison with the overwhelming effluence and affluence of the estuary up the Thames.

I passed through Great Wakering and was heading for Wakering Stairs and Foulness Island when I hit another barrier, as the whole area is closed to the public because of MOD 'activities'.

'Oh,' I said in disappointed tone to the barrel-chested and bull-necked military man on the gate, 'I was looking forward to riding up to Foulness. It looks nice and empty on my map!'

'We don't like to advertise where we are,' he replied stonefaced, trained to indifference.

But it may not be this way for too much longer: one of the last bastions of Cold War paranoia – the ban on identifying defence establishments on Ordnance Survey maps – has recently fallen victim to advances in technology. Now that every inch of the British Isles has been commercially mapped from the air with close-ups being available on the internet, the Ministry of Defence has had to change tack. It admits that it is silly to keep these top-secret defence installations off the map; if they can be seen from the air or from the road, then they can be shown on a map.

The decision to remove military installations from maps pre-dates the Second World War when Whitehall set up a unit to expunge sensitive sites from public documents. The same unit also removed street signs to confuse any invading force. So now dozens of top-secret places like the Flyingdales Early Warning Station in North Yorkshire (former home of the famous 'golf balls'), the chemical and biological research station at Porton Down in Wiltshire and the Royal Ordnance factory at Burghfield in Berkshire, where Britain's atomic weapons are assembled, are being added to Britain's maps. Until now they did not officially exist. Even the Atomic Weapons Establishment just southwest of Reading is to be identified, which is a good thing as it could help homing pigeons who risk getting caught in the rain over Reading. This Aldermaston base, the size of a small town, is currently depicted on my OS map as open countryside, fields and trees, which to us roving cyclists is really very cruel. There you are, eyeing up a nice bit of map-marked camouflaged shrubbery for a much-needed widdle, only to find the Ministry of Defence staring up your rear.

And so was the case with Foulness Island, which may sound like a malodorous place but it derives its name from the Old English *fugol* (bird) and *naess* (promontory). The island's thirty-five square miles of offshore sandbanks attract enormous flocks of geese and wildfowl. If the proposal some forty-odd years ago that Maplin Sands should be the site of a deep-sea port and London's third airport with connecting road and rail links had been accepted, this lonely stretch of land of wildflowers and 10,000 wintering Brent geese would have become unrecognisable.

Although it was still three months till Christmas I passed a festively premature sight in the village of Barling: Santa stuck in the top of the chimney of Jail Farm Cottage and festooned with fairy lights. I think he had peaked too early myself. Then, in the garden of the house next door, another oddity: among the roses and antirrhinums sat a very large propeller off an aeroplane, which to my unaccustomed aviation eye looked like something off a Messerschmidt. All these incongruous garden ornaments were confusing me. Then I put two and two together. Santa, having obviously had enough of sledges and wayward reindeers that end up getting clamped in Piccadilly Circus, had, somewhere along his return route to the North Pole, hijacked a light German aircraft, lost control of it over Essex and crashed into Jail House Farm. There was no other explanation.

Essex villagers are an enterprisingly self-sufficient lot, judging from the amount of home-grown goods for sale beside 'honesty boxes' of jam jars and old biscuit tins on tables and stalls outside their garden gates. There were stacks of eggs (hen and duck), bags of fruit and vegetables (tomatoes, cucumbers, cabbages, onions, runner beans, beetroot, courgettes, corn cobs, potatoes, parsley, apples, plums, damsons), jars of jam, honey, marmalade, chutney and pickle, bags of manure, litters of kittens and garden furniture and birdtables and nestboxes ('MORE SELECTION INSIDE!'). I also passed an inordinate number of antique shops and garden centres, and catteries with names like Pampurred Pets and Pussy Palace.

I was a bit disappointed with Essex because I thought I would be cycling through its flat(ish) lands in no time, but then I discovered it was full of meandering river estuaries to follow (Roach, Crouch, Blackwater, Colne and Stour). Daniel Defoe's progress on his travels round England was similarly hampered when he wrote: 'From the marshes and low ground, not being able to travel without many windings and indentures, by reason of the creeks and waters . . .'

Then the headwinds and rains returned with a vengeance to set me back further. Radio 4's weathermen and women (or, as I believe they are now supposed to be called, 'broadcasting meteorologists') all seemed to find this bad weather terribly funny. Isobel Lang had the audacity actually to laugh when she forecast storms and gales, while Philip Avery, who has the horrible habit of describing the odd shower as 'bits and pieces of rain' (bits and pieces of paper, maybe, but please, not rain) got all poetical and said, 'So much for seasons of mists and mellow fruitfulness – it's more a tempest we've got on the cards today, *chuckle, chuckle.*' Their chummy terminology quite put me off my porridge.

By the time I reached Ipswich my feet had been swimming in my shoes for five days on the hop. Crawling into my leaking tent at night felt like lying beneath a giant colander through which 'bits and pieces' of rain would trickle. Added to that, it was getting harder to camp, what with the evenings drawing in and the nights turning chilly. So, on a roundabout at the base of the towering concrete Orwell Bridge, I treated myself to a bed and a bath at the Travel Inn. I was glad not to have room service because I think the 'room servicer', on setting eyes on my room, would have immediately thrown me off the premises. I had rigged up an elaborate lattice work of bungee-cord washing lines that criss-crossed over each other a multitude of times from window frame to door handle to television wall mount to bedboard fixing. Upon these was strung an array of dripping gloves, socks, clothes, jackets, bivvy bags, sleeping bags, inner tent, fly sheet, ground sheet, sleeping mats, upturned panniers, map bags and stuff sacks. It may have made my nocturnal visit to the bathroom feel more like a trek through the virgin jungles of Papua New Guinea, with all manner of strange tangled objects trying to snap at me and trip me up while horrible green flapping things thrashed around in my face, but at least it was a good security measure: anyone trying to climb through the window or steal through the door would have caused a complete collapse of several furlongs of bungees festooned with an extensive collection of camping clobber to land with a wallop upon my bed.

Beyond my primeval rainforest of Chinese laundry, the storm raged on.

My only gripe with the Travel Inn was two stickers I found stuck on the wall in the bathroom. One, placed over the hot water tap, said:

CAUTION! HOT WATER.

The other, attached to the tiles over the towel rail warned:

CAUTION! THIS TOWEL RAIL CAN GET HOT.

Do we really need to be told that heated towel rails can get heated or hot water can get hot? And why stop at hot water? Surely the Travel Inn's bedroom kettle should come with a sticker alerting its user to the fact that:

WHEN THIS KETTLE IS BOILING IT IS BOILING.

Or maybe a bedside sticker drawing one's attention to the naked truth that:

DANGER – THIS BED IS A BED

because you never know, someone might just mistake it for a light switch or a telephone directory or possibly even a complimentary shower cap.

CHAPTER 36

The flat, windswept watercolour lands of East Anglia swallowed me whole with their huge inverted bowls of wide skies and horizon-racing clouds. Suffolk had started out as watery as Essex, with the Rivers Orwell, Deben, Ore, Alde and Blyth, and I wound my way around their snaking banks.

Two notable things happened in Woodbridge. First, the rain stopped. Then, as I was standing outside a store called Loaves and Fishes in a bedazzling burst of sunshine, I heard someone call my name. I turned round and there, smiling broadly, was someone I hadn't seen for ten years. In 1990, I had been cycling across Romania six months after Ceauşescu was shot, when I reached a town called Sibiu, many of whose buildings were riddled with bullet holes from the previous December's uprising. It was here that I had met Brian Dale-Thomas and his wife Aminge, the first Britons to cross my path since I had been cycling across Western Europe a couple of months before. At first I noticed they had both been giving me very strange looks and it was only when I got round to looking in a mirror that I realised why. I had been cycling close to Copşa Mićă, which was then Europe's most polluted town, with chimneys belching out thick clouds of industrial poisons that covered everything – houses, cars, animals, vegetation – with black carbon, my body included. I looked as if I had been clambering around in a coal mine.

'I will never forget the state of your filthy face!' laughed Brian, as we stood in spick-and-span Woodbridge.

I had met up with Brian and Aminge a couple of times not long after I got back from Eastern Europe. But then I had gone away again and had my address book stolen so we lost contact. On one of our meet-ups I had met their daughter Clare, an anorexic, who was a few years older than me. I asked Brian how Clare was now.

'She died in Thailand,' he said, 'of pneumonia. She was too weak to survive.'

I was shocked. I knew she had been suffering from anorexia for twenty years, but when I met her she was actually going through a better period and was putting on a bit of weight. But then she slid downwards and became so thin and weak she was susceptible to almost any infection going.

Brian couldn't linger because he was off to pick up Aminge who was 'having her neck done'. He gave me his address, together with a huge hug, and then he was gone. For the rest of the day I kept thinking about Clare.

Following the coast and estuaries from Woodbridge to Southwold was the best riding I'd had for weeks. Even the returned rain and the deep-flooded lanes didn't mar the enjoyment of spinning along Suffolk's quiet narrow byways lined with hedgerows heaving with blackberries and bursting with birds packing their bags for winter.

A continuous flow of sights came and went as I rode past Sutton Hoo, where in 1939 the richest and most spectacular hoard of treasure ever found in Britain was unearthed from the elaborate grave of a Saxon king, and Bawdsey, where radar was first developed before the Second World War and where, as I discovered, wild celery grows beneath the hedgerows. Orford Ness was good too because it is full of superlatives: the largest cuspate shingle spit in Europe (it's about ten miles long) and the most easterly point in Britain (a joint equal with Lowestoft). And like the Fleet, the salty lagoon behind Chesil Beach, it is also where Barnes Wallis experimented with bouncing bombs.

Aldeburgh was good for feminism because it was the home of the first woman doctor in England and the first woman mayor. More importantly, it was good for my stomach, because the town's Co-op was the only shop I found open late, saving me from a hungry night. The night got off to a bad start, though, because I couldn't find anywhere to camp. I had been hoping to find a tent-spot somewhere along the River Alde but it was all very marshy, as George Crabbe, Suffolk's best known poet (who was born in Aldeburgh), attests in his verse story *The Borough*:

Here samphire banks and saltwort bound the flood,
There stakes and sea weed withering in the mud:
And higher up a ridge of all things base
Which some strong tide has rolled upon the place.

Aldeburgh itself was an incredibly picturesque little place of Georgian houses surrounded by nature reserves, heaths and commons. But then, cycling north out of the town, I found an ugly caravan park the size of several football pitches and resembling a jerry-built estate. Unfortunately tents were prohibited, which was strange: an eyesore covered with scores of vast, boxy static caravans was permitted to defile the landscape, but a small green tent that would blend in unnoticed and which, apart from a six-foot patch of flattened ground, would leave no traces by morning? An emphatic 'NO!'

When I stumble upon irritatingly nonsensical bans like this, I find the best thing is simply to ignore them. Especially when I'm in need of a shower. So, as a damp dusk fell and the chill of the autumn night air tightened around me, I skulked on to the site and put up my tent on a very nice patch of billiard-table lawn behind the back of an unoccupied wall of caravan (sometimes their preposterous size can have their benefits). I then managed to enter the locked toilet block (I'm giving away no secrets here except to say I vandalised nothing), helped myself to a hot shower, washed out some socks and a few other essentials, and warmed myself up under the electric hand dryer. Early the next morning I was gone before anyone nabbed me. That'll teach them, I thought.

I gave the vast and intimidating grey concrete hulk of Sizewell Nuclear Power Station a wide berth not least because it was rumoured the next terrorist attacks could be on Britain's plutonium-making reactors. And what a balls-up of my cycling plans that would be! I had to get to Scarborough yet.

All down the east of England the coast is slowly, or in some places speedily, being swallowed up by the ravaging North Sea. One of the most dramatic sites where this has happened is medieval Dunwich, where the sea has been taking the town away from Suffolk for over 800 years. The original settlement, founded by St Felix in 632, grew into a flourishing trading port on the River Blythe; its deep-sea fleet traded timber, grain, salt, hides, wool and herring with Iceland, Norway and Bordeaux and it thrived on fishing and shipbuilding.

There were more than fifty churches, monasteries and convents and as many as 5000 inhabitants, many of whom, in 1241, had a hand in building no fewer than eighty ships for the King. Then, towards the middle of the fourteenth century, a northeasterly gale coincided with a high tide, and in a single night of devastation much of Dunwich was dissolved into the immensity of the sea, effectively killing the town's trade dead.

Thereafter the relentless forces of nature continued to take their toll; whole streets and buildings tumbled from the cliffs and by 1753 two-thirds of Dunwich had disappeared without trace. All that is left now of ancient Dunwich is a church buttress, the archways of a medieval friary and the remains of a Norman leper hospital. The locals say that when a storm is approaching, the sound of submerged church bells can still be heard eerily tolling beneath the waves.

CHAPTER 37

Some say the start of winter is when the clocks go back. Others say it is when you can no longer sit comfortably on the soil with your bare backside because of the cold, or that it is when a winter's fog will freeze a dog. In Suffolk, winter begins at the onset of the sugar-beet processing season. So, according to BBC Radio Suffolk, Tuesday 2nd October was the official start of winter.

But after the rain cleared it turned into a very unwintery day – big bursts of sunshine that felt even a little back-warming out of the whipping wind. That morning, weatherman Everton Fox had talked about a lot of rain around with 'tricky driving conditions' before describing the temperatures as 'somewhat academic'. What the sweet Fanny Adams is that supposed to mean? That the temperatures are feeling very scholarly today and can be found walking around with educational textbooks under their arms and mortarboards on their heads? Please, Everton, if you could just talk in centigrade or fahrenheit, that would be fine by me.

Past High Health Pigs, a very large pig farm with very large rootling pigs and very large 'KEEP OUT!' foot-and-mouth signs, I turned off on to the quiet dead-end road to Walberswick, which led me towards the sea across a nature reserve. My map wasn't detailed enough to tell me if there was any way I could cross the River Blyth, like on a little passenger ferry, perhaps. If there wasn't, I would have to backtrack on a fairly lengthy detour to join the main road north of the river. There was no one around to ask and so I kept going.

Then, near a tumulus and Tinker's Walks, I came upon a man sitting in the passenger seat of a car parked in the entrance to a field. He held a clipboard and wore a yellow fluorescent jacket. Having seen men like that before, I reckoned I knew what he was up to so I bumped off the road on to the potholed track and peered at his surprised expression through the window. On his lap sat an Ordnance Survey Explorer map (1:25,000 scale) of the area. He wound down the window and I said, 'Hello! I think you're just the man I'm looking for!'

'Not a lot of people say that to me! Must be my lucky day!' he replied.

The man was a traffic survey man logging, with a tick on his clipboard, the few forms of traffic that were passing on this road that ran out at the sea. He knew the area well and went into great detail with the aid of his map showing me how I could cross the Blythe by way of the old railway bridge, which had now been pedestrianised. As he was talking to me, head in the map, a rare burst of motor traffic shot past and the Tick Man then got in a sudden flap because he had been taken unawares and thought he might lose track of his ticks. (It was nice to see a man take a pride in his ticks.)

'It's all right,' I said, 'I've got them imprinted in my sights.' And I assured him that it had been one transit van, one pick-up and three cars – and not one van and four cars like he thought.

'You'd better watch out,' I said, 'or you'll find yourself out of a job.' Then I asked him what he did with all the ticks and numbers.

'I send them off to the Number Crunchers,' he replied.

'What are Number Crunchers?' I asked.

'People who sit in offices poring over figures.'

'Oh, and then they decide whether the quiet dead-end road to Walberswick should have a bypass or be made into a motorway?'

'Something like that,' he said.

'Are you going to count me?' I asked (I was in one of my overly inquisitive moods).

'No,' he said, 'I'm only doing vehicles.'

'But I'm a vehicle – a self-propelling one.'

'I'm afraid I'm only doing motor vehicles.'

'Does that mean I don't exist?'

'To the Number Crunchers you don't. But you do in my eyes!' he added with a wink.

That was quite enough, so I said, 'I think I'd better be on my way now!'

And after thanking him for his help I cycled off in the direction of Walberswick.

Opposite East Sheep Walk I came across someone else who didn't exist – a fast-moving cyclist on a road bike. He was travelling in the opposite direction but we had time to bid each other a cheery 'halloo'. The next thing I knew he was riding beside me having executed a swift U-turn. Over the next five minutes I learnt that his name was Jamie, that he had read my first book, that the tyres I was using (Continental Top Touring 26in × 1.75s) were the same ones that he used on his mountain bike, that he wasn't really working at the moment and that he preferred hiking to biking and had just come back from hiking in Switzerland with his dad. He was, I believe he said, about forty and living at home with his heartily hiking father. Then he said he would like to join me cycling for the rest of the day. *Ah, such music to my ears!*

'But I'm going in the opposite direction to you,' I said, falling back on that old onion.

'Oh, that's no problem,' he replied, 'I'm happy going anywhere.'

Well, it might not be a problem for him, I thought, but what about for me?

'I think you'll get very bored riding with me,' I said. 'I'm a slow-moving vehicle and I stop and start a lot to look at things. And I also can't seem to talk and cycle at the same time' (*hint, hint, hint*).

None of this seemed to faze Jamie or lead him off the scent, but then serial killers are notoriously tenacious. Not that I'm saying Jamie was a serial killer, mind, but it was best to treat him as one until proven otherwise.

Fortunately, my life-saving knight in shining armour came in the form of a red British Telecom phone box. I jammed on my brakes.

'Sorry,' I said, 'I've got to make a phone call.'

And then, because I suddenly thought Jamie might wait for me, I added in well-worn Polar-exploring style, 'And I could be some time.'

It did the trick. I entered the red tardis and made myself look very busy making very important phone calls to Mr and Mrs Dial Tone. Jamie gave up and took off up the road towards the clipboard-tick man. Good, I thought. That's three tag-along men down. How many more to go?

I rode into time-warped Southwold (where beer is still delivered to pubs by horse) and on past the rows of smart and brightly painted beach huts which, having featured on TV a few times, could even qualify as celebrity beach huts (I'm sure a lot of drizzling of olive oil goes on around them). Whatever they are, they don't come cheap – the going rate is £40,000. There was the time when beach huts were the 15-bob-a-day holidaying sanctuary of the toiling classes at leisure, but not any more. They are now *de rigueur* for people who prefer *frangipane* to fish and chips.

249

I spent the night camping in the rain lying rigid with cold in a vicious nor'easter up at Chestnuts Farm, which sits entwined among a maze of gorgeous country lanes between Rushmere and Black Street.

By nine o'clock the next morning the sun had resurfaced and I set off in fine spirits down the road towards Lowestoft. I had been going no more than five minutes when a cyclist appeared around the corner ahead of me. *Oh no!* I thought. *It's him!* It was Jamie, the cycling serial killer. I couldn't believe it! Of all the unlikely places! Of all the untimely timing! Here I was, up on an empty web-work of lanes so confusing that even with a satellite phone and GPS it would be a challenge to meet up with someone of your own intentional choosing. Now, miles away from where I had last tried to shake him off my tail, here was Jamie. How unlucky can you get?

Jamie didn't quite see it like this. He was cock-a-hoop over the coincidence of it all and felt it was our destiny to be together, if not in marriage, then in a day's riding. Lacking in phone boxes or other convenient life-saving roadside furniture into which I could dive and hide, I agreed, purely out of common courtesy, that he could cycle with me. Well, it is a shame to offend – even if you are about to be murdered. So off we went, riding along two abreast, him all interrogatively chatty, me all frostily curt (my guard was up).

Before long, my fast-filling bladder was calling to me, but I couldn't stop to release its contents behind a hedge because, alas, I was not alone. And if I did stop to excuse myself, he might come too and heaven only knows what might happen then. I did not want to end up a corpse in Mutford Little Wood – or even Mutford Big Wood for that matter. So putting on a brave face and tucking away an even braver bladder, I kept going.

As time progressed I became more and more agitated. All I wanted to do was cycle along these lanes in the safety of silence and solitude – listening to birds, peering in hedgerows, watching beetles scuttling across the road, gazing at moats (Suffolk has got a lot of moats) – instead of answering questions about what tent I took to Iceland or what did I think of Switzerland?

When we arrived on the outskirts of Lowestoft I stopped to look at my map. But my lycra-shorted serial killer told me I need not do this as he knew the area and could show me which way to go. He was all very nice about it but then I've read mass murderers can be very nice before they turn very un-nice. And anyway, I didn't want to be shown the way because I like plotting my own route and ending up lost by myself.

This time my life was spared by a table on the pavement outside a house groaning under the weight of home-grown apples for sale. I screeched to a halt and spent so long dithering over which particular apples I wanted to buy, and so long finding the right change to put in the 'honesty box' before laboriously unbungeeing and unpacking half the contents of my panniers in order to locate a space in which to cram them, that I felt certain that Jamie-the-Ripper would lose interest and go off to find someone else to kill. Not so. He even offered to buy the apples for me! I recognised this as being typical premeditated murderer's behaviour – be all nice and charming one moment, then slit your throat the next (not that I was paranoid or anything, of course). Oh no, I was not going to let myself fall through that old trap door, thank you very much.

The time had come for decisive action. So, adopting my politest parlance, I turned to the Likely Lycra Killer and said, 'Excuse me, but could you please just fuck off!' Actually, I said no such thing. Colourful language does not become me. Instead, by way of a little surreptitious but firm wording and impressive acceleration (on a bike as heavy as a fruit-heavy apple tree), I finally shook him off my tail and rode into Lowestoft mightily relieved to be free and alone again.

I didn't spend long in Lowestoft – just long enough to claim my easternmost point at Lowestoft Ness (only two more 'points' and several thousands of miles and islands and Ireland to go). Then, before I knew it, I had passed from the county of the 'southern folk' of Suffolk into the county of 'northern folk', or Norfolk, and its prolific supply of marshes, rivers, broads and windmills.

Not on the road to anywhere, Norfolk juts out into a forbiddingly scowling North Sea, buffeted by Siberian gales that come shrieking over the vast flatness of the north European plains. Beneath an immense sky, I whipped across the hedgeless prairies where the black earth stretched to the windswept horizon, and steamed through Great Yarmouth (but not so great traffic), Caister-on-Sea (old Roman port that once stood on an island now transmuted into caravan park and holiday camp mecca – oh, and site of a butchers called Tubby & Sons), California (not the one north of Mexico but the one south of Scratby), Horsey Mere (lake where Nelson learnt to sail), Eccles (not cakes, but site of another village lost to the sea), Bacton (formidably large and whiffy gas terminal), Cromer (used to be an inland town, now good place for watching the rare spectacle of the sun rising and setting in the sea) and Weybourne, where the shingle beach shelves so steeply that invading ships could come so close inshore that it spurred the verse:

> He who would old English win
> Must at Waborne Hoop begin.

CHAPTER 38

All of a sudden it was summer again. At least for a day. I was down to T-shirt and shorts and seeking out shade for my churchyard lunch spot. To savour this one-hit winter wonder of a heatwave, I headed inland to cycle for miles among the glorious car-free country lanes flaming and flaring with red poppies and gorse, drifts of crackling leaves and deep-goldening oaks. The air was all a-buzz and a-flutter with season-confused bees and butterflies and dragonflies, while haydust, sent billowing out from a burst of frenetic combine harvesting, wafted and whirled across my face.

So by the time I arrived in Stiffkey I was feeling a bit hot and floppy. The old pronunciation 'Stewkey' for Stiffkey has more or less died out, which is a shame because it conjures up such interesting culinary connotations. Keeping to a food theme, the name does still live on in the local delicacy – the prized cockles known as 'Stewkey Blues'.

I camped on the outskirts of the village down near Cabbage Creek amidst the wide expanse of salt marshes. The north Norfolk shore is like one long nature reserve, riddled and riven with marshes and dunes and spurs and spits and creeks and channels and shingle ridges and reedbeds and sandflats and mudflats. As a fireball sun sank towards the horizon, vast skeins of low-flying Brent geese honked cacophonously overhead, their striking V-shaped white rumps visible against a reddening sky.

Later on I rang mum from the local phone box and discovered that her back-door rats had now migrated to the house. Apples had been gnawed, droppings had been found. This was not good news. But as the rat population is growing by leaps and bounds annually, it is, to pest people, not rare (or bad) news at all.

In towns, urban legend has it, you are never more than twenty-five paces from a rat. In the country, the pest experts say, you are never more than ten strides from our furry friends. Well, mum and dad could beat that, they had them at their feet! But you don't want them there for long because a pair of breeding rats can produce a dynasty of up to 600 – an amount that pales into insignificance compared with mice, which can manage 2000. And I know, because I've got mice – the large and lively and agile and aggressive-when-cornered, pec-flexing yellow-necked variety, to be precise (I also have the smaller wood mice and house mice, which come with additional limbo-in-under-the-door abilities). Anyway, our local pest-destructing friend, Tim Hubbard, ran to mum's rescue and hit said rats on the head. He's good like that.

Back in my tent I tuned in to Radio Norfolk and heard a woman from the local diocese talking about how her church was lacking an organ. Moments later a woman rang in and saved the day by saying she had a spare one. But then they hit upon an organ transportation problem. Mrs Diocese said she had no suitable vehicle at her disposal. No sooner had she said this than another woman rang in to say she had a spare van that could take an organ. Matter resolved.

'That's public broadcasting for you!' said the presenter.

Switching stations, I momentarily came to rest upon one of Bach's harpsichord concertos on Radio 3, which reminded me of what Beecham once said about likening the sometimes discordant-sounding harpsichord to a skeleton

copulating on a tin roof. As I drifted off to the tunes of the radio with my tent
door open wide to the vast star-spangled skies, I was rudely awoken by a squirrel sniffing at my sleeping bag. This didn't worry me in the least, which is
strange really, seeing as the pesky grey squirrel is little more than a rat with a
spin doctor.

I know a man, Les Woodland, who used to live in the land of the 'northern
folk' before he migrated south to France. Although Norfolk is not the most
populated of counties by a long chalk, it still has a good smattering of people.
And Les appears to have known every one of them and has a story about everything.

One such story is about Stiffkey, where the rector started his career con-
sorting with prostitutes and ended it by being eaten by a lion called, Les thinks,
Alfred. The rector was defrocked on the steps of Norwich cathedral for his
adventurous and liberated ways and protested to the end that his interests
were merely for the girls' souls. He took to living in a barrel on Skegness
seafront without eating and then said he would get into a cage with a lion, possibly to prove that the lion, if not the bishop, was on his side. For a while it
looked as though he was right. But then he made a regrettable error. He
stepped on the lion's tail. If you have ever stepped on a cat's tail you will know
it is bad news. Step on a lion's tail and it is a little bit worse. Alfred took exception to the wayward rector and ate him.

Before Les moved to France, he could be found dwelling in Wymondham, a
town just southwest of Norwich. According to Les's reckoning, Wymondham is
worth a look for its batty abbey. The interior is spectacular, but from outside the
two towers are quite different and both unfinished, because the monks and the
townspeople fell out and each insisted on building their own tower, racing to see
who would finish first. While they were busy building, the abbey was walled off
down the middle to stop one side trespassing into the other. They made friends
again before they had finished and so the towers remain unfinished.

Wymondham also has a guildhall on stilts. It has sagged over the years and,
so Les tells me, when it was used for town council meetings, the legs on the
chairs and table were cut shorter on one side than the other so everyone could
sit level.

One more thing about Wymondham: the town has a station that is privately
owned, and is possibly the only one on the network that sells pianos.

I couldn't travel very far in Norfolk without recalling something that Les had told me about the place. At one stage, when I was sick of the heavy traffic on the coast road, I headed inland along some of the best cycling lanes in the land. By simply letting my wheels lead the way, I passed one Slipper Chapel, several tumuli, moats and windmills, and lots of farms with names like Top Farm, Frog Farm, Edgar Farm, Crabbe Castle Farm, Leicester Square Farm, Long Lane Farm, Short Lane Farm and Whey Curd Farm. I also rode through the villages of Great Snoring and Little Snoring. Not far from Les is a village called Seething which Les, a journalist, told me had provided the headline 'SEETHING WOMAN KILLS SNORING MAN'.

Norfolk may have more than its fair share of Snorings, but there are even more Burnhams. Six of them in all: Burnham Market, Burnham Norton, Burnham Deepdale, Burnham Overy Staithe, Burnham Overy Town and Burnham Thorpe, where Nelson was born. Les finds it hard to imagine that Nelson spoke, or 'spook' in a 'rumpty-tumpty' Norfolk accent when he said, 'England expects . . .', but supposes he must have done.

Les knows Les Winter, who for many years had the pub in Burnham Thorpe and ran it as a museum to Nelson as much as a drinking den. The pub has never had a bar. You simply enter – it's all wooden seats and tables, all original rather than styled on an Old Worlde theme – and eventually someone will find you and ask you what you want to drink before they go off into a back room and pour it for you.

Down at Burnham Deepdale I ate lunch sitting among the gravestones of a Norman church, built of flint. The church has a stocky round tower peculiar to Norfolk; apparently flint was easier to build into a circular shape than a square. Norfolk is an incredibly flinty place. The lanes are strewn with a particularly sharp tyre-ripping variety of flinty gravel and grit, which seems to be the building blocks of which the county is made. The trouble is it's chipping away, which probably explains why the land of the northern folk is tipping into the sea.

I was reminded again of the disappearing coast at Brancaster, where the horizons are low and broad and the shoreline constantly changing through the action of wind and waves on shingle and sand. It is a capricious landscape and seascape rolled into one and caught in a continual shifting drifting flux. It was funny to think that in medieval times, herring were caught almost as far 'inland' as Norwich.

At its western end the Norfolk coast abuts The Wash, which stretches across to Gibraltar Point in Lincolnshire, forming the second largest area of inter-tidal mudflats in Britain. The only seaside town in East Anglia to face west is Hunstanton, or 'Hunston', as locals call it, which was developed in the 1860s by a local landowner, Mr Hamon L'Estrange (or Le Strange, as they called him), of nearby Hunstanton Hall to take advantage of the Great Eastern Railway there. Being an out-on-a-limb branch line, the railway has of course long been demolished, along with the grand Victorian pier.

After riding along to Stubborn Sand I took my excursionist inclinations inland where, just north of Snettisham, I passed Norfolk Lavender, the oldest and largest full-scale lavender-growing and distilling operation in the country, which, being established in 1932, I noticed is the same age as my mother. They both seem to be bearing up well.

I pedalled over the Peddars Way (a grass-covered Roman road that runs dyke-straight from Ixworth in Suffolk to Norfolk's Holme-next-the-Sea), passed through Docking (which at one time was called Dry Docking because, perched on a hilltop 300 feet above sea level, it had no water supply of its own) and Sandringham (site of large royal beach hut) to King's Lynn (another regal-sounding place just south of Seal, Breast and Bulldog Sands). And if I was in King's Lynn that meant I was nearly in Boston, which meant that I was nearly in Lincolnshire. Suddenly I felt I was moving up the map, so much so that I could almost smell those wee bonny sporrans of Scotland.

Then, not for the first time, my coastal voyage capsized because from King's Lynn I had to take an unprecedented swing south to Downham Market to catch the train as I had once again been summoned to give a bout of cycling-cum-book-flogging talks around the country. I also needed to make a bit more money to see me on my way.

As I was cycling down towards Downham Market following the great River Ouse through Saddle Bow, Wiggenhall St Germans, Wiggenhall St Mary the Virgin and Wiggenhall St Mary Magdalen, I had to stop to pull on full waterproof apparatus as the weather had turned wild, the ruthless wind racing across the flat fenland into my face. The Met Office had been busy on the airwaves issuing severe weather warnings: forget 'bits and pieces' of rain, apparently a mini hurricane was storming across the Atlantic waging on a warpath to hit the south.

Swaddled from tip to toe in full Goretex glory and slapping my helmet on for good measure (I didn't want a lamppost landing on my head), I was in the middle of making secure my last flap of Velcro when a Thorn tandem drew up alongside. It was a husband-and-wife team who lived just up the road in Tilney

All Saints, which made a pleasant change from a Wiggenhall St Something. They were on their way to meet up with the local cycle club for their 'Sunday run', and had mistaken me for one of their club riders waylaid by the roadside. Then they took in the spectacle of my multi-storeyed pannier collection and thought that, unless one of their members had had a brainstorm to come out cycling with such a monumental load, I must be someone else.

'You look like you're on a grand tour!' said him up at helm.

I said I was, of sorts, but was now on my way home for a short intermission. He asked me what my 'grand tour' involved so I gave him a quick coastal run-down. He seemed quite impressed that my trek had no particular time limit.

'Are you on your gap year?' he asked.

'No,' I said, 'just a very large holiday.'

'I read a book once about a girl doing a similar thing,' said Mr Tandem Man, 'but she walked round the coast with a dog. I can't remember the name of it now apart from the fact that the girl had a dog's name and the dog had a girl's name.'

'Spud,' I said. 'Spud Talbot-Ponsonby! I've read that – *Two Feet, Four Paws.*'

'That's the one,' said Tandem Man.

And we talked about it for a few moments before Mrs Tandem interjected by asking me if I had ever read *The Wind in my Wheels* by Julie Drew. I let out a gasp of a laugh and then promptly turned the colour of a burning beetroot (which was quite some accomplishment as it was Siberian cold out there) before admitting, 'Yes. I wrote it!'

A short intermission of exclamations ensued. I was then invited to battle into the wind with them as far as their club rendez-vous point. As they didn't look like the sort to go round slitting the throats of straying cyclists in Wiggenhall St Mary the Virgin (too cold and too exposed for that sort of caper), I agreed.

'Felicity, my wife, was thinking of getting a Roberts,' said Captain Tandem, glancing down in mid-spin to my bike.

'Was she? I mean . . . are you?' I said, obviously still a little ruffled as I couldn't even get my tenses right. But I soon regained my composure and recommended she go out right now and buy one.

I made it in the nick of time on to the 12.39 to King's Cross. There was no guard's van so I had to drag my laden bike directly into the passenger carriage, where there was no space to put it other than half-blocking the gangway. I prepared myself for a barrage of 'bloody cyclist!' abuse, but everyone was all very nice and surprisingly chatty for a busy carriage. One young mum, with a little boy called Daniel, made some comment about how she once had a cycle trailer but her son kept falling out through the holes. Another woman with a dog, whose tail I accidentally stepped on, said, 'Are you Dutch?' as if that explained the reason I had flattened her mutt's tail.

Then a man got on with a bike, which he leant against mine, thus effectively making the aisle completely impassable. But still no one seemed to mind. The cycling man could see I was loaded for touring, which prompted him into telling me that he once spent three months cycling round Spain. He had evidently loved it.

'I want to do more of that sort of thing,' he said, 'getting away on my bike, but . . .' and he pointed to his head, 'it's all in here, isn't it? It's that mentality thing of deciding to give up your job and the life that you know and then go.'

His name was Andrew and he told me he was a gardener from Hackney who worked with disadvantaged children in and around the East End. I could see him being very good at that because he seemed a thoughtful and patient and generous person, not least because he gave me a bag of his dad's windfall apples.

'Have you ever tried cycling abroad?' asked Andrew as we crunched into an apple or two.

'Yes, a bit,' I said, keeping my cards close to my chest, before sliding on to the subject of Anne Mustoe, the headmistress who cycled round the world without knowing how to mend a puncture.

Then a girl leant across Andrew and said, 'Excuse me. You're Rosie Dew aren't you? My dad's a big fan. He made me read your book about cycling round the world!'

'Oh, sorry!' I said, because I was, sorry. I didn't like the sound of being force-fed down somebody's throat. I wanted to slip down nice and smoothly. With a ball-batting Wimbledon head, Andrew looked from her to me and me to her before shooting me a very strange look.

The 'mini' hurricane caught up with me an hour's cycle from home. It struck with a sudden ferocity sending water falling in a curtain of solid shafts and a wind that screeched through the cables and roared through the trees. It was a scene of pure and wonderful and terrorising chaos as ancient oaks crashed down around me, and branches and wooded debris rained through the air – the land and the elements colliding together in a primeval vortex of fury.

CHAPTER 39

Winter came. Winter went. Spring sprang. Spring sprung. For months I had been meaning to pack up and pedal off onwards around the coast, but never quite making it. Instead I found myself doing things like cycling across Holland with my ageing mother in the depths of winter, or hugging my knees in a freezing cold guard's van marooned for two hours with my bike on a broken-down Virgin train outside Manchester.

I should have left in April because the sun came out. Had I known it was going to come out and, more to the point, stay out (no April showers were there this year), I would of course have pushed myself up a notch or two and taken off. Instead I found myself warbling on about the wonders of two-wheeled travel to the likes of RAF revellers and the local WI. I also became preoccupied with squashing every good-for-nothing deathwatch beetle I found crawling about my floors and walls. This took the better part of June because there were a hell of a lot of the blighters to squash. Which was just as well, I suppose, because it didn't stop raining all June.

Didn't stop raining all July either. The Met Office said that the average amount of rain for July fell in the first thirteen days alone. On the fourteenth day it was still raining and I woke up to find a hornet a foot from my face. That was enough to make me decide to leave my livestock-crawling home behind for a while and take off back to Norfolk.

It was St Swithin's Day and I was all ready to leave when my tooth started hurting. I decided the best thing to do was ignore it, but mum decided that was the worst thing to do.

So late St Swithin's afternoon I cycled off on the eighteen-mile round trip to the dentist, who said I needed a filling. Holding aloft a large and very painful-looking needle, he also said I needed an anaesthetic. I said yes to the filling but no to the anaesthetic. I didn't want to lose contact with my mouth because I had trains to be catching and needed to remain coherent to purchase tickets and persuade irascible guards to allow me into their vans to berth my bulging bike. The dentist said it would hurt. I said that was okay, I could take it, it's all good practice for childbirth. (Not that I was planning on birthing a child, mind, but sometimes I think it's good to test your limits.) More concerning than the needle was what he was going to fill my tooth with. After reading numerous horror stories in the press, I was worried about mercury. I didn't want one of the most poisonous metals known to man leaching into my system and reacting with my bottom bracket. I aired my concerns to the dentist and he assured me not to worry as he was going to patch me up with home-cured Fiji. At least that's what it sounded like he said. Having a bit of ham-like tropical island wedged in your tooth seemed not enough to make a song and dance about and so I lay back in the reclining chair, donned his dark glasses and thought of England.

On the WAGN (Waiting Ages Going Nowhere, or West Anglia Great Northern) train to King's Lynn, I picked up a discarded newspaper and read how a seventeen-year-old woman had been detained at Manchester airport after trying to smuggle a chameleon into the country by disguising it as a hat. It was perched on her headscarf when she arrived on a flight from Dubai. As I was contemplating this gloriously fanciful scene, and wondering whether searching for the likes of such contraband headgear was what the old poem 'Cock up your beaver, brave Johnnie my lad' was really all about, a white-haired woman in her early sixties and a pair of trousers that converted into shorts leant across the aisle and said, 'Going far?'

My bike, groaning beneath a preposterous assortment of lead-heavy panniers, was bungeed across a line of seats (there were no guard's vans on the train), looking for all the world as if it was going to take me on some grand expeditionary trek south across the Hammer House Horrors of Africa, perhaps, never minding it was in fact heading north towards . . . well, Spalding.

'A little way,' I said. And I briefly told her about my cycling voyage around the coast.

'How lovely to be so free!' she said. 'This is the time to do it when you're young – before you get tied down with a job or family. Are you on your gap year?'

Yes, another one. I'm having a double bill. What with all my deathwatch beetle and wet-weather worries, I'd been hoping that over the past gap year I had aged considerably. But apparently not. This revelation was most depressing. My high hopes of looking decrepit dashed on Day 1 (of Year 2). But I didn't hold it against Mrs Shorts Conversion – she was a nice woman.

'I cycle too!' she said enthusiastically as she picked up her Blacks backpack and moved into the seat opposite. 'I can cycle up to twenty-five miles in one go! At least that's what I could manage last year. I used to go hostelling. I won't tell you how many years ago that was, but I once spent a week hostelling in France. The whole trip cost £9 and that included the £5 airfare! It was a cargo plane; we rolled our bikes up a ramp to board and then sat in hard seats opposite each other like a train. It was only a twenty-minute flight. Felt like we'd hardly taken off before we landed again.'

'Where did you fly from?' I asked.

'Lydd, a small place near Dover.'

Lydd. That rang a bell. And then I remembered The Two Bob Shop and my lunch stop – stamping my feet for warmth as I tried to shelter from the whistling wind behind the Cathedral of Romney Marsh. For no apparent reason, the train then rolled to a halt. In the middle of nowhere. It then lurched forwards, changed its mind, and then lurched forwards again and took off.

Mrs Shorts Conversion went on to tell me about her husband Reg, a carpenter and joiner, and that she had two grown-up children, Peter and Sally, and four grandchildren and that she worked as a cashier in Woolworths in Ely and lived just up the road in Littleport. She said she'd lived on the Bedford Level all her life.

'But of course it's changed a lot since I was young. It was a quiet place back then. Whenever we wanted to go anywhere we either walked or cycled. Never thought twice about it. Now there're cars everywhere and all these new boxy houses being built on the edge of every village. Dormitory towns – that's what they call them isn't it?'

We both turned to look out of the window and on cue we caught a glimpse of some semi-built boxes, topped with a few men in yellow hats, torn backwards by our galloping rush. Moments later, in direct contrast to the poxy boxes, the wide fenland-dominating bulk of Ely cathedral hove into view, its magnificent multi-turreted towers and octagonal lantern rising like wraiths above the misty haze of the city.

'Littleport's the next stop,' said Mrs Reg. 'Used to be a port too you know, when all this area was covered in water.' And eels. For most of its history, the 68-foot mound of Ely was an island surrounded by mile upon mile of swamp and fen, and known as 'Eel Island' because of the abundance of eels. Then the marshes were drained in the seventeenth century, leaving a flat and curious landscape of fertile black-earthed fields and rivers banked higher than the roads.

As Mrs Reg stood up ready for her stop, she patted my helmet hanging from its straps off the back of my bike.

'Glad to see you've got one of these,' she said. 'I don't cycle anywhere without my helmet these days. I've worn one for thirteen or fourteen years – ever since Reg was riding back from work one day and fell off and hit his head. He got "brainlash", that's when the brain hits the back of the head before hitting the front. It caused a big personality change in him. He lost all motivation to do anything – he was always so busy and keen before that – and his short-term memory went and he'd get all emotional about things, which wasn't like my Reg at all.'

She stopped and her eyes went all watery and I could tell that ever since her husband's accident she had had a hard time at home. 'Yes, I wear mine all the time,' she went on, 'and I hope you do too!'

I felt a guilty pang slither down my neck at the thought of how little I wore it.

'You know what,' said Mrs Reg, 'if I walk down to the village instead of cycling, people say to me: "I don't recognise you without your helmet on!"'

The train slugged to a jolty halt at Littleport. Waiting for the electric doors to open, Mrs Reg gave me a perky look and said, 'Here's a quick tip: wear a plastic bag under your helmet – keeps your head dry in the rain and warm in the wind!'

She stepped out on to the platform where she waved to another woman, who greeted her with a kiss, and then the train lurched forwards and they were gone.

CHAPTER 40

It was in King's Lynn that Henry VIII poked his head above the parapet of my travels again. Until his meddlings, King's Lynn was known as Bishop's Lynn (and before that, in Domesday Book times, it was just plain old Lena or Lun). But then our Henry wanted this prospering port that belonged to the manor of the Bishop of Norwich as part of his royal property and so seized it during his Dissolution of the Monasteries and it became known as Lynn Regis.

In a burst of half-hearted sunshine I rode down to the quayside and passed a bony and angular man who was walking as if he had sand in his swimming trunks. Not that, as far as I could tell, he was wearing any swimming trunks (he was kitted out in a tight tracksuit); he just displayed that uncomfortable gait common to seaside folk who look very unhappy with the fact that they seem to have half the contents of the beach wedged up their bottom.

I bumped over the cobbles, stopped to admire the seagull-shat statue built in memory of Captain George Vancouver, 'A great navigator and surveyor', who was born in King's Lynn and went on to charter thousands of miles of the Northwest Pacific coastline from San Diego to Alaska – which, never mind sailing, is a top-notch cycle.

Just beyond Captain Van Man, I found the grand Great Ouse stretched across my path. I thought it might be nice to get in the watery spirit of things and take the little passenger ferry to West Lynn – a ferry which, a local woman proudly told me, had been running for well over a thousand years.

'A thousand years?' I said, gazing across the water towards this most ancient of relics. 'They certainly knew how to make boats in those days!'

The woman gave me a funny look and walked on. And she was right, that wasn't very funny at all. But that's one of the perilous things when you travel alone: you lose it fast. Anyway, I then espied the large arm-quivering number of steps I would have to carry my incredible hulk of a bulk of a bike down (all the more so because it was low tide) so decided to cycle the much busier bridge way round instead.

Once over the Ouse I passed through the village of Clenchwarton, which struck me as an excellent name to describe people who walk along looking as if they have a lorry load of sand caught in unmentionable crevices. From now on, such hapless souls would be known as Clenchwartons.

The land lay flat and wide-angled as I wiggled my way over Wingland Marsh. It felt good to be off again, spinning along lanes in sporadic bursts of warm sunshine past fields of strawberries and acres of cultivated roses. The air smelt sweet and edible, like a potful of jam. That's one of the addictive things about cycling – you're out there and in it and the most fleeting of moments suddenly becomes very intense. You start noticing the minutest of details: the petrol-blue iridescence of a scuttling road-crossing beetle; the breeze catching the wind-weathered edge of a discarded McDonald's bag; a bank of small flies lifting like a gauze cloud off a fresh mound of still-steaming horse muck; a jay's tiny blue and black-barred feather caught in a spider's web.

People sometimes exhibit a tendency to do funny things when they see someone on a bike. Beside the River Nene, up near Guy's Head lighthouse, a farmer, trundling along towards me in his beefy high-rise tractor-truck stretched his arms out wide as if to embrace an invisible form, before applauding me with a cheeky-chappy face. Then, a bit further along the road in Gedney Drove End, a big, well-upholstered man stepped out of his house just as I was passing, took one look at me and said, 'Morning!' even though it was in fact about 5.30 p.m. Which reminded me that I had better start looking for a place to camp soon. Before long I was pitching my tent on a grassy swathe behind the Rose and Crown in Holbeach Hurn.

I was now in the thick of fenland. Lincolnshire fenland. Around me lay a wonderfully watery-sounding world seared by straight-cut fields, drains and dykes, marshes and washes: Spalding Marsh, Moulton Marsh, Whaplode Marsh, Pinchbeck Marsh, Fosdyke Wash, Risegate Outfall, Moulton Mere Drain, South Holland Main Drain and a slightly provocative Lady Nunn's Old Eau.

As I set sail the following morning, there appeared an abundance of magpies

too. I'm not a superstitious sort, but I couldn't help thinking that such a prolif-
eration of these harsh rattling-voiced birds spelt a spell of bad luck. Lots of
explanations abound as to why they should be associated with such hapless
happenings. One is that they refused to go into the Ark and instead remained
outside chattering. A more likely one is because they are carrion eaters and
often congregate on a corpse. But vultures and hyenas are particularly partial to
a pile of carrion too, yet you don't go round counting 'One for sorrow, two for
joy, three for a girl, four for a boy . . .' every time you see a flock of hyenas or a
pandemonium of vultures veering off over a hedge. Personally I think the
magpie's tarnished image is down to its collective noun: murder. At least I think
that's its collective noun, because you get a murder of crows, and magpies
belong to the same cunningly crafty family, do they not? They come in a parliament too, and there's something decidedly doomy and gloomy and inauspicious
about such ministerial mutterings. Coincidentally, a Lincolnshire version of
counting magpies goes: 'One for sorrow, two for mirth, three for a wedding,
four for a death'. No wonder I was feeling a calamity lay just around the corner,
ready to pounce; I kept passing packs of four.

My ill-omened magpie struck on a long straight stretch (there were lots of
long straight stretches round here – it was all very Dutch-like and dyke-like) not
far from Middle Marsh farm. It struck in the form of a dispiriting clonking
sound from my rear cassette (rear wheel sprocket cluster, for the uninitiated)
along with a clunking jumping chain. I frowned and I fretted and I dismounted. Then I fiddled and fuddled and wiggled and woggled the notchy
cable down in my rear derailleur department and, miraculously, life on the
gear-changing front returned to a silky-smooth transmission. My diagnosis was
an index gearing malfunction. Until setting out on this cycle-coasting voyage,
I had never used index (pre-programmed) notchy gearing before. I had always
relied on my faultless twenty-three-year-old Campag Gran Sport friction (self-
assessing-where-your-gears-are) levers. (Sorry if I'm getting a bit
bike-boffin-like, but bear with me.) I liked what I knew and I liked what worked
and I liked what lasted. So why was I now an index-geared guru? Well, I had
been cajoled into trying it, not least because it was more compatible with my
new bike set-up. But I distrusted it because I didn't really understand how it
worked. That is, until I was servicing it down on my hands and knees on a dyke
(if you'll pardon the expression). I had faced and fought my malicious magpie
head on, and won. And I felt good about that.

My spirits soared all the more when the wide-skied clouds scudded off over
the horizon to reveal a vast dome of sky – an achingly brilliant blue. For the first

time all summer, it actually felt hot. High above me larks hung hovering on fluttering wings, singing their hearts out with their uplifting and persistent warbling flight songs. Red heads of poppies grew at random by the roadside, some splashing their dashing scarlet among a field of green or gold crops. Every house I passed appeared to have an abundant bush of mallow planted outside as a standard fixture, their purple-veined, hollyhock-like pink flowers dancing in the frisky wind.

I bowled along the pancake flats and crossed over the South Forty Foot Drain into Boston, where I climbed up to the first balcony of St Botolph's church (the biggest parish church in the country) locally known as The Stump – its tower was 272 feet tall. I had been able to see the tower from twenty miles away. Now, on the first balcony (the top was closed), I could just make out the hefty hulk of Lincoln Cathedral some thirty-two miles to the north. It was up here I met a big-boned, sweaty-browed Scotsman who had apparently passed me back on Fosdyke Bridge. When he asked where I was cycling to and I said Skegness, he said, 'Fair play to ye!' Which made me laugh because that's not a sort of reply I'd expect.

The sky, as immense as ever, had turned from a clear blue to blue and billowy with friendly clouds. But it didn't stay that way for long. By late afternoon, it looked sour and moody, a great band of dirty grey consuming the last of the blue. With the darkening day came a strengthening wind, which swept across that unhidden bare soul of the flat table-top world of wolds and marshes, hitting me broadside with full force. The air smelt leaden with rain and I began to fret about the inevitable soaking heading my way.

The A52 was heaving traffic, and made all the more horrible by the capricious blasts from the keen but constant wind that kept knocking me off course into the path of vehicles – vehicles that seemed to have no understanding of what the weather was doing to me. To them I was a crazy overladen cyclist, obviously drunk from my failure to keep to a straight course. But they couldn't feel the banging wind or the passing, sucking undertow of every trailer-pulling truck – not while they sat in sealed-in comfort, their heads absorbing the sounds from the radio or the voice from the mobile pinned between shoulder and crook of the neck. Their minds were anywhere other than how to compensate for the cycle-unfriendly elements that their vehicle simply carved through with rushing ease. And no matter that I might be riding down the road in the style of a wave-tossed dinghy, they continued to overtake me at 60 mph, inches from my elbow.

Although the A52 was the road nearest to the coast, I decided that as I didn't fancy the very real possibility of dying beneath the wheels of a motorist more intent on pushing buttons on a mobile phone than watching where they were going, I would pack in this fast-flying highway and head inland. So at Friskney Tofts I turned off across Friskney Fen and although I was riding in a completely sideways direction to my intended route, the contrast of the quiet lanes was suddenly so enjoyable that I followed Fodder Dike all the way to Hobhole Drain.

It was at Hobhole Drain that the rain caught me. It seemed to fall in sheets, layers and layers of rain smacking into my jacket and bouncing off the road and the long straight canal. The temperature must have dropped ten degrees. My fingertips turned white with cold. Every now and then a car passed, the passengers' breath fogging the windows.

I splashed onwards down Bell Water Drain, through Thorpe Fendykes till, with sixty-two miles under my belt, I found another pub to camp behind at Wainfleet Bank. The ground was sodden and sliming with slugs. The day had turned into one of those days that never really come to an end; it just fizzled out damply.

CHAPTER 41

On opening my eyes the next morning I found my inner tent covered in dome-shaped and keel-shaped and sausage-shaped slugs, which I took great delight in flicking off to smack into my fly-sheet. There were a few tiny pearls, no bigger than my little fingernail, but most of them were either long and shiny and black, or fat and pale and brown with orange skirts. In my haste to escape my tent for a much needed pee, I forced a bare foot into a cold damp shoe and squashed a slug, which burst all over my toes.

In a petering-out drizzle, I shook the rain off my tent and packed it into a pannier before flying off up the road to Skegness in a wind-assisted gallop. This wind was a rather fitting way in which to arrive in this seaside town because, in the words of John Hassall's jolly fisherman railway poster so ubiquitously used since 1908:

SKEGNESS is SO bracing.

I pulled up outside Safeway to restock front-pannier larder supplies. As I was locking up my bike a medium-old woman, with big hair piled high, walked by and sneezed.

'Bless you!' I said.

She turned to look at me before saying, 'It's not contagious! It's . . . you know . . .'

And there she paused, not knowing quite what it was.

'An allergy to supermarkets?' I proffered.

'Aye, summat like that!' she laughed, before trundling off with her trolley. And it dawned on me that that was the first thing I'd said all day. It also dawned on me that accents were turning more northern and that made me feel good; there is something about northern tones that is as solid and reassuring as a good dry stone wall.

Down on the promenade the sun poked out from behind a bank of troubled cloud. The wind was as bracing as ever and the cold forbidding North Sea looked dirty grey and ruffled. But in true British holidaymaker 'I'm-going-to-bloody-well-bask-on-the-beach-whatever-the-bloody-weather' spirit, there was a good smattering of hardy souls braving the bracing elements. I was delighted to note there were plenty of Clenchwartons walking uncomfortably about with bucketloads of Skeggi's castling sand caught in tender cracks and clefts.

I was also delighted to note a sign advertising

JUGS OF TEA/COFFEE For the Beach.
JUGS OF ICE COLD ORANGE TO TAKE AWAY.

And all 'only available at CHERYL'S PIER KIOSK ON THE PIER DECK'. I'd never before seen kiosks selling *jugs* of tea and coffee and juice for the beach. Cups, yes, but not jugs. And I thought: what a good idea – that is, as long as Cheryl got her jugs back, because I felt certain a jugless Cheryl would be a cheerless Cheryl.

I utilised and maximised the slither of sun that shone my way by commandeering a prom-side deckchair, which was just perfect for a well-wrapped-up lazy loll. It was also perfect for people-watching – a fine sport if ever there was one. I watched chirpy children flying kites and biffing balls. I watched pre-teen gangs of sullen boys scuffing along in their untied trainers, kicking cans, looking for trouble. Too close for comfort, I watched a slimy character shuffle past, with a whiff of the mingled odours of spilled beer and fried grease. His big-as-a-barn gut tumbled out over his shorts, semi-covered by a taut T-shirt emblazoned with the words: 'Over Thirty and Feeling Dirty'.

Against the railings leant a man with a bleached blond boot-camp cut. He wore a ground-scraping pair of baggy combats and glugged Beck's from the bottle. He was tall and heavy shouldered and stripped to the waist, revealing a rising phoenix tattoo outstretched across his back. I watched him watching a tall, willowy girl, her fragile, bird-like limbs swathed in diaphanous flimsies. He watched her with what American feminists call 'elevator eyes' – his gaze scanning appreciatively up and down her almost fey female form. Next, heaving themselves up from the beach, came an overweight trio of facial hair-sporting pensioners, one of them a woman. This sudden flux of beards struck me as quite fitting, seeing as Skeggi, the affectionate name for the resort, means 'bearded one'.

Regimented barracks of holiday villages, holiday camps, retirement bungalows, hotels, chalet parks and caravan encampments abounded up the coast from Skeggi to Ingoldmells – which is where, in 1936, Billy Butlin built his first Butlins. There were lots of family-themed-for-fun things like Fantasy Island ('The Multi Award Winning Family Visitor Attraction!'), but not a lot was on offer for family-less cycling spinsters.

Although I was riding beside the sea, I couldn't actually see it because of the massive bank of sea walls and twenty-foot-high sand dunes obscuring my view. At Chapel Six Marshes I clambered up through the calf-scratching marram grass over said sandy dunes just to make sure the sea was actually there – well you never know, things that you think are where they are, are often nowhere near where they are actually supposed to be. Anyway, it was there all right, and looked as cold and grey and lumpy as ever. Reassured with my findings, I planted myself at one of the picnic tables as I felt it was high time for a spot of lunch.

I was mid banana and honey and avocado concoction when a man, who had pulled up in a VW Compass Navigator motorhome, ambled over to me cradling a mug of coffee and said, 'That's some load you've got on there, pet!'

'It is a bit,' I said. 'I'm trying to eat my way through some of it now.'

'I cycle a fair amount meself,' he told me. 'It's a good excuse to get away from the wife!'

'The wife' had just emerged from the Compass camper and called over to 'the husband' saying she was going to see if she could see the sea. (See, I wasn't the only one who mistrusted its existence.)

'I'll tell you what,' said the man, who had also told me he was sixty-five and from Huddersfield, 'the wife bought me a radio for me bike. Sits on me handlebars, like. Right good it is because it doubles up as a combination light and horn. Mind you, the horn's a bit effeminate-sounding like. A sort of *peep-peep*! Well, summat like that!'

He told me that on Sunday mornings he now rode into town in style, listening to Steve Wright's *Sunday Love Songs*. He glugged down the rest of his coffee, emitted a big sigh and said, 'Don't see many young people like you touring around on bikes these days. It don't seem to attract the youngsters. It's the different lifestyle I suppose. They don't want to get wet or hack up hills and stuff. In my opinion they're all turning too soft like, and want to get everywhere too fast. They should slow down a bit!'

I liked Mr Compass Camper, he expressed similar views to me, and we chatted further (the wife was obviously having trouble locating the sea). After I mentioned something high falutin about how I could do my journey so much easier by car, but that it just wouldn't be the same because of there being something about the intimacy of cycling that gives you such a lovely sense of gradual transition from one place to another, we were soon on to the subject of local dialects.

'Us Yorkshire folk have the reputation of being offensively blunt,' he said. 'We seem to give the impression of being as hard as nails. We just don't like no la-di-da talk, that's all!'

He then lost me a bit because he went off on a slight tangent about how, where he was from, the folk were all Anglo-Saxon, like.

'Suppose we're all Anglo-Saxon, really,' he said, 'Or Danish. Vikings, like!'

As it was, I met a Viking a little further up the coast near Moggs Eye. At least he looked like a Viking, because he had platinum blond hair and Viking cheekbones. On his head he wore a wheelbarrow. Don't ask me what he was doing walking along the side of the road with an upturned wheelbarrow on his head because I didn't ask him. I nearly did, though, when he lifted it slightly off his head to see where he was going, then spotted me and promptly doffed his wheelbarrow as he might a cap. But I bottled out from enquiring because I thought: sometimes you've just got to accept the fact that a Viking wants to go for a walk with a wheelbarrow on his head. Whatever the reason, it reminded me of the Albanian proverb: 'An upside-down wheelbarrow is no good to anyone, but at least it is dry on the inside.' If you're not familiar with Albanian proverbs, they tend to be vaguely poetical and mostly unhelpful. Unlike ours, that is, which tend to be plain bossy: 'Do as I say, not as I do'; 'Look before you leap!'; 'Don't count your chickens before the horse has bolted!'

The joined forces of the ferocious tides and hurricane winds of the 1953 storm surge had caused yet more flooding and havoc up along this flat east coast. Sutton-on-Sea had had to be evacuated, and afterwards the sea walls had been bolstered and strengthened. Near the low-water line of spring tides it is supposed to be possible to see the remains of stumps of trees of a submerged forest, which dates from around 2500 BC. But no stumpy trees did I see as I sailed through Sutton at the peak of high tide. More sea-swallowings occurred around here too, when, in the sixteenth century, the parish church vanished into the hungry ocean. And just down the coast, in Chapel St Leonards, during a 'tempest of wind and rain' in 1571, 'the whole towne was lost except three cottages . . . the church was wholly overthrown, except the steeple'.

Outside the Spar in Sutton-on-Sea an elderly man wearing a flat cap and holding a canvas shopping bag said, 'That's some load you've got on there! How far you going?'

'Newcastle,' I replied, because I thought that sounded a lot less complicated than a tangled tale of where I was ultimately trying to go.

He looked at me with a deadpan expression and said, 'Don't be stupid!'

Then he walked off, leaving me to think how fortunate it was that I hadn't revealed my true destination or else he might have walloped me one.

Forth through the 'Thorpes' I sallied: Trusthorpe, Mablethorpe and Theddlethorpe. For someone who can't say their 'th's, this was a bit of a nightmare area for me so I kept my mouth shut and my head down and whirled my wheels ever onward. ('Thorpe', incidentally, is Old Norse for an outlying farm or hamlet, so I blame those burly Vikings for furthering my speech impediment.) Big black rainclouds fast-forwarded across the flat fertile land of wolds from the southwest. I did my best to ignore them, even to the extent of not glancing over my left shoulder, as massive, anvil-shaped monsters, preparing to shed their load over vulnerable cyclists, are not a comforting sight. Near Donna Nook I happened upon a heron, which, on espying me, was suddenly on its way, rising on its great wings with neck still awkwardly outstretched. It then drew its head back into its shoulders as it flew ponderously over the swampy field, a dark grey disappearing M-shape in the sky.

After fifty-five miles of cycling with an unhelpfully whipping wind punctuated with boisterous bursts of squally showers, I made it to Humberston Fitties, just south of Cleethorpes. It was here, at the mighty Mouth of the Humber, that I decided to call it a day, mainly because I liked the sound of camping in a 'fittie', whatever a fine 'fittie' might be.

'It's a local word for salt marsh,' a local fittie-dweller told me, answering that little hiccup in my knowledge.

Against my better judgement I pulled up at Thorpe Park-cum-theme-park-Caravan Park, mainly because of a definite dearth of anywhere else to put my tent. If they took tents, that is.

'Do you take tents?' I asked a girl in the extravagant reception building.

'Tents? Oh, no, we don't,' she said breezily, whereupon a man over her shoulder said, 'Oh, yes we do.'

It was a bit early for pantomime season so I ended up looking confused.

Then, as I preferred the sound of the man's answer, I asked how much it was for one very small tent, one very small bicycle, and one very small (but perfectly proportioned) person.

'Fifteen pounds,' he said.

Had I had anything in my mouth on which to splutter, I would undoubtedly have spluttered. Instead I did a John McEnroe and said, 'You can naaat be SERIOUS!' Actually I didn't. But I did say, in a typically unflappable and unemotional British style, 'Fifteen pounds? Are you sure?'

'Yes, £15 is the going rate,' said the man.

But all I want to do is brush my teeth and go to bed.

'How much would it cost to camp here if I was a family of four with a ten-ton tent and a car?' I asked, because it's always worthwhile to ascertain exactly how much cycling spinsters of lowly means are being ripped off if they don't happen to have a petrol-polluting machine and a handy family unit about their person.

'Fifteen pounds,' said the man.

That's discriminatory daylight robbery, I thought, and stomped off.

But I camped at Thorpe Park anyway. I sneaked round the back and over the top and in the side, all the time on the watch-out for any patrolling tent police who might upset my plot. My major obstacle was not having a key for the locked toilet block and as I didn't think the surrounding families of four would appreciate me lifting my leg in the bushes or sluicing out my front and back bottoms with my water bottle while in full view of their barbecued dining, I needed to find an alternative. This momentary dilemma was soon solved by falling into step behind the slipstream of a buttock-clenching woman, travelling with an urgent gait towards the block of my desires. Once inside I partook of all procedures of a cleansing nature, doing my damnedest to use as much hot water as possible in revenge for such silly pricing policies. Not that I'm a revengeful sort as a rule, but singleton discrimination does tend to get my goat.

The next morning I had one of those experiences that nearly make you cack your pants. After visiting Grimsby's fishy-whiffing fish dock, I somehow found myself channelled on to the monster-truck-snarling, motorway-like trunk road that runs in a great rushing roar from the centre of the city to the Humber Bridge and the scary M180. My intention had been to find an alternative route through Pyewipe and Healing but something had obviously gone wrong some-where along the line and I found myself sandwiched in a suicidal situation between fast-moving lanes of killer juggernauts. As I approached a compli-cated junction of overpasses and underpasses, I tried my utmost to veer off down a slip road, but the truck behind was having none of it, so the safest thing in a devilishly dangerous situation was to retain a straight course and hold on tight for the ride. In this heart-in-mouth manner I was sucked up and over the overpass. As I saw my only means of escape fast disappearing in my rear-view mirror with, up ahead, a vast fast vision of a road ready to eat me alive, the voice in my head screamed, *Ohh, FUUUCK! This is not where I want to be!*

The only reassuring thought I could muster was that at least I was dressed for the occasion, clad as I was in full city-survival traffic-warfare battledress: a brain-bucket helmet and a fluorescent yellow 'I'm-from-the-council-come-to-mend-the-drains' reflective vest. It wasn't quite the shell of indestructible armoured coating needed to survive a jammy-dodgering juggernaut sandwiching, but it definitely helped to suggest *YOU'VE NO BLOODY RIGHT TO RUN OVER ME IN THIS HIGHLY VISIBLE SCREECHINGLY YELLOW NON-FASHION-ITEM KIT!*

Okay, don't panic, I thought, as a cold finger ran up my spine. Just cycle on a wing and a prayer and keep to an even keel and turn off at the first opportunity. But then, glancing down at my handlebar-bag-mounted map, I immediately broke into a cold sweat of panic on noting that, because this thundering trunk road was essentially a motorway, it ploughed recklessly onwards over bridges, under bridges, blocking all hope of a saviour sideroad emergency exit. I won't tell you the string of expletive thoughts that raced through my head at this stage because I fear they wouldn't sit easily with my mother. I now knew I had to make a spontaneous decision: either be truck-sucked all the way to bloody Scunthorpe or conduct one of those lunatic manoeuvres familiar to viewers of *POLICE CAMERA ACTION*, when you watch with laughable and unbelievable horror a deranged motorist reversing back down a motorway slip road among swerving and skidding vehicles when they realise they've taken the wrong exit.

Still within sight of the overpassing-underpassing junction behind me, I admit I did briefly entertain the harebrained and suicidal thought of running back along the verge, inches away from the full force of a barrage of body-flattening oncoming trucks, only to meet certain death when pushing my bike the wrong way down a vehicle-rushing frenzy. Instead I pulled on my brakes and stopped on the hard shoulder. But knowing that hard shoulders are the most likely place to die on a motorway, I didn't linger there. I tumbled with bike down the embankment, dismounted all bags and, with super-human strength, hurled them and bike over a high fence before climbing over after them. I could feel the eyes of rubbernecking motorists upon me. *What the BLOODY HELL does she think she's doing?* I could hear them say. Well, what I was doing, thank you very much, was reconnecting baggage to bike and dragging my mount round the muddy perimeters of a field, and another field, and another field, until I hit a road near Great Coates that didn't look like it was out to kill me. And I thought: *Ahh, the things we do all in the name of fun.*

It just wasn't going to be my morning, though, because no sooner had I escaped from the city limits when I suddenly found myself under aerial attack from flies. Not just normal flies, but swarms of tiny and itchy black midge-like flies in their thousands. They got in my hair, they got in my eyes, they crawled in my ears and down my bra, and they stuck in such excess to my arms and my legs and my face that I resembled a giant fly-paper on wheels. I was later told that these were harvest flies – peculiar to this region and all points north – and for the next month, whenever I passed an area of harvesting pea fields or wheat fields, my body would blacken and bristle and itchingly prickle.

A skyline filled with a massive forest of flaring chimneys grew ever bigger as I approached the strangely mesmerising sight of Immingham's oil refineries and oil terminals and power stations. What a different scene from the one the Pilgrim Fathers would have left when they set sail from here, bound for their illegal emigration to Holland, on the first stage of the voyage that finally took them to America. The muddy creek where they climbed aboard has long since disappeared beneath the concrete and steel of the vast deep-water docks and the impressively complex industrial landscape.

From out of these docks emerged a metallic flood of articulated lorries from Holland and Germany and Scandinavia, and for a while I shared the road with their skull-rattlingly noisy hulking great forms. But before long I was riding down a long, rain-streaked and rather bleak street in New Holland. It was from here that the old paddle-steamer, *Lincoln Castle*, used to ferry passengers from the wooden pier across the Humber to Hull. Until the suspension bridge was opened by the Queen in 1981, New Holland used to have the strangest vehicle ferry terminal in the country: cars using the Hull ferry would drive on and off it along the railway station platform.

Ah, what fun the old days were! Motoring with gay abandon around British Rail passengers waiting for their trains, driving over a few unattended suitcases in the process, bumper-biffing the odd porter in the kneecaps for a laugh, and whoops! – what's this? – just swerved off the edge of the platform to land in the middle of the tracks? Never mind, we'll try and get her under way before the 11.07 from Cleethorpes comes steaming down the line, but fancy a cup of tea first? Oh, to live back in a carefree risky world! Now the Nannying State won't so much as trust you to open a train door or window by yourself so we have to sit in airconditioned, window-sealed nastiness. What's wrong with all you poncy Nannies? All we want is a bit of spicy-life danger and to make risk-assessing decisions for ourselves.

Things turned quite exciting in Barrow-upon-Humber because something black in the gutter caught my eye as I was cycling out of the village. I immediately performed an about turn for further inspection. Thinking it was probably only a bit of broken bumper, I was most pleasantly surprised to discover it was a wallet. A fat, bulging, credit card-stashed wallet, 'n' all, complete with pin-numbers and cash. Well, what can I say apart from what a tremendous find! And crikey, what a thrill to hold such a handful of riches! With pound signs pinging up in front of my eyes and visions of lying sprawled in sumptuous five-star splendour in a hotel in Hull, I pocketed my booty and cycled off up the road to find the nearest cash machine.

Oh, all right then, I didn't. I'm sorry to disappoint you but I am of course a model citizen and after establishing that the wallet wasn't attached to a piece of invisible thread for *Candid Camera*, I noted the name of the credit card holder, a certain Mr Rowe, and thinking that he had perchance dropped the offending article when climbing into the car, I went a-knocking on neigh-bouring doors to make my enquiries.

But no Mr Rowe rose my way. Indeed, no one rose my way. I rattled on doors and ding-donged on bells and the only reception I received was from a ginger cat that wrapped itself around my ankles with touching affection. Then, in one house, I could see the shadowy form of a woman in a room out the back. As she obviously couldn't hear my rat-a-tat-tat on the door, I finally, and rather brazenly, strolled purposefully round to where I took her unawares from the rear, as it were.

'Ooh,' she oohed, surprised by my surprising her.

But she could shed no light on the identification of Mr Rowe. Then, with a faintly guilty (albeit thoroughly enjoyable) voyeuristic curiosity, I launched into a more meticulous wallet-rifling procedure in search of a possible clue that would lead me henceforth to my man (handing the wallet in to the nearest police station was my last option – I fancied getting to the bottom of this mystery myself). Sandwiched between a wodge of various credit cards I found a store's own-brand card for a place called Spencer. Is this Marks's other half, breaking out on a solo career in utilitarian underwear, I wondered?

'No, it's a builder's place up the road,' said the surprised woman, who was now displaying more a state of surmise than surprise.

'How far up the road?' I asked.

'Not far,' she replied. 'Turn left here, then take the second right. Keep on up the hill, go straight across the junction, then just keep going straight and it's down there somewhere.'

So off I went to Spencer's to see if they held the object of my investigations on their books. What I found, not so much on their books as on their dinner breaks, were four bulgy-muscled builders, lounging on the railings beside a Portakabin. As I cycled up to them I could see them nudging and winking and thinking, *Aye, aye! What have we got here, then?* But I can handle builders, I thought, training a practised eye over them, and before they could give me any lip, I asked if they knew my Mr Rowe.

'What, Nic Rowe?' said one, 'Yeah, he's the contracts manager. I think he's out though at the moment.'

'No, I saw him come back,' said another. 'Do you want to see him?'

'That'd be good,' I said. 'I think I've found his wallet.'

'Bloody hell! He's been going spare about that. Said he'd given up ever finding it!'

Five minutes later, an emotionally ecstatic Nic Rowe had me in his arms, planting me with one of the biggest relief kisses I've ever felt.

'Oh, Jesus!' he said, 'you're a darling! You've saved me fucking life!'

It turned out that Nic had stopped in Barrow to buy something, put his wallet on the roof of his car, and driven off. In return for 'saving his life', he wanted to foist a hefty cash reward upon me. Of course, being the innocent that I am, such a rewarding thought had never even crossed my mind.

'No, no, really, I don't want anything!' I protested, with not so much as even a momentary hesitation of lying through my teeth. 'It's enough to have just made your day!'

But Nic was having none of it. He wanted to buy me a crate of beer, he wanted to take me out to dinner, and he wanted, successfully, to stuff a rolled-up £20 note into a vent of the upturned helmet hanging off the back of my bike (I knew my helmet would have a use). He then gave me his work number, his home number and his mobile number (steady on!) and insisted I ring him later to meet up. But I never did because I was more than content with my lot: lying beneath the Humber Bridge in a rain-lashed campsite where, in the washing-up room, hung a sign that warned:

UNATTENDED CHILDREN WILL BE SOLD AS SLAVES.

How much more exciting can you get than that?

CHAPTER 42

The next morning I awoke to a fine spectacle: the neighbour's ample underwear hanging limply in the rain, a mere bra-twanging strap length from my front door. Behind a pair of extraordinarily big green pants, of such expansive proportion they could double up as a court cover at Wimbledon, stood the pants wearer's two-berth Swift Silhouette Diamond caravan (complete with porch awning, fridge, shower, cassette toilet, blinds and flyscreens). In the doorway, semi-submerged from view by a pair of her husband's unwholesomely saggy grey Y-fronts, stood an enormous woman shouting very loudly into a mobile with a 'hard as nails' Yorkshire accent.

'. . . Yer don't know what day it is, mother! . . . I said yer DON'T KNOW WHAT DAY IT IS! . . . Yer what? All rhaat, what day is it then? . . . See, I told yer, yer don't know what day it is! Yer had yer dinner out on Tuesday, not Thursday! . . . What? . . . No, yer next pension day's the 25th! All rhaat? . . . All rhaat mother, I'll ring yer tomorrow, then . . . No, I told yer, yer can't ring me, I'm in Baaarton! . . . What? Oh, it was quite nice yesterday morning, but it's raining now . . . yeah, that's rhaat, it's RAINING. It's not cold though . . . I said, IT'S NOT TOO COLD! . . . Yes . . . Yeah . . . all rhaat mother, I'll speak to yer tomorrow then . . . yeah, that's rhaat. Bye, then . . . yeah, that's rhaat, tomorrow . . . Bye, then mother, bye . . . What? . . . Yeah, love you too!'

On the other side of some dripping bushes I found a pale, pug-faced German cyclist packing up a capacious tent. We had a bit of where-you-from-where-you-going make-conversation chat before he revealed he was based in

Berlin, working in a factory as an industrial electrical engineer. When he asked me what I did and I told him I was a cook (this was the simpler option than disclosing I was on a lifelong gapyear) we hit an obvious hiatus in cross-Channel humour.

'So!' he said, suddenly becoming animated for the first time, 'in 10 hours time you vill have my dinner ready for me on zee table! Yah?'

And he burst into a howl of most unamusing laughter. I looked at him and thought: *Christ! I'm glad I'm not married to you, matey, or else you'd get a smack around the chops!*

There is something very special about cycling over big bridges like the Severn Road Bridge or the Clifton Suspension Bridge or the Firth of Forth or the Golden Gate. And the Humber Bridge was no exception. On a wide cycle path where pedestrians and cyclists were completely segregated from the flood of rushing traffic by a metal barrier, I swooped over the horizontal greyness of the flat landscape and the churning grey waters of the river (which is not really a river but the estuary of the Yorkshire Ouse and the River Trent) for nearly one-and-a-half miles. It was so enjoyable that I turned round to do it all over again. To savour every moment I kept stopping to peer over the side and watch the water, swashing around uninvitingly a good 100 feet below, and wondered what it would feel like to jump. As I stood I could feel the slightly stomach-fluttery sensation of the bridge quivering and vibrating and trembling beneath the weight of the heavy throbbing traffic as it rumbled along on the A15, passing over the wide waters that separated Lincolnshire from Yorkshire. Looking upwards I stared at the phenomenal mass of cables in which there are altogether 44,000 miles of wire – enough to go round the world one and a half times. It's at contemplative moments like this that it strikes me what seriously clever people engineers are.

After spending nearly five miles cycling back and forth across the Humber Bridge (no wonder it takes me a long time to get anywhere) I descended off the suspended ramp at an exhilaratingly high velocity – my first bit of proper speed since I started riding up from King's Lynn on this hill-less fen-filled coast. Thus, in such fine wheel-whirring style, I rode into Yorkshire's East Riding.

Hull was horrible in a fun sort of way. The cycle path I'd been half-heartedly following suddenly left me high and dry on the approach through Hessle, so I ended up being filtered back into the flood of city-bound traffic which thickened into a fetid stew of metal that clogged the road and gummed up the air. On top of this, it started to rain with such extravagance that within half and hour I was wet through and could feel water slopping back and forth in my shoes.

In a state of urban frenzy, I rode like a wild thing along the deathly dual-carriageway that follows the length of Hull's modern docks, which line seven miles of Humber waterfront. At one stage I caught sight of the *Pride of Rotterdam*, berthed at the North Sea Ferry terminal, and, with a sudden shiver of excitement, thought: *shall I bypass the delights of Paull power station and go to Holland instead?*

Instead I went to Thorngumbald along the unpleasantly fast straight of the A1033. At the side of this road I passed a big sign that said:

A1033: 124 TRAFFIC CASUALTIES.
51 SPEEDSTERS CAUGHT.

At that point a boy racer sped past my unamused funny bone as if he was trying to break the world land-speed record. All in all, the best thing about my haul through Hull was passing Humbolls Airfix Factory (quashing the myth that all those model Spitfires that I so painstakingly assembled and painted with my brothers were made in Santa's grotto) and a fodder stop called SCOFF-A-LOT CAFÉ. Oh, and I also hit a major mile mark of my coastal jaunt: looking down at my bike computer I noticed that the distance between Land's End to Hull was 3000 miles. At least it is my way, though I'm not quite sure how – I cycled across America in less.

It continued to rain vindictively. Among the smashed bottles outside Keyingham's locked church, I stopped to hastily down two bananas and an energy bar while trying to shelter from the cold slanting hail that suddenly bombarded the village. Thankfully it was only short-lived, but by the time I got going again I was frozen through. Oh the joys of an English July!

Near Whinhill Farm I stopped for a pee in a field of broad beans, podding a few for good measure while down on my haunches and eating them raw (it is nice to do two things for the price of one). On the other side of the hedge, feet from my moony-white bare buttocks, cars sped past in a splash of spray, oblivious to the fact that I was peeing and podding in the rain. Once all peed and podded out, I squelched back to my bike across mud so sticky it turned my shoes into platforms.

Just up the road in Patrington, I was purchasing a pack of porridge from the village store when a man walked through the door and, having noticed my bike, said, 'That's some load you got on there! Still, saves having to carry it!' Then he asked me where I had started from.

'Land's End,' I said, because that was the less convoluted answer.

'Oh, rhaat. We're off to Plymouth next week with the kids. Can you recommend a route?'

'Are you cycling?'

'No way! We're driving.'

'Well, in that case, definitely don't go the way I came unless you've got a year in hand, because my route took me via the Channel Islands, Kent, France and Essex.'

'Bloody hell! You need to get yourself a better map, me petal!' he said, before walking off behind a shelf of tins.

As I was remounting my steed, a big, wide and very yellow New Holland combine harvester came trundling through the village, narrowly avoiding hacking off a few ancient-walled buildings in the process. I know a wind-shielding gift horse in the mouth when I see one, and I was soon slipstreaming it at a super-suck-along 17 mph all the way to Weeton.

That night I camped just north of the spit of Spurn in a soggy field in torrential rain and tent-flattening winds. The sound of the hammering rain was so loud that I could only hear the radio if I held it next to my ear in the manner of a nerdy man in a bobble hat and milk-bottle glasses walking along the street listening to the football results. But it was worth looking nerdy, even if no one could see me, because the phone-ins on Radio Humberside proved most entertaining. The *Peter Something Show* (I didn't catch his surname, thanks to a thunderclap clattering above my tent) was having a competition about trying to guess the exact distance between certain towns like Market Weighton and Driffield. Local radio seems to excel at serving up copious preamble while luxuriating in the superabundance of idle chat (the complete antithesis of curt Radio 4, where you're not even allowed to say hello or goodbye).

Peter Presenter asked one caller what she was doing this weekend.

'Well, I'm just getting t'tea ready at t'moment,' she said. 'Me and me 'usband, we've not long been back from Beverley. Me husband, 'ere, 'e plays in t'Beverley Brass Band. But 'e never got to play today, because it got rained off, like. It were ever such a shame.'

Peter Presenter commiserated a moment, agreeing that, aye, it had been rhaat wet, like.

He then asked what instrument the woman's husband played.

'What's that, love? Oh, it's a big one. It's a bass trombone.'

Peter Presenter didn't seem to have a reply to that. But that didn't matter because Mrs Brass Band was off on a yabbering roll.

'Yer know what? I've been hoping to get a new Magnet kitchen for ever such a long time now, but me husband said there's no need for a new kitchen, not when he can varnish the old units, like. So that's what he's doing at t'moment. He's on t'floor by me feet. Says when he's finished, this kitchen will be as good as new – so I suppose it'll just have to do!'

'Isn't he in the way if you're getting the tea?' asked the presenter.

'Aye, we're getting in each other's way, really. I'm trying me best to manoeuvre around him!'

As the rain continued to pelt my tent, I lay bundled up in my sleeping bag, staring into the blackness with mini trannie pinned to lughole, visualizing the lovely scene of a house somewhere on Humberside, containing a wife in pinnie and slippers, trying to prepare the tea while tripping over her husband who's crawling around on the floor with a lethally sticky brush trying to varnish the kitchen cabinets because he's too tight a bastard to go to Magnet Kitchens and buy her a new one. And somewhere, sitting proud in a corner, is a big shiny brass bass trombone that has just had a most unfulfilling journey to Beverley and back. Because it rained.

Anyway, after all that, Mrs Brass Band guessed the wrong distance between the two towns, so she hung up to concentrate on getting the tea and falling over her husband.

The next caller was a young lad from Hull who, speaking in a phlegmatic monotone, didn't sound like the most frolicsome person in the world.

'What have you been up to today?' asked Peter Presenter.

'Nowt much – listening t'radio or watching TV,' replied the scintillating bundle of fun.

'Anything good on?'

'What, on TV? No, it's all boring, in't it?'

'What do you like watching?'

Pause (for possible deep and philosophical thought).

'Films, I suppose.'

'What sort of films do you like?'

Silence. Hmm, difficult one this. Might have to phone a friend.

'Horror? Westerns?' prompted Peter Presenter perseveringly. (Talk about pulling teeth. Had I been in his shoes, I think I would have given up long ago on this one – sparkling live wire that he was.)

More silence. Helloo? Do we have life down the line?

No, seems we have a bit more silence.

Then finally, from out of the deadened darkness, came the reply, 'Dunno. Anything really.'

To give him credit, Monotone Man might not have known what he likes to watch on TV, but he knew his distance between the two towns because his answer, 'twelve mile', was the correct one and he won the allotted prize. The usual overboard cock-a-hoop victorious quiz-caller response of, 'Oh, my God! I can't *believe* it! Thank you *so* much!' followed by the inevitable, 'Can I just say hello to my husband Percy and my three kids Pandora, Pamela and Paula and my dog, Panta, and my cat, Purra, and my fish, Puffa, and my neighbours Paul and Pauline and my work mates Philaminor, Philamajor, and Phil-her-up-Please and . . . anyone else who knows me!' was not the sort of vanquished reply heard coming from Monotone Man. He emitted a toneless grunt and then hung up.

'Well, he sounded excited!' said Peter Presenter.

And then I fell asleep.

CHAPTER 43

The weather seemed to be fulfilling Shakespeare's gloomy forecast to a tee: 'For the rain it raineth every day.' And it haileth too. At least it did again today. Rob McElwee came on Radio 4's pre-news weather bulletin and said, 'You don't often get reports of snow in July, but we've had some calls to the Met Office today – it's hailed so hard it's left a snow scene.' Classic FM's brief post-news three-day forecast sounded none the brighter: 'Tomorrow – showers turning to rain; cloud and rain on Tuesday; cloud and heavy rain on Wednesday'. *Showers turning to rain*? Excuse me, but how can rain turn to rain? When I get caught in a shower of rain it tends to be rainy. And wet. But maybe I'm missing something.

Sadly, my non-rainy shower never came. Instead, a steady downpour developed into a more determined deluge. The irregular road surfaces turned from puddled wind-whipped lagoons into a veritable boiling sea. Trying to find a field to piss in was no mean task; at every field gate, any trace of grass had long since vanished into a calf-deep mire, which, to negotiate, I needed waders, not trainers.

Cycling down the three-and-a-half mile long, narrow spit of sand and shingle to Spurn Head was fun – it was so wet and so windy, and so utterly horribly cold, that by the time I had fought my way to the extreme tip overlooking the notorious tide-race and shallow shoals of Stony Blinks and the Humber's gaping Mouth, I was well and truly weatherlogged. The fact that I was able to stand where I was standing was a feat in itself as Spurn, scoured from the fluid landscape of the Yorkshire coast, is a shifting no-man's-land on the verge of destruction. Some time in the next few years, storms will finally wash it all away, taking the lighthouse and lifeboat station with it.

The extraordinary phenomenon of Spurn's flimsy and thin hooked spit, which in places is no more than a few yards across from each high-tide mark on either side of it, appears to hang on for dear life to Holderness – which is itself yet another piece of flat east coast land with a wild, weather-ravaged sea-stolen coastline. Kilnsea, the last place on the 'mainland' that sits at the base of this tendril of land, has a history that typifies most of the Holderness settlements. For 700 years or more, it has been virtually powerless to prevent the relentless encroachment of the sea and huge areas of the parish have been swallowed up (Old Kilnsea has long gone). A plaque set into the wall of the former Blue Bell Inn (now a shop) records that in 1847 – the year it was built – the building stood 534 yards from the sea. Today it is well under half that distance. The erodable boulder-clay land has been vanishing at the rate of about seven-and-a-half feet a year.

I fancied that Holderness must derive its name from an essential Hold-on-Tightness for the inevitable rough and rocky ride of its fragile existence. But it is never as simple as that: 'ness' refers to the promontory, whereas the 'hold' has absolutely nothing to do with clinging on to your hat and your life and your land and everything to do with the title of a high-ranking yeoman in the Danelaw (the word is related to the German *Held*, 'hero') who would have once ruled the promontory. Now why didn't I know that?

Soaked from the slanting rain and the salty spray of a fiercely ruffled sea, I pushed my bike the three miles or more back up Spurn's sandy rough-roaded spit (it was too impossibly windy to stay upright to ride). The Sunk Roads and Hawke Channel lay in the more sheltered west as part of the Humber Estuary, Spurn's spindly cradling arm doing its best to protect the lone rock and shingle banks of Dolphin, Old Den and Greedy Gut, and the more distant Skeffling Clays, Hole Bars and The Plumbs, all the way to Cherry Cob Sands.

It continued to rain, hard. At one point, I dived into an open barn littered with spilt grain to put another layer on under my jacket and a cornered rat ran out between my legs. A little later I took shelter standing in a semi-enclosed bus shelter to put more clothes on and to eat a few fast handfuls of food before I froze (I had to keep standing because if I sat down my muscles grew cold and seized up). A dog came along, loping beside his aged and angular owner, and I watched the wind catch the big floppy dog's ears and send them aloft. The man leant into the wet and wild weather, holding tight on to his cap.

'Blowin' a bit,' he remarked in a rusty voice. 'Fair drop o' rain too.'

'You could say that,' I said.

The man moved on, but not before his dog had stuck his wet sniffing nozzle (or whatever dogs have) up my arse.

I carried on, past a spate of discarded cigarette packets drowning in mud on the verge, past the vast imprisoned North Sea Gas Terminal brooding menacingly behind miles of security camera-topped razor-wire fencing, past an abandoned high-ankled Doctor Marten boot and two cracked plastic wheel trims, past a supermarket in Withernsea called Proudfoot, past wreaths of sodden brown-rimmed flowers marking the spot of a road-death victim, past huge hedgeless fields of wheat – the rain beating down the stalks, flooding the black rutted soil.

I followed the ever-retreating sea-snatched coast of Holderness all the way to Bridlington where, outside the tourist office, I dropped a handful of maps on the ground. Before I had a chance to bend down to retrieve them, an elderly woman walking past with her granddaughter turned to her and said, 'Pick up t'maps for t' young lassie, will yer, pet?' Afterwards I thought: how nice to be called a young lassie when really I'm an old maid.

Moments later a loud bunch of boozed-up lads piled out of the pub and came swaying down the street. One bloke, built like a brick shithouse, stumbled against me and slurred, 'Wha's tha'? Some fookin' bike under all tha'? I know me bikes, like. Tha's made in York, in't it?'

'No,' I said, 'South London.'

He took a step forward, sandwiching me between my bike, propped against the wall, and his pneumatic lardy beer gut. Then his eyes went all funny and he thrust his pushy jaw so close to mine I could smell his stinking brewery breath.

'Coome 'ere, gorgeous,' he said, flicking out his fat ugly tongue, 'and give us a kiss.'

By this stage I was practically bent backwards over my bike. I heartily swore at him as I quickly turned my face away from his slobbering mouth while trying to shove him off me. I could easily have kneed him in the bollocks but I knew that a drunk man was one thing and an angry drunk man was quite another.

'C'mon, yer sad wanker!' shouted one of his mates, and he moved off on unsteady legs down the street. As I pushed my bike down the shopping precinct, muttering obscenities to myself, I thought: *funny how I can drop my map and people run to my aid, yet pin me up against the wall beneath a fat drunken bastard who would probably rape me if I gave him half a chance, and no one wants to know.*

Outside Holland and Barratt, I was piling a big sack of rolled oats on board my bike (can't let being molested in the street put me off my porridge, you know) when I overheard a conversation between two women standing in front of the shop window beside my bike.

One of the women, in her fifties, asked the much younger woman, 'Who yer seeing at t' moment?'

'I'm not seeing anyone.'

'Wise decision,' said the older woman, 'Very wise decision. This coming from someone who's spent thirty years trying to get rid of t'man they've got!'

And being in an anti-man mood myself, I thought: *how wise indeed!*

As I was cycling up a bit of a hill out of Bridlington, the pavements were filling with pushing and shoving school kids spilling out of the local school. One beefy young lad with a head of cropped stubble shouted, 'Why yer got all them bags?'

'I'm moving house,' I said.

But over the last couple of days I had begun to suffer from the effects of moving my house around; my dicky knee of yore was hurting. *Oh no!* I thought. *Not again!* I had been hoping to push on up the coast to Scarborough, but instead I made it no further than Sewerby, where I limped into the Poplars campsite. The packed site was run by a chatty couple who at first said they were full. After one crestfallen look, they said they were sure they could find a small space to squeeze me in. Trouble was they wanted £9.50 for the pleasure of pitching my tent next to a big pile of dog poo. Time to adopt my Moroccan carpet-selling hat of bartering, I thought, and I got them down to a fiver, which I still thought was daylight robbery to pay for taking up a minute space of grass, but then maybe I'm just a tight-arsed cyclist.

Anyway, unless I wanted to aggravate my knee more by pressing on to find a different camp spot, I had no alternative other than to be grateful for small mercies and put up my tent. As I was doing so a man from the caravan next door came and brought me a steaming mug of coffee.

'Weather's not been kind to yer,' he said in a deadpan sort of way.

'You can say that again!' I replied.

He walked back to his caravan without saying another word. When I returned his mug he said, 'I've just seen t' weather forecast on t' TV.'

'Oh,' I said, 'is it good? Are we all going to be basking in hot sunshine by the morning?'

'No,' said Deadpan Man, 'they've got flood warnings out for all of east Yorkshire.'

'Oh, how lovely!' I replied, 'That's just what we need!'

Back at base I found a long gangly man in glasses standing with a short woman dressed in a strange sort of body suit which was tight in all the right places and tighter still in some of the wrong ones. Apparently they had been discussing the smallness and compactability of my tent, so I had to spend the next few moments immersed in boffin tent-talk, answering questions on weight and length of poles before moving on to the lofting properties of my sleeping bag, when all I really wanted to do was to lie down to take the pressure off my knee. Then they told me they lived on a crap housing estate in Sheffield and that getting away to this campsite meant that they could actually relax for the first time in months.

'The kids down our street are a fookin' nightmare,' the gangly man said. 'They keep setting bins on fire, smashing windows, nicking cars. We can't step outside door, like, without being shouted and sworn at.'

'Aye,' said the woman, 'it feels rhaat good to get away from them four walls, like. We don't even mind camping in t' rain, it's just nice to escape. Them kids, they've made our home feel like a fookin' prison.'

The next person to come calling at my tent was a character of a completely different nature – and nation. Cameron ('call me Cam') was a young Canadian on a mountain bike and a two-year working visa. He had just spent a month cycling in Holland and had ridden up here from Hull after getting off the ferry.

'My grandfather was from Apeldoorn,' he told me, 'so I was kind of inter- ested to see what the place was like.'

I asked him if he had a Dutch surname.

'Well, it was originally Logtenburg,' he said, 'but when my family emigrated to Canada they changed it to Logenburg because dropping the 't' made it much easier for North Americans to say!'

Cam had spent all his life living in Winnipeg (most of it with his dad, a suc- cessful importer of tropical plants) and had never been to another country apart from when he went on a family cruise to Puerto Rico.

'So landing in Holland was kind of awesome!' he told me. 'It's a completely different culture to anything I've ever known.'

Then he asked me to clear up a bit of trans-Atlantic misinterpretation for him.

'What do you guys call this?' he asked, indicating the money pouch strapped round his waist. 'A woman in Hull looked at me real strange when I referred to it as my fanny pack.'

'It's probably best to call it a bumbag,' I said.

'A *bum*bag? Oh, right. That's cool.'

Behind Cam's bike he was pulling a Bob Yak trailer piled high with gear.

'Know what I did today?' he said. 'I lost my pants! I strapped them to the top of my trailer, but I can't have fixed them on properly because they flew off. They were the only pants I've got. God, I was so mad!'

For two days my knee had me confined to barracks so I wallowed in my tent in the rain. Wallowing in tents is a pastime that comes quite naturally to me and is always a good time to catch up on those bits of housekeeping that slip through the net when on a journey of perpetual movement. By virtue of its simplicity, tentwifery becomes almost pleasant, for a one-berth tent needs very little dusting or polishing or sweeping. So all that's left to do is round up a surplus of escaped porridge oats (they make good ground insulation though) and nail clippings (not good news for punctured ground sheets) before scraping off the remains of a few shrivelled slugs that have sneaked in the back door in their typically underhand slimy way. With such inner tent challenges accomplished, I could lie back with a sense of achievement and listen to the rain.

And what rain it was! It came plashing and pouring and teeming and drenching and driving and dripping and dropping and storming and sheeting. Some areas in North Yorkshire, not far from where I lay subsiding in the mire, recorded twice the monthly rainfall levels in just one night. No surprise, then, that July was to be the wettest for forty years. And no surprise either that once again I had attracted the worst of the weather, because while I wallowed in the wet the remote islands of Orkney (where I would have been had it not taken me so much longer than the long time that I thought it would take me to get me to where I was) were enjoying almost three months of unbroken sunshine. But despite the dismal summer that had saturated the majority of the British Isles, the British Tourist Authority and the English Tourism Council had taken to looking on the bright side of life by saying that the British tourist industry was weatherproof – because visitors had no great expectation of sunshine. Ah, that's the spirit! Think dull and damp and anything other than a drowning is a bonus.

As I packed up a wet tent in the wet rain and placed a wet body on to a wet bike, I rather fancied booking in at the Snugglepuss Cats Hotel where, so a notice in the window of Bempton post office informed me, I could expect to find:

All chalets built to Feline Advisory Bureau Standards overlooking a central courtyard in a rural garden setting. Each chalet is individually heated and has floor level entry to cater for old and infirm cats. All diets can be catered for.

But I'm not a cat.

Aren't village post offices splendid things? Sociologically speaking, I'm sure that you can tell a lot about the psyche of our island nation simply by reading the notices and 'For Sale' cards Blu-tacked to their windows. Whereas in the United States a 'WANTED' poster might be alerting its citizens that the hunt is on for a psychotic serial killer who eats his victims' brains and is 'WANTED' dead or alive, things that us folks are requested to track down on this side of the water tend to be a little more tame. 'WANTED,' said a notice in Brampton post office, 'Clean jam jars (will collect)'. It's all so very reassuring.

Another reassuring thing I learnt on this very wet summer's day was that cows reared on flat land do not a hiking herd make. Picking up a copy of the local paper, I read how Mr Scarr, a farmer from Bainbridge in the Yorkshire Dales, had lost his herd to foot-and-mouth the previous year. He had recently returned from a Norfolk sales spree with thirty-three feisty Friesians. The only problem was that, according to Farmer Scarr, the cows – bred on flat land – didn't take kindly to hills. 'We have to push them up,' said our good farmer, 'but then as soon as you turn your back, they come down again.'

On Cam-the-Canadian's recommendation that I stop by Bempton Cliffs which, to his mind, were 'awesome', I dutifully paid a visit. These 400-foot walls of chalk, stretching for four miles along the crumbling coast, are riddled with ledges and crannies and crevices where an estimated 75,000 wailing kittiwakes build their nests together with tens of thousands of puffins and razorbills and fulmars and gannets and guillemots. On top of this heady winged mix, there's the bonus of a few shags to be had if your luck is in. The area is an RSPB nature reserve and on one of the RSPB viewing platforms overlooking the plunging cliffs alive with the cryings and chatterings and circlings and swirlings of a prodigious amount of seabirds, I met an RSPB man with a telescope.

Obviously I didn't look much of a twitcher to him because he turned to me and said, 'Do you know what you're looking at?'

I managed to bite a facetious comment in the bud by replying, ever so sensibly, 'Well I know my puffins and my fulmars and my gannets, but I'm having a spot of difficulty on the razorbills and guillemots because they seem to be wearing the same dinner jackets.'

So the kindly and good-natured RSPB man invited me to grab a hold of his huge telescope (ooh, yes please!) and, as I peered down its impressive orifice secretly hoping to score a shag, he told me how to differentiate my black-and-white-clad ornithological stumbling block. Easy really: razorbills have razor bills and guillemots have gills. No, only joking, apart from the razor bill bit. With their stocky build, razorbills are more nightclub bouncer to the more effeminate slender and sleek girls-night-out guillemots.

I homed in on a pod of puffins perched precariously on a piece of precipitous cliff (don't try saying that with a portion of pelican pie in your mouth). The thing I love about puffins, apart from their colourfully clownish bright boots, is that slightly sheepish and wistful expression they wear that says: *I can't possibly let the neighbours see me out in a beak like this!* And they're probably right – the Great Creator of Puffins did go pretty OTT on the lipstick. But if you've got a bizarre bill you might as well flaunt it, and this our dumpy friends have got down to a fine art when they come hurrying home, rapidly wing-beating, with sand-eel moustaches. How much more comical can you look?

In contrast to the decidedly frumpy and farcical puffins, it's the pointed black wing-tipped gannets (Europe's largest breeding seabird) that are the streamlined torpedo killers of the cliffs. To watch them on a fishing mission, skydiving from heights up to 130 feet, spearing the water with yellow heads at 60 mph, is truly mesmerising.

'In 1957,' my RSPB man told me, 'there were fifteen pairs of gannets nesting on these cliffs. Now we've got over two-and-a-half thousand pairs.'

'How have they done so well?' I asked him.

'Well, back then there used to be a lot of "climmers" – that's the local word for men who used to climb down the cliffs to steal the eggs. Because they didn't want chicks in the eggs, they would knock all the eggs off over the edge and then return two days later to collect the freshly laid eggs. So Bempton has gone from having nearly nothing to being the largest mainland gannet colony in Britain.'

I spent a day walking up and down the cliff-lined coastline between Flamborough Head and Speeton Cliffs, passing as I did such tantalisingly named places as Scale Nab, Cat Nab, Gull Nook, Cradle Head, Stottle Bank Nook, Crab Rocks, King and Queen Rocks and Dulcey Dock. Later, when cycling in heavy rain past the track to Hoddy Cows, the road was a memorable one for being covered with a glut of tyre-squashed worms. What is it about worms that make them so suicidally intent on crossing roads? Don't they know they're out of their depth? I can understand the logic behind beetles busily scuttling in a mad-hatted dash to get to the other side – after all, if a road is in their way, then they haven't got much choice other than taking their life in their legs and legging across; but worms are some of the world's greatest ground excavating creatures, for heaven's sake, so why can't they just get burrowing and tunnel a safe path beneath the road? I know I shouldn't let such trifling issues worry me so, but oh, how they do! Were I travelling by car I probably wouldn't even give them a second thought because I wouldn't even notice them before I'd flattened them. But on a bike you're out there with the worms in all weathers and it brings home to you the stresses and strains of an earthworm's life.

Anyway, all these flattened worms put me in mind of a piece I once read in the *Independent* about a junior agriculture minister who recommended stamping on the accidentally imported New Zealand flatworms as the best way of eradicating them. When a Parliamentary Lord Somebody then asked, 'Are you sure it's effective to stamp on a worm that's already flat?' the junior minister assured him that the flatworm was triangular in cross-section.

CHAPTER 44

There's history a-plenty along Yorkshire's east coast, with Romans and Saxons and Vikings and Roundheads and Cavaliers and even the Imperial German Navy all leaving their mark. Something else that has left its mark is an asteroid crater under the sea off Scarborough. Scientists made this discovery as I was passing this way and the local news was excitedly reporting about the crater, seven miles wide and 900 feet deep, which is thought to have been caused 60 million years ago by an asteroid 1500 feet wide. Normally I would have been quite excited about this discovery too; after all, geologists thought it could hold unique clues to asteroids like the one thought to have wiped out the dinosaurs 65 million years ago. But I was still more concerned about my worms. Well, not *my* worms, you understand (I'm fine down there, thanks), but my road-flattened ones.

Talking of 'down there', I was pushing my bike along Scarborough's pedestrianised shopping precinct when, outside the Link store, I was intercepted by a vivacious woman in her fifties who said breathlessly, 'Ooh! I would just *love* to do that! But I'd be too scared! I've got a Puch and a Dawes, a six-speed and a twelve-speed.'

I uttered some suitably impressed utterances.

Then she said, 'Do you get mash, love?'

I looked at her in a state of non-comprehension. She couldn't be alluding in some sort of druggie code to hash, could she? No, surely not – I look far too pure and cherubic and concerned for a worm's welfare to indulge in such a pastime. In that case, she could only mean one thing – bangers and mash. Obviously I was displaying a mashed potato aura about me, which was a bit disappointing, as I would prefer a porridge-flavoured one, really.

'Mash?' I said tentatively. 'Do you mean a sort of Mash-means-Smash mash?'

'No, love,' laughed the woman. Pointing to her front bottom, she explained, 'I mean the sort of sitting-on-saddle fungal mash you can get down here!'

Dear heaven, I thought, they're not half forward, these northerners! Here I am talking to a complete stranger in the street about what might or might not be occurring between my legs. (For the record, I would like to make it clear that I have neither thrushes nor worms playing havoc with my undercarriage – though I did once have something quite interesting drop out of my bottom in India, but I'd rather not go down that road right now.)

It turned out that whenever the woman spent any substantial time on her bike she would get . . . well, let's just say 'problems' in her downstairs department. We then progressed to saddle-comparison talk, and I recommended she try a specifically female one like mine, which comes with a hole in the middle for refreshing those parts that even Heineken cannot reach.

So, with a possible bottom solution in hand, we cheerily parted company and went on our separate ways.

Earlier on in the year, Scarborough beat Hastings and Weymouth to win the Safeway Excellence in England award 2002 for Most Improved Resort. I presume that this is a compliment but, like my old school reports, 'most improved' can mean you're still pretty crap; you're just not as crap as you were.

Whatever it meant, Scarborough was looking good and seemed to be holding its head up high, trumpeting in the wake of winning this apparently prestigious award. It also seemed to be trumpeting its history which, depending on which tourist leaflet or local newspaper I picked up, was either proudly declaring its distinction as being the oldest seaside resort in the country (the 'Queen of Watering Places' and the 'Queen of the Yorkshire coast') or claiming that it's 'probably the world's first seaside resort'. Which, read another way, probably means that it isn't.

What was slightly more certain was that it was 'probably' the Vikings who gave Scarborough its name, founded, as it is thought to be, by a Norseman named Four Gills . . . I mean, Thorgils Skarthi. If that is more probable than improbable, then Scarborough can be understood as meaning 'Skarthi's Fort'.

What is definitely a lot more definite is that the pilgrimage to Scarborough began back in the 1620s when a certain Mrs Farrow proclaimed the health-giving properties of a small, reddish-coloured stream flowing across South Sands. It was said that these mineral waters were 'a most Sovereign remedy against Hypondriack, Melancholly and Windiness' and 'cleanses the stomach, opens the lungs, cures asthma and scurvy, purifies the blood, cures jaunders, both yellow and black, and the Leprosie'. Towards the end of the seventeenth century, Mrs Farrow's capitalisation of the mineral waters had turned the wells of Scarborough into a famous spa town. At the same time, Dr Whittie became an enthusiastic advocate of sea-bathing, even going so far as to do a Dr Brighton by advising people to drink sea water for its 'medicinal' properties. Not long after that the first bathing machine appeared at Scarborough (the town claims that this modesty-protecting contraption was invented there) and, before you knew it, it had soon become fashionable for men and women to leap naked into the sea for a frolic.

As a chill wind swept the pier, I sat huddled on a step eating a banana while watching people watching the donkeys tramping up and down the littered sand. Above us all hung a low, leaden grey Yorkshire sky that merged with the cold waters of an equally grey North Sea.

Although it was Friday, it was not yet Friday night but already a group of students, decked out in hip-hop glad rags, were well on their way to getting bladdered, while a pack of Red Bull-swilling girls were parading along the prom in micro-skirts and halter tops, their thighs stark white as plucked chickens. I was so busy people-watching that I had forgotten that people might be watching me. As apparently they had. (*Urgh! Scary thought!*) A small boy armed with a plastic Kalashnikov had crept up from behind me. He was kitted out in full camouflage gear. Even his hard-fisted face was daubed with jungle-coloured war paint so that he looked like a Macbeth moving bush. I felt he had confused his environments. He should really have been decked out in Desert Storm gear if he wanted to blend with Scarborough sands. Oh, and eating an ice cream while straddling a donkey would help a lot too. But I didn't tell him so. Instead he told me he was out on patrol and that there were some snipers in them fish warehouse things over there.

'Well, we better take cover behind this wall,' I said. 'I don't want to be getting any holes in my head – I've got to get to Hartlepool yet!'

Then the moving bush said, 'Are yer one of them travellers, like?'

'Well, sort of,' I replied, 'I'm travelling by bike round the coast.'

'Do yer sleep out, and tha'?'

'Yes,' I said, 'in a camouflaged tent.'

'Do people try and kill yer?'

'Hopefully not! I've been all right so far, but I have to keep a wary eye out for suspect characters.'

'Have yer got a gun?'

'No,' I laughed, though I know it's no laughing matter (as my mother would say). 'I travel unarmed.'

'Yer can have me gun if yer want.'

'That's very charitable of you! But I'm okay, thanks. I've got my bicycle pump I can use as my walloping weapon.'

'But yer can't shoot no one with tha', can yer? Me mum and dad can buy me a new gun. They said yer probably not got much money because yer one of them travellers, like.'

Then it started raining, hard, and my moving bush jumped up and ran back to Parental HQ across the open sand without zig-zagging in a low-to-the-ground secret-service way as laid down by the Geneva Convention, which was a bit of a rash move, I thought, seeing as there were snipers in the fish sheds.

Near Scalby Mills I veered off the busy main road on to the disused Whitby–Scarborough railway line, which Sustrans have turned into an 18-mile cycle trail. It was lovely! No cars, no people. Just dripping woodland, heady wafts of wild garlic and arched brick bridges. It took me close by to the cliffs of the Cleveland Way, from the likes of Sailor's Grave to Rodger Trod and beyond. In fact it was not far from where Rodger had Trod that I got caught up in a cow-jam. A local farmer was using the trail to walk his 'gurls' from one field to another. So I sat on my crossbar for all of the 270 buxom beauties to sway past in a dignified convoy. Every now and then, one of them would stop to look at me. Then another would do the same. Not to be outdone, I stared back, gazing questioningly into their moist black eyes, which regarded me with that special clueless intensity peculiar to cattle. It was all very slow and all very nice.

Other moments of high excitement were scaring a blackbird, which came cannoning out of the bottom of a hedgerow in full metallic alarm-call fluster, and rounding up an escaped sheep that must have limbo-danced under a gate.

There was no other explanation. *Flippin' heck!* I thought, *who would be a sheep farmer when every sheep is a potential Houdini?* It took me the best part of an hour to try to convince the barmy bleating animal that it was far easier to return to its woolly companions through an open gate (which I devilishly opened at the risk of losing the rest of the scatterbrained flock seeking a break for freedom in a mad stampede to Scarborough) rather than keep ram-raiding headlong into the wire-netting fence. But still, you can't help feeling sorry for sheep occasionally. They plainly suffer from a bad press, not helped by the Tibetan saying: 'It is better to have lived one day as a tiger, than a thousand years as a sheep.'

Up high on the red cliffs of Ravenscar, the rain stopped and the sun came out. Gratefully, I peeled off all clammy layers and stood on the cliff in the luxurious warmth, gazing down upon the unexpected splendours of Robin Hood's Bay. All of a sudden Yorkshire had become Cornwall without the tourists, or the Jurassic Coast without the punter-pulling 'branding'. For, like Lyme Regis and Charmouth, here be dinosaurs too, embedded in the red rocks and shales that form the beach's cliffhanging backdrop. By revealing a history of the last 180 million years, this sea-snatched stretch of coast, eroding at the rate of some two inches a year, read like some gigantic geological textbook. If you're a dab hand with the investigative *tappety-tap* of the hammer, a prehistoric treasure trove of cigar-shaped belemnites and coiled ammonites, spiralling like beetle grubs, are up for grabs – every whorl a unique fingerprint of the past.

Stacked up behind the beach roost the russet pantiled cottages of Robin Hood's Bay's steep-twisting, cobble-alleywayed fishing-cum-artists' hamlet, the houses clinging precariously to the steep slopes like nests of sand martins, each buttressing the one above. So compact do they stand that eighteenth-century smugglers could outwit the Revenue men by passing contraband from hand to hand through the tunnels and cellars from one end of the village to the other without it ever having to see the light of day.

On down past Stoupe Beck Sands and Boggle Hole I went till I ground to a halt outside Fylingdales Cricket and Football Club, where I sat on a welcoming bench in the sun to eat half a pannier of food. The bench had a plaque that told me it had been placed there 'IN MEMORY OF HAROLD SCARGILL OF WAKEFIELD 1916–1993'. And I thought, *Blimey! Is that Arthur's dad?*

With batteries nicely recharged, I then sped off to the clifftops over Whitby, taking in the jagged skeletal sandstone ruins of Whitby Abbey on the way. This stark, brooding marvel was founded by the Benedictines in the eleventh century after those storming warpath Vikings, with horned wheelbarrows on their heads, had destroyed the original church. Along with our Scandinavian seafaring pirates, that monastic meddler, Henry VIII, had helped to play a part in the destruction of this magnificent but slightly sinister abbey (it was one of the settings for Bram Stoker's fiendishly vampirical *Dracula*). In 1914, it was even shelled during a German warship attack on the coastguard station.

More pantiled roofs greeted me in the old whaling town of Whitby. It would have been a lovely place to linger, but its narrow curving streets like Flowergate and Baxtergate were heaving with holidaymakers, many of whom were off to join a long serpentine queue to walk round a replica of the *Endeavour*, which had sailed to Whitby amidst much publicity from Australia. When an ovoid-shaped man walked past me in cluster-revealing shiny nylon shorts and a T-shirt emblazoned with 'Wine Me, Dine Me, 69 Me', I decided to leave a visit to Captain Cook's house in Grape Lane to another day.

There was nothing flat about the road out of Whitby, which climbs up out of the deep gorge-like Esk Valley before leading you up round Raven Hill. Down on the coast ribboned the stretched sands of Upgang Beach and before I knew it I was freefalling at such eye-watering velocity into the village of Sandsend that when I jammed on my brakes at the bottom, a whole café of people sitting at tables outside turned to stare at the suddenness of my arrival. At moments like this, it's very tempting to do something very silly like ripping off all your clothes and running up and down the road howling with demented laughter. I think this reaction must have something to do with the flushed excitement of a hilarious descent combined with being glared at by a sea of gobsmacked faces. Anyway, demonstrating remarkable self-control, all I ended up doing was paying a visit to the public conveniences.

When I remounted my bike, all those slack-jawed faces turned to stare at me again (it's most off-putting to think how many people have been timing you at your toilet). *She's not going to cycle up that, is she?* I could see them thinking – *that* being a severe, double-arrow hill that rose away from the café at a dizzy vertical. And they were right – I wasn't. At least I wasn't until I decided that I was – well, just as far as the first few feet and then I would get off and push. So, with a reckless leg-whirring run-up, I flung myself with gay abandon into the gravity-defying obstacle. Twenty seconds later, with exploding lungs and zonked-out limbs, I was on the point of defeat and dismount when an old lady, with elaborate silver hair, leant out of an engine-straining passing car and called, 'Keep goin', lassie!' So I did. Funny how so few words can go so far.

More few words that have no doubt gone far were inscribed on the clock war memorial in the village of Hinderwell:

> Pass not this stone in sorrow but in pride
> And live your lives as nobly as they died.

In order to walk around the steep narrow alleys of Gun Gutter and Dog Loup (which is all of one-and-a-half feet wide) I had first to plunge down the drastic one-in-five descent to the entrance of a constricted valley in the lee of Cowbar Nab and into the twisting, cobbled fishing village of Staithes – the village where Captain George Vancouver's idol, Captain Cook, worked in a haberdashery and grocery store before he took to sea in a Whitby collier. And then I had to cycle all the way back up again. Up. Down. Up. Down. It was all very Cornwall, with its hills and coves and mines. I passed Boulby Potash Mine (near Twizziegill Farm, which lies just inland from Boulby – the tallest cliffs in England), climbed up over Downdinner Hill, before plummeting back down (dinner) into the village of Skinningrove, where iron mines and blast furnaces and a steel works acropolis have all taken their toll on the land and the people.

In the First World War, the Skinningrove Steel Works became a number one target for the huge German Zeppelin airships. During the critical stages of the U-boat campaigns of 1914, Skinningrove not only added two more steel furnaces and a mixer to the plant, but it also doubled the size of its coke-oven installations to manufacture shell steel for the badly needed guns on the war fronts. On top of that, scientists at Skinningrove were researching the possibility of using the ethylene present in coke gas to produce mustard gas, one of the principal and most horrific weapons of the First World War. One night the massive 804-foot Zeppelins dropped over a hundred high-explosive bombs on the Works, including incendiaries on the naphthalene plant and the roof of the benzol house. Incredibly, only the steel plant offices were badly damaged and there were no reports of injuries.

Saltburn, where the Cleveland Hills meet the coast, came and went in a burst of more leg-quaking hair-pinned gradients. Then, near Tofts Farm, I was turning right on a roundabout when an erratically driven car cut me up. Inside were four crop-skulled thugs throwing obscenities and empty beer bottles out of the windows. They howled with laughter and tore round the roundabout again on squealing tyres. By this stage I had just joined the road to Marske when they slewed up alongside, yelling their ugly bulldog-pinched heads off. Then one of them leant out of a back window and gobbed me full in the face. The driver stuck his arm out above the roof, gave me the finger, and then they careered off down the road straight through the red flashing lights of the rail-way crossing dropping its barriers.

In the space of about twenty seconds my happy, untroubled mood had been transformed into one of raging fury. I pulled over to the side of the road, stood astride my bike to wash off my face and, under my breath (I don't like to cause a scene), promptly turned the air a very deep shade of blue. I went all trembly and felt like blubbing out of sheer frustration. I had never been spat at before and, to put it mildly, it's feckin' horrible. On top of that, I was at that lovely moment of the menstrual month when the slightest little thing can upset the applecart. But being spat at and sworn at and almost flattened by four foul-mouthed thugs was the cherry on the cake. And all for what? One moment I had been merrily riding along, minding my own business, and the next I was a wobbly wreck. Quite comical really, when I thought about it in the aftermath, but at the time it was an experience not to be cherished.

CHAPTER 45

Redcar might have a lot to do with racing horses, but it has nothing to do with racing-red cars. Instead the 'Red' is Old English for 'reed' (*hreod*) and the 'car' is Old Norse for marsh (*kjarr*). Bring them together and you get the 'reedy marshland'. But I didn't see much in the way of reedy marshlands – Redcar was all a bit built up for that.

Redcar has had an illustrious past. To combat the German Zeppelin raids on the Skinningrove Steel Works during the First World War, a Royal Naval Air Service aerodrome was set up near the present race course so that aircrews could hunt and attack the enemy before they could reach their targets. It was also a training airfield and one of the instructors was Captain W.E. Johns, who later became the author of the *Biggles* stories.

It was an arduous course, with pilots having to learn to fly their machines and at the same time cope with having to unjam, reload and aim their guns. It can't have been a very restful time for the nearby residents either as the Sopwith Camels skimmed over their rooftops, often to crash before they made the airfield.

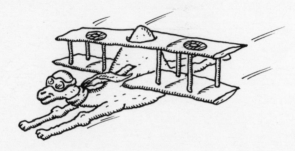

Getting nowhere fast – mum and me in a state of post-lunch lethargy.
South Harting recreation ground, West Sussex

Berthed at Beachy Head, East Sussex

Trying not to run over my self-timing camera. Near Bowmont Forest,
Scottish Borders, Scotland

Hot, tired and rattled around. Near Oh Me Edge, Redesdale Forest, Northumberland

Resting in peace. St Mary's Church, Reculver, Kent

Mum hoofing-it across the sands of Woolacombe. Morte Bay, North Devon

Running to the rescue of my camera and mini tripod when a car suddenly looms into camera-crunching view. Near Foxhole Point, Bude Bay, North Cornwall

Flat out in the Lake District when it all gets too much for an aching Achilles.
(I might look happy but I'm not!) Stickle Pike, Cumbria

The joys of travelling light. Camping near Cleethorpes, North Lincolnshire

Damp camp . . . and cold. Camping in early winter on a farm near
Bethania, Ceredigion, Wales

Wide skies. Beachy Head, East Sussex

Wet winter in Wales. Near Llwyndafydd,
Ceredigion, Wales

Cormac man to the rescue to ferry
me across a four-foot deep flood.
Near Gwithian, North Cornwall

The end of the road. Land's End, Cornwall

Rolling on. Near St Catherine's Chapel, Abbotsbury, Dorset

All these steely-nerved tales of derring-do rather made my worries (like being spat at) seem decidedly frivolous. My real worry was trying to find somewhere to camp. I was told there was a caravan park down near the dismantled railway at Warrenby, but then, when asking directions from someone else, I was advised not to stay there – it was a rough place, they said, and only the previous night some shady characters had been picked up by the police.

So I ended up sleeping on a rugby pitch that I found beside the railway line on the edge of Redcar. It was not a secluded location. First there were the faces from the trains gazing down upon me, including the drivers, who inevitably tooted their horns in greeting whenever they saw me. Even the freight train drivers gave me a cheery I-can-see-you! wave. Then there was the wall of houses that backed on to the rugby club – rows and rows of windows overlooking my bedroom – out of which people occasionally emerged to let their dogs foul the playing fields. Finally there was the dark and dodgy broken-glass footpath, frequented by gangs of local lads and the odd male jogger (potential flasher material?), that led from the housing estate up to the railway line and along to Marske. My major problem (apart from surviving the night with my life intact) was tending to my toilet. Number Ones were fine – I simply pee'd into an empty 450g yoghurt pot (I recommend Rachel's Organic Dairy for the secure snap-shut lids, a most reassuring feature when manoeuvring on shaky ground about the tent) and hurled the golden contents out of the door into the hedge.

But what to do with the more pressing Number Twos? *Please God,* I thought, *make me constipated – just for a day.* But He obviously didn't hear me, because when that crucial early morning moment came upon me there was not a moment to waste. I couldn't go anywhere outside because I could bet my bottom dollar that there would be a curtain twitcher in one of those houses watching my every move through boggle-eyed binoculars. Not only that, I was bound to time my toilet just as a train rushed into view, the driver waving and tooting his horn when he clapped eyes upon my activities. I decided there was only one thing for it: re-enact a part of Andy McNab's *Bravo Two Zero* and do an SAS job. Well, if our boys in the Special Air Service could crap into a plastic bag, then so could I.

The whole undercover operation went exceedingly swimmingly – no mistakes anywhere, which I thought was rather splendid for a first-time learner. I tied a nice neat knot in the top of my bag, picked up my produce and then hurled the whole lot into a doggie deposit bin. I returned to base light in spirit, and even lighter in buttock, with that rewarding feeling of a job well done.

The road from Redcar to Middlesbrough led me along a fast dual carriageway flanked by a vast industrial complex of steelworks and petrochemical plants, Teesport container and ore terminals, car depots, and a mesmerising forest of flaring chimneys that glared golden against a sky of coal-black rain cloud. The slightly freakish but wholly charming Transporter Bridge swung me across the overworked murk of the Tees on a compact cradle-caged car-deck suspended 160 feet above the river. It's an intriguing chimera of a construction, giving the appearance of being unable to decide whether it wants to be a ferry or a bridge.

From the Tees to the Tyne is one of the most industrialised coastlines in the country – a succession of harbour towns and urban sprawl, with the intervening stretches riddled with the vast complexes of modern industry and the forlorn remnants of a great ship-building and coal-mining past. Riding into a strong chemical-smelling wind on the flat road to Hartlepool, I was surrounded by an incongruous confusion of nature battling it out with a chaotic scene of heavy industrialisation. Much of Cowpen Marsh bird reserve and Seal Sands has been rudely invaded and reclaimed by an area traversed with armies of marching pylons, wires and cables and undulating pipelines, whole tracts of land populated with oil tanks and gantries, cooling towers and chemical globes imprisoned behind miles of high security fences. When industry suddenly assailed this marshy and creek-weaving no-man's-land, the conservationists resisted its advance mainly on behalf of the birds that use this damp muddy spot as a migratory stepping-stone. To an extent the conservationists were successful. The birds still have a portion of mud and water on which to come skidding in to land, but their flight path takes them winging past the power station, the chemical works, an oil refinery and a major section of the national grid.

Nearing Graythorp I passed more oil storage depots and huge industrial sites belonging to Petroplus and Huntsman Tioxide and the touch-of-Viagra Hartlepool Erection Group. My first inhabited landfall since Middlesbrough was Seaton Carew (the seaside resort for Stockton and Hartlepool), where I washed up amid a torrential downpour of rain. Taking cover in a graffiti-defaced phone box I learnt, among many other delightful scrawlings, how 'SAMMY IS A SPUNK BUCKET'. *Well, that's good to know.*

There were buckets filled with other things (like castle-building sand) down on Seaton beach. In a sudden change of tack, the weather had switched from wet to not so wet to a strange, and almost eerie, sepia-skied atmosphere. It even felt half hot. Packs of people piled on to the litter-strewn sands, which, despite blatant industry on every side, looked quite nice through eyes wide shut. I watched a little girl filling her bucket with unsavoury-looking sand. Then she held something up in her hand to show her mother, who was sitting close by. I couldn't see from where I was standing on the sea wall what it was. But the mother was able to identify her catch all right and she yelled at her daughter to drop it. The girl recoiled about four feet in a state of frightened incomprehension. I thought at first it was a dog deposit, but it was only when a whole crowd had gathered round and an official in a yellow coat had been called that I knew it was something more serious. There were a lot of discussions and disgusted faces and then the yellow coat man bent down and picked up the little girl's find with tough industrial-strength gloves. He walked back in my direction and I saw, hanging from his gloved fingers, a hypodermic syringe. Spunk buckets and druggies' detritus – Seaton wasn't painting a particularly pretty picture.

A mean wind whipped up and I took shelter from its sharper edges by standing behind a church I found down a side street so that I could eat my mish-mash of a lunch without it being coated in a layer of soiled sand. The church was a fortified one; all doors locked and bolted, all windows caged and barred. Broken glass carpeted the ground while litter swirled around my feet in the erratic eddying wind. I was on my last banana when the local vicar turned up prior to a funeral taking place there later that afternoon. He was a nice man, asking me if I was all right or needed any help. Then I asked him about his church, incarcerated behind a seal of impregnable shields.

'We get a lot of problems with teenagers drinking round here,' he said. 'They'll steal anything given half a chance. There're a lot of drug addicts too that hang around the doss house down on the seafront. We don't like having to lock everything up like this, but it's just the way it has to be.'

That night I spent sleeping in one of the back streets of Hartlepool in the home of Dennis and Edith Wilson. I have only met Dennis and Edith a handful of times but I feel I know them well because they're the parents of Peter, an old boyfriend with whom I had an on-off, off-on hurly-burly relationship for about five years. Despite often infuriating Peter with my inability to give him any definite signs of 'commitment' (scary word and an even scarier prospect of waving goodbye to freedom!), we had some good times together from cycling across the North York Moors in the dark, to riding through Nepal and into India (including a fun but mad month spent side by side in a hospital in Delhi), to biking down the Mexican cactus-crowded deserts of Baja California. Very wisely, he finally gave up on me and, like his dad, married a German girl. They now live near Munich with Maya, my little flaxen-haired goddaughter.

I had never stayed in Dennis and Edith's home without Peter and I was a bit worried about going back down memory lane in case it rekindled feelings from the past. But in the event, I felt fine. Edith, a big warm-hearted German who, despite having lived in England for over fifty years, still bore strong Teutonic tones, had laid on a grand smorgasbord-type tea of cheese, heavy dark Germanic bread and salad. As we ate, Dennis told me that not long after he had first met her at a dance in Germany in 1946 (he had been posted near Hanover to serve with a Royal Signals squadron), she had enrolled in a night-school class to learn English. When Dennis asked her what she had learnt, she said, 'I would like to have a cup of tea.'

'You would like to have a *what* of tea?' asked Dennis.

'I would like to have a cup of tea,' repeated Edith.

Having been taught to pronounce her words in Standard BBC English, Edith made the 'u' in 'cup' sound like an 'a'.

'It's not a *cap* of tea,' said Dennis. 'A cap is something you put on your head! It's a *coopertea*.'

He then told her to stop going to her classes because he would teach her proper Hartlepool English instead.

Cousin Marilyn, who lived in the next street, dropped round for a chat while waiting for her husband, Ricky (a tower crane driver who didn't like heights), to get home from work. Putting the cheese away in the fridge, I noticed a fridge magnet that said: 'The difference between cats and dogs is that dogs come when called and cats take a message and get back to you.' Dennis and Edith had two message-taking cats.

Later on, after Edith had gone to bed, Dennis, a small, baldpated and convivial man, poured himself a whisky and sat down next to me on the settee to show me some photographs and newspaper cuttings of him from the *Hartlepool Mail*. To compensate for having left school at thirteen, Dennis had spent the past few years making up for lost educational time and seemed to have studied virtually every Open University course under the sun. I could never keep up; every time I spoke to him he was undertaking some other new, big mind-boggling subject and earlier that year he had been selected as North East of England Region Outstanding Adult Learner of 2002. Radio Cleveland and local newspapers all interviewed him regarding his scholarly achievements. Part of his award included a £200 voucher, which he used as part-payment for an Open University course on 'State, Economy and Nation in Nineteenth Century Europe'. He was also currently completing various computer courses and a Learning Mentor Course and a German Level 3 course. I felt very woolly-headed in comparison.

As we sat chatting into the night, Dennis told me that after he left school a couple of months before his fourteenth birthday, he had worked for two years as an office boy at a local brewery for a wage of ten shillings (50p) a week.

'This may sound like slave labour compared with wages today,' said Dennis, 'but fish and chips cost only three old pence, which is just over one new penny, and there were 240 of them to the pound then.'

He changed jobs to serve as an apprentice die-sinker at a nearby drop forging engineering firm.

'It was a process,' said Dennis, 'whereby two blocks of steel in cubes of about two feet were machined so that each block had one half of the finished product cut into it. One block was secured at the base of a drop forging hammer and the other block was secured to the part of the hammer which was raised up high and allowed to fall on to a rough red-hot forging, which after a few blows took the shape of the product.'

'I see,' I said, with glazed expression. Well, it was all a bit late in the day for my yawning brain.

Anyway, a few years later, Dennis was sacked from this job for 'cheeking the General Manager' (turning his back on him) and found he had a choice of either working in the coal mines or being conscripted into HM Forces. As he didn't fancy working down a shaft three-and-a-half miles under the sea (he went down for a taster) he became, after basic training, a wireless operator in Morse code. With a surplus of wireless operators, he later became an army clerk, then a steelworks clerk, a postman and, in 1975, a driving instructor, setting up his own Denwil (a truncated Dennis Wilson) driving school, which he kept up for twenty-two years.

We progressed from car-talk to bike-talk and Denwil regaled me with a little story about how, during the war, he had finished work at the drop forging firm on a Sunday afternoon and suddenly got wind of the idea that he wanted to see how far he could ride his bike with no hands.

'I had ridden it all the way down Brenda Road into Stockton Road with my hands mostly in my trouser pockets,' he said. 'As I was crossing Oxford Road a policeman ran out from the police station house near the corner, put his arms around me and held me up on my bike with my hands still in my pockets. It was a fair cop and cost me a fifteen-shilling fine, almost a week's wages.'

'What were you charged with? I asked.

'Propelling a pedal cycle in a manner likely to cause danger to the general public!'

It felt strange sleeping inside for the first time since leaving King's Lynn – a bit claustrophobic but a welcome change from being bombarded by a profusion of either slugs or flying ants. And quite good timing, too, seeing as a violent thunderstorm struck in the night. Denwil was off early in the morning to go to his computer class and after a big hug with Edith, I left her to watch the tears and arguments of Kilroy's TV audience debating, in typically squabblesome fashion, the heady subject of 'Slimming for Summer'.

Threatened by a heavily oppressive storm-scowling sky, there was nothing much to dally for on the road from Hartlepool to Sunderland. I followed a coast whose cliffs, not so many years ago, would have been lined with working collieries spewing their mine waste directly on to sludge-blackened beaches and into a filthily polluted and greasy sea. But 'Turning The Tide', the five-year £10 million regeneration scheme to restore this blighted and blasted part of East Durham after the last collieries closed in 1993, has returned twelve miles of this once scarred and blackened-dead coastline to its former glory – so much so that it has now been designated as a Site of Special Scientific Interest, as well as a Heritage Coast and a Special Area of Conservation.

The storm struck as I laboured up the steep hill into the former mining village of Easington Colliery. Within minutes the gullies were gurgling with torrents of water, the scummy gutters awash with the careless cast-offs of discarded drink cans and crisp bags and packets of cigarettes scudding off down the cliff. Ranks of low grey-slate roofs and acid rain-stained terrace houses that you could buy for £20,000 lined the wet, grey street. It all looked very melancholy and depressing. Ever since the pit closed some nine years ago, unemployment has rocketed.

In a family-run shop where I stopped to buy my lunch supplies, the people looked cheerful enough. But you could tell that times were extremely tough. A string bean of a man, all sharp edges and in his fifties, who quipped that my bike must be over the weight limit, knotted his brow into a scowl and told me that since he'd lost his job down the pits his marriage had fallen apart and that every day was a struggle. His frowning features seemed to epitomise the rained-on faces of those that I passed further up the street. Every one of them looked tired and run-down and worn out.

Before I knew it, Durham had jettisoned me into Tyne and Wear – the only county in Britain to comprise two river names. The first relaxed and smiling face I found belonged to Steve, a jovial street cleaner in the centre of Sunderland. He had intercepted me as I emerged from the tourist office in Fawcett Street laden with leaflets.

'I bet they've sent you on a wild goose chase too!' said Steve, by means of a conversational opening gambit. 'Yesterday I had to redirect two German girls on bikes after those muppets in there sent them in completely the opposite direction to the one they wanted to go!'

Steve was sitting on his street-cleaning Green Machine (which was actually blue), a sort of mini tractor with bumpers of brushes and pavement-dousing water jets.

'I've always been into bikes myself,' he said, before launching into a slightly convoluted tale about how he used to race but then got a bit bored with all the training so was about to buy a mountain bike so that he could go riding up on the moors when he had an accident on his road bike which meant he then couldn't afford to buy a new bike because it was his road bike that he was going to sell to get money to buy his mountain bike.

He then had an accident at work. One day, ten years ago (he's been a street cleaner for twenty-one years), he was lifting an inner bin out of an outer bin when the sharp rim of the bin sliced through his little finger till it was hanging from a white thread of tendon.

'My boss was totally unsympathetic,' said Steve. 'He told me to keep working and then to go to hospital if I really must.'

Steve had four operations to reattach his finger to his left hand, but none of them worked because the tendon kept snapping. Finally he had to have it amputated. After a long drawn-out battle in which his union fought it out with his employer, Steve received £7500 in compensation.

'I went straight out and bought a mountain bike,' said Steve, 'which I now use to take my eight-year-old daughter cycle camping. And the wife got a new kitchen. So we decided losing my finger was all worth it in the end!'

I was now well into Geordie land – though supposedly you're not a true Geordie unless you've been born north of the Tyne – surrounded by that melodious dialect that always sounds so tunefully optimistic. But what wasn't so optimistic was the weather, which was hammering parts of Britain with what the meteorologists described as 'extreme weather'; mini tornadoes in Leatherhead, extreme flooding in Glasgow and flash floods in South Shields. South Shields is where I ended up spending a very wet night within the caged-in walls of Lizard Lane Caravan Site. Booking in, I was asked by the warden to write my name on her receipt form. When she saw 'J. Dew', she suddenly became most animated.

'I know a J. Dew!' she said. 'Where I also work as a dinner lady at a school, the headmaster there is called John Dew. Now isn't that funny! I had never met another Dew until I worked there and now I know two of you! And you're both Js! Maybe you're related, like!'

'Maybe,' I said. 'Though probably not! But then we are nearer to Scotland up here and I have got some Scottish blood in me.'

To be honest I couldn't summon up that much enthusiasm about a possible Dew Clan link (unlikely as it was) when I had wet tents to be putting up to get even wetter.

It was a dismal night – wet, cold and horrible. By morning the soaking and oppressively dirty mist was so low that you couldn't even see the tops of the houses. And Souter Lighthouse had been cut off at its knees.

As I was leaving the caravan site, the warden called after me, 'I'm going to tell my J. Dew that I've met his namesake. You're a rarity, you Dews!'

Which is more than can be said for 270 million Chinese, a quarter of the population, who share the same surnames – Li, Wang and Zhang. I learnt this riveting fact from the local *Metro* newspaper that I picked up later that morning, my eye having been caught by the headline: 'Wang for all and all for Wang (and Li)'.

CHAPTER 46

The South Shields ferry whisked me over to North Shields across the murky Tyne. Sandwiched between these 'Shields' I pondered on the possibility that the name might refer to the rows of Viking shields that flanked the sides of their double-ended longships as they rowed across the rough North Sea. Once again my conjectures couldn't have been more hopelessly wrong. In Middle English 'shields' meant 'sheds', referring specifically to the fishermen's huts, which formed the hub of the settlements that grew into the present towns that face each other on either side of the Tyne.

Once off the ferry I rode along the Fish Quay, stopping opposite a row of fishmongers and fish restaurants and fish markets to use a public toilet. A sign attached to the outside wall beside the one for 'LADIES' declared:

NO FISH BOXES IN TOILETS.

Ooh! How crude! I thought.

There were more words on walls to read down at the mouth of the Tyne. Daubed in angry big-lettered aerosol paint across the side of a derelict building on a disused wharf that faced the toing and froings of the North Sea ferries was scrawled the greeting:

WELCOME TO ENGLAND. VASSEL STATE OF GERMANY. BLAIRS SUCCESS TO BRING THE COUNTRY DOWN WHERE HITLER FAILED.

A beaten-up red Mini pulled into the car park that overlooked the beach and the fog-eaten Black Middens. The two occupants watched me writing down the 'vassel state' graffiti into my diary. Then the driver, a man in an NYC base-ball cap, wound down the window and called, ' 'Ere, man, where you from?'

'Near Portsmouth,' I said.

'Portsmouth? You English, then? Me, I thought you had come off the boat and were maybes . . . Scandinavian, like.'

Then he lit a fag and drove away. I had no sooner tucked my diary back into my handlebar bag than a man in glasses and a pork pie hat came wandering down the derelict wharf, dragging a reluctant rain-bedraggled dog.

'Bloody hell fire!' he said in a very un-Geordie-like accent. 'What are you, some sort of Russian refugee carrying all them bags?'

'No, I'm Scandinavian,' I heard myself saying.

'Ha!' said the pork-pie man, 'I guessed you was a foreigner!' Then he turned to his miserable-looking dog and said, 'C'mon mate, we've gotta get back to Wantage.'

As I cycled away I tried to remember where Wantage was because I always get Wantage mixed up with Wanage, I mean Swanage, and Weybridge and Wadebridge and Wanstead and Watford, which makes it sound like I must get very lost; but I don't get lost, it's just that sometimes I'm not quite sure where I am.

But Wantage – how could I possibly forget Wantage when only one Wantage fits into Anon's immortal rhyme:

> There was a Young Lady of Wantage
> Of whom the Town Clerk took advantage;
> Said the Borough Surveyor
> 'Indeed you must pay her
> You've totally altered her frontage.'

Tynemouth, Sharpness Point, Long Sands, Cullercoats, Smuggler's Cave, Whitley Bay and Seaton Sluice all passed beneath my wheels in a mist-draped blur laden with cold summer rain. I stopped in the covered gateway of a cemetery to put on two more layers of clothes and wolf down a quick lunch, and by the time I got going again I was tremblingly cold – so cold, in fact, that I had to march up and down the glaring strip-lit aisles of a LIDL store in Blyth to warm up. While I was at it, I bought a tin of tuna for 12p, which quite pleased me until I discovered it tasted of a mix between an oil slick and a dead hamster.

Once past Blyth and the Rockers rocks and the Spital Carrs of Newbiggin-by-the-Sea, my mood was a merry one despite the downpours because I was now well and truly past the worst of the industrialised north. More momentously, I had entered the big and relatively empty wilds of the northeasternmost county of England and there's nothing like an easternmost or northernmost or on-top-of-most to gladden the spirit. You could, if you felt so inclined, read Northumberland as the land of the 'North Humberlanders' because Northumberland was the land of the tribe of the North Humberlanders who lived north of the Humber. Douglas Adams, in his little book *The Meaning of Liff*, a 'dictionary of things that there aren't any words for yet', offers an interpretation for the useful term 'Humber' as the movement of a very fat person's cheeks when driving over a cattle grid. Anyway, the true North Humberlanders were a rough and hairy lot, by all accounts, always at each other's bearded throats and nicking each other's cattle.

Funnily enough, bearded throats were what I ended up sleeping next to that night – not the throats of the hirsute fellas of the North Humberlander tribe, but the hairy throats of goats. Looking for a place to camp, I had cycled past a long wet grassy field containing one solitary tent. Five minutes later I was sitting on the outhouse toilet of Mr and Mrs Sanderson. Yes, they had said, I was most welcome to camp in their field if I didn't mind goats and lone men. Smelly-bottomed goats and the unknown aromas of a lone man do not happy bed-partners make, but daylight was fading and I fancied laying myself to rest before night was nigh.

'Are they good goats?' I asked. (I was more concerned with the antics of the goats than I was about the lone man because, as far as I knew, lone men don't chew tents.)

'They're show goats,' said Mrs Sanderson.

'Show goats?' I said. 'That's nice! Are they rare species to behold?'

'They're not really that special!' said Mr Sanderson. 'The wife only takes them to the shows so that she can go and chat up the other contestants!'

The wife shot him a withering look.

'I'm sure they're all lovely!' I said, trying to act as peacemaker in this small-holding domestic dispute.

And then I went to meet the goats. Thankfully there was a fence between me and them which is more than can be said for what stood between me and the lone man – about four feet of air and some squelchy grassy ground. I wouldn't normally pitch myself on top of a lone man like this (no, no, really I wouldn't – I have my standards) but the only patch of slightly less lumpy and swampy ground was in this one little corner that backed directly on to a busily buzzing electricity substation. So I was sandwiched between a herd of smelly billies and kiddies and nannies on one side, and a lone man of unknown quantity on the other. All I knew about him was all I could see: that he slept in a big green Vango tent and drove a Mondeo. At first I thought he must be out for a walk because his tent was all zipped up and not a sound did stir. But then, just as I was pushing in my last peg, a sudden slapping sound materialised in sporadic bursts from the inner confines of his tent. To anyone other than a camper, such a sound could be good reason for concern, but to the trained ear of those who spend any time under canvas (or rip-stop nylon), the slappings meant only one thing: the frenzied slaughter of flies from within.

The fact that I had now ascertained that there was an insect-killing man in the tent did nothing to lessen my growing concern of quite what it was I had planted myself up against. So, under the pretext of filling my water bottles, I walked back across the sodden field and up the track to the Sandersons' abode, getting half-mauled by their ferocious guard dog on the way.

When Mrs Sanderson came out to restrain her barking hound, I took the opportunity of asking her what she knew about my neighbour.

'Not that much,' she said, 'apart from he's here for another two weeks or so, and he works nights in Newcastle.'

Back at the gate to the field, I met the man himself. Pony-tailed and topped in a Craghoppers fleece, he said hello to me and I said hello to him. Then he apologised in advance should he wake me up later tonight on his return from Newcastle, which I thought rather dashingly touching. A bit more leaning-on-gate chat entailed, during which I discovered he was a musician, a guitarist, and was on tour with Andrew Lloyd Webber's musical, *Whistle down the Wind*. Having unearthed this information I then felt completely fine about him. Though I did think it a bit funny that he was camping. And camping so far north of Newcastle, too. At least, it felt a long way north because it had taken me a day to get here from there. But there I went again – a self-propelled person forgetting once more how cars crush distances in a trice.

'What makes you camp all the way up here?' I asked. 'Don't most of the musicians stay in hotels in Newcastle?'

'Well, although the job pays quite well,' he said, 'the type of hotels I can afford are the cheap and nasty sort where you get difficult landladies and might find half a dog decomposing in the corner. I also don't eat breakfast – the smell of cheap greasy bacon cooking has put me off breakfast for life! When I told the band that I was sick of hotels and was going to buy a tent, they thought I was mad, but now a few of the others are thinking of doing the same. And it's better for me too because it means I don't end up drinking all night with the group after we've finished the show.'

Much as I would have liked to quiz him further, he had to get off to Newcastle. But the next morning, as I was cramming my clobber into my panniers, he crawled out of his Vango and came over for a chat.

'How did last night go?' I asked him.

He told me it went well. Then he told me quite a lot more. Like, he had a ten-year-old daughter – not a musician but a very good mathematician, who 'sadly I no longer live with' but whom he was going to take up to Loch Ness on his 'busman's holiday' the following week, before heading to Southend where *Whistle down the Wind* was next playing; that when he wasn't touring he lived in Manchester; that he could play anything – rock 'n' roll, country, jazz, classical – on anything that 'had a stret' (guitar, mandolin, banjo, whatever); that along with musicals he also performed on TV, the last one being a programme on a Saturday night presented by a Spice Girl.

'So for something like that,' I said, 'how much practice do you have to do? Do you have to spend weeks and weeks going over it again and again?'

'No, never,' he said. 'Because I can sight-read I usually just launch straight into it. Sometimes, if there are other musicians, we might run through it a couple of times, and then go.'

I was most impressed.

'What's your name?' I asked. 'If I ever see you in, or on anything, then I can tell people I've slept next to you!'

He laughed.

'Steve Willingham,' he said.

Then he asked me what I did and how long I was cycling around for and I told him that I was a cook and wrote for the odd bike mag and that I didn't really know how long I was on the move for – just as long as it took to follow the coast back to Land's End.

Steve looked all thoughtful and said, 'I'd love to do that.'

This surprised me, because I thought what he did sounded rather exciting.

'I feel I've wasted too much of my life getting drunk,' said Steve, suddenly looking regretful. 'I've always wanted to go cycling or backpacking. For years I've been buying stuff on account of how small or light it is to pack, but I've never been able to make that final big decision and go. Probably because I know that I could never really do it, let alone leave behind all the things that I'd want to take with me like my guitars and CD player!'

We hob-nobbed for the better part of an hour. Even so, I felt I could have stood all morning in that field happily talking to Steve next to the potently whiffy ruminating goats. He was funny and interesting and seemed to have a lot to say. But the rain was coming and I had to get going. As I cycled off to Widdrington, I thought about how certain strange circumstances turn up and turn out. There I'd been, not knowing where I was going to camp, only to end up sleeping in a soggy field squeezed between some whiffy goats and a man I'd at first been worried about, but who turns out to be a top-touring musician and someone with whom in the space of a few intense minutes I find myself on the same wavelength. And then, although we both might feel there's probably a lot more to say to each other, I'm off down the road rolling past Stobswood opencast coalmines, leaving in my wake a chance encounter with a man whom I will most likely never see or hear of again.

That's where I was wrong. Although we hadn't exchanged addresses, Steve tracked me down and wrote to me. Just in case all memories of him had been wiped clean from my memory, he reminded me that he was 'the goat on the Northumberland campsite with the musicians in the next field'.

Ah, yes. Mondeo Goat. How could I forget?

'After our all too short meeting,' he wrote, 'I had visions of you pedalling through all that filthy weather and despite all of what I said I didn't envy you at all! . . . I enjoyed our talk about what one does with one's life and finding your own niche – I've realised that my current gig (yes I can say that without a hint of pretension!) has me nailed down so I've given notice and am going back to my usual far less regimented bits and pieces.' *Oh no! Not bits and pieces of rain?* He went on to tell me that 'lo and behold THREE members of the band want to do the camping bit at the next venue so maybe the message is getting across.' Further on he recommended a few good nooks and crannies to camp, one of which was on the Gower: '. . . it's a very special place and it's my Swiss Army knife on the beach somewhere if you come across it.' He finished off by saying, 'Hope you don't mind me getting in touch – just felt our meeting was too short, but perhaps they are the best ones!'

And maybe they are. Maybe it's best to keep it like that. But somehow I felt that somewhere I would meet the old goat again. And when I did, I had a feeling it would be fun.

CHAPTER 47

August was upon me again. And still there was no summer in sight. There wasn't even any sky in sight. All the weather could offer me was a wet and persistent mist hanging heavily over my head before turning to drip down my neck.

To take shelter from the shivery summer, I piled through the doors of St John the Baptist Church in Alnmouth where, in the middle of the aisle, I undertook a vigorous bout of star jumps in order to reconnect me to my numb and soaked-sock toes. Thankfully there was no one around (apart from God) to question my sanity. Near the door I found a copy of *The Bridge*, the magazine of the five local parishes, in which I read of quite a hoo-hah going on between the vicar, the Rev. Canon Brian Cowen, and a few of the church-going parishioners who had felt he had 'got rid of John'. John was John Cooke, who had apparently resigned as a Reader of the parishes. It was all a bit complicated and long-winded for me to grasp but it would seem that John was opposed to the ordination of women as well as the date of the Carol Service. In a copy of the letter from the Rev. to John (which the Rev. wanted published to 'dispel the gossip' as John's 'resignation was contrary to what I had suggested'), I learnt: 'At my second PCC meeting you told me that I could not have the Carol Service on the Sunday evening before Christmas because it was still Advent. Despite the fact that the choir trainer was the person making the request.' Further on in the letter the Rev. wrote, 'Following the PCC's agreement to share in the training of Marion you declared very strongly your

disagreement to ordained women and showed that disapproval in a very forthright way.'

Ooh, how exciting! A *forthright way*, eh? What was that, I wonder, a shouting
match or a biff on the nose or did he take one of Mrs Sloggle-Bottom's village-
fête custard pies full in the face? Was Alnmouth turning into Ambridge? Could
there be a dirty-scoundrel Brian Aldridge lurking somewhere among their
midst? I could feel myself being drawn in, eager to know the sequel and the
inner happenings – the sort of scandal and slander and backbiting and trifling
and frivolous gossip that makes our spark-flying village lives go round.

On a lighter note, *The Bridge* featured a 'TO MAKE YOU SMILE' page,
which incidentally was, shock-horror, '*Sponsored by BMW*'. (Is that allowed, a village mag sponsored by a village-ruining vehicle? Should the page not be
sponsored by a more congruously harmonising hay bale or cow pat or self-
righteous cyclist, the latter two perhaps seen in some villagers' eyes as one of
the same?) Anyway, the 'SMILE LINES' included a tale entitled 'A lot to ask'.
So, heard the one about . . .?

A man walking along a Californian beach was deep in prayer. 'Lord grant
me one wish.' Suddenly the sky clouded above his head and in a booming voice the Lord said, 'Because you TRIED to be faithful to me in all
ways, I will grant you one wish.'

The man said, 'Build a bridge to Hawaii, so I can drive over any time
I want.'

The Lord said, 'Your request is very materialistic. Think of the enormous challenges for that kind of undertaking. The supports required to
reach the bottom of the Pacific! The concrete and steel it would take! I
can do it, but it is hard for me to justify your desire for worldly things.
Take a little more time and think of another wish, a wish you think would
honour and glorify me.'

The man thought about it for a long time. Finally he said, 'Lord, I wish
that I could understand women, I want to know how they feel inside, what
they are thinking when they give me the silent treatment, why they cry,
what they mean when they say "nothing", and how I can make a woman
truly happy'.

The Lord thought a moment, and then replied: 'You want two lanes or
four on that bridge?'

It was still raining by the time I emerged from the church. If I thought it was wet before, then it was nothing compared with what was to come. As I rode past Fluke Hole, North Reins, Boulmer Steel, Red Ends, Howdiemont Sands, Sugar Sands, Rumbling Kern, Peep O' Sea, Hips Heugh, Black Hole, Jenny Bells Carr, Football Hole, Faggot, Robin's Wood Rock and the Long Nanny Burn to the vaguely saucy-sounding Lady's Hole and Nacker Hole, the downpour was so violent and so prolonged and led to such massive flash-flooding that it was like cycling underwater. A gentle August cycle had suddenly turned into an extreme sport. I felt I needed oxygen tanks for survival. Later, I read in the *Observer* that, on that decidedly damp day, North East England recorded its highest ever daily rainfall – 61 mm. In other words, it had rained the month's average in twenty-four hours.

But I didn't really mind. It was all quite exciting and, looking on the shinier side of life, at least I wasn't going to die from sunburn. Also this part of Northumberland's 'Castles Coast', from Craster (tiny harbour famed for its oak-smoked kippers, but fuming more with motors than herrings) to Bamburgh (site of massive crag-perched castle – its Norman keep looking exactly like the sort of thing I saw tipped out of a shiny plastic bucket on Scarborough beach after four good whacks with a spade) was spectacular, with its columnar cliffs and the beaches that alternated between bright white sand or big, blackish rounded cobbles where narrow gashes marked the faults where the sea had been able to scoop out the crushed rock.

Just off shore lay the Farne Islands, thirty or so bits of sea-lapped dolerite rock full of cliffs and stacks and seabirds. I thought about taking a boat trip over from Seahouses but, apart from the fact that I couldn't take my bike, I didn't much fancy facing the packs of holidaymakers queuing at the quayside. Anyway, not being a great people-person, I think I would have preferred it in St Aidan's time when, around 651, he used Inner Farne as a retreat for lonesome prayer and meditation. As did St Cuthbert, the Northumbrian shepherd boy who became the north of England's most admired saint, and had a monastic cell of stone and turf on the island. For a saintly soul it seems he used to get a bit het up about some of the seabirds, reproving them for being greedy and thoughtless and encouraging them to conduct themselves in a more Christian manner. He did have a fond spot for the eider ducks, which is why some of the locals still call them cuddy ducks. Another local bird name is for the ubiquitous puffins that pretend to be either moles, making tunnels in the sand, or terrorists, taking over rabbit burrows. Tommy Noddies, they're called, on account of the way that their clownish heads bob noddingly as they walk around.

Taking advantage of a sudden crack in the clouds, I clambered round the hulking square-jawed, red-sandstone battlements of Bamburgh Castle, a formidable edifice that appears to grow straight out of the imposing bulwark of rock on which it stands. This rock must have seen a lot of action in its time, as there has been a fortress of one kind or another at Bamburgh for over 2000 years. The rock seemed particularly good at attracting people with faintly farcical names. The Saxon, Ida the Flamebearer, became King of Bernicia (as the area was known) in 547 and founded his capital at the site. His grandson, Ethelfrith, became king of all Northumbria and named the capital Bebbanburh in honour of Bebba, his wife. Three times it survived ferocious Viking attacks. Then the Normans took it from Matilda, Countess of Northumberland, who surrendered it to William Rufus rather than have him put out the eyes of her captive husband, Robert. Finally, in 1464 during the Wars of the Roses, it gained eminent notoriety when it became the first English castle to fall to gunfire.

Another church that sheltered me from the rain was St Aidan's in Bamburgh. In the churchyard I found an elaborate shrine-like tomb, all fancy filigrees and carved columns and arches. After a little investigation I discovered it was the memorial to Grace Darling who, during a terrible storm in 1838, rowed with her father in a Northumbrian fishing coble to rescue most of the crew of the *Forfarshire*, a paddle steamer that had struck Big Harcar rock on the Farne Islands at four in the morning, half a mile to the west of Longstone where her father was a lighthouse keeper. She was only twenty-two at the time and her bravery made her a national heroine overnight. She died four years later of tuberculosis.

In Middleton, a little huddle of houses overlooking Holy Island, I stopped at a public phone box to ring the builder to see when he could come out and meet me. With all this rain and murk I felt I needed a dose of him to boost me forth for more inevitable soakings. But there was no reply so I left a suitably inappropriate message on his machine and walked out of the phone box into Peter Anderson. Peter Anderson was an elderly gent in rolled up shirt sleeves and suit trousers tucked into a pair of Wellington boots. He lived in the house across the road.

'How much weight you got there, pet?' he asked, indicating my bike with big earthy hands.

'About sixty kilos,' I said.

He bent forwards to feel my tyres.

'Many punctures?'

'No,' I said, 'I've had two in three-and-a-half thousand miles.'

Moments later I was in his kitchen, standing in front of the Rayburn, with a mug of steaming tea in my hand. Looking out of the window I could see Holy Island, or Lindisfarne, that sacred Northumbrian rock, engine-room of early English Christianity, where Aidan and Cuthbert led the good life, and a handful of islanders still try not to lead a bad one.

'I suppose you're heading over to the Rock?' asked Peter, following my gaze towards the island, which had suddenly burst into brilliance beneath a hallowed shaft of sunlight.

'Not today, the tides are all wrong,' I said. 'I think I'll save it for when I come back down from Scotland. Should be quieter then too, which will be nice.'

'You like me – an introvert?'

'Well, not really,' I replied. 'I'm just not that keen on being surrounded by lots of people.'

'It's parties I don't like,' said Peter, handing me an open tin of biscuits. 'Never know what to say to people, that's my trouble.'

We moved into the dark, cluttered front room where Peter sat me down in a soggy armchair. Over the course of two mugs of tea I caught a sneak snapshot of his life. He had two daughters, one of whom lived nearby. She was now holidaying on Orkney with her daughters.

'They drove up there with their bikes on the back of the car,' said Peter. 'They rang me the first day after they had cycled six miles and said they were all exhausted!' He gave a little laugh. 'How my granddaughters will cope without a TV I just don't know. They're usually glued to it for most of the day.'

His other daughter lived in London, though Peter wasn't quite sure where because he didn't know London at all.

'Just a moment,' he said, reaching for an address book. 'It's somewhere beginning with "S". Ah, here we are . . . Streatham. Ever heard of it?

'Yes,' I said. 'It's south London, not far from where my bike frame was built.'

'The place means nothing to me,' he said.

This wasn't really surprising, seeing as he had lived in the North East all his life.

'We had a house in Hexham for many years' he said. 'We were always assured that the fields we looked out over would forever be for sheep. Then they built rows and rows of houses. "Not in my back yard!" we said. So we moved. For twenty-five years we rented an apartment up the road in Middleton Hall.'

Who was the other part of the 'we', I wondered? No wife appeared or was mentioned so I just presumed, in a presumptive way, that she was dead.

Including the time that he had been in this house, I worked out that Peter must have lived in Middleton for about thirty years. So, basing my extensive calculations on this, I assumed, in an assumptive way, that he must know all his neighbours.

'No, don't rightly know any of them,' he said. 'We like to keep ourselves to ourselves.'

A dog started barking outside the door. I found it a bit distracting because whenever I hear a barking dog within close proximity, I prepare myself for the imminent canine fang-clamped destruction of half my lower leg. This could have something to do with my past experiences of bike-chasing dogs who make no bones about wanting to eat me. That's why I prefer aloof, message-taking cats.

Peter didn't appear to hear the high-decibel skull-rattling barking. He was away on a life history roll.

'. . . then from '47 to 1970, I worked in Newcastle – this side of the Tyne – making clay drainpipes. But then they brought plastic ones in, didn't they, so I was made redundant. I became a civil servant – very boring – till I retired when I was sixty-five. I still needed to work, but no one would have me. Finally I found a job working in the canteen up at the new power station they built near Berwick.'

With a few more added extras, that more or less brought us up to date, so I drained the last dank dregs of my tea and stood up, making to be on my way.

'Must you go so soon?' said Peter, though I'd been there almost an hour. I managed to convince him that I must and we moved down the front hall, wading through a blur of dancing, yelping dog.

CHAPTER 48

The border town of Berwick is in England. At least I think it is, as there has always been some doubt as to which country Berwick belongs. During 300 years of medieval warfare it kept getting batted back and forth between English and Scottish rule – so much so that from 1296 to 1482 the castle and town changed hands at least thirteen times. Then, just to add to the confusion, from the sixteenth century until 1836 Berwick was an independent borough, neither in Scotland nor in England. The historical anomaly that Berwick is still at war with Russia is based upon a popular belief that Queen Victoria used to sign herself in a nice and snappy 'Queen of Great Britain, Ireland, Berwick-upon-Tweed and the British Dominions beyond the sea'. But then, through administrative error, she carelessly dropped the habit. Berwick, according to this tale, was officially party to the declaration of war but not to the subsequent treaty affirming peace.

And still the bat-back game rumbles on. A few months before I arrived in Berwick, the Scots had been celebrating after an important concession was made on its claim that Berwick, which had been captured 800 years ago by Richard I, should be returned to Scotland. Reacting to the Scottish Borders Tourist Board's offer of 10,000 merks (silver pennies to you and me) to buy back the town, the mayor of Berwick, Rae Huntly, said: 'While the offer is welcome, we haven't had the "For Sale" board out. I would suspect they would have to up their price quite considerably to something approaching the £10–20 million mark.'

As far as I know, the carpet-salesman haggling still continues. And probably will for the next 800 years.

On a map, the River Tweed looks like the natural border. But as part of that very delightful historical peculiarity, it's actually three miles further to the north, which leaves this strange little chunk of land looking so obviously Scottish. The A1 carves a frenetic path straight through the side and as I followed its horribly busy course north I suddenly, on a whim, turned left and went like the clappers through Clappers.

A new idea had taken hold.

Seeing as I had made such a spectacular meal out of cycling this far (nearly 3500 miles from Land's End to Scotland and more months than I'd care to mention), I decided I would 'do' England and Wales this year (and last year) and save riding around the coast of Scotland and Ireland until another rainy day. At my snail-in-labour rate, it was going to be enough of a challenge to try to get back down to Land's End before the thick of winter. Though heaven knows, if it was cold and wet now at the beginning of August, maybe it would be hot and sunny by December. In this A-over-T global-warming world, you can only but hope and guess and expect the unexpected.

Just up the road from Clappers, I climbed up a narrow lane to the summit of Halidon Hill where, had the weather been willing, I could have had a dazzling view of the sea and the Tweed and the wild Cheviot Hills. Instead the dismal murk allowed me just enough mist-draped leeway to take a bearing on the nearby battlefield where, in the summer of 1333, the English army first experimented with the longbow and turned their Scottish neighbours into 14,000 pincushions. All in the name of Berwick.

Later that day, the unexpected came my way. In the morning I had been fording through floods up to my hubs, yet by the afternoon the dirty squally rain clouds were hurtling off northwards towards the Southern Uplands leaving me to roast and redden beneath a crackling sun.

That evening I camped in a high grassy field overlooking the rolling Cheviot Hills on Farmer Younger's farm. Farmer Younger was a kind old man with a weather-battered face who lived in a farmhouse surrounded by a thick moat of mud with his daughter and clutch of grandchildren. In the corner of one of his fields stood an old moss-smeared Monza caravan, which he unlocked so I could use the tilted Elsan toilet.

'If ye want tae sleep in here, ye'll be verry welcome,' he said, with a generous gesture of a thumbless hand. But my tent won the day with its compact and cosy containment and superior view.

With tent all set up and sleeping bag airing in the steadily ripening rays of a rare setting sun, Farmer Younger tramped over, trousers tucked into his big black wellie boots and said, 'I'll be going down tae the Plough for a couple – will ye be joining me?'

The Plough, I discovered, was his local a mere mile down the road, but I didn't join him because I wanted to wash my clothes and hair and various body parts under the outside tap at the bottom of the field before it got dark. Farmer Tucker wasn't in the least bit put out that I had turned him down.

'Ye're probably verry wise tae keep ye head clear!' he said, in his melodious Border Country dialect – a sort of busy mix between Scottish colliding into Geordie. 'Ye sleep well now, me lassie, and I'll be seeing ye in the morning.'

He turned to trudge off across the field, sights set on the Plough.

'Are you walking there and back?' I asked.

'Aye,' he said, before adding with a winking nod, 'I may be having a few more than a couple and then I tend to be getting a wee bit excited, like!'

And off he went, flattening a trail through the long, dew-tinged grass.

The next morning he came and propped himself against the dry stone wall, part of which was draped with my drying tent, and told me that though this farm had been in his family for over a hundred years, he had recently been forced to sell all of the outbuildings.

'My grandfather used tae have 500 acres here with fifteen full-time farm workers. They lived in the farm cottages just down the road there. Then I took over with my uncle and then with my brother, but that didnae work out. So they left me tae farm by meself, like.'

'What sort of farming?' I asked.

'Arable and livestock. But with the way farming was going, I had tae sell off half the land. Then last year in foot-and-mouth, a farmer friend of mine committed suicide. Those government health people wouldn't leave him alone, like.'

He sighed and looked out over the fields towards the distant and rounded volcanic hills of the Cheviots, their great crags and cairns and tors and moors catching the first spoked rays of early morning sun. Down in the valley, scarves of mist threaded slowly among the opulent trees.

'Aye,' said Farmer Younger, 'there's nae future in farming for my family any more.'

None of his three daughters and eight grandchildren – six girls and two boys – was interested in farming. His daughters all had their own very different lives to lead. One was a travelling hairdresser, another worked in a doctor's surgery, while the third seemed to enjoy spending a lot of time on holiday in the New Forest. Farmer Younger found it a shame how his grandchildren appeared quite happy to spend all day indoors, either on the computer or watching TV. It was so different from his childhood, he said, when he used to be outdoors all day helping his grandfather on the farm.

'One of the ten-year-old bairns,' he said, 'will be lying on the sofa watching television even on a fine morning like this. I'll say tae him, "Get ye-self outside lad! Ye cannae beat the outdoors!"'

Farmer Younger showed me round the old stone and oak-beamed farm buildings undergoing massive renovation. Where one apartment was taking shape (soon to be housing a well-off commuter), he told me that this was where his grandmother used to make butter from the cow she kept across the yard. A property dealer had bought up the farm buildings from Farmer Younger in one lump sum. Each small apartment would sell for well over £100,000 each.

'I hope you did all right from the sale,' I said.

'Och, it was nae sae bad,' he replied. 'I could have done better but ye cannae be greedy can ye?'

Property dealers can, I thought.

With all my camping kit packed away, I was ready to hit the road. With his horny-hard palm, Farmer Younger shook my hand, mangling all the bones inside, and clapped me affectionately on the shoulder.

'If ye ever find yeself this way again, me lassie,' he said, 'ye'll know where tae come.'

I was now on a westward course, crossing the great neck of land from the sullen North Sea to the frisky Solway Firth – a sheltered stretch of water bordered to the north by the jutting jaw of Dumfries and Galloway, and to the south by the protuberance of Carlisle's Adam's apple. I followed the high rushing torrents of the Tweed as closely as I could, flipping back and forth from England to Scotland first near Honey Farm over Union Bridge, then over the broad span of stone arches that linked the Tweed's muddy banks between Norham and Ladykirk.

I loved every minute. This stretch of the Borders, low on population, high on hills, was perfect cycling country. As, unusually, was the weather. It had turned into one of those hot, still summer days where a hazy cobalt sky lies clamped like a shimmering bowl of heat across the land. At some stage I looked up and saw nothing in the sky but sun and a whorl of buzzards that dipped and corkscrewed on the thermals overhead. Later on I scared a hare into turning a half-somersault before it ran away, thumping the ground.

The first and last time I had been to Coldstream was some thirteen years before, when I stopped over to visit Graham Bell, the importer of the wheelchair bike that I was cumbersomely cycling up to John O' Groats. Graham had pulled out the stops by arranging for me to be marched across the border accompanied by a real live bagpipe-blowing Scotsman kitted out in fetching kilt and full sporran splendour. This time, though, things were slightly different. I had told not a soul I was coming, yet the town was bedecked with colourful streams of welcoming bunting. Even more touchingly, crowds of smiling and waving people clutching cameras lined the pavements, while the whole of the Coldstream Guards turned out in top piping parading form to herald my impressively grand entrance. *Thank you! Thank you boys!* I tried to tell them above the bellowing bladdering of their cacophonous pipes. *You really shouldn't have gone to so much trouble! A big bowl of porridge would have been more than sufficient!* But they didn't seem to understand and it suddenly dawned on me that this fine fanfare wasn't actually put on for me.

Oh. How bitterly disappointing.

As coincidence would have it, I had chanced upon Coldstream in Civic Week, just as they were celebrating the 'Riding the Borders' festivities. According to tradition, this is when a popular citizen is elected to lead a rollicking ride around the statutory boundaries of the borough. The lucky man is the Cornet or Standard-bearer. From what I could gather by talking to a big, bearskin-topped Coldstreamer who cornered me to tell me he used to be a keen cyclist, the Ride commemorates bygone times when common property rights were reinforced by an annual show of strength called a 'wapynshawe'. Or something like that. The riders rode hard and drank even harder, bringing apparent confusion to any of their enemy encroachers. By this stage, my bearskin lost me somewhere down the foggy paths of history, and I felt much more at home when he turned his attention to my triple chain set and the smooth lubrications of my bottom bracket.

There was more flitting between the two countries as I crossed back over the Tweed (which only two days before had flooded the lower town) into England before returning to Scotland a few miles down the road near Nottylees. It was a good road, fast, flattish, scenic and empty. Aided by a whipping tailwind, I was swept along at such a delirious speed that before I knew it, I was being rattled

by the cobbles in Kelso, a bright and bustling market town standing at the con-
fluence of the salmon-rich Teviot and Tweed. For centuries, Kelso was a
strategic point in the relentless and barbarous Border wars between the Scots
and the English, and now lies amidst a region of rolling hills and ruined
abbeys.

CHAPTER 49

Windywalls, Spylaw, Pylafoot, Middle Softlaw, Ladyrig, Whinnyhouse and Wilyrigg Strips were just some of the enticing places I passed as I followed a weave of empty, and sometimes steep, country lanes to Jedburgh. At one point, near Cappuck, I crossed over the straight line of Dere Street , the Roman road built unusually wide by Agricola (Coca-Cola's rural brother) to take two lanes of chariots.

Jedburgh was another battleground in the tempestuous wars between the Scots and the English. Despite being the target of years of bombardments and burnings and much sacking and pillaging, the beautiful rich red sandstone abbey, once a retreat of Augustinian monks, still looks magnificent even though it may be windowless and roofless.

Jedburgh was also another place where I was presumed to be foreign. A large square Scotsman, with fiery red hair and a thicket of flaming beard, homed in on me as I was pushing my bike past the sixteenth-century rough-hewn stone house of Mary, Queen of Scots.

'Ye cannae ride tha' with-oote stabilisers!' he said.

'I can,' I said in defiant spirit. 'And I do!'

'Och! Ye from Sweden?'

'Yes,' I said. 'From Västerbotten.'

Because if he wanted to think I was from Sweden, well, that was fine by me. It also gave me a perfect opportunity to air that Västerbotten word, which has struck me as faintly comical ever since I cycled up that wooded way in 1987.

Anyhow, I don't know why he jumped to the conclusion that I was from the land of the krona and the tent-tripping moose, because most of the foreigners up this way were, judging from their registration plates, Germans or Belgians or Dutch. There were a fair few Mancs thrown in for good measure too. One lot trooping out of the off-licence were skull-cropped, beer-swilling and loud-mouthed.

'Bloody rip-off!' shouted one in a Man. United strip. 'It's only £1.78 a litre in Safeway!'

One of his mates who joined him in mouthing off about the expense of the offie was wearing an ENGLAND tracksuit, which struck me as risky kit to be sporting in such historically turbulent territory as this. His 'woman', who was dragging an eight-year-old with a David Beckham mohican, said in a voice so loud that everyone in the street turned round, 'Don't yer DARE talk to yer mother like that!' WHAACK!

What a relief it was that these weren't my countrymen. Hailing from the land of the Västerbottens can certainly have its advantages.

From Jedburgh I followed the course of the winding Jed, which rushes down through Camptown and scampers under an immense cliff so high that its deep, dark shadows cooled me from the searing sun, before losing its tributary identity, first in the Teviot and then in the Tweed. Before me lay the Border bulwark of the Cheviots. Bleakly beautiful, deceptively benign, these round-topped hills extend for about thirty-seven miles along the border of Scotland and Northumberland and, like New Zealand, have more sheep than people. I climbed steadily upwards, enjoying every minute of this mini mountain pass. First on one side rose Dod Hill, on the other Mervins Law, then further on past Edgerston Rig I spun along between Hareshaw Knowe and the knobbly granite hills of Knock Hills and Hophills Nob. A few wide-open hairpins later and I had peaked at Carter Bar, which, at 1371 feet, may only be a pinhead in the face of the high-rise Himalayas, but to me it felt on top of the world.

Feeling suitably triumphant, I gazed out over a remote and lonely landscape. The weather was so good I could see as far as the softly rounded 2036-foot lava flow of Windy Gyle, which itself lies within easy striking distance of a multitude of similar ancient flows like Beefstand, Russell's Cairn, Cushat Law, Comb Hill and Bloodybush Edge. I was standing on an ancient border that had been here for nearly a thousand years. Until James VI, King of the Scots (he of King James Version of the Bible fame), 'acquired' the English Crown in 1603 as James I, England and Scotland were separate kingdoms. And they remained that way, at each other's throats, happily slaughtering each

331

other for about the next hundred years until, in 1707, the Scottish government in Edinburgh was absorbed by the Treaty of Union into the Westminster Parliament of a United Kingdom. To signify the Union, the Scottish flag of the Cross of St Andrew was joined with the English Cross of St George to form the Union Jack. And now, what with everyone wanting to reiterate their national identities, look what trouble that's brought. Believe me, it's a whole lot simpler being Swedish.

Over in the lay-by, I met a grave-faced couple from Hamburg. This was the first time they had ever been to Britain, they told me in rather sketchy English, and they were now heading to Hull to catch the ferry to Rotterdam.

'Vee vant to go home tonight,' said the woman, who looked like a scary form of Betty Boothroyd.

'Oh. Have you not enjoyed it here?' I asked, taking immediate offence.

'Excuse me?'

'You said you want to go home tonight. Have you not enjoyed yourselves here very much?'

'Yar, yar. Vee have to very much,' said mein frosty-faced Frau.

'So do you mean you *have* to go home, rather than you *want* to go home?' I do like to establish my facts.

'Excuse me?'

'Are you returning home because you are at the end of your holiday, or because you've had enough of people like me not knowing what they are talking about?'

'Excuse me?'

'I'm glad to hear you've enjoyed yourselves,' I said, hastily veering off down a verbal escape route, 'because I believe they've had a lot of rain in Västerbotten.'

Plainly, the altitude was affecting the thread in my head. The Teutonic Two gave me a strange look and then wisely moved away. Sometimes some points are just not worth pursuing.

In preparations for a swift descent, I fastened down flight goggles, checked runway wheels, secured all pannier vents and gave a quick surreptitious glance to the hydraulics of my wayward undercarriage. Apart from an annoying pair of knickers that insisted on riding up the lesser known ridges and crags of my *västerbotten*, everything looked good, all systems were go. But as soon as I had taken off and was building up throttle speed to full hair-raising hurtle, I found myself having an exciting Indiana Jones moment involving a runaway Sholley trolley. Quite what an old woman's tartan-bagged, high-street wheelie shopper was doing making a rapid break for freedom on a roof-of-the-world road between Wooplaw Rig and Catcleuch Shin, you may well ask. I certainly did. Actually I didn't. I was too busy trying to avoid a nasty tangle of wheels and topical tartan. One emergency landing later, I ascertained the following: a camper-van family had recklessly pulled over to the side of the road to embark upon a perilously perched location for picnicking. This family favoured not a picnic basket but a picnicking shopping trolley for conveying their picnicking produce. Only trouble was, trolleys have wheels, and hills have hills, and wheels on hills are not good thrills if left to their own devices.

Things went a little smoother and a lot more swiftly as I raced past Echo Crags and Hungry Law. Talking of hungry, I realised I was, so pulled on my brakes in the wooded wilds of Cottonshopeburnfoot (don't try saying that with a hopeful foot of burnt cotton in your mouth) where Northumberland National Park very kindly provided me with a special pine-shaded picnic table. As I munched my lunch I leant an ear to my travelling trannie. *You and Yours* on Radio 4 had Peter White at the helm conducting a phone-in. Following a 'Driver fury over Euro cycle laws' lead story in the *Observer* two days earlier, he was asking listeners to call in to air their views on this proposed legislation that would make motorists responsible on a no-fault basis for all 'accidents' involving cyclists and other vulnerable road users. All it meant was that the UK would fall into line with France, Belgium, Scandinavia, Holland and Germany so that drivers' insurance policies would automatically pay out for injuries and damage to cyclists and pedestrians, regardless of where the fault lay. Which to my mind is very sensible as, after all, it's not cyclists and pedestrians who go round injuring or maiming or killing those people who sit in their fast-moving air-bagged, ten-ton boxes of steel, useful though they may be. But straight away things started inflating out of all proportion. Citing the RAC, the *Observer* claimed that the measure would raise car insurance premiums by an average £50, even though the Association of British Insurers said there was no evidence that premiums would rise. Even the EU said it was not aware of any extra costs to the insurance industry in countries where the scheme was operating. But these facts went wholly ignored by the national press who, for two days, had been having a bike-bashing field day. Anyone on two wheels came under fire from a colourful tirade of tabloid and broadsheet vitriol. Suddenly we were being called anything from Lycra Nazis to bicycle guerrillas, hairy-armed men to belligerent yobs, suicide jockeys in Lycra to demonic biomechanical centaurs, from pampered cyclists to card-carrying car terrorists bent on revenge. *Please, please, People of the Pen, calm your abusive tongues. All we want to do is to travel holier than thou without causing destruction, safely and serenely under our own steam.*

But they wouldn't calm down. Jeremy 'Motor Mouth' Clarkson, writing in the *Sun*, said:

> They have already taken over a third of the roads with their green Tarmac cycle lanes. Now the Lycra Nazis want to take over the whole lot! And they still don't pay a penny for going on the roads which the poor old motorist pay through the nose for.

(Actually, we do. Anybody who pays income tax contributes towards the roads.)

Or take the *Daily Mirror* columnist, Tony Parsons, getting thoroughly het up and making it about as personal as you can get:

> Bicycles are like masturbation – something you should grow out of. There is something seriously sick and stunted about grown men who want to ride a bike . . . if we truly cared about safety on our roads, then we would make a bonfire of all those stupid hats, all that hideous Lycra and every bicycle in the land.

Ooh, feel that hatred! Feel that rage! Feel that fiery heat of a hot steaming cyclist misanthropist. I can tell you, Tone, I've got a thing or two I could say to you (like if we truly cared about safety on our roads, we would ban bull-bars and talking on mobiles while motoring, for starters), but I can't really be bothered as I'd rather go and ride my bike instead.

Most of the listeners calling in to *You and Yours* were typically anti-cyclist: bikes should be taxed, cyclists insured, licence plates made compulsory, bicycles kept separate from cars and pedestrians, keep them out-of-sight, out-of-mind, leave-the-roads-to-us, blah, blah, blah. One man ringing from Nottingham said he thought bikes were just as dangerous as cars! I nearly choked on my banana when I heard that. Seeing as, shock horror, I had recently relaxed my nimby mast-erecting stance and relentingly bought a mobile phone, I thought about ringing in myself, not so much to air my views (I prefer to go for a cheering cycle rather than get all heatedly demonstrative about things) but because when Peter White asked me where I was calling from, I could say, 'Cottonshopeburnfoot.'

Because I thought that might make history.

And then Peter White would say, 'Where the devil is that?'

And I could say, 'It's in between Three Kings and Mally's Crag – just south of Harry's Pike and Middle Shank, which if you're still a bit lost, is down the hill from Hungry Law and The Hearts Toe.'

And then Peter would think I was a loony on the line, talking in tongues like that, and throw the phone down on me. Well, it would be worth it, wouldn't it? Actually it wouldn't, because apart from the fact that I hadn't once used my mobile yet for speaking on, my battery was running low and I wanted to save it for sending saucy textings to the builder. Which is the only reason I bought the phone in the first place.

Taking off along the wild and lonely twelve miles of rough dirt track that leads from Blakehopeburnhaugh to Kielder Castle, I was immediately swallowed up by the thick plantations of Redesdale Forest. As I climbed past Witch Holes to over 1500 feet across some of the most beautifully bleak and remote moorland in England, only three cars passed in two hours, which reinforced the fact that I was now in the least densely populated county in the country. And it felt wonderful. Some of the surrounding hills and wild moorland sounded wonderful too, like Smallhope Rig, Girdle Fell (it did?) and Oh Me Edge. Or is that what you're supposed to say when your Girdle Falls?

Soon after passing close to Devil's Lapful, I arrived at Kielder Castle tired, hot, dusty and thirsty. Kielder Castle, an elaborate eighteenth-century hunting lodge built for the Dukes of Northumberland, lies deep in the heart of Kielder Forest. This vast, dark, dank forest is an expansive hill-carpeting crop of mostly spruce, pine and larch plantations, which, since 1926, the Forestry Commission has created to become Europe's largest man-made forest. Everything round here is large, from the forests to the landscapes to the lakes. The biggest lake of all is Kielder Water, and I suppose it is only fitting that Europe's largest man-made forest should also contain Europe's largest man-made lake.

'It was a ruse, you know,' a local woman, who stopped to offer to take my photograph, told me with evident bitterness in her tone, 'flooding the valley like this. They told us they had to build a reservoir to provide for Tyneside. But that was never the case. They just told us that to hoodwink us into acceptance.'

I found more resentful feelings lingering in Kielder village store.

'We weren't happy about the flooding at all,' said the husband and wife team behind the counter. 'Yes, the shimmering water may look very nice in certain lights, but look behind you on that postcard. That's what the valley used to look like twenty years ago and you can't beat that sort of natural beauty.'

They were right. The valley a-flame in all its autumn glory looked gorgeous: dry stone walls, winding lanes, old stone farmhouses. Now 2684 acres of centuries and centuries of sheep-farming and life, were all drowned out beneath an artificial sea.

'Our neighbour lost his farm,' said the proprietor. 'Been in the family for generations. It was all very well being told the reservoir was needed to provide the North East with a much-needed water supply, but it was all a scam.'

That night in a valley bisected by the deep waters of the North Tyne, I camped in the rain on a sheep farm right in the middle of Bellingham, a small market town surrounded by a mix of bare fells and lush grazing lands, and busy with well-equipped walkers weighed down with rucksacks. For Bellingham, which the local greengrocer told me is pronounced 'Bellinjum', has the final stage of the 250-mile course of the Pennine Way on its muddy doorstep. Camping down the slope from me on Demesne Farm lay a mixed troop of hardy hikers scattered among a colourful array of flysheets. They had come up from Sheffield, where they all belonged to the same running club, and for about a week were walking a section of the Pennine Way. Big-booted and iron-calved, they looked like they could walk the hind legs off a donkey. But I was wrong.

'We're definitely struggling,' said Ann, a librarian who had worked at Sheffield library for twenty years. 'Running marathons is easy compared with walking eight miles with a heavy pack on your back!'

Kathy, a slim and sprightly blonde who I thought at first was in her mid twenties until I discovered she was travelling with her two children, both young adults, said, 'The thing with walking in a group is that you're only as strong as your weakest link.'

Their weakest link today was Kathy's daughter, who had pulled a muscle in her leg. Because of this, they were stalling in Bellingham to give her a day of rest.

It's funny to compare the different food fetishes that some walkers rely on to fuel them up and down the fells. In the past I have met people who live on nothing but Mars Bars, lardy cake, Wine Gums, Kendal Mint Cake, pork pies, or fruitcake sandwiched with doorstops of strong Cheddar. I could now add another gastronomic delight to this list: when Ann's mum and dad, keen day hikers, escaped to the hills, they packed nothing but packets of Jacob's Cream Crackers.

Using Bellingham as my base, I spent three days riding through the dense conifer forests and across the sprawling barren brown moors of Northumberland National Park. All around me lay reminders of a past filled with strife and bloodshed and violent death. Some of it was a recent past, like on a dangerous stretch of the A68 (Dere Street again), where, in the hope of deterring speeding motorists, a road sign declared: 3 YEARS – 75 ACCIDENTS. But most of it was of a stormy past filled with Border raids and bloody battles. Flodden Field, just south of Coldstream, is legendary for being the bloodiest battle ever fought on English soil (15,000 men were killed) and the Scots suffered the bitterest defeat of all, but the battle of Chevy Chase nearly 130 years earlier in 1388 at Otterburn was very terrible too: 200 Scots and 2000 English were killed, and Hotspur (which I'd always thought was a football club in north London) was taken prisoner. Incidentally it's his son, the East End gangster-sounding Harry Hotspur, who features in Shakespeare's *Henry IV*. Just thought I'd throw that one in.

After three nights at Demesne Farm, I thought perhaps it was time to get moving back in search of the sea, though I could have camped there a week or two quite happily. The farm had been in the Telfer family since 1942. Robert Telfer, who ran the farm with his father, was also a call-out fireman. He was one of a team of twelve men and carried a pager about him at all times.

'I can get to the station in two minutes flat,' he said. 'The first six go. That's the number of men we're supposed to have, though if we can't wait, we sometimes leave with four. If we're stretched, we get help from Hexham.'

He told me he had about sixty to seventy call-outs a year, and when I mentioned the '3 YEARS – 75 ACCIDENTS' sign on the A68, he told me he had attended a lot of those crashes himself.

'It's simply people driving too fast,' he said. 'They see a stretch of straight road and put their foot down. But there're some nasty dips along there like, and we get to pick up the pieces.'

Another morning, leaning against my tent-sheltering dry stone wall, Robert bemoaned the fact that the government had no idea about farming.

'They tell us to "diversify",' he said, 'and get a job in a factory!'

Robert had his biblical-sounding nephew staying with him for a week or two. Nazareth was half-Greek, with striking blond hair and olive black eyes.

'He lives in Athens,' said Robert, 'so being here on the farm with our 300 breeding ewes is like another planet to him!'

When Nazareth came to watch me take my bike apart on a maintenance mission, he told me he loved the farm and wanted to take a sheep and a cow home with him to show his friends.

The morning I packed up my tent, ready to hit the road, Robert's dad leant over the wall and said, 'You're not leaving us are you, pet? Sometimes you get used to faces and it's a shame when they move on, like.'

Robert turned up too to say goodbye. But it wasn't a very quick one because we got on to the subject of the 'reservoir'.

'Two of my great uncles were displaced from Kielder valley when they flooded it,' he said. 'They were moved into Bellingham from their farm lodge, but they didn't feel settled here and neither of them lasted long. I think it was because they had never lived in a town that they died so quickly. They loved the valley – and to be forced to abandon a place where you've lived all your life – to see it disappear under water – can't be good for you.'

CHAPTER 50

Reivers is the romantic name given to the thieves and outlaws and cattle-raiders that once ruled the Borders. Their name lives on in various tourist-drawing guises, one of which was the Reivers Cycle Route, which I briefly linked up with near the coarse-sounding Shitlington Crags. More coarseness lay in store just across the way at Bog Shield and Rubbingstob Hill. From there it was down to Pity Me and Cockplay and Hadrian's very large Wall. At least, it *used* to be very large, because these days it's a lot easier to miss than it was 2000 years ago when the wall, the Romans' northernmost frontier of a far-reaching empire, built as an impregnable barrier to separate the land of the Britons from the land of the Picts, stood too high to be scaled by a man standing on another man's shoulders.

Still, England's Great Wall, originally spanning the neck of the country for seventy-three miles from Wallsend-on-Tyne to Bowness-on-Solway, has its impressive moments. These are mostly along the central section between Chollerford and Gilsland, where the wall marches across the starkly stunning Northumberland countryside with the ruins of forts, mile-castles and signal turrets set along its length at regular intervals. And this was the long, straight switchback stretch I whipped along in the wind, following a scalloped horizon past Fozy Moss, Sewing Shield, Beggar Bog, Hotbank, Once Brewed, Twice Brewed, Haltwhistle (which flaunts itself as 'The Centre of Britain' – true if you chop off a few bothersome outgrowths like Anglesey and the Scilly Isles), Sunny Rigg, Fell End, Burnt Walls and Runner Foot.

But I didn't whistle along it all in one fell swoop. I paused at Beggar Bog, where I made full use of the PCs in the car park at the excavated ruins of Housesteads (Vercovicium), which along with Chesters and Vindolanda is one of the best-preserved Roman forts in Britain. It could garrison troops from a thousand-strong infantry unit within its five acres, and was built to guard the point where the Knag Burn breaches the ridge of whinstone cliff. This craggy ridge of land, rising like massive crests of petrified waves, played right into the hands of the invaders, as the steep banks virtually doubled the height of the wall, and, where they did not, great ditches were dug.

A few years ago, on a cold, dark, drippy wintry afternoon, I had cycled up this way and explored the fort's rugged ruins alone – a very different scene from the one now crawling with car-trippers and back-packers. So, with light-ning illuminating a bruised summer sky, I saddled up and galloped off with that air of suspense that a storm always arouses.

But I didn't get very far. The wind swung round and the rain was fast moving. With a sense of urgency, I dived down a dip and hurriedly put up my tent. The storm hit just as I was throwing myself, together with the last of my rain-splattered panniers, into my small sheltered space. All zipped up, I sat with satisfaction eating and listening to the noisy rain drumming down on the tent. As the storm moved overhead, sharp claps of ear-bursting thunder sporadically shook the earth, making me flinch automatically. The air smelt raw and fresh and wild and very angry. And I loved every apprehensive minute of it all. Why anyone would favour a one-star, or even a five-star hotel over sleeping out on the bare brutal land of a storm-pounded Roman barricade, heaven only knows. Right now, you couldn't get any better than this.

Just up the rise from my camp spot reared Winshields Crag, which at 1200 feet is the highest point of Hadrian's Wall. Early the next morning I climbed up there, blowing hot breath on my hands to warm them from the damp, dawn chill. In Hadrian's day, and for the 300 years following his day when this area was a heavily defended frontier zone, sentries on a nearby turret would have been watching my every move. But today, the only thing observing me with sus-picious eyes was a hovering kestrel, hanging head down in the wind, tail outstretched like a fan.

The passing rain had left a clear and acutely honed morning in its wake. The lower slopes were rinsed and iridescently green. To the south rose the backbone of England – the round-topped Pennines, with their highest peak, Cross Fell, just visible in the dim-lit distance. Looking west I could see the hills of Dumfries and Galloway, while to the northwest lay the Bewcastle Fells and Scotland. As if that wasn't enough to stand and stare at, the North Humberlanders' whale-back moors in the due north rolled gradually upwards, in various shades of golds and browns and purples, to the Cheviots. I could see a dark wedge of Wark Forest, the southern section of Kielder Forest, and the early-warning mast of Hopealone. The only trees I could see in detail were the indigenous hardy species of hawthorns and mountain ash, growing vertically out of the rocks. No wonder, then, that Lord Trevelyan described Northumberland in the early 1900s as 'the land of the far horizons'. It was also the land of the dry stone walls, built in the eighteenth century to contain stock and to clear pastures of stones. The wildlife love them: they provide wonderful shelter and habitation for nesting birds like wheateaters and dunnocks, as well as mice, weasels and stoats.

The Romans withdrew from the Wall late in the fourth century, when Rome itself was under threat from the invading Goths, Vandals and Huns, and troops were needed to defend the city. Eventually Rome fell, but the Wall survived. And it would have survived a whole lot more intact had not people, over the centuries, adopted the canny habit of helping themselves to this grand source of free building material when building a cottage, a church, or even a castle. The scalloped horizon, formerly called the Nine Nicks of Thirlwall, has, thanks to extensive quarrying by Tarmac, turned into a mere five 'Nicks'. It's almost inconceivable now to think that only fifty years ago it was considered quite acceptable to dig up a 2000-year-old monument for roadstone.

I was reunited with the coast again on the wide, tide-washed estuary of the Solway Firth. This sea-gash of fast currents and all-engulfing tides, separating southwest Scotland from northwest England, is rimmed on the north Cumbrian side with salt-marshes and mud-flats, boggy cow-grazed meadows and silent sands. As I cycled across this elemental landscape of air and water, I was greeted by semi-submerged road signs, warning me of treacherous tides, quicksands and dangerous bathing. None of this worried the thousands of wading birds busily skimming over the surface or scuttling along the edges searching for mud-buried food.

It was lovely to be back on the coast, with the calls and cries of the birds and the salty smack of the sea. The weather was wildly windy, and even sometimes sunny. But judging from the morass of dirty cloud marching over the purple hills of Galloway, and the thick band of dreary grey hanging over the Lake District's distant peaks, rain was not far away.

Hadrian's Wall reaches its western limit at Bowness-on-Sea, but because the ramparts are made of turf at this point, precious little remains to be seen. It's here that the salt-marshes face the narrowest point of the Solway Firth, with fine sea-sweeping views over to Scotland just two miles away. In the seventeenth century, the English and Scottish raiders kept up a steady feud across the firth and most of this feuding seemed to involve an unhealthy fetish for church bells. One party of Scots sailed across the water and stole Bowness church bells, but they only managed to get halfway back across the estuary before, hotly pursued by the much-piqued English, they were forced to abandon them mid-stream. The bells now in the porch of St Michael's Church, Bowness, were seized from villages on the Scottish side of the Solway during avenging raids. Wouldn't it be nice if that gung-ho Texan cowboy, George Bush, could be content with nicking a few bells, or any other dangly things, off Saddam Insane instead of gagging for mass destruction and all-out warfare? Then Saddam could get in his kayak and paddle off down the Tigris and up the Potomac to Washington to swipe back his objects of chiming delight. That way we could leave those troublesome two to it, bobbing back and forth across the oceans aboard their ill-equipped sea-going crafts until they got swallowed up by either an oil tanker or a whale with questionable taste.

Once round the Cardurnock Peninsula with its salt-marsh and raised beach, I followed the Moricambe marshes along flat and virtually car-free lanes as the tide stole up a myriad of narrow creeks. The rain reached me as I stood on the end of the arm of Grune Point, a shingle spit which watches over the very liquid-sounding Channel of River Waver and the Channel of River Wampool. So I pulled on my waterproofs, put my head down and rode, and rode, and rode. Though the weather was wet and the wind most unhelpful, and though the road became more flooded with cars the further south I sank, I didn't mind as I had suddenly hit one of those days when your energy never ebbs. I charged down the Cumbrian coast, eating up the miles through Maryport, Workington, Whitehaven, flashing by pylons and ports, wind farms and forts, and railways used and disused. I passed steel works and chemical works and other workings of an opencast nature. Things grew wilder with Whitehaven in my wake.

On the clifftop at St Bees Head, from where on a good day you could see the Isle of Man (all I could see was a sullen grey sea merging with an equally sullen grey sky), the only other person fighting to stand upright in the berserkly blowing wind was a woman with long, black, tossy, swishy hair like an Icelandic hippy horse. Unlike me, zipped and Velcroed up to my neck in fetching Goretex, she was facing the bracing wet wind in nothing more than tassled jeans and tie-dye T-shirt. When she turned and saw me she emitted a shriek of maniacal laughter. Then, clawing the air for balance, she stumbled over to me and said, shouting against the roar of the wind, 'It's so much better now that I know how I'm going to do it!'

I stared at her for a minute, certain I had a mad witch on my hands. Her face was unnaturally shiny and, despite the rain, bore the wink of polished brass.

'Going to do what?' I shouted back. But she just threw back her head and howled with demented laughter. A shiver shot down my spine. *Oh no!* I thought. *She's going to plunge to her death off the cliff!* Maybe St Bees Head, being the only cliffs on the Cumbrian coast, was like a northern Beachy Head. A suicidal black spot.

'Are you all right?' I asked, when clearly she wasn't.

But what else could I do, short of jumping on her to pin her to the ground? I looked into her eyes and saw pupils as big and black as bottomless pits staring psychotically back at me. Then, before I could do anything, she ran like an oscillating drunk back to the lighthouse, jumped in a car and drove away. *Yikes! She's not going to commit suicide! She's going to murder a philandering husband!*

Oh well, I thought, as I walked into the wind back to my bike. He probably deserves it.

A sharp rise and fall saw me flying into St Bees, leaping across Pow Beck, forking near Fairladies Farm, and in questioning mood at How Man. The nuclear monstrosities of Sellafield looked balefully bleak and foreboding, so I pushed down on the pedals, ratcheted up a gear and scuttled by. Before I knew it I was in the MOD's big gun-booming DANGER AREA of Eskmeals Dunes, so I beetled on to Bootle. With the peaks and crags of Corny Fell, Bootle Fell and the outlying peak of Black Combe rearing up into the rain off my portside elbow, I shot down the Cumbria Cycleway to the ravaged shore around Millom. From here I had to track back north to Duddon Bridge to skirt Duddon Sands, all the time watched over by the not overly dramatic heap of Black Combe. But this nigh-on 2000-foot fell has attracted a fair share of folk-lore in its time. Its lure as a supernatural hot spot most likely has something to do with the Swinside Bronze Age stone circle, known locally as Sunken Kirk, on its northeastern flank. According to legend, Black Combe bees wake from their winter slumber to hum in unison at midnight on Christmas Eve, and cattle kneel in bovine adoration. But the tradition I can most identify with is the one in which the mountain is possessed by a much less Christian spirit who answers to the name of Hob Thross, or Hob Thrust, 'a body all over rough'. (Steady on!) It was believed that Hot Hob could be summoned to do Hob

Thross's bidding in the early hours – so long as he was rewarded with a big dish of thick porridge with butter in it. That's my man!

Suddenly I was into the land of the 'Furnesses': Broughton-in-Furness, Kirby-in-Furness, Askam-in-Furness, Dalton-in-Furness, and the big Barrow-in-Furness. I had always presumed that 'Furness' was just an adaptation of 'furnace', since the first of many blast-furnaces were built in the area in the eighteenth century for the exploitation of the local iron ore deposits. But don't presuppose your suppositions before the horse has bolted. The peninsula is what its name says it is – the 'fur ness', or the 'far peninsula', marooned by the sandy reaches of Morecambe Bay. Or, to take it down a peg or two, Furness is a combination of the Old Norse words *futh* (buttock) and *nes* (headland).

Barrow was once the world's biggest producer of iron and steel. The census of 1851 showed a mere handful of people living beside the banks of the Walney Channel, but by 1873 there was a port of over 40,000 inhabitants with a thriving engineering and shipbuilding industry. Since that time Barrow docks have supplied ships for the Royal Navy, from ironclads to HMS *Invincible*, and from Britain's first submarine to the scary Trident nuclear submarines of more recent times. Until the 1980s, Barrow's shipbuilding company was VSEL, Vickers Shipbuilding and Engineering Ltd, or, as the locals called it due to the impending redundancies, 'Very Soon Everyone's Leaving' (the acronym was an apt one; five months after I cycled past the shipyard's doors, 700 workers were made redundant and Barrow is now an unemployment black spot). Then it changed to GEC Marconi Marine and now it's BAE Systems and making such delights as Assault Craft Landing Vessels, Auxiliary Oil Tankers and Astute Hunter Killer Submarines.

With headlines like 'New legionnaires' victim set to be named' blazing out from local and national newspapers, I gave the centre of Barrow a wide berth. Six people in all were to die from the largest outbreak of legionnaires' disease in the UK for ten years. About 150 people were confirmed as having contracted the disease, which was traced to a faulty air-conditioning unit in the town's arts centre.

Sea air mixed with a dose of car-spewing carbon monoxide was all I breathed as I nipped down the skinny length of the Isle of Walney, passing through Barrow's early twentieth-century-planned suburb of Vickerstown, the island's only built-up area – the rest is mainly rocks, sand, dunes and grassland. I rode beside Biggar Bank and Snab Sands to Rape Haw, and walked down to the nature reserve where my ears were assailed with the shrieking cries and squabbling complaints emanating from the largest ground-nesting gull colony in Europe (I would have lasted a lot longer there had I worn my bike helmet to protect me against the vicious dive-bombings and aerial attacks of the angry adults). And then I rode all the way back again, veering off on a slight variation to follow the touristy 'Cistercian Way' and a dyke that, as early as the fourteenth century, had been erected by the iron-smelting monks of Furness Abbey to prevent flooding. Walney, which derives its name from Old English *wagen* (quicksands), is only a quarter of a mile wide in places and mountainous seas sometimes crash right across the island during violent storms.

It was still raining by the time I joined the coastal road around the peninsula from Barrow, past Point of Comfort (which, with shoes sloshing like water butts, I had long since left behind), Elbow and Wadhead Scars to Ulverston. One of the very agreeable advantages of cycling is that it gives you such an unstinting amount of time to muse and mull over the sometimes comical, not to mention deeply perplexing names of the places through which you pass. Take Ulverston, for instance, which was providing me with endless hours of conjecturing pleasure (yes, I'm sorry, but you've got to amuse yourself somehow in this lone-wheeling game). After serious pedalling ponderations, I concluded it could only be a truncated form, meaning 'the town of the ulnar (nerve)'. Either that or 'the town of the vulva'.

Disappointingly, Ulverston has nothing to do with ulnars or vulvas but more to do with a Saxon landowner whose Old English name, Wulfhere, delightfully translates as 'Wolf Army'.

Stand almost anywhere on the shores of south Cumbria and you can't fail to notice that Morecambe Bay is more than big. In fact, it's more than 190 square miles of water, which at low tide drains away to leave a vast expanse of quaking and burbling tide-shifting sand, drawing in the crowds of wading birds. It also has on occasion drawn in unsuspecting pedestrians who, putting a step in the wrong direction, can be sucked and slurped into oblivion. The whole huge area is washed out twice a day by urgent tides. I flew up the bay when the tide was racingly high and watched vast concentrations of waders pack together on the last available space, producing an extravaganza of feathered sight and sound. All I needed to top it off was the spectacle of a plundering peregrine launching an attack, creating all-out havoc.

To make up for the lack of peregrine falcon, what I did see were the Alps, Arrad Foot, Lady Skye, Pool Foot, Speel Bank, Bigland Scar, Cark, Humphrey Head, Eden Mount, Eggerslack Wood, and Meathop Marsh. Having completed all the upping and downing of Cumbria's fat tentacle-hanging southern coast, I finally turned the corner at Levens all ready to storm on south. But instead I headed directly northwest, deep into the Lakes and high into the fells. And that's where I spent several days, in atrocious weather conditions (the rest of the country was flopped out in a heatwave), taking perverse pleasure in the physical discomfort and pain of dragging over a hundred pounds of kit over every pass I could possibly fling my wheels at. No, I hadn't lost my marbles: I was simply stalling for time as the builder had suddenly decided to take his two weeks' holiday and come out to meet me.

As he had never been north of York in his life, nor for that matter seen a real live mountain, we decided that, rather than cycle together down the flats of the more industrialised and built-up northwest coast of Lancaster and Merseyside into north Wales, it would be more scenically fun and muscularly testing to spend the whole frolicking fortnight cycling in a climbing and falling fashion about the fells.

But things got off to a bad start. Two days before I was due to rendezvous with builder and bike at Windermere railway station, I was cycling over Hardknott Pass to scoot between Swirl How and Cold Pike along Wrynose

Bottom and Wrynose Pass on my way to Side Pike, Stool End and the perfect Pike of Stickle, when, on a rain-lashed mountainside, I stopped for a pee. The way that I went about doing this, so as to hunker down out of sight of the road, involved clambering over an obstacle course of rocky outcrops, dry stone walls (which were actually very wet stone in the rain) and a clump of batty-brained sheep in brown overcoats. I was in the final stages of mounting a skew-whiff gate when a whipped-up wind-devil, lurking in wait behind Hell Gill, Black Wars, Long Scar, Cam Spout, Crinkle Crags, or possibly even Dollywaggon Pike, pounced for the kill. Caught in the uncompromising position of getting my leg over (the gate's top bar), the sudden violence of a storm-tossed gust blew me clean off my hurdle and I had one of those moments when your whole world turns turtle. I banged down on to the boggy rocky ground, missing a too-close inspection of the finer details of the dreggy dags of an ill-positioned sheep's rump by a mere dropping's breath. The ground cover of muddy dung and matted wool was not spongy or springy enough to prevent something pinging disconcertingly in my left Achilles tendon.

Had I lain down there and then and stayed still for three days, my ankle would probably have righted itself enough for me to proceed unhindered along my pedalling way. But when you're alone in the mountains in the mud and the rain with just a pandemonium of some poggle-headed sheep for company, you can't just lie down and pretend you're not where you are with a foot that's not feeling as it should. And anyway, I had a builder to be meeting. So I scooped myself up, shook myself down, and limped off on my way.

CHAPTER 51

By the time I fell into the builder's arms at Windermere station, my tendon was well and truly twanged. I couldn't walk, I couldn't cycle; I couldn't even camp, because that involved having to walk or cycle somewhere uphill and out of town to find a suitable grassy-knolled location. To cap it all, just as I was immobilised, the sun came out, shining down hard and hot, and it was forecast to stay hotly shining for the next two weeks.

If you don't revel in jams of cars and coaches disgorging crowds of OAPs, Japanese and families, together with the odd Costa Brit-style mob – all beer belly and mooning bum, falling over drunk in the street at ten o'clock in the morning – Windermere, with all its Wordsworthian hype, is not the best place to find yourself marooned in, specially during the prelude to a blazing hot August bank holiday.

I felt terrible. Terrible for ruining the builder's hard-earned holiday. But, apart from expressing touching concern for my malfunctioning leg-part, he didn't seem to mind in the least. He said he was quite happy to stay in Windermere for as long as it took for my ankle to get better, even if that was the whole of his holiday. One of the benefits, I was discovering, with going out with a man who had barely ever been outside Hampshire, let alone England, was that he found anywhere south of Dibden Purlieu or north of Reading to be of the utmost excitement. So Windermere, with its lengthy lake and picture-postcard panorama of protecting mountains (the builder's first sighting of anything higher than a Sussex Down or a Yorkshire moor), was to him a scene of Shangri-la perfection. Even the holidaymaking hordes were a welcome diversion, providing an endless source of entertaining contemplation. Like two old dears, we spent our days sitting on lakeside benches watching the world go by.

For five nights we stayed on the edge of town in a cheap bed-and-breakfast. The house belonged to Geoff and Pat, a couple in their early fifties who had just started to let out their spare bedroom – a small but clean, white bright room overlooking the cemetery. We immediately set about cluttering the place with our excessive combination of seventeen various panniers that spewed a variety of sweaty clothes, musty sleeping bags and whiffy food. Added to that was my mountain of plastic bags and a very wet tent and groundsheet, which I draped across every drapable surface. Within ten minutes our room looked like a post-traumatic disaster area, seriously in need of emergency aid.

Originally from Yorkshire, but having only recently moved to Windermere from Swindon, Geoff, a computer programmer, and Pat, a head of some sort of educational college, were great talkers. Such was the continuous flow of their rattling chatter that when they first showed us to our quarters it was a full hour before they finally shut the door and left us to it. This was fine by me as I am easily entertained by other people's verbiage, but for Gary, who had just endured a harrowing journey sitting for hours on the floor, crammed in the corridor of a broken-down, over-crowded Virgin train, it was all a bit overwhelming. Specially as he was suffering from north-of-Reading culture shock.

The toilet and bathroom, which we shared with Geoff and Pat, were situated across the landing, a mere two steps away from their open bedroom door and three steps from Geoff's office, where he sat glued to his computer in full view of the toilet door. To be within such close earshot rather put a restraining order on any untoward resonances that might inopportunely emit from one's person.

The location of our shared facilities provided another cause for anxiety: both Geoff and Pat possessed an alarming ability to detect our toileting needs. No matter how mouse-like we were, every time we opened our door with the sole mission of hot-footing it up and down the steps of the landing to Destination Toilet, one or other of them would inevitably pounce on us to engage us in an hour or so of one-sided, station-platform small talk. Such yakety jabberings are all very well when waiting at Didcot Parkway for the delayed 11.07 to Leamington Spa, but take on quite a different meaning when the contents of your lower intestine are stacking up, desperate to come in to land like a backlog of aircraft circling over Heathrow. Sometimes it was almost easier to climb out of the bedroom window, drop down to the patio one floor below, and run across the road to use the public toilets in the car park opposite. None of which was good news for a buggered Achilles tendon.

Though Geoff and Pat were in their fifties, they had a surprisingly young daughter, five-year-old Kay. I thought that either they had hit jackpot and got a late one in there, or she was adopted. It wasn't until the second morning of our stay that I discovered her true story.

Gary and I were sitting at the one little table having breakfast in their front room. We never had a chance to talk to each other because either Geoff or Pat would stand over us, convivially babbling on about one thing or another. Talking away to itself in the corner sat a flickering TV, which none of us was paying much attention to until the news suddenly broke that the bodies of Holly Wells and Jessica Chapman, the two ten-year-old Cambridgeshire school-girls who had been missing for nearly a fortnight, sparking off the biggest manhunt in British criminal history, had been found in some Suffolk wood-land, seventeen miles from their homes in Soham.

As if this wasn't enough of a tragedy, Pat stood in the middle of the room, hands on her ample hips, eyes locked on to the TV, and said very matter-of-factly, 'Our daughter was murdered.'

I stopped chewing mid-mouthful and stared at her disbelievingly. Gary, never one to express his emotions in public, continued chomping on his fry-up. I was shocked. I've met plenty of people before whose child has died through illness or accident, but never murder. Pat saw that I was shocked, and then calmly, and almost coldly, explained.

'Her boyfriend killed her and then he threw himself in front of a train. Kay may call us mummy and daddy,' she said, 'but she's really our granddaughter.'

She told us how beautiful and bright her daughter, Sue, had been. She was only nineteen when she died. That was two years ago, when Kay was just three. Matt, her father, killed Sue because he was angry and jealous when she tried to split up with him. He was besotted with her and didn't want to live without her.

Two days later, when I was sitting on a step outside the garage, taking my bike apart, Pat walked over to see what I was doing. Then, unprompted, and scarcely pausing to draw breath, she just talked and talked to me about her daughter. For a while, when they were looking for a place of their own, Sue and Matt had moved in with them, so Pat knew Matt very well. He was a good lad, she liked him a lot. Trouble was, Sue was a terrible flirt, and men were con-stantly falling at her feet. On the night of the murder, Pat said that she just knew something terrible had happened to her daughter. It was just a feeling, she said, an almost sickening pain. She had gone straight down to the sports club community centre where Sue sometimes went. Sue wasn't there, but Pat overheard a conversation between a group of teenagers sitting at a table, saying they couldn't take the train to the place they were planning on having a night out in because someone had thrown themselves on the line.

'Straight away I knew that was Matt,' said Pat.

She raced over to their flat, arriving seconds before the police. Inside, Sue lay dead. But the police wouldn't let her in to see her. It was a crime scene, they said, and it had to be forensically investigated. This was the point at which Pat exploded.

'That's my daughter in there!' she shouted. 'You have no right to tell me I can't see or hold her. I'm her MOTHER, for God's sake! DON'T YOU UNDERSTAND?'

From the moment I first met Pat, it was obvious she was a strong-minded and extremely determined woman. And her resolute iron will was no match for the police on that awful night. They caved in to her demands and she got to hold her beautiful daughter in her arms for the last time. While she was telling me this, her eyes filled with tears and she turned both lips into her mouth and pressed them together. I hobbled over to her and gave her a hug. The awfulness of it all was just too unimaginable. I wondered at her ability to appear so strong, so 'normal' – cooking dinner, cleaning the car, hanging out the washing. Life has to go on, she said. You can't simply sit around moping all day, doing nothing. And anyway, there was Kay to think about.

'She's a very demanding child,' said Pat. 'She rushes us off our feet so that we're almost in a perpetual state of exhaustion. But we're determined to give her a good life.'

Kay knew exactly what had happened to her parents. If her school friends or football team pals (Pat said she was a right little tomboy) ever asked her about them, she would simply say, 'Daddy killed Mummy and then Daddy died when he jumped in front of a train.'

Pat had one other child, a son, who was at college in Bristol. He had reacted very badly to the death of his sister; he was angry and depressed and withdrawn. Pat worried about him, but she said his friends had been fantastic.

'They could have easily given up on him,' said Pat. 'He's been a very difficult person to be with because of all his moods, but most of them have stuck by him, which is some comfort at least.'

What Pat occasionally begrudged was the freedom that she had been looking forward to, suddenly whisked away.

'I chose to have my children,' she said, 'so I didn't mind never having a moment to myself. But then, just when I reach the age when my son and daughter can look after themselves, I find myself starting all over again. Much as I love Kay, she's a handful! And Geoff and I have had to put off any plans we had of travelling. Sometimes it's hard to accept that we're tied down with Kay for the next thirteen or fourteen years.'

One of the things Pat regretted missing the most was that unique mother—daughter relationship.

'Sue had been a difficult teenager,' said Pat, 'but she'd reached that age when we suddenly hit the same wavelength and could really understand each other. I think it's a very special girls-together thing. It's just not the same with boys.'

I knew what she meant. When I'm not away cycling, mum and me either see or speak to each other every day. We know exactly what the other is thinking – a line of thought that seems to escape the three men in our family completely. For better or for worse, we also both possess the same silly sense of humour and can be guffawing uproariously about something when all dad does is look at us as if we are psychotically unbalanced. When I was attacked and beaten up by a man in Bulgaria, mum woke up in the middle of the night and had a feeling in the pit of her stomach that all was not well with me. Dad, meanwhile, slept a deep and untroubled sleep.

Lacking a pair of crutches, or an ankle strong enough to push a pedal, my only form of transport about Windermere was on the back of the builder. So as we moved from old codger bench to chip shop to old codger bench (ooh, what a riveting time we had!), I held on limpet tight to his broad-beamed back, steering him with my knees or whacking him one when he strayed off course or tried to knock me out when he forgot to duck when passing beneath a low-lying bough or doorway.

Gary had a lot to put up with; deprived of my bike I was moody, tetchy, prickly, fidgety and frustrated. I have a rather inconvenient and desperate need to cycle every day and if I'm unable to because of injury, I turn into a highly charged and volatile ball of pent-up frustration and cabin-fever horribleness. To add to this ugly Molotov cocktail of delights, I was also menstrually unstable. Gary was definitely seeing me at my worst. I told him that if we could survive these two weeks together (the longest time we'd ever had), we stood a good chance of surviving anything.

After four days off the bike, I could stand it no longer. I strapped up my ankle and, all packed up, cycled one-leggedly with Gary about five miles up the road to Ambleside. The ride was beneficial for clearing a bit of fiery excess baggage out of my head, but not so favourable for the recuperation of my malfunctioning tendon. But at least Ambleside, being a ramble-sided Mecca, was more our cup of tea than Windermere, being crampon-packed with climbing shops and camping shops and all things packable and wickable and foldable.

At one point Gary piggy-backed me down to the Health Centre where I placed my injured extremity into the hands of Dr Sloss. Dr Sloss touched and tweaked, prodded and poked before declaring my Achilles tendon severely twanged. He said he recommended, and could refer me for, a course of physio – only trouble was there was a six-week waiting list. I said I can't wait that long, I've got Land's End to be cycling to. He advised me not to do any cycling for at least two weeks, minimum. He then broke the news that Achilles tendons can take up to a couple of months to heal. *Oh hallelujah!* I thought, as I felt the depression levels rolling up their sleeves and rising into action. What was I going to do? I *need* exercise! If only for sanity's sake.

I asked Dr Sloss about walking. He said don't. I asked him about crutches (I was panickingly plotting whether I could crutch-it to Land's End). He said he didn't have any. I asked him about swimming (I was panickingly plotting whether I could swim-it to Land's End). He said that was okay, but only kick with the good leg. I asked him if he knew of a place where I could hire a kayak (I was panickingly plotting whether I could . . .). He looked at me as if I was barking bonkers. And then I laughed and told him that I forgot he was a doctor and not a tourist office. By this stage he appeared more concerned for my mental health than for my Achilles. When I got up to leave, he looked a very relieved man.

When my piggy-backing taxi service picked me up, I was not in the happiest of moods. To cheer me up, he transported me to one of the outdoor stores in Cheapside Street where I could drool over the lightweight likes of titanium mugs and titanium spoons. Next stop was of a more educational nature; an ambling trip around Ambleside museum where I was enlightened by a deeply cultural ditty:

> It's baa, ye bonny, harmless sheep,
> Feeding on yon mountain steep.

The builder and I spent six nights in Ambleside, two of them in a dark dingy outhouse on top of a car park. The remaining four were spent high up in the eaves of the friendly Brantholme Guest House overlooking Loughrigg Fell with its Todd and Ivy Crags. Apart from the uplifting view, we also had an en suite bathroom, albeit dodgy-stain carpeted and coffin-sized. I was the first to christen the toilet and, as I did so, I noticed a slowly dripping commotion dropping out of a rear-end pipe. Whereas most people would probably choose to ignore it, or, at best, mention it to the management when checking out, builders seem to need to demonstrate their can-cure-anything qualities by rolling up their sleeves, removing cistern lids, and acting all cocksure with their ball floats, split pins, lever arms and ball valves. At least, my builder does.

I left him tinkering in his fix-it-all element while I busied myself with the constructive pastime of furnishing the room with plastic bags. Just as I was happily rustling away amid a chaotic sea of polythene, I became aware of a call for assistance emanating from the bathroom. (Let it be known here that *never*, unless exceptional circumstances dictate, am I *ever* called to assist. For, in similar vein to 'he who may not always be right, but is never wrong', 'he who may not always be able to fix, will fix it with no help from others'). Sweeping aside a pluming cloud of carriers, I hastily hobbled over to the in-house guesthouse plumber. At first I failed to grasp the gravity of the potentially flood-disastrous scene. This was because the plumber was fighting with his thumb to hold back the equivalent gushing pressure jet of Yellowstone's Old Faithful sky-spouting geyser. In fact, so blissfully unaware was I of the calamity unfolding within our en suite cistern that I even ventured to make light of the situation, enquiring of the plumber if he would care to have me see to his stopcock.

Well! It's not often that such offers of pressure-relieving benevolence are so briskly rebuffed. But oh! how they were this time around! I was about to storm off in an offended sulk, to drown my sorrows in an ocean of plastic bags, which, thanks to a freshening wind blowing merry hell through the flung-open windows, were ballooning across the carpet like an army of Arizonian tumbleweeds, when I was ordered into action.

'Leatherman's flat-headed screwdriver blade!' said he calmly, but firmly, in a state of admirable restrained distress. (To those not in the multi-tooled know, a Leatherman is the Big Boy's equivalent of a Swiss Army knife.) At this juncture, I dared myself a brief raising of one's eyebrows in tilted-head, quizzical stance because, as a rule of thumb (not the one currently holding back the cataclysmic force of Old Faithful), the builder's sizeable and indispensable tool is unfailingly found to be attached to the lower-to-middle reaches of his person.

The reason for its absence now, however, was down to the fact that it was currently stabbing a loaf of bread on the bedside table (my cistern-dripping discovery had interrupted the builder while in mid-sarnie-preparing sawings).

I handed said blade to the great Mending Maestro. And then he set to work, kindly informing me as he did so, albeit in dentist-to-dentist-assistant garbled technical speak, of the can of worms on his hands. Should you be fool enough to express a desire to know just what the devil the plumbing problem was with the cistern's internal organs, then please, let me, a mere layman, explain.

Apparently we had a blocked-off overflow on our plate. To add to its woes, the cistern contained a cheap plastic ball valve, which in turn led to a cheap plastic lever arm that blew off at the valve. This then blew the right-angled pipe off the top, resulting in the mains-pressure water hitting the ceiling. Having called his serf to assistance, the Leatherman-clutching plumberman turned off the ball-a-fix valve under the cistern. The valve, incidentally, was a Portsmouth valve with a horizontal piston as opposed to a Croydon valve with a vertical piston. (When I dared to enquire if there was such a thing as a Melton Mowbray or possibly even a Piddletrenthide valve, I was severely reprimanded and told to pipe down.) Exhibiting a fine display of Blue Petering apparatus, the undisciplined cistern was at last patched up by way of elaborate vocabulary, a zip-tie and a cardboard packer. Glowing with the flush of success, the plumber then strutted about the room like a plump rooster fluffing out his feathers. A most irksome spectacle if ever there was one. Rather disappointingly, no further near-cistern drownings or great geyser jettings were experienced during the rest of our stay.

Saying that, we did nearly end up being wiped-out by water. Not the gushing, spouting fountain of the toilet-top sort, but by the treacherous seas of Windermere. It all began when I was having one of my '*aarrrggghhhhhhh*-can't-cycle', cold-turkey moments. Feeling all crabby and crotchety and restless and twitchy from my lack of heavy-panting exercise, I hitched a lift on the builder's back down to Ambleside's Waterhead Pier. Here we hired a Beatrix Potter, dabbling-about-on-rivers-style wooden rowing boat for an hour. In order to release over a week's worth of pent-up energy, my plan was to sit the builder in the back to act as my big, ballasting cox, while I rowed hell-for-leather up and down the largest lake in England until I expired and could return to being a nice and gentle normal person again.

So, all oared up, off we soared at such fine, water-slicing speed that I scattered half the waterfowl of Windermere in my wake. For the first few minutes, I even gave the Bowness ferry a run for its money. A couple of millennia earlier and I could have been giving the Romans a run for their money too; they used Windermere as a waterway for transporting stones and iron ore northwards on the lake. I also gave the builder more than he bargained for by way of several mis-fired strokes and paddle-drenching baths, which, in the rowing-boat trade, I believe is called 'catching a crab'. Had my arms been my legs, I felt quietly con-fident that I could have rowed the ten-mile length of the lake no trouble, and then rowed all the way back again within the allotted hour. But as I don't tend to cycle with my arms, my biceps soon wilted and our speed steadily diminished to a more sedate pace. Also, because my legs were too short to reach the bracing sliders, I kept slipping clean off my thwart, the oars flying out of their thole-pins, which contributes nothing towards a smooth and efficient passage.

The builder, reclining in style in the rear like a parasol-twirling damsel, spent most of his leisurely time revelling in the panoramas and peaks of the sur-rounding Fairfield Horseshoe, High Sweden Bridge, Snarker and Randy Pikes. At times he became so distracted by the all-encompassing mountains that his coxswain duties fell by the wayside, and we ended up having some overly close bow-ramming misses with inconveniently placed rocky outcrops and gin palaces at anchor.

At one point we were chatting away while I was rowing away when the coxswain's placid, sun-dappled features suddenly acquired a countenance of impending doom. Instinctively, I turned to look over my shoulder. A surfer's dream wall of a wave, as fearsome as a Hawaiian curling-cusped Bonsai Pipeline, was hungrily steamrolling towards us. With oars flailing wildly in a state of uncertain anticipation, I emitted a colourful yelp of panic, certain we were about to be swallowed alive by the Loch Ness Tsunami of Windermere.

'She cannae take it, cap'n!' I cried, perhaps a tad melodramatically.

The coxswain, never one to let his feathers ruffle, assessed the situation in a millisecond, before calmly and unflappably advising his oarsman to 'bring her round Jose!' This statement (which has since gone down in the annals of history and been applied to manoeuvring anything from a wheelbarrow to a supermarket shopping trolley) sent me into fits of uncontrollable laughter, but, in the name of self-preservation, I dutifully kept my head and, as instructed, brought the nose of the flimsy craft round to face the menacing maws of the killer wave head-on.

Then, we waited.

White-knuckled and tight-lunged with sickening suspense, I suddenly got hit by another cacophonous fit of nervous laughter. But it was a short-lived fit because, with the black wall of wave almost upon us, everything then went into slow motion. The sun disappeared. The mountains vanished. All forms of life and land were suddenly lost behind an oceanic swell of biblical proportions. There was nothing else for it but to brace ourselves for impact and cling on to the skiff's gunwale, tooth and nail. But it was obvious that without so much as a buoyancy aid between us, she was going to take us under.

When the wave hit, our vessel scaled the cliff of the lip-curling breaker, tottered precariously on the crest for a dubious instant, before plunging over the edge into the snarling jaws of the dark valley below. Here our worst dreams were realised. The wave was not just a rogue – there was a whole wave-train to be sucked into and spat out of. Coaxed by the cox, I hurriedly brought the bow round again for our valiant watercraft to look the heaped and growling, teeth-baring waves full in the face.

Miraculously, and quite unexpectedly, we surged and plunged up and over the whole Titanic roller-coasting wash. Flushed with the elation of survival, we immediately fell into an extended spasm of raucous cock-a-hoop hysterics. Though we had taken several bucketloads of Windermere's waters on board, it was nothing serious enough to warrant a Mayday. But another rowing boat was not so lucky. Packed with a crazy scrum of people, it had taken the waves badly – sideways on. Lying low in the water, there were arms and oars draped all over the side. They looked like a shipwreck crew, the last dregs of survivors from a Cape Horn rip-snorter, adrift for months in the southern ocean. It was a most amusing sight. I couldn't stop guffawing with helpless laughter. The coxswain and I feared if we got any closer we would find a scene of shocking cannibalism with remnants of marrow-sucked limbs lying in the footwell. With a sense of desperate urgency, they rapidly headed back to shore, bailing out as they went.

The question was, where had the waves come from?

'BLOODY SPEEDBOAT!' was the answer, yelled by a most irate man on board a moored sloop. He had been having a quiet glass of wine with his wife in the cockpit when their whole world had turned into a pitching and swinging roll, their single mast pendulously veering from horizon to horizon. Wine, glasses and unwinding crew had gone flying.

'EVERY NOW AND THEN YOU GET SOME RICH GIT THRUSTING HIS SPEED WAY OVER THE LIMIT!' came the shouted explanation.

Mr Sloop was clearly not a happy man.

And so from Mr Sloop to Mr Sloss, the good doctor of Ambleside. He may have told me not to cycle, but that's like telling a sheep not to ruminate. It's an automatic reaction. So, three days before the builder was due to depart the fine tidal wave-washed shores of Windermere, I pretended my foot was all dapper and dandy and we spent the day cycling a phenomenally outstanding 5.5 miles to camp in the lush and brilliantly verdant skirtings of Kirkstone Pass.

That disobedient portion of exercise paid me back by laying me up good and proper for two days flat. On the third day I rose again and mounted the builder's back as far as the bus stop. Here, with our roving Stagecoach Explorer Tickets, we were conveyed in an '*aaarrrrggghhhhhh*-can't-open-the-windows' air-conditioned bus over Kirkstone Pass, which snaked its way between John Bell's Banner, High Hartsop Dod, Lord's Seat, Lingy Crag, Lanty's Tarn, Swineside Knott, Shooting Box, Birk Fell (he was if he did) and Great Mell Fell (really now, you must learn to look before you leap!) to Keswick. This was the first time I had been transported by a motorised vehicle for weeks, if not months, and it only went to emphasise that buses are not a patch on pedals.

The purpose of our machine-driven mission to Keswick was to visit Vic and Karin Gibson and their two boys, twelve-year-old Sam and young teenager Joe. I had known Vic and Karin for nearly twenty years because we all used to see each other a lot in my Liverpool days when I went out with Ward. (Vic and Ward, both journalists, had worked together at the *Wallasey News*.) It was only recently that they had moved from Merseyside to Cumbria, mainly to give Joe and Sam more freedom from the city, to run around in the hills and to play more sports, at which they both excel. Being Scousers at heart, although they made the right move and love it in the Lakes, they have to head south about every six weeks for a goodly dose of Liverpool.

Gary and I found Karin and the boys in Keswick Perfumery, the small, cosy corner shop that Karin opened after giving up working as a nursery nurse in Borrowdale. Because the builder was leaving the next day to get back to his chippying, we only had time for a fleeting visit. Vic works in Carlisle, as News Editor on the *News and Star*, and couldn't get back in time before we had to catch the bus back to base camp. But the rest of us had lunch together in the café across the street and here we caught up on all the hot gossip, which included filling me in on the chaotic love life of Ward. The rest of his life's been pretty chaotic too, by all accounts. Although he's now doing very well living in Glasgow and working as Features Editor on the *Daily Record*, his career has jumped about all over the place over the years since we split up. It seems to have encompassed everything from working as a TV presenter on Janet Street-Porter's *Network 7*, plus a dodgy period working on various sex shows on Channel 5, to moving to Spain to sunbathe on a rooftop (oh, and to do some writing) before moving back to Blighty where he found a job with *Loaded*, the lager-loutish lads' mag, which sent him off on shark-diving missions and suchlike. He then embarked on a Tante Marie cookery course with the idea of becoming a superstar chef and opening a restaurant. (When he rang me up out of the blue one day to ask me for some cheffing tips, I emitted a small guffaw as I visualised his blackened, major fire-and-health-hazard chip pan from our Bournemouth days of yore.) That idea didn't quite materialise as he had envisaged, though he can now rustle up an impressively hearty meal of top-notch restaurant standards. Then it was off to live in Egypt, where he worked as a tour guide for a while.

When he was sacked from that job, he made his way home via Syria. It was here that he very nearly met his maker for the second time (his first near-death experience was when we were cycling to Morocco together and a van crashed into him in Southern Spain). This time around, he was late on joining a bus for a tortuous one-and-a-half-day journey. He had a ticket to sit on the left-hand side of the bus, but when he arrived on board, he found his seat already taken. This wasn't a problem, because there was another seat free on the right-hand side, so he sat there and had quite a fun time chatting to some young army lads who were sitting in the seats around him. At one point on the journey, he suddenly looked up and saw a truck thundering down the road towards them. It hit their bus head on. The impact sent Ward crashing through the window to land in the dirt with his bags. Amazingly, he was okay, but out of a bus of forty-three passengers, he was one of only five survivors. Had he sat in his intended seat, he wouldn't have been so lucky. Everyone down the left-hand side of the bus was killed.

CHAPTER 52

All of a sudden it was time to tally-ho off to dainty dead-end Windermere railway station, where everything suddenly turned into a black-and-white *Brief Encounters* moment as I bid farewell to the builder. I returned to tented base, forlorn, woebegone and heart sore. The next four days were spent eating and ankle-resting in a state of cheerless builder bereavement. Up until this point of my camping career, I had never once been lonesome. Now I felt all pitifully melancholic and pointlessly isolated. But my crestfallen mood of mourning didn't last long. As soon as I stopped moping around by putting mind over wonked Achilles and hitting the road again, I felt fine. Didn't even miss the builder. Well, maybe just a touch, but nothing to make a song and dance about.

Cycling in a mostly one-legged fashion in my lowest gears, I inched southwards in the sun along twisting rolling lanes that climbed among bright green fields speckled with sheep. Some of the sheep were such shirkers that they chomped the grass while kneeling, as if in worship of the sun. I passed Near Orrest, Mislet, Heaning, Hill, Ings, Stavely and Crook. After a mere 15.92 miles, my ankle had had it and I checked into a campsite at Bonning Gate.

It was Sunday, 1st September, a good day to camp at an official site as this weekend had seen a mass exodus of campers and caravanners; the schools went back the following day. The only other tent on site belonged to Harry and Chris, a father and son, and their dog Bonny. When I arrived they were sitting silently side by side in the sun beside their camouflage-green 1973 Land Rover.

To their side, a battered camper's kettle was on the brew, chugging away on a little Trangia stove. Pitched behind them rose their big, no-messing A-frame army surplus Arctic tent containing two army surplus camp beds and two army surplus Arctic sleeping bags. On the floor of the tent was splayed the furry residue of a polar bear cub. At least, that's what it looked like. This was Bonny's bed. I knew all this because after they had finished silently staring at me as I pitched my tent and unpacked my panniers, they showed me the sights of their Arctic home. It smelt something special too.

Both Harry and Chris were big, beefy fellas. Chris, who must have been in his thirties, seemed quite timorous and withdrawn. But Harry, who looked like an East End thug with a squashed nose and cauliflower ears, made up for any taciturnity by talking twenty thousand to the dozen. This was the seventh year in a row they had driven up to Bonning Gate from their home in Diseworth, a small village in Leicestershire. Harry, now an engineer, had been a miner at Diseworth colliery from 1958 to 1984.

'That's when Maggie closed the mines down,' he said. 'Because she knew we were stronger than them. That we could break them, like. Used to earn 60 bob a day, I did, to dig nine linear yards of coal six-foot high. From 6 a.m. till 2.30. Sometimes you'd have to walk three to four mile before you'd even get to t'pit face. If you didn't fill the truck, you were made to stay there till you'd done it – till ten at night if you had to. We worked 3000 foot under ground. Just wore a pair of shorts, like, nothing else. Some parts was a sauna. Other parts could have icicles. It were a hard life, but I loved it. The men, you could trust your life with them, you could. Not where I am now, like, where they stab you in the back.'

Chris, standing at the rear of the open Land Rover where the dog-haired floor served as the kitchen, was making three mugs of tea. Wordlessly, he handed me one. Coal-black, it looked like it had been brewing since the dawn of time. It tasted of musty tents and dead polar bears.

Harry was still breathlessly talking away.

'I'd get back from t'pit,' he said, 'and fall asleep in me dinner. That were how tired I were. All you wanted to do when you got home was sleep. You had no energy to go out, to kick people's doors in like they do today. I tell you, youngsters today, like, they don't know what hard work is. All they want is to get as much money for as little work as possible. That's why this country's gone to the dogs. There's no hope now. I'll tell you something else. The biggest mistake this country ever made was opening the Channel Tunnel. It let all them rag-heads in to take our money, our houses.'

Ooh, a racist rant, eh? I was about to do my bit to 'Say No' to anti-foreigner slurrings, but I couldn't get a word in edgeways. Harry was on the white-supremacy tribal roll. There was no stopping him now.

'Keep all them bloody imports out, I say. They're watering down all us true English blood. You're not daft. You've been to France. You must have seen them all trying to get over here. I'll tell you what, the people I feel sorry for are the old folk. I know I'm getting on meself, like. But it's the old people what put the Great into Britain. They worked hard, like, all their lives and now what do they get?'

I was on the point of opening my mouth to tell Harry he was being a bit out-rageous here, but I wasn't quick enough off the mark because he got in before me and said, 'I'll tell you something else.' (He was telling me a lot here, Harry was. Whether I wanted to hear it or not, which I didn't. At least not the anti-immigrant party political broadcast. But I wasn't here to make wars. All I wanted to do was to go and wash out my socks.)

'The gospel truth, this is. Now, you see this?'

Harry gave his Castrol Oil baseball cap a little nudge upwards, before he dug into the pocket of his army camouflage tracksuit bottoms and pulled out a two-pence piece.

'See that? What's that?' he said, pointing to the object in the palm of his hand.

'It looks like a coin, to me,' I replied, not sure if I liked being tested.

'No!' he laughed, failing me at the first hurdle. 'What's that, right there?'

A dirty-nailed finger pointed directly on top of the tuppence.

'The Queen's head,' I said.

'You're right,' he said.

And I emitted a mini sigh of relief. I've always hated difficult questions.

'And you know what? When she's gone, this country's really going down the plughole. They're all trying to get rid of her, that Blair and Brown. Because of them politician people, this country's gone to ruin. Look at farming. A friend of mine was a pig farmer up till last year. Then we get all that foot-and-mouth fiasco, and now he's got nothing, like.'

At last, I managed to escape to the toilets to have a shower and wash my smalls. On the way back to my tent, I tried to skirt round the side of an empty caravan to avoid any further grilling from Harry. But he detected my presence and homed in on me. For the next forty minutes he told me how he didn't enjoy his engineering job at all, how all the employees come and go and you can't trust anyone. Not like the miners, like, who were there for life. Chris, he could have had a job for life, but Maggie Thatcher put paid to that.

The next morning, when I was packing up my tent, Harry strolled over.

'Tell me something,' he said (and I thought, that makes a change, me telling *him* something). 'What is it about all them fourteen- and fifteen-year-olds getting pregnant and that?'

Oh no, I thought, *he probably thinks I'm a teenager. One of their peers.* I was about to say something banal about, well, how times change and that most girls like a little how's your father. But Harry wasn't really looking for an answer.

'That's what I mean,' he said. 'The country, going to the wall, like. Things were different in my day. You just didn't go round messing with girls and all that at that age.'

When I mounted my steed, ready to take off for Mount Joy, Harry shook my hand in a most notably firm fashion, almost turning it into a crumple zone. For no particular reason that I could fathom, he said, 'I believe what goes around, comes around. If you're good to people, they're good to you back.'

If he conveyed that stance to the 'imports', I thought, then the world would be a rounder and rosier place.

The lane south from Crook to Underbarrow and through Honeybee Wood to Brigsteer was startlingly green and rolling and happily traffic-free. After a clear cold night that had rimmed my tent with the starry sparkle of frost, it turned into a blue, sun-on-back-warming morning. The early air seemed thin and rarified. All I needed for the picture to be perfect was to have an ankle that behaved itself. It wasn't too bad though, as I had adapted a skewed method of cycling that involved not having to extend my Achilles tendon fully. It was not an ideal route to recovery, specially as this weird technique would probably end up bedevilling my knee. I suppose it was a sort of bloody-mindedness, a self-preservation order I had put on myself. Inside I knew I shouldn't really be cycling at all, that I should have gone home with the builder like we had discussed, and given it a proper rest and some physio. Instead I ended up having a tussle between mind and malfunctioning body part. The body part was saying, *Nooooo morrrrre!* While the mind was saying, *Come, come now. Shirk not your ankling duties!* So here I was, cycling down towards Lancashire, enjoying what my eyes were seeing, but not what my foot was feeling.

The first vehicle to pass me in a long time was a tractor. The tractor man leant out of his high-rise cab and shouted, 'You got another person in those

bags?' Then he gave me a little cheering wave and a cheeky face before rumbling off round the corner. A little gesture that made me think it was perhaps
worth knackering my ankle for after all.

But I didn't feel like that for long. The next thing to come my way was a
vehicular fashion show – two tough-as-tanks tower blocks on wheels. The first
was a demonically dashing, four-wheel-drive Freelander, which blasted past in
an unscratched dark green metallic blur. No doubt running late taking tiny
Tristan to school. The second was a pacier-than-a-Porsche Mercedes off-roader.
All spit-and-polish bodywork, and flash twat blacked-out windows. Probably,
more precious little darlings on board. Left in a diesel cloud, I steered myself
back out of the sodden verge and, dusting down my elbows, felt that maybe
such activities as gently wandering the country lanes by bike should be
restricted to experienced members of the Dangerous Sports Club.

At Brigsteer, I dropped down to the pancake-flat of Lythe Valley and skedad-
dled along an exposed, dead-straight lane that cornered only once on a small
stone bridge. It felt slightly dyke-like and the sky suddenly seemed very wide-
screen – all big and blue and billowy with puffy dollops of Persil-white cloud,
skimming along in the lively wind. In the far distance rose the Furness Fells,
while tracking the skyline to the east snaked the chain of the Yorkshire
Pennines.

I rejoined the shoreside at Sandside on the sandy estuary where the River
Kent's broad mud-flats – which provide a home to one of the largest concentrations of birds in Europe – enter the great enclave of Morecambe Bay. A
spectacular railway viaduct, a third of a mile long, connects the two banks at
Arnside, which is where a man, bearded like some Visigoth, collared me.
Bobble-hatted and bifocaled, he was cycling along on a rusty old Rockhopper,
his knees angling outwards like a swaggering cowboy. Obviously not taking
kindly to my overtaking him (dented male pride and all that), he gave chase.
With my wide-eared wing-mirrors, I had him in my sights, so upped the pace
without having to look over my shoulder to monitor the progress of the pedalling pursuer. As I was whipping along at a keen lick, the road suddenly ran
out, not into the sea, but into a footpath that led to the National Trust land of
Arnside Park. This was just as well, really, as there wasn't much point in further
ruining my ankle for the sake of a man in a bobble-hat.

'Where d'ya think ya going with all them bags, like?' he said in an accusato-
rial tone once he had caught his breath.

'Västerbotten,' I replied, mild of manner.

'Oh, rhaat. Yer Scottish?'

This made me laugh. I don't think Västerbotten could sound less Scottish if it tried. Maybe Mr Bobble Hat thought I was swearing in Gallic.

'No,' I said, 'Swedish.'

'Ha! The Land of the Cuckoo Clocks, eh?' he said, very authoritatively.

'No,' I said. 'That's Switzerland.'

Mr Bobble Hat then turned his attention from clocks to computers – cycle computers. Like the one attached to my handlebar stem.

'Look,' he said, 'I've got one of them computer things too. But it don't work. Can ya get it going for me?'

I leant over and had a look. The screen looked a bit dead to me.

'Has it got any batteries in it?' I asked.

'I dunno. S'pose so.'

Then I saw his computer cable was all wrapped round his headset, going nowhere. I looked at his wheel and noticed he was lacking a sensor on his spokes.

'Have you got a sensor for the computer?' I asked.

'A sensor? What's one of them things, like?' he said, adjusting his bifocals.

I was not getting a good vibe from Visigoth Man. There was something unctuous and very creepy-making about him. As I turned to him suggesting he take his bike to a bike shop, I noticed that among all that wiry facial hair he had incredibly glossy lips, as though he had just kissed a toffee apple. He looked at me and I could tell he was not the least bit interested in the workings of his bike computer. He had other things on his mind, none of which I felt were pleasant. When he started enquiring about my saddle, I felt it was high time to be on my way.

Up a steep, ankle-breaking hill I struggled, to the 521-foot grey limestone craggy viewpoint at Arnside Knott, which offered a grand view almost worth re-twanging my tendon for. To the north reared the rugged broken peaks of Cumbria's highest mountains, with Shap Fell tucked further round to the side. Then the ever-perfect presence of the Pennines swept south to the isolated mass of the Bowland Fells, whose gritstone moorland stretches from Botton Head to Wolf Fell. Proffered to me on my panoramic plate down below I had the speed-skimming tides of Morecambe Bay, while beyond that spread the injury-pleasing levelness of the Lancashire Plain.

Before I hit the plain, I had a little dawdle to the Shilla Slopes to see the ruins of Arnside Tower, one of a whole chain of forts built in the fourteenth century as a defence against raids across the Scottish border. Honestly, those mischievous Scots! Why couldn't they be content with staying put in

Västerbotten? Either that or go and nick some of Sweden's cuckoo clocks instead of running amok down here.

And so to silted-up Silverdale. Strange to think that pleasure steamers from Morecambe used to land passengers here, because the deep-water channel of the Kent is now about four miles away. The turn-around occurred in the early 1920s when the river's channel swung westwards, leaving the village high and dry. From here I followed a narrow lane down to Jack Scout and Jenny Brown's Point, once a centre for copper smelting. Now, save for the forlorn gulls, it's all very quiet. Apart from the remains of a slender stone chimney stack there's not a lot to see, except for a vast carpet of springy turf that used to be carved up into strips to surface bowling greens. I cycled back up the lane, skirted the reed and willow marshes of the RSPB reserve at Leighton Moss (where if, unlike me, you're in the right place at the right time, you can see the explosively ping-singing bearded tits – or 'pingers', as twitchers call them – and hear the booming calls of the secretive bittern), careered over Crag Foot, dodged Dog Holes and Three Brothers and let the Lancashire Cycleway carry me to Carnforth.

Speeding cock-leggedly down the traffic-growling A6 towards Morecambe and Heysham, from where I planned to catch the ferry to the Isle of Man, I suddenly decided to 'abandon mission, abandon mission'. The ankle-crumpling hills of the Isle of Man could wait until next year. Instead I would keep to the flatter lands of the Lancashire Plain, where I stood more chance of survival.

But then I paid no heed to my heel and headed off into the killer hills of the Lune Valley. This may sound a foolhardy move in itself, but the mighty River Lune, which rises north of Sedburgh and flows southwestwards to Morecambe, has a name of Celtic origin meaning 'health-giving one', most likely referring to its water god. So to cheer my ankle, I thought I'd offer it a dose of the healing waters. Actually, I thought no such giddy nonsense. I simply fancied escaping inland off the thundering A6 and it was by pure good fortune that the River Lune should lie in my way.

It was also by pure good fortune that, just as my stomach was telling me it would like to find an agreeable location to take on board a spot of lunch, the Crook o' Lune presented itself in the form of a perfectly positioned picnic table overlooking that dogleg crook in the Lune, together with a fine vista of the emerald valley. Just up river lay Kirkby Lonsdale, the town that Charlotte Brontë called Lowton in *Jane Eyre*, and the view from which the nineteenth-century art critic John Ruskin described rather fulsomely as 'one of the loveliest scenes in England – therefore in the world'. Still, there was no getting away from it: the Lune valley was something special all right.

As I was sitting munching my lunch a man on a mountain bike pulled up alongside my table and, standing astride his crossbar, gazed out over the green scene and ribboning river running below us. He exhaled a big sigh of satisfaction.

'Ahh,' he said, 'I can never tire of this view!'

And I knew what he meant; I could imagine it lovely in every light.

The man was not one of Jeremy Clarkson's 'Lycra Nazis'. He was dressed in normal clothes and riding a not very flash bike. His name was Gary and the fact that he was standing beside me, looking out over the waters of 'the health-giving one', was a miracle in itself. By rights, Gary should have been dead. A few years before, when he was 51, he had been working at the nuclear power station in Heysham. He had worked there for years.

'I loved the job,' he said, 'climbing up pylons and working with a good bunch of lads.' Then his bones started to ache. 'I might have been a bit over-weight,' he said. 'I liked my drink – perhaps a little too much. Being a little heavy made climbing up the pylons hard work, but I had never been ill in my life.'

His doctor thought the aches and pains were down to rheumatism, but Gary wasn't convinced. He felt there was something more to it. It took second and third opinions and four months of blood tests before he was diagnosed with leukaemia. Endless sessions of chemotherapy ensued. For two years he was life-threateningly ill. He got septicaemia. Then his lungs collapsed, his liver col-lapsed and virtually every other organ caved in. For two-and-a-half months he was in a coma. When he finally woke up he thought he had just been asleep for a night. But he couldn't ask anyone what was going on because he was full of tubes and so drugged-up to the eyeballs he kept hallucinating. The doctors couldn't believe he was still alive. Nor could his family.

Now, with his cancer in remission, he had given up drink and bought a bike.

'Someone had given me a second chance at life, so I thought I'd show my appreciation by bloody well getting healthy!' he said.

Instead of going back to work he decided to take early retirement because he didn't want to keep working only to find he would never have a chance to do all the things that he had wanted to do with his family. So he bought a camper van and toured Spain for three months with his wife.

'I don't have so much money now, but money isn't everything,' said Gary. 'Instead I can come down here every day if I want. I tell you, after what I've been through, a view like this even looks good in the rain now!'

No sooner had Gary gone when a silver-haired woman on a small-wheeled shopper pulled up at my table beside her burly, bike-pushing husband.

'Excuse me, luv,' she said, indicating the bench seat on the opposite side of the table. 'Would you mind if we sat here for a moment?'

I didn't mind at all, so they sat down, backs towards me, faces facing the Lune, and proceeded to unpack their picnic lunch from parcels of carefully wrapped tinfoil. I started writing my diary, but I couldn't concentrate because it was too exciting waiting to see what was about to appear from the silvery packs of foil.

' 'Ere you are, luv,' she said, handing her husband a white ham sandwich. He took it without saying a word, just kept looking at the Lune as he took a hulking mouthful.

'Lovely 'ere, in't it?' she said all chirpy.

'Aye,' he said.

A moment elapsed. She handed him a square of kitchen towel. He took it, wordlessly. Another moment elapsed. They continued to sit, view-gazing.

'Ooh, look. Are they fishing?' she said.

'Aye,' he replied.

And that was it for a while. They both sat in silence as they ate their sandwiches, a pork pie and a scotch egg. And I thought: *I bet this is what it's like at home. She's all bright and breezy, running around making his dinner, washing his clothes, and he just sits in his chair, reading his paper, being Mr Monologue.*

' 'Ave you finished, luv?' she asked.

'Aye,' he said.

She retrieved the opened tinfoil pack off his lap, shook it free of crumbs, and folded it very carefully into four. *I bet she's going to reuse that,* I thought. Because that's exactly what I would do.

'Are you ready for your coffee now?' she asked.

'Aye,' he said. 'That would be nice.'

And I thought: *Ooh! We have a development here! He's turning conversational!*

A thermos appeared, a lid was unscrewed, and a plastic mug of coffee was poured.

' 'Ere you are, luv,' she said, handing it to him.

He took it without a word of thanks and then said, 'They're fly-fishing, you know.'

'Oh, is that right, luv?'

And nothing else was said.

I wrote all this down in my diary and then gathered all my plastic food bags together, ready to leave. When I cycled with my sister-in-law Mel to Morocco, she would dare me to go up to complete strangers (usually middle-aged Brits holidaying in Spain) and proffer the opener, 'I hear they've had a lot of rain in Vlissingen!' While they stared at me in a state of stunned bafflement, I would glance over their shoulder and catch sight of Mel creased up in hysterics. Some people might consider this as rather strange behaviour, but it wasn't half fun, and we did get to meet some quite splendid people this way. Anyway, as I stood at the Crook o' Lune packing up my food pannier, I suddenly felt sorely tempted to say to my table-sharers, 'I hear they've had a lot of rain in Vlissingen!' But instead, I heard myself saying, 'Do you come here often?' Which is probably just as bad.

'No, luv,' said the woman, swivelling her silver perm to talk to me. 'We just thought that now that they've built the Lune cycle path, we'd try riding up here from Lancaster. It's only a couple of mile from where we live.'

Then she told me it was the first time she had ridden a bike for forty years.

'I feel ever so unsteady,' she said. 'I think I need some "L" plates! I suppose I just need to get my confidence. But I can't imagine ever feeling brave enough to cycle on the road. I don't know how you do it – what with carrying all that load, like. You must be a right plucky little thing!'

As I cycled off, heading for Caton, Corney Hill, Windy Clough and Shooters Pile, it struck me that when Mrs Silver Perm last rode a bike there were about 5 million vehicles registered in Britain, half of them cars. In 1951 there had been 4 million vehicles in Britain (of which 2 million were cars). Fifty years later there were nearly 30 million vehicles, 25 million of which were cars. Only the previous week I had read in the *Observer* how 'Gridlock is here to stay as traffic hits record level'. An article written by Kamal Ahmed, the Political Editor, said:

A future of massive traffic jams and gridlock across Britain will move a step closer this week as new figures reveal that traffic on the country's congested roads has reached record levels . . . Transport analysts are now predicting rising numbers of 'mega-jams' – tailbacks of more than 10 miles – as cars try to squeeze on to ever busier roads.

Further on I read of a report from the Office of National Statistics (ooh, don't we love them?) that would reveal that Britons drove nearly 296 billion miles on the roads in 2001, an increase of 5 billion miles on the year before. If the increases were maintained it was predicted that, by early 2003, the figure was likely to break the 300-billion-mile mark for the first time. So, let me see now.

We're a small island nation of 59 million people owning 30 million vehicles, driving 300 billion miles a year. That seems to me to be equivalent to driving around the earth several thousand million times a year.

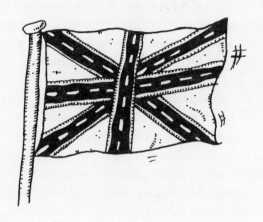

CHAPTER 53

The wild collision of moorland fells on the Yorkshire border is Lancashire at its loneliest. Instead of cycling on the flats beside the sea, I felt myself drawn upwards to the isolated gritstone moors of the Bowland Fells. I blame a signpost for my misdemeanours in leading me so astray. The 'Trough of Bowland', it said in alluring tongue. How could anyone heading to Blackpool ignore that? I certainly couldn't – even with an angry ankle. So up I went to the desolate pass of Bowland's Trough, bidding good day as I did so to the likes of Rotten Hill, Balderstones, Swine Crag, Sniddle Holes and Shooting Box. It was wild and wonderful and I sped back downwards by way of the deeply incised river valley of the Wyre.

I camped that night on the Lancaster Canal. It's a busy bit of land round here, severed by the north–south arteries of the M6, the A6, the mainline railway and the canal. The tent spot I found was on a farm. A few caravans were lined in a row, all (save two) closed up for winter. The field belonged to Olive Halton. I only knew this because just as I was knocking on the door of the bungalow to ask if I could camp at the bottom of the field, a car pulled up and a small stocky man in his late sixties said, 'You looking for Ollie Halton?'

'I suppose I could be,' I said.

'Ollie's on 'oliday!' called a head over a hedge. It was attached to a grey-bearded man standing on the roof of a moored canal boat. 'Won't be back for a week.'

'That's a bother!' said the stocky man, 'I was looking for her myself.' Then, leaning into his car, he pulled out a white plastic tube. 'Know what this is?' he said.

And I thought: *Oh no! Not more difficult questions!* At least it didn't have the Queen's Head on it to trip me up.

'It's a white plastic tube,' I said, because I felt I couldn't go too far wrong if I stated the obvious.

'It's one of five posts I use to keep cars from driving on to the grass verge outside my house.' *How the sweet Douglas Adams was I supposed to know that?* 'The other four have been stolen. That's the second time. I bet it's them bloody lads again. I was wondering if Ollie had seen any lying around. They tend to throw them over the hedge.'

Then he pointed to the top of the tube and fired me with Testing Question No. 2.

'Know what this is?' he said. *Hands on the buzzer. Starter for 10. No conferring.*

'It looks like a castor-protector.'

'Correct. And you know what they're for?' (Testing Question No. 3.)

'What, castor-protectors? They prevent furniture wheels from leaving a dent in the carpet.'

'That's right.' *Advance to Pall Mall. If you pass 'GO' collect £200.* 'I found they were just the right size to fit the tube-ends. Gives them a neat finish.'

And I thought: *Do I really need to know this?*

'I'm Gerald, by the way,' said Gerald, and he put out his hand and I shook it. 'You an Ozzie?'

'No,' I said, 'I'm English.'

'You sound like an Ozzie. Been watching too much *Neighbours*?'

'No,' I said. 'I've never watched *Neighbours* in my life. I haven't got a television.'

'Oh. Must be the way young people talk these days. My daughter's the same. She's from Lancashire but she lives in Milton Keynes and now sounds like an Ozzie. It's the questioneering intonation you young things stick on the end of words.'

I felt a bit put out. I didn't think I sounded like Kylie Minogue on the rear of my words.

'I haven't had a lot of practice at talking lately,' I said in my defence. 'So whatever I say is going to come out funny.'

Then Gerald patted me on the bum with the end of his tube.

'You're a lovely girl!' he said. 'You not wed yet?'

I suppose there are some women who would be most affronted by this, and give him a good theatrical slap about the chops. But I didn't really have the energy to get all het up. Instead I simply said, 'No, I'm a lesbian.' Just in case he was thinking of proposing. I also thought that it might pipe him down a bit, though on the other hand, it could of course pipe him up even more.

With a downward pipe he drove off back home, no doubt looking behind hedges for castor-covered white plastic tubes, leaving me to have a little weather-talk with a retired couple in a caravan ('I hear they've had a lot of rain in Vlissingen' – or something like that) and put my tent up in the corner of the field.

A little later on Gerald returned. I was hanging my washing – namely knickers and socks – off the sheep-netting fence and my looped brake cables.

'It's all right, I'm not looking!' he said, looking. 'You probably don't want me to see your smaller garments!'

I could see I had a bit of a dirty old duffer on my hands.

'I was just wondering if you fancied a tipple,' he said. 'Or a cup of tea if you prefer. I was telling the wife about you. Says she'd love to meet you.'

I thanked him, but said I didn't have the energy. He was quite pushy and said it was only for a quick chat and he could give me a lift back to his house right now. I said it was against my policy to get in cars with strange men. He laughed and said he could understand. Then he told me I could walk there as it was only a hundred yards down the road. I said I couldn't walk as I'd hurt my ankle. He suggested I cycle, then. I said I didn't want to cycle because that would disturb my washing line. In the end he gave up, which is what I had been hoping he'd do.

My ankle could at last breathe a sigh of relief – I had finally reached the broad, flat peninsula of the Fylde, which lies between the estuaries of the Lune and the Ribble. 'Fylde' is an old name meaning simply 'plain'. The Fylde is not only flat, but fertile farmland too. Quite fen-like in its dyke-like ways. There's even the odd windmill thrown in for good measure.

At one point I passed a phone box on a small, quiet junction outside Cogie Hill Farm. I had just turned right for Cumming Carr and Stake Pool, when I heard the phone start ringing. There was no one around so I turned back and went to answer it.

'Hello?' I said.

'Hello?' said a woman's voice.

'Hello!' I said, adopting a slightly different tone.

'You've just rung my number,' said the woman, sounding a bit cross.

'No, I haven't,' I replied, thinking: *keep your hair on!* 'I was just cycling past this phone box so I thought I'd answer it!'

'Who am I speaking to?' asked the woman.

'A cyclist!' I said. 'You won't know me. I'm from Västerbotten.' Or was I from Australia? It was all getting so confusing.

There was a moment's silence.

'I've just rung 1471,' said the woman, 'and your number came up. I thought you might be ringing about the chickens.'

'Chickens?' I said, emitting a mini splutter of astonished laughter. 'No, that wasn't me. I don't need any chickens. I haven't got room in my panniers.'

'What?'

'I don't need any chickens. I'm in a phone box. Maybe the person before me wanted your chickens . . .'

And then the line went dead. Oh well, I was only trying to help.

The next oddity to come my way was a sun-shimmering sheep mirage: waves of white wool pitching and rolling up and down the slight undulations of the narrow, straight lane. A farmer was moving his flock of sheep down the road in front of me. I brought up the rear and was rewarded with the fine spectacle of a hundred rollicking rumps charging into the distance. It seemed so rural out here that it was strange to think the busy bustle of Blackpool lay a mere willy warmer away. To put off the city life for as long as possible, I looped-the-loop up and down the lanes around Pilling Moss, Hale Nook and Out Rawcliffe – jerky cornering ways with names like Turkey Street and Knitting Row Lane. I passed fields of Friesians and ripening corn-cobs and hectic haymaking. The black-berries were blackening and furry-leafed applemint grew in profusion in the sheltered base of the hedgerows. The wasps were awake, the bees were abuzz, and the busily chattering swallows lined up for roll-call on the telephone wires in preparation for their long trek south for winter.

After pedalling through Pilling and reaching a dead-end at Knott End, I headed south down the Wyre through Height o' th' Hill and Hambleton. I wasn't in the mood for urbanisation, so I hurried through Skippool and Thornton, past the electricity sub-station and the chemical works to Fleetwood.

Here I took flight to Cleveleys and shot down through North Shore, tracking the tramway to Blackpool.

A steep, chill, sun-gilded cloud covered the darkened city as I glided along the Golden Mile, glancing towards the steel ice-cream-cone Tower, the Prom, the Pleasure Beach and the blue curving spinal columns of the Big One (Europe's tallest roller-coaster). I didn't do anything that most people come to Blackpool for because I didn't come to Blackpool to do anything other than slide down its side in a spin. I didn't enter the giant, pirate's skull portals of Coral Island bemusement arcade to play psychotic video games. I didn't wander around any Winter Gardens or waxworks of Madame T's, or see any life in the Sea Life Centre. I saw no shows nor sucked no rock. I didn't turn my knuckles white or chill my spine on any clattering roller-coaster rides, or spend any dosh on jellied eels, false ears or willy warmers. I didn't straddle any donkeys on the sands of the windswept beach or take a promenade down a finger of pier.

But I did do something. I navigated a treacherous route around a swarming straggle of tourist coaches disgorging gaggles of rebellious geriatrics. And I bought a stash of saucy but corny postcards. One of these I sent to my mother. It pictured a couple sitting side by side in bed. A big, buxom woman with long-lashed eyebrows and hair in rollers sat looking fed up with a worried and wimpy bald man with a moustache wearing green, stripy winceyette pyjamas. From out of his head ballooned a speech bubble:

'Do you think the doctor could give me some pills to improve my sex urge?'

'No lad,' replies Mrs Buxom with hands on hips. 'He can only heal the sick – not raise the dead!'

Down the coast at the mouth of the Ribble sits the more upmarket Lytham St Anne's – or, as this four miles of sea-fronted buzz-cut lawns and gardens and parkland is known, Leafy Lytham. With its four surrounding golf courses, the town seemed to be full of putting greens and bowling greens and cricket greens. I wound round the edge of the Fylde's southwest corner, the onshore wind whipping me along to Warton, Freckleton, Clifton and Preston.

Preston was mayhem. Unfortunately I had arrived in time for the afternoon rush-hour. I paused only to use the toilets in strip-lit Morrisons, and read the headline in the *Lancashire Evening Post*: 'Maniacs Attack Preston Schoolgirls'. Well, that's nice, I thought, and hurried on to Hutton. By the time I got there

I was feeling all pent up from the mad dashing down death-trap dual car-riageways and the troubling clouds of a darkening day. So, at West Lancs Police HQ, I veered off for New Longton where I found three dilapidated moss-stained caravans sitting in a road-enclosed, dog-fouled field. The caravans belonged to a bunch of builders working on a site in Preston and were clearly their homes. The field belonged to Madge, a strong Lancs-accented woman in a nearby bungalow.

'Want a brew, luv?' she asked after allowing me to camp on her land.

Ben, a chained-up sheepdog, went berserk when I biked in, straining at its leash, snapping at my tyres.

'I wish a vehicle would clip 'im one to teach 'im not to run after cars, like,' she said.

Madge was having an extra room built on to the end of her bungalow. It was still only in its skeletal stage of construction.

'You know, luv,' said Madge, 'it's taken seven weeks just to get this far because them builders can't stop falling off the roof, like. They keep taking time off in hospital. At this rate, I reckon it'll be Christmas by the time them lot get finished.'

That evening I walked along the road to a phone box and rang mum. She said she'd been to the dentist that day and had to have a tooth pulled out. But it was a stubborn tooth – fixed in there so firmly that the dentist had to put his knee on mum's chest and pull with all his might.

'We're having a bit of trouble here,' said the dentist, somewhat understat-edly.

But even with the aid of the knee, it still took over ten minutes of tugging and wrenching and yanking before the tooth gave up the fight and pulled free. The dentist, drenched in sweat, had to have a sit down. The dentist's assistant looked like she had seen a ghost.

'And I went all shaky,' said mum, laughing down the line.

By this stage I was laughing so much that people walking past the phone box were giving me a strange look. The dentist asked mum how she had got to the surgery.

'I cycled,' said mum.

'Well, I think you had better go and have a lie down before you get back on your bike,' advised the dentist.

Mum had felt no such horizontal desires and cycled the nine hilly miles home.

Next I rang the builder. Since I first met him when he worked for a firm of builders, he had now switched jobs and become a carpenter with the Green Oak Carpentry Company, which makes traditional bespoke oak-framed buildings (yes, I'll be taking orders after the show). After a bit of chat I made the mistake of asking him what he had been making that day. Well, it would seem that earlier on he had cut some jack rafters which were joined to pre-Georgian hips with a nun's crutch (chippy-speak for a cradle joint). This was followed by some dihedral angles on hip rafters and some side-halved and bridled butts. Then he turned his attention to a counter-tongued and grooved, stop-splayed and tabled scarf with sallied abutment, under-squinted with a transverse key and wedged and fixed with four-edge pegs and eight-face pegs. Apparently, if you're still with me, this thirteenth-century technique is the best joint in framing as the strength exceeds half that of unjointed timber. This was more information than I needed so I went to wash my socks.

CHAPTER 54

Beneath a spongy sky, I hurtled off to Much Hoole, turned off at Tarleton and took the back roads to Banks, criss-crossing a straight, flat grid of salad-growing fields and furlongs of greenhouses. Most of the pickers and packers were East Europeans and Asians, prepared to work hard for little reward. Despite the wet and muddy conditions, they seemed a cheerful lot and waved to me merrily as I bowled on by.

At Fiddler's Ferry, Merseyside greeted me by way of a sewage works and a sand extraction plant that hoovers the sand off Southport beach, reputedly to send it off to the Middle East. It was a hard, straight stretch past Angry Brow into a fierce, teeth-snarling headwind as I followed the endless road that ran bang beside the ceaseless miles of bleak, featureless, rain-lashed beach. In town, I picked up a copy of the *Parish Newsletter* of St Marie's, Southport, in which I later read the small ad: 'Has anyone got a bike for a man that they don't want any more?'

Further on, past the oceans of dunes and the holiday centre, I stopped to use the toilets in the caravan park beside Woodvale Airfield. Norman, the man at the busy reception (they were having a Caravan Club meet), greeted everyone, whether in person or on the phone as, 'All right me son?' When a police siren sped by on the A565, he said, 'I better hide, like. That'll be me mother-in-law coming to get me!'

I had to head on to the A565 myself – a horrible road of dual carriageways and speeding traffic. Earlier that day, as I was adding a bunch of bananas to my cargo in Tarleton, a man had drawn up beside me in his car. He told me he was a cyclist but no longer rode along the A565 after a car tried to knock him off, which wasn't the sort of goodwill message I wanted to hear before diving on to it myself.

Unfortunately, there's no alternative coast road from Southport to Liverpool. I toyed with the idea of heading way off course inland to ride beside the Leeds and Liverpool canal, but then the man told me that he'd ridden down there the other day and some parts were so overgrown with skin-ripping brambles and briars that he had almost fallen in trying to avoid them. On top of this, the headline on the local paper told of an Ormskirk man who had drowned yesterday after coming off his mountain bike and falling into the canal. As I didn't fancy adding to the canal's collection of corpses, rusty bicycles and shopping trolleys, the A565 it was.

So, riding assertively, which is just another way of saying I rode with a defensive '*don't even think about messing with me*' demeanour, I pounced on my pedals and careered past Formby, Ince Blundell and Crosby to Bootle. On the finishing straight into Liverpool, I followed the seven-mile length of the once-great docks that had boomed during the eighteenth and nineteenth centuries, making Liverpool one of the biggest and most prosperous ports in the world.

In a blink of sun I pulled up at Pier Head at the Mersey Ferry and was just in time to roll straight on board for take-off. It's funny how little things fix themselves in your memory: standing on deck the thought of Ward suddenly came flooding back. I was just eighteen, he was nearly twenty-five and in his tasteful wooing ways he was so busy snogging me on my first trip across the Mersey that he pressed me backwards over the upper-deck railings to such a back-breaking extent that I could see the petrified effigies of the Liver Birds, with wide wings outstretched, upside down.

Disembarking on the other side, I was wheeling my mount past the barricades of people when I heard someone calling me. I turned and saw some wildly semaphoring arms and moments later I was being bear-hugged by Paul and Hazel, Keswick Perfumery Karin's ever-vivacious mum and dad who lived just up the road in Wallasey. It was a lovely surprise to see them. They bought me tea in the ferry terminal café and we caught up on news and gossip. Since I last saw them, Paul had had not so much a triple-heart bypass as a 'cinque' by-pass.

'They pulled my heart out,' said Paul very matter-of-factly, 'took a vein from my leg, then flopped my heart back in. Now I've never felt better!'

Paul used to be a merchant seaman and remembers the days when the docks were a hive of activity and massive ships were lined up and down the Mersey. Both he and Hazel wanted me to come and stay with them, but I had to press on as mum and dad had suddenly decided to go holidaying in Wales and were keen to meet me somewhere along the north coast.

New Brighton, Wallasey's Mockbeggar Wharf, Hoylake and West Kirby all seemed very familiar despite the fact that I hadn't been there for years. Ward and I used to spend a lot of time up here on the tip of the Wirral, the peninsula washed on the west with the estuary of the Dee, and to the east with the mighty Mersey. After Ward, I still came up here to see Vic and Karin. Sometimes, when they were having one of their parties, I would finish cooking in London on Friday night, then get on my bike and cycle to Wallasey in time for the Saturday night happenings. At some unearthly hour of the morning, I would leave the party when it was still in full swing and cycle off into the eerie, sodium-lit night through the industrial and port conurbations of Birkenhead and Bebington where, down at the docks, the darkness was punctuated by splashes of surreal light from arc lamps and welders' blow torches. Then it was on to Eastham, Hooton, Sutton, Moston and Chester and its empty, dark, cold railway station to lie on a bone-chilling metal bench waiting in the pre-dawn an hour or more for the boat train from Holyhead to scoop me up and trundle me back to London in time to start cooking again.

This time round things were slightly more civilised and I weaved my way down the Wirral's west coast through Heswall, Neston and Puddington before I was sucked up at Shotwick by the boorish antics of a truck-rumbling trunk road hell-bent on spitting me out into Wales. But I said no to death at the Dee and swerved off at a life-snuffing flyover to re-establish my pulse on a pavement bordering an army camp. By lucky chance I looked up and saw a Sustrans National Route Network sign. I followed the wheeled way, which led me at a sedate and pensive pace past an industrial estate, a steel works, a sewage works and over the clack-eting-racketing wooden slats of a railway bridge. Sometimes cycle paths are the most insane, hair-tearing things in the world when they are mined with multiple vehicle-priority pavement-painted markings, six-inch kerb-drops, shattered glass and parked cars, or planted with bus shelters and lampposts and bollards perfectly positioned to send you colliding and careering head first over the handlebars. Other times they are a gift from the gods, especially when they prevent you from becoming overfamiliar with the undertowing undercarriage of a road-roaring juggernaut on an overpass outside Queensferry.

I found a place to camp up near Pabo and Pydew in a sloping garden full of butt-biting geese. I'd stopped there because I had spotted a caravan tucked behind a bush and in the same way as what's good for a goose is good for a gander, I thought what's good for a caravan is good for a camper. Sitting in the window of the caravan were a man and a woman. When they saw me squelch up, they gave me a little 'bloody-awful-weather!' wave. Attached to the caravan was a tent-awning carbuncle. Moments later the arched doorway zip was unzipped and the woman said, 'We're just having a cuppa, luv. Want to join us?'

Under normal circumstances (whatever *they* are) I would have, but at that moment I was too road-lagged and too wet and too intent on pitching my tent before I lost more of my rump to the bill-hissing geese. No sooner had I erected my sopping home than the caravanning woman appeared beneath a halo of brolly.

'I don't accept "no" as an answer!' she said, handing me a fat flask of tea, a jug of milk and a saucer of Hob-Nobs. She told me she was from Salford, just outside Manchester.

'We got kids your age,' she said. 'So we want to look after you proper!'

Later I discovered her two children were mere teenagers. How depressing.

My dawn was damp, still and dirty grey. But by the time I was cycling up round the snake's head of Great Orme, a massive limestone headland nearly 700 feet high, a small sun showed dimly through the thinning gauze of cloud, like a shadowy headlamp, silvering a ruffled streak of water across Llandudno Bay.

Because I like to cycle round coastal lumps and headlands and islands as close to the sea as possible, I chose to ride round Great Ormes Head in a clockwise direction. But, according to the road-planning gods, who like to make finger-shaking rules, I shouldn't have done because, unbeknownst to me, Marine Drive (the toll road that loops the Great Head) is a one-way only-way roadway.

And I was going the wrong way.

How the sweet Bryan Adams was I supposed to know that? I wasn't born with a coagulating one-way system in my blood. I was born with a whichever-way-is-fine-way flowing fancy-freely on the highway through my veins. And anyway, there was nothing to tell me on the Gogarth side that it was a one-way only-way silly-way road. Apart from a big red no-entry sign. But I didn't hit that till I was halfway up the precipice, and when you've got a saggy ankle to pacify, you're in no position to tell it to re-do what you've just done, only the other way round.

So yes, you oncoming motorists, you may look daggers and shake your fists at me. But, see here, I'm forcing myself to yield unto thee, by keeping tucked in tight to the pathway, and walking where I must so not to vex you further on your vehicular way. Still, I think the Marine Driveway should be a Marine Cycleway, as this is the only way to travel in a flexi-way either way up and down the narrow way of this most spectacular of snaking-head byways.

Someone else who was not ecstatic about the motor traffic round here was Jane Jones. I met her round the other side as I was falling (the wrong way) down the cliff-hanging drop towards Great Ormes Happy Valley. She was cycling up (the right way on the one-way) on a Scott mountain bike. Because of my past penned offerings, she seemed to know all about me. I did my best on catching up on knowing her. She was forty-two, had a six-year-old daughter, Katy, and was married to Graham, who ran the outdoor centre somewhere near Llandudno. Jane hailed from Stoke, had lived in Wales a while and would be in Llandudno for at least another five years. She and Graham had once talked about living abroad.

'But we're getting a bit old for that now!'

Jane was also super-fit. She was once a top runner but then her hip gave up the ghost so two years ago she took to her bike and now loves it. She wasn't so keen on the taxi drivers of Llandudno, who kept cutting her up, as did the town's copious supply of oldies hunched behind the wheel.

'There're so many pensioners living here who are such bad drivers,' said Jane. 'They just can't seem to see cyclists!'

As a result she was campaigning to try to allow cycling on the prom.

At Llandudno Junction I was swept across a sandy span of tide-swept estuary into the medieval garrison town of Conwy. With the foothills of Snowdonia providing a dramatic backdrop, Conwy is dominated by the magnificent crenellated, gritty-stoned bulk of Edward I's military masterpiece, the thirteenth-century Conwy Castle. This mother of all castles, with its soaring curtain walls, indented-edged battlements and eight massive round towers, was strategically placed in this corner of northwest Wales in order to subdue and contain the Welsh. (Don't tell me they were nicking church bells too.) Anyway, Conwy's walled town is also most enchanting although Thomas Pennant, the eighteenth-century writer and traveller, didn't seem to think so. 'A more ragged town is scarcely to be seen, within', he said, though he did add 'or a more beautiful, without'. I think that is what's called talking in swings and roundabouts.

The only road to follow the mountainous coast is the motorway-like A55 (T) – 'T' for terrible Trunk. This road, reverberating with the tremors of traffic, is hemmed in by quarried scarps of ancient limestone and granite, and has the inconvenient habit of diving in and out of NO CYCLISTS ALLOWED tunnels. *Oh no! Not Terrible Tunnels as well as Terrible Trunks!* Struck down in a dithering dilemma as I was, Sustrans suddenly came up trumps with a quandary-saving cyclepath. So while the swishes of fast-growling traffic disappeared into the gaping black mouths of the tunnels (one of which, I noted, was built in my mother's year of birth, and again I'm pleased to say both mother and tunnel are ageing well), Sustrans took me on a jolly seaside caper right around the rocky projections of the 1000-foot walls of the over-quarried mountain of Penmaen Mawr into the squeezed-between-mountain-and-sea coastal resort of Penmaenmawr itself.

Earlier in the day, when I had said the word 'Penmaenmawr' to a Welshman, he had looked at me as if I was from Västerbotten, but then this could have been because of my hugely unwholesome mispronunciation. I still don't know how to pronounce it correctly, but what I can do is to dissect it into three: *pen* means 'head', *maen* means 'stone' and *mawr* means 'big'. Hence, Big Stony Head mountain, which is a hell of a lot easier to say. Big Stony Head Mountain would be even bigger and stonier and headier if all the years of extensive quarrying hadn't removed so much of its granite. Many a millennium ago, Penmaenmawr's mountain was losing its rocks for other reasons; in Neolithic times it was the centre of an axe factory, as its particular igneous-rock outcrop was just the ticket for shaping into implements. Nearby at Graig, the slopes are still strewn with the waste from the prehistoric workshops, from where axe-heads, adzes, chisels and hammerstones found their way to various parts of the country.

It was all going so well on my super-smooth super-cycling highway, happily void of all other forms of pedalling or perambulating life (I even spotted a couple of whiskery seals' faces bobbing like upturned bottles offshore) when, all of a sudden, I was rudely jettisoned back to join the thundering tyre-swishing expressway. I survived as far as Llanfairfechan (don't you swear at me), where I spun up the first escape route and then proceeded to Bangor on minor roads through Nant-y-Pandy (which I always thought was a children's TV programme), Gorddinog, Abergwyngregyn, Ty' n-yr-hendre (I'll tie what I want, thanks), Tal-y-bont and Penryn's nineteenth-century neo-Norman castle with its one-ton slate bed (made for Queen Victoria) and a slate Grand Staircase that took ten years to build. (Ten years? Don't tell me her builders kept falling through the roof like Madge's.)

And so to 'upper row of rods in a wattle fence', the university town more - commonly known as Bangor. It made a change to arrive in a place that I could actually pronounce, which is more than can be said for Llanfairpwllgwyngyllgogerychwyrndrobwllllantysiliogogogoch, the village that lies in long-winded saliva-flying style on the other side of the Menai Straits. My map had this Anglesey village written as Llanfairpwllgwyngyll, the shortest postally acceptable version. The full teeth-rattling mouthful, apparently devised by a local tailor in late Victorian times, is based on blending the names of two parishes together and translates as 'St Mary's Church in the hollow of the white hazel near the fierce whirlpool, with the Church of St Tysilio close by the Red Cave'.

After taking the obligatory snapshot of the platform sign at Llanfairpwllgwyngyllgogerychwyrndrobwllllantysiliogogogoch railway station (due to popular tourist-attraction demand, British Rail reopened the village's station in 1973, several years after it had been closed as part of Beeching's cuts), I sped northwards past the fancy cliff-clinging villas facing the racing waters of the Strait and the distant knife-edge ridges of Snowdonia. On through Beaumaris ('beautiful marsh'), which owes its name not to the Welsh but to the Norman-French of Edward I who built the last castle here as part of his 'iron ring' chain of north Wales fortresses. Further on, just past the ruined priory at Penmon, I came to a halt at the rocky spur on Anglesey's eastern tip. After days of rain, ensconced in a uniform wash-grey of sea and sky, now, as I stood near Black Point lighthouse, the sun came back from exile.

The view was spectacularly sparkling. Across the Menai Straits I could see the serrated bastions of Snowdonia. To the east over Conwy Bay I was able to trace my route all the way from the one-way system of Great Ormes Head, past the quarries of Big Stony Head Mountain to Bangor. Closer by, less than a mile off shore, rose the craggy lozenge of Puffin Island. Although vast numbers of birds like cormorants, fulmars and shags flock to the island to populate the blue-grey limestone cliffs, the puffins that gave the island its name are a lot less numerous now than they used to be, thanks to copious quantities of rats robbing the puffin burrows of eggs and young. Also, over the centuries, French and English gourmets' taste for pickled puffin didn't help matters by decimating the birds' numbers. Every year for many years, thousands of boned puffin carcasses were exported in barrels of spiced vinegar.

If I was to walk from here to Holyhead, I would be treading where the saints had trod. St Seiriol the White, who in the sixth century established a monastic community at Penmon, and his friend, Sy Cybi the Yellow, who created a monastery at Holyhead, used to walk daily the twenty-five miles between the opposite tips of Anglesey to meet and discuss matters spiritual. Seiriol, who had to walk west in the morning and east in the afternoon, always had his back to the sun and so remained pasty faced. Cybi, on the other hand, was always facing the sun and so acquired a tan of bronze.

This made me think that if Cybi was always facing the sun, then the weather was definitely better in the good old days of yore. Now it's all doom and gloom and sopping socks. According to the latest UK Climate Impacts Programme report (a stormy mouthful in itself), British winters will become fives times wetter over the next 100 years with the season marked by a string of ferocious storms. The weather people, who apparently know these things, say that the sodden summer I had just cycled through has merely marked the latest watershed in the rising volatility of Britain's weather. Those in the know hark on about how evidence that Europe is entering a new climatic age, characterised by unforgiving downpours and flooding, has become compelling. While I'd thought I had it wet when I had been riding through the mountains and moorlands and downlands and dales of the north a month or two ago, in August, the Continent had been buckling under its worst storms for 2000 years. Two of central Europe's architectural gems – Prague and Dresden – suffered massive flood damage that summer: I later discovered that the entire rainfall of a typical August had fallen in thirty-six hours and that Belgium, not wanting to be outdone, had endured the wettest year on record for 150 years in 2002. The year was not a dry one for Ireland, either: it would turn into the wettest since records had begun 110 years before. Irish weather became so miserable that it rained almost half the time during 2002.

Going back to 'real time' in mid September, the good news was that, as I had taken so long to do so little in so far as I had never made it round the intended coast of Scotland, I had missed out on joining the Scots as they suffered their soggiest summer for sixty-four years, nor did I celebrate with them their wettest October on record.

And the reason for all this? Climatologists maintain that weather patterns are cyclical, pointing their climatological fingers at fundamental changes in climate throughout history. It would seem the UK was warmer only a thousand years ago. Evidence has it that grapes were grown then in the lowlands of Scotland, a feat that is impossible today – thankfully, as who wants a lily-livered glass of wine when you can have a strapping bowl of stodgy porridge?

Along with the summers that used to be more summery, winters used to be more wintery. Nigel Bolton, the national forecaster for the Met Office, recently warned us in the *Observer* not to forget that '200–300 years ago the River Thames was freezing with ice thick enough to bear an elephant'. Just what the good folk of Georgian London were doing taking an elephant on to the ice in the first place, he didn't explain.

CHAPTER 55

My wonked ankle held out just long enough to get me to Holyhead and the 4000-mile mark. It then collapsed in a helpful heap, threatening to leave me high and dry. But at least mum and dad hadn't. Not yet anyway. They had been walking in Snowdonia and so came to the rescue by treating me to a night in a hotel in Trearddur Bay where, in the bathroom, I found the toilet paper had been specially folded into a pointed end, presumably for aerodynamic reasons.

I looked in the Yellow Pages and rang every physio on Anglesey. But they were all either on holiday or booked up for a week. Hmm. Time to hum and haw. How long would my Achilles take to get better? Or had I pushed it to the point of no return? It felt all prickly and needly and horrible – a sure sign of tendonitis is what I suspected a tut-tutting Dr Sloss would diagnose. Should I rest here a week or two and see if it improved? Or should I let the train take the strain and head home to get some proper advice and manipulations?

Mum and dad said, in that motherly fatherly way of mothers and fathers, that they couldn't decide for me because, whatever they suggested, I would most likely do the opposite. What are they saying here? That I'm a 'difficult child'? A stubborn-muled teenager in my gap year? Don't believe a word of it! I'm an angel. A cherubim. A pleasure to behold.

So, in a slouchy sulky way, I slumped off and went to ring the builder from the phone box down the road. Just as he was in the middle of enlightening me about the joys of cripple jack rafters and a straight bridling of three-quarters depth with squinted abutments, an over-lipped face-edge pegged scarf, an Audi estate pulled up in the lay-by beside the phone box. Up in the flight deck sat a man and a woman of middling years. They looked at me. I looked at them. They kept looking at me. Having spent the better part of my life loitering around in phone boxes, I felt I knew that look. It was the look that said: *How long are you going to be? Two minutes or all bloody day?*

I said to the builder, 'I've got to go, someone's waiting for the phone.'

The builder said to me, '. . . stop-splayed joints, then a soffit tenon with a diminished haunch for joining floor joints into main bridging joints . . .'

Splayed joints? I didn't like the sound of that. So coarse, these builders.

When I stepped outside the phone box, the driver stepped out of his car. I presumed he wanted to use the phone but he wanted me. Or to put it another way, he wanted to speak to me. His name was Mike Venables. I only knew that because he told me. But I didn't tell him my name because he already knew it. Bike talk ensued as did an invitation to stay with him and his wife, Pam, at their house on the other side of Trearddur Bay. But for once I didn't need to, as I had a hotel down the road. They invited me to coffee the following morning instead, so over I went.

For three hours I sat enrapt in chat on Pam and Mike's sea-view balcony, drinking tea and eating bananas (the menu had undergone a slight change). Pam was a musician – a pianist and a top-of-the-range choir singer. Earlier that year she had gone with her choir to sing in a cathedral in Barcelona and said to Mike, a retired vet and a keen cyclist, why didn't he cycle down to Spain to meet her. So he did just that with Pedalling Pete from Pickmere, a George Longstaff-mounted engineer friend of his. Before that he had cycled the End to End and down the Pacific coast to San Diego. Mike said he'd love it if Pam cycled, so that she could join him on his rides, but she wasn't keen, she didn't want to push herself.

'I don't like the idea of it being hard work,' she said. 'I don't have any desire to test myself.'

Mike, being a vet, offered me some advice on my twanged fetlock. But as he was used to hairier and hoofier things, he said the best person to speak to was Sally, his daughter. As handiness would have it, Sally was a doctor. Mike rang her up, said a few words and handed me the receiver. Sally quizzed me about what hurt where before giving her verdict on my predicament. It was best to head home, give it a proper rest and some physio to prevent possibly turning it into a chronic tendonitis.

That's all I needed to hear. I left Mike and Pam to drive back to their home in Cheshire (Anglesey was their holiday home). After bidding farewell to mum and dad, who were going to continue tramping round Wales, I one-legged it down to Holyhead railway station to catch the train to London.

As I was hobbling along, pushing my bike down the platform, I saw a notice pinned to a sandwich board warning of the dire penalties that would befall any traveller who assaulted a member of staff. This struck me as not a particularly reassuring start to my journey: it seemed to imply that things were going to be so bad that I might be hit by rail-rage and feel the urge to lash out at some poor guard or ticket collector or 'revenue inspection officer' in order to release my anger and frustration.

As it was, the guards and platform staff couldn't have been more helpful or good-humoured if they tried, all quipping and muscling in to heave and haul my hopelessly heavy bike into an impossibly small guard's van, or lugging it up and down the station's back-breaking steps to change trains. I must remember to limp more often when travelling by train with an impregnated bicycle – it works marvels. Just a shame the standard of the railways couldn't match the efficiency of its employees; within the space of six hours I had one broken-down train, two signal failures, and a dose of what was apparently the 'wrong kind of hail'.

It was October by the time I made it back to Holyhead with ankle intact. Keeping true to the tradition of attracting the wrong sort of weather at the worst sort of time, I had timed it perfectly to miss the sunniest September in Wales for decades.

'This is the first rain we've had for three weeks!' the toilet cleaner in Holyhead station told me as she saw me changing into my waterproofs and warming my hands under the hot air dryer.

Outside, 40 mph winds blew blinding stinging rain across the street. The good news was that at least I didn't have to camp in it. Not tonight anyway. This was thanks to Mike and Pam, who had insisted I keep them abreast of Achilles' developments and my ETA back in Holyhead, because they wanted to drive the 100 miles from their home near Manchester airport just to meet me and give me a night in their Anglesey abode.

It felt strange to be in Holyhead and not using the island as a stepping stone for the ferry to Ireland. I went down to the harbour anyway because there's something about the constant restlessness of a port's passengers and ships that is palpably exciting. Leaning into the wind, I pushed out past

Soldiers' Point and the harbour's massive breakwater, which reaches out for almost two miles into Holyhead Bay. Its incredible length took the nineteenth-century workers nearly thirty years to build.

Had it been a bright and sparkling day, I would have climbed up Holyhead Mountain. At only 720 feet high, it is more Holyhead Hillock, but still, it is said to offer one of the best viewpoints in Wales, embracing in its sweeping panorama the high-rise ranges of Snowdonia, the Lake District and the Isle of Man, as well as the mountains of Mourne and Wicklow in Ireland.

As it was no longer a sunny September, but a stormy October, I had to content myself by coping with the savage conditions as I battled out to the contorted rock formations at South Stack. I'd been up here to the bird reserve before, but in much gentler weather when I could stand in comfort watching guillemots in their thousands, along with razorbills, peregrines, karronking ravens and chee-owing choughs. It had even been calm enough to hear the mournful call of a clan of grey seals, as the rugged bay between South Stack and North Stack is one of their few safe hauling-out spots on this wild and rocky coast.

But not this time. Even the evil-eyed herring gulls were struggling to keep their cool with the rumbustious winds – either going nowhere as they tried to fight into it, or torpedoing off into the distance when they turned to go with the flow.

I had never seen a gull make a cock-up of a landing until that afternoon at South Stack. There it was, trying to be all clever, performing acrobatics in the big squally sky, when it thought it would show off by coming in to land an inch from a grounded gull. Things started promising. It took a wildly windy gust well, swooping at an impressive angle towards its sighted target. Its aeronautic aerofoils were looking good, tweaking a little expert hydraulic adjustment here and there on its black-tipped white-flecked wing-flaps, followed by a smooth releasing of the pink-webbed undercarriage.

Then it all went horribly wrong.

Instead of a light-footed landing, it appeared to fall about four feet to the ground in a sudden embarrassing sack-of-potato heap beside its surprised mewing mate. As if that wasn't bad enough, it then seemed to lose its balance and practically fell over backwards, out of control. Its mate gave it a sort of 'Blimey! Having a spot of trouble, are we?' look.

Dusting down its silver-grey mantle and rearranging its upperwings, the pride-dented gull flashed its mate the most sheepish and shamefaced look I've ever had the pleasure to behold in a bird.

'Sorry about that!' it seemed to say. 'But I just completely lost it!'

By the time I had cycled down the hill to the bay of Abraham's Bosom, the sea was heaped and growling, every wave baring its teeth. As a result, water and air were practically indistinguishable as the wind whipped the sea's surface into spume as dense as a dark fog. The gusts hit the island even stronger this side, slamming into me with such force that, if I wasn't careful, I would end up being hurled over the edge, lost to the boiling white-watered cleavage of Abraham's Bosom, never to be seen again.

I made it to Trearddur Bay, forced to walk most of the way, and sheltered in the entrance of the same hotel I had stayed at with mum and dad. I waited for three hours while the doors swung and banged in the wind and the window-panes rattled in their frame and the rain drummed down on the conservatory roof. Just before six, I took off across the bay to Ravens Point to knock on the door of Mike and Pam, who had arrived from Manchester way only moments before. Spark on cue, the rain stopped the minute I walked through the door.

For two hours we sat drinking tea in their upside-down house – you sleep and bathe on ground level; eat, cook, chat and piano-play up near the stars. Mike was originally from Sheffield, whereas Pam hailed from Oswestry ('Oswald's tree' – St Oswald was King of Northumbria a very long time ago) in Shropshire. Her father was a painter and decorator with the council.

'We lived in a council house and never had any money,' said Pam. 'But I had no concept of ever being poor until I went to college where Rita, who's now one of my best friends, laughed at me for living in a council house.'

One day, Pam was invited to go 'MSB' with a group of girls, all richer than her. Pam didn't know what they were talking about. But it turned out that 'MSB' was their acronym for Maximum Sun Bathing. Sun bathing? This was a new concept to Pam. And an odd one at that.

'Lying in the sun out of choice was just not something we did at home when I was growing up,' she said. 'It's not what poor people did!'

Later on Mike and Pam took me out for an Indian up Holyhead high street. Over our dhaals and vindaloos and peshwaris and bhunas, I discovered that Mike played a starring roll once a week on GMR (Greater Manchester Radio) as the phone-in vet on the Phil Wood show, having to answer callers' queries ranging anywhere from dominant dogs who refuse to move from your favourite chair, to sorting out eating disorders with red-kneed Mexican spiders. I also discovered that Mike was minus three discs and had metal plates, plus twelve screws, in his neck. Not that I was looking for any plates or screws – it was just something he told me over a mouthful of shashlik.

Although he looked in great shape to me, Mike had had a bit of bad luck with bad backs and broken collarbones, which made it awkward looking over his shoulder on his bike. A mirror was his saviour in that department. Before he worked in a large vet practice, Mike had been a farm vet in Cheshire for ten years (he was involved in the foot-and-mouth outbreak in '68), but his bad back and an illness put paid to that. At one point in our conversation – I think it was not long after he was describing what it felt like to put your arm up a cow's arse, well, not exactly the arse but that sort of Ulverston area, if you know what I mean, and help to birth twin calves (the people at the table next to us weren't half giving us some odd looks) – Mike told me he had contracted brucellosis from calving cows. This condition, which sounds like an unpleasant reaction to bad breath-inflicted people who answer to the name of Bruce, is in fact a bacterial disease typically affecting cattle and causes undulant fever in humans. Val, my neighbour, who has written a book about vets, says in her chapter entitled 'Chickens, Chimps and Halibuts' (don't ask me where the cows are) that a woman she knew who contracted the disease from cattle said the treatment was worse than the disease. Which doesn't mean to say that the disease is any fun. Mike certainly had a not very enjoyable time with it all; along with the never-ending fever and rashes, it also affected his eyesight. Finally, after giving up being a farm vet, the brucellosis seemed to burn itself out of his system. (By the way, just in case you were wondering, like I was wondering, who the heifer was Bruce, he was Sir David Bruce, a Scottish physician who identified the bacterium.)

By the end of our Indian, I'm sorry to announce that I had dropped considerably in Mike's estimation. Before he met me, he seemed to think I was some sort of cycling goddess. This made me laugh because how many goddesses do you know who can crap into plastic bags? Not that I told him I could, as such. Anyway, he was very disappointed that I hadn't eaten nearly as much as he thought I would eat. But I told him I didn't like to over-indulge seeing as he was paying, and also, I wasn't my normal hungry self as all I had done that day to build up an appetite was sit on a train and watch seagulls crash-landing out of the sky.

The next thing to disappoint Mike, prompting him to say I had 'feet of clay', was when he asked me whether I was going to continue cycling around the world alone. I said yes, I was still keen to keep cycling through as many countries as possible, but that I might go with the builder. This was not the gung-ho answer Mike wanted to hear; he much more fancied the idea of me forging a trail-blazing path around the big, bad world alone.

'Pack him in!' he said, referring to the builder. 'Pack him in!'

But I didn't want to pack him in, even if he was full of splayed table scarves and under-squinted abutments.

CHAPTER 56

The next day dawned bright and blue and breezy. Big hugs all round and then off we went on our separate ways – Pam and Mike back to Cheshire, me towards Land's End.

At least, that was the idea. In practice I ended up going in completely the opposite direction from Land's End. Not because I got lost (please, perish the thought!) but because the lovely lanes of Anglesey led me astray. Away from the main roads, the island is made for cycling. So over the next three days I rode all over the flat, rolling and sometimes hilly countryside – passing windmills and windfarms, standing stones and Neolithic burial chambers, giant early seventeenth-century stone dovecotes and churches containing painted skeletons, smugglers' old haunts and coves and castellated lighthouses, warrens of dunes and villages ransacked by Viking raiders, hedgerows laden with blackberries the size of strawberries and the red, orange and gold-brown hued left-over lunar landscape of Parys Mountain, once the largest copper mine in the world. There were meadows too, and moorlands of flowering heather shagpiles and gorses exploding with fiery fusions of brilliant colour.

One evening, just outside the village of Penmynydd, I stopped to knock on the door of a farmhouse at a place called Dragon. Three sheep dogs tried their best to maul me, but their lengthy leashed chains restrained them inches from my ankles. Mrs Maple, the young farmer's wife, answered the door. I asked her if she had a corner of a field I could camp in. She said she did but asked me to give her an hour so she could move the cows out of the field. I said I didn't want her moving cows just for me. But she insisted because the field with the cows in was on a hill and looked out over the sea and the jagged crests of Snowdonia. Talk about room service – first I have my quarters cleared of cows, then I'm given the finest bedroom view to be found.

While waiting for my room to be prepared, I cycled up the hill to the village petrol pump and store to buy my food supplies. As I was packing my freshly purchased produce into my panniers outside, a man wandered out of the garage and came to talk to me. He was a Brummie, a big one at that, but had lived on Anglesey for fourteen years. He used to own a brewery, taking £3 million a day from his vast chain of pubs.

'It was a nightmare,' he said. 'I had to give it all up – the stress was too much. You couldn't trust anybody. All the pub landlords, they were all fiddling the accounts.'

Then he went into a bit of a rambling story about how he had a mate, or his mate had a mate, called Bob Mateland who used to babysit for him as a boy and who was a bit of a top cyclist and hit big times when he rode in the 1948 Olympics, and that Bob Mateland's missus was also a top cyclist and beat the London to Land's End record, but then she got tinnitus and couldn't cycle anymore so committed suicide.

And then he said to me, did I know that Jimmy Savile used to be a good competitive cyclist too, as well as a boxer? And I said no, I thought he just sat in a big chair wearing lots of medallions and chunky rings fixing things for people. And then he said, did I know what Jimmy Savile's real name was, and I said, no, because I thought it was Jimmy Savile. And he said, 'That's where you're wrong, sunshine, it's Oscar Pennyfeather.'

I emitted a mini guffaw because when you're so used to someone being called Jimmy Savile, you don't expect them to be called Oscar Pennyfeather. It's just not right.

Conversation then changed course when a 4×4 pulled in at the pump and a big chap got out who was a mate, not a Mateland mate, of Brummie Man. The Mate Man called us over and opened up the back of his vehicle to reveal a dog the size of a small horse. It was a big black Newfie with a huge soppy face.

'He's called Branston,' said Mate Man. 'Three years old.' Then he said, 'Know why his paws are like webbed feet?'

I looked down and saw that just one of Branston's feet was big enough to smother my face.

'They're for pulling in fishing nets!' said Mate Man, not waiting for an answer, which was good because, as we've established earlier, I don't like being tested.

I fair flew down the coast to Caernarfon where our Ed had built another one of his moated and massive-walled castles to subdue those fiery Welsh. Then it was on and round the lovely water-laced lanes of Ysgubor Isaf, Llandwrog and Dinas Dinlle, only marred by my hopeless inability to pronounce them, and a bonanza of hedge-cutting throwing spiky caltrops of tyre-exploding hawthorn all over the road. Oh, and I also got stung on my bum by a savage stinging nettle when I dived behind one of these viciously freshly flailed hedges for a pee. It was one of the most eye-watering things I'd had taking me unawares from the rear for a long time. Just a shame I didn't have anyone with me to monitor the cheek-smarting damage.

Then came the bit I had been looking forward to – the lonely Lleyn Peninsula, 'The Land's End of North Wales' (said the tourist office). This pointy peninsula in Gwynedd, that cups the lid on Cardigan Bay, is rough and rugged and virtually treeless and bounded by cliffs. The headlands were ideally positioned to go flying off in the thick, drizzly gauze-grey mist if I didn't watch my saddled step. The area is littered with dairy farms, Iron Age hill forts, Neolithic tombs and small green fields quartered by furzy hedgerows perfect for pitching a tent behind, while dominating the whole fine finger are the bare, sharply pointed triple summits of Yr Eifl, 'The Fork', thrusting up from the sea. This sturdy trident of boulder-scattered coned mountains is known in English as The Rivals, which for once is a more poetic name than the Welsh.

My ankle, which was just about holding body and bottom bracket together, survived a couple of killer hills as I skirted this three-for-the-price-of-one moun-tain. After buying some food supplies in the Spar in Nefyn, I cycled round the corner to eat them, sheltering from the wind and rain in the porch of Eglarys Dewi Sant (St David's Church). As I stood by my bike stamping my feet and speed-piling my Spar produce into my mouth, a small, elderly woman in a headscarf crossed the road and walked up the path specially to say, 'The door's open, you know, my love. You can go in and have a look if you like. We take pride in keeping our church unlocked.'

As I was finishing my third banana, another woman poked her head around the side of the door and looked at me. This took me by surprise as I wasn't really expecting anyone to be inside; virtually every church I had stopped at on my ride around the coast had been either locked or empty.

'Have you come to decorate the church?' asked the woman.

Decorate the church? How odd. Huddled in my dripping cycling garb and keeping company in the porch with a ponderous machine, I hardly think I looked like your average overalled P & D with paint brushes at the ready to slap on a coat of gloss. But then, as I peered over the woman's shoulder and caught a glimpse of a table groaning beneath the weight of strings of onions and phenomenal pounds of pumpkins, I realised she meant the Harvest Festival decorations. After she had left the church to go home for lunch, I took a look inside and saw window ledges adorned with generous bunches of grapes and bananas, cascading with apples and pears and oranges. On the dried food front, FOX'S ('est. 1853') Butter Crinkle Crunch biscuits appeared to be a firm favourite. I counted nine packets in all.

Just as I was going out, another woman was coming in. When she saw the size of my ten-ton load she said, 'My goodness! What do you do with all those bags on the hills?'

'They come up with me,' I replied.

There's something about being in a slightly out of the way place that seems to spur people into acknowledging your presence with a cheery wave. As I continued riding down the Lleyn's lanes – narrow twisting roads edged with high banks and tall hedges – the few people that I did see all waved: a farmer, a postman, a motorcyclist, a minibus driver, a woman feeding her chickens and a little boy on a micro scooter. An old man pulled up alongside me in his rust bucket of a Ford Fiesta Popular and said, 'By Jove! You've got some gear on there, gal!'

I passed unpronounceable Rhwngyddwyborth and the 'Whistling Sands' of Porth Oer (which, at certain states of the tide, emit a squeak when walked over, supposedly through the tiny sand-grains rubbing together) and the tiny whitewashed walled fishing village of Aberdaron. Up the hill I camped on a farm on a cliff and slept surrounded by the fragrant flavours of rain-beaten blackberries and fresh cow pats.

The next morning I awoke beneath a bright and hollow sky and could see across the tidal races and whirlpools that gave Bardsey Island its Welsh name of Ynys Enlli, 'Isle of the Eddies'. The religious Celts were deeply drawn to remote islands in the west and a monastery was built on Bardsey in the Dark Ages. So many pilgrims left their bones there (how forgetful!) that it became known as 'The Island of 20,000 Saints'. Bardsey was also the retirement home of Merlin, the masterly wizard of the Arthurian legends, who retreated to the House of Glass, which I suspect is just a rather fancy name for an Everest conservatory. He's never been seen since, by all accounts. Though, to semi-misquote Kirsty MacColl, 'there's a guy works down our chip shop swears he's Merlin . . .'

From Rhiw, I plummeted down a spectacular triple-arrowed hill into the teeth of Hell's Mouth Bay. The road was closed to motor traffic because of a meaty landslide, but any fleet-of-foot cyclestrians and pedecyclists could squeeze by and enjoy a peaceful passage along the fringes of Lleyn's southern extremities.

At Abersoch, the modern world crashed back with a bang. It was Sunday and the weekenders were clogging the roads with their Barbour-green Freelanders, £60,000 Range Rover Vogues and other various 4×4 weapons of mass consumption, or playing in their powerboats – Sport's Utility Vehicle's marine equivalent – on the Bay.

What could have been a fine ride was ruined by stampeding convoys of vehicles and so I hurried up the under arm of the Lleyn Peninsula until I came to rest in its armpit at Porthmadog, the former port for the region's slate industry. It was now raining heavily and as I was standing in a phonebox talking to the builder (yes, the counter-tongue and grooved table scarves together with the diminished haunches for joining floor joints into main bridging joints were coming on nicely, thank you) a small man in his seventies and a German Army surplus overcoat stood beside my bike, rubbing his chin while scrutinising my equipment. The moment I emerged from the phone box he pounced, quizzing me on the material of my panniers and my jacket. The answering of these two questions seemed to warrant a hand sandwich: he took my gloved hand between his and then gently squeezed it slightly – an action that made me retrieve it as quickly as possible.

Unfortunately he was on to me again as I was packing food supplies into my panniers outside the local Co-op. He was clutching a rolled up magazine.

'See this,' he said, unfurling it and pointing to a mud-splattered page full of small-ads ringed in red pen. 'I'm going to buy a life-raft and adapt it to sail to Australia. Should take about six months. Round the Horn.'

The magazine was some sort of specialised boating rag and the two types of lifeboat that the man had his eye on cost around £12,000. He would buy it from a life-raft supplier in either Scotland or Norway. As I grew steadily colder in the biting wind that ripped through the precinct, the man launched into a lengthy explanation about how he was going to use something like a 'windmill' sail that could be shut down and reefed when the winds came on too strong. He was also going to adapt the bow with a couple of twelve-foot lengths of 4×2 ash beams.

'Oh yes,' he said, 'it's got to be ash – young and supple.'

The next unbelievable stage would involve going down the local B&Q to buy a stash of shower mats ('just the right material for the job'), which he would then glue with epoxy resin to the covered fo'c'sle. The mind boggled. Was it really possible to sail a small craft comprising B&Q shower mats around the village duck pond, let alone the heaped, godforsaken seas off Cape Horn?

Before I had a chance to ask him he said, 'You don't need sextants to navigate any more, you know?' *You don't?* 'There's a method I know where by giving your date of birth and horoscope . . .' *What, to the oceanic gods?* '. . . you can tick off the days on a calendar and always know where you are.'

Oh, I know that method. It's called pie-in-the-sky navigation. All you do is stick your head in the clouds and hope for the best.

Then Mad Mat Man said, 'I was interested in your jacket because I want to take something like that with me.'

This was getting sillier by the minute. You don't sail a boat made up of non-slip shower mats around Cape Horn while dressed in a lightweight and hoodless cyclist's jacket with a bum-flap and headlight-reflecting Scotchlite down the arms.

'Wouldn't a survival suit be more the sort of thing you need?' I asked gingerly, not wanting to belittle the man's plans of adventurous shower-mat exploration, or anything.

'I've got one of those,' he said. 'It's in the trunk.'

'What trunk?' I asked.

'The trunk full of equipment I'm taking with me.'

'Have you ever done anything like this before?' I asked, beginning to feel genuinely concerned about the arduous undertaking he was taking on board.

'No,' he said. 'And it will probably be the last thing I do.'

This worrying and fatalistic attitude prompted me to ask, 'Will there be a life-raft on your life-raft?'

'You know what it says in the Bible?' he said. *Yes, don't meddle with men and their serpents if your name's Eve. Oh, and the waves come big on the Red Sea.* 'Don't mess with David if you're Goliath . . .'

He then launched into a giddy reel of evangelising holy talk, which was all very well but, unless I was missing something, didn't answer the life-saving salient point of rafts on rafts. There again, he could just be saying: why take a raft when you can take God?

To which I would reply: Give God a hand – he may not be *au fait* with sea-going shower mats.

When Mad Mat Man started on to me about repenting of my sins, and I shall be forgiven, I felt it was high time to make my escape.

The only place I managed to escape to was the public toilets across the street. I was just in the process of parking my bike when a well-upholstered woman of menopausal age, dressed in a floral raincoat, offered to guard my mount for me while I went within to do what I could do without.

'Thank you,' I said to the woman who bore all the homely and comforting feel of a favourite flocked wallpaper, and accepted her offer, even though I didn't think there would be many people jumping at the opportunity to ride off in the lashing rain on a bike big enough to fit a toddler and heavy enough to give an impregnated hippopotamus a run for its money.

Even so, when I was locked in my cubicle the thought still struck that maybe, at that precise moment when I was in no position to act, the woman was doing a runner with my mount.

But of course she wasn't. She was standing like a sentry beside my steed while gazing attentively at the dripping tree that draped itself over the toilet block.

'Do you know,' she said, and I thought: *Oh no! No taxing questions, please!* 'All the times I've walked past these toilets and I've never noticed this tree. And now look, even in the rain, doesn't it look beautiful with the leaves changing. Sometimes I think it's good to just stop rushing around and take time to look at the world around us. Wouldn't you agree?'

'Yes,' I said, wondering what it was about me that attracted philosophical ruminations outside cold, wet toilet blocks. 'I perhaps do it more than I should.'

Then the woman woke up out of her dreamy tree-appreciation state and said, 'I'm Sue by the way – it's lovely to meet you!' Reaching for my frozen fingertipped hand, she shook it warmly and said, 'God bless, love. And take care.'

CHAPTER 57

I love cycling in Wales. I love the feeling of the sea on three sides, the continuous presence, if not views, of mountains, the spaciousness of it all. All of this I had in abundance as I bowled along the Snowdonian coast south to Barmouth. It was here that I met a man whose recent disability just went to reinforce how fortunate I was to have such freedom to roam at will through the roominess of Wales. I was on the harbour front at the time, eating hunched down on my haunches opposite a moored yacht with the unfortunate name of *NautiLadi*, sheltering from the strong, bone-chilling south-easterly behind a mountainous pile of lobster-smelling pots. As I rocked back and forth on my hunkers, shivering uncontrollably while wolfing down as much food as I could before hypothermia set in, the man rolled up in his wheelchair, enwrapped in rugs. He was a Brummie, but had worked for years in Wales as a Mountain Rescuer. Then he had a terrible accident. And now this. A life confined to a wheelchair.

'Well, these things happen,' he said, putting on a brave face.

But then his eyes teared when he told me how much he loved the mountains and what was so hard was sitting here immobilised in his wheelchair and looking up at the mountains, knowing that he can't go climbing up there alone ever again.

'For most of my adult life,' he said, 'I've helped other people. Now I have to rely on people helping me. That's hard. That's very hard.'

Buffeted by the keen and constant wind, I crossed the Mawddach estuary on the wooden-slatted walkway of the mile-long railway bridge. The tide was low and a broad expanse of cockle-buried firm sand, woven with skirls and curlicues of watery channels, was busy with a riot of oystercatchers, filling the clean bracing air with the shrill call of their far-carrying pipings. Dominating the views upstream rose the distant peak of Cadair Idris, standing proud among a swirling and menacing morass of squid-ink black squally clouds rimmed with the odd dramatic burst of glaring sunlight.

The road south through Friog had me compressed up high between a cold grey shadowy cliff-face and the vast primeval soup of a deep, dark, indifferent sea. In the summer I could imagine this twisting road being a nightmare of caravanning holiday traffic. But now, on a wild October day, feeling the excitement of the season closing in around me, I had the road through Gwastadgoed, Llwyngwril, Llangelynnin, Rhoslefain, Bwlch, Tonfanau, Pen-y-wern, Pant and Talybont virtually to myself.

By the time I got to Tywyn, the wind was ripping down through the valleys with such strength that it kept throwing me across the road. The A493 to Aberdyfi was now laden with lorries and impatient motorists who seemed impervious to the fresh gale blowing outside their vehicles. Someone once said that 'real life happens outdoors', so these drivers were in a make-believe world of their quasi-front rooms and offices – lounging in easy chairs, throwing another log on the central heating, conducting business deals on their mobiles, dining to the audio system's stereophonic sounds of 'Relax! Smooth Classics for Rough Days!' on Classic FM. Worrying about being hit or run over doesn't make for a placid state of mind, so when I passed a sign pointing off down a narrow country lane to a place called Happy Valley, I readily allowed myself to be enticed off course and headed that way.

As I passed by Bod Talog, along a winding lane roofed over with trees, and kept company with a chattering valley river watched over by Dauddyffryn and the glorious bare-backed ridge of the Tyddynbriddell Hills, the only vehicle to pass me was a badly corroded car with a whinnying fan belt.

Rolling through the woods of Llechwedd Melyn, the narrow lane became wind-tunnelled by the growing gale, emptying oceans of leaves and a fusillade of twigs and small branches across the road. I had to put on my helmet to avoid being conked on the noddle. Trying to ride into this Force 8 gale was no breeze. The way the wind gets funnelled and channelled by valleys and mountains is teasingly cruel to cyclists. One minute I would be in my lowest gear, straining and wrestling into its furious face, while the next it would either slam into me from the side, slewing me on to the opposite bank, or completely change its tune and playfully hurl me along from the rear. It was hopeless trying to keep any sort of steady course or cadence – any gear I flicked into was never right, the wind ruining any momentary rhythm by its capricious antics. My forearms ached with keeping such a tight and rigid hold at the helm. But I didn't mind in the least – there were no distracted or short-tempered drivers to fret over or be run over by, leaving me simply to concentrate on hanging on for the neurotic fun of the ride.

The Dyfi Estuary is the last of the major submerged valleys that make up such major indentations into the coast of Cardigan Bay. Like the others, it owes its great giant-wielding axe-clefts to crazy and complex events in the Ice Age when the sea level moved up and down as warm phases succeeded cold. It was about a twelve-mile detour inland to Machynlleth, the small market town built at the last crossing point of the Dyfi before the estuary widens into the open sea. Possibly because of the Centre for Alternative Technology up the road, Machynlleth seemed like quite a New Age, artsy-crafty town, being well adorned with health food shops and health food cafés, pin boards and windows filled with notices advertising every alternative going. It was also well adorned with women in big boots and Teva sandals and diaphanous tie-dyes, all looking slightly spacey. As I was locking my bike against the railings, I overheard one of these women, with cropped, electric red hair, say to her sandalled and kaftan-clad companion, '. . . my health's suffering . . . it's the changing seasons . . . I need more love . . .'

When I turned the corner to ride back down the southern side of the Dyfi, the wind proved more a help than a hindrance and I flew through Furnace, Tre'r-ddol, Llancynfelyn and Ynyslas to Borth. Here I hit a death-defying ascent which fair put a spanner in the workings of my Achilles again. But I cajoled it onwards. It had to hold out. Land's End was calling.

On Aberystwyth seafront, a man with a shaven head and a physique like a rugby scrum-half asked me what the devil I was doing cycle touring in cold, wet weather like this. I told him and then asked what the devil he was doing in bare feet and sandals on an arctic windswept prom in October. He said he was a

cameraman and had just come back from Africa, where he'd been filming
Tomb Raider.

I said, 'But Aberystwyth's not Africa,' and that he could at least have pulled
on a pair of socks before going out.

He said, 'There's no point – I wear sandals all year.'

Feeling this conversation was getting us nowhere, I went on my way.

That night I camped in the rain and the rocketing wind up high in the hills on
a sheep farm at Pant-y-gwair. Now in Ceredigion, I had veered inland towards
the Cambrian Mountains, the stark, bare backbone of Wales that extends about
85 miles between Snowdonia in the north and the Brecon Beacons in the
south, to visit Chris and Di Bell. So the following morning, beneath a slate grey
sky of winter, I packed up a sopping tent and cycled off to where they lived on
an unpopulated lane near Cribyn.

I had first met Chris, an engineer specialising in precision-made indestructible chainrings, and Di, a social worker for disabled children, when riding my
wheelchair bike from Land's End to John O' Groats. This sounds like I had got
very lost, ending up in Wales, but they were living in Bristol at the time. We had
kept in touch on and off since then and now they offered to put me up for the
night, feed me and do my washing. An offer I couldn't refuse, specially as it
came on to rain buckets and continued that way for the rest of the afternoon
and all the night.

I was introduced to the animals – sheep, ducks, a door-opening-and-shutting
dog called Judy, a short-haired tabby called Jay, and a rotund white cat called
Pauper. As my clothes were drying on the airer hanging over the coal-fired
Stanley, Di had a heart to heart with me and revealed that one of the problems
with Chris was that he always did the tops of things up so tight. She would try
her damnedest to get into a jar of jam or the toothpaste and get nowhere.

And there was more. Sometimes she would come back exhausted from work
in the evening and mention a difficult case she had been working on that day
that was troubling her.

'Chris will sit in his chair and nod and grunt as if he's listening, but I know
that all he's thinking about is chainrings.'

Talking of chainrings, Chris rubbed his bushy beard while surveying my bike
and said, 'You could go down to a twenty on the front.'

For those not in the bike-boffin know, allow me to translate. Chris's 'twenty' was referring to twenty teeth on the small chainring on the front triple chain-set, which in other words translates as 'bloody small'. Using a twenty in conjunction with a thirty-four toothed sprocket on the rear cassette – yes, yes, I know this is boffinly boring but bear with me – meant that I would have a hilariously low (i.e. v. easy) gear. My ankle liked the sound of this, so I granted Chris permission to strut his chainring stuff upon my mount in his compact and tidy workshop adjoining the house.

After swapping my forty-two toothed large chainring for a forty, and with the aid of some 4.8 mm spacers (sorry, am I losing you again?), the whole opera-tion went swimmingly and we emerged into the morning sunshine with a bike with a stupidly low gear. Thanks to this twenty-tooth chainring, I now felt that no mountain was too high (nor river deep enough) in my ever-searching quest for an easy life.

Chris was far too enthusiastic for my liking about wanting me to experience an injurious dive-bombing from an insane and notoriously vicious buzzard that attacked cyclists along a quiet stretch of hilly lane to Dihewyd. Chris regaled with masochistic glee how he had recently suffered a violent aerial assault himself – the dive-bomber leaving him to nurse blood-oozing, sharp talon-inflicted tramlines down his scalp.

'Made me shake all over,' said Chris. 'I was in a right state!'

Other neighbourhood cyclists, similarly left to nurse scarified war wounds meted out by the bicyclist-hating buzzard, now gave the road to Dihewyd a wide berth. I told Chris that, in the name of goodwill to all mounted-kind, he should erect a hazard sign forewarning cyclists to:

> BEWARE! YOU HAVE NOW ENTERED A DIVE-BOMBING
> BUZZARD AREA. BE PREPARED TO TAKE PRECAUTIONARY
> SCALP-SAVING ACTION!

In the name of pate preservation, I bottled out and instead cycled to Dihewyd along a lane a mile to the west of the one patrolled by the demented beast of beyond. Chris had assured me that I would be quite safe along this route from any bird bombardment.

I was in the process of making steady progress past Feinog-uchaf, when my ears picked up the tell-tale mewings of a buzzard in the vicinity. Swivelling my head in a panic-scanning 360 degrees, I caught sight of the ominous dark brown-dressed bird, eyeing me up as potential pedalling prey from its prominent perch on a distant telegraph pole. *Don't even THINK about it,* I thought. But think about it, it did, because the next thing I knew it had sighted its target and was scudding at hedge-height along the lane towards me. There was no time to take avoiding action. All I could do was clamp my handlebars, clench my saddle and marvel at the burning-red eyes and the whitish, boldly barred brown breast of the buzzard as it swooped straight towards my quaking bonce. Then, at the eleventh second, it veered upwards, missing me by a magnificent millimetre.

Onwards I went. Northwards I went. Passing Pantyrhen, Pandy and Wig-wen until I rejoined the coast at Aberaeron – an immediately appealing little harbour town with its bustle of boats and its ranks of gracious Regency houses painted in a blaze of brilliant colours. There was quite a pull-up out of Aberaeron, but travelling slowly has its benefits and the benefit to befall me on the long hill to Ffos-y-ffin was finding a £10 note in the gutter. It was a bit wet, a bit muddy, but nothing that a bit of air-drying on my handlebar bag couldn't render usable. Along with the pound coins, twenty-pence pieces, allen keys, 10 mm spanners, torch, bulging wallet and self-tapping screws I had so far found at the side of the road, I was doing quite well. Add that to the £20 that the builder had found in a lay-by, and which we subsequently spent on a splash-out feast, things were turning positively rich.

I plunged virtually out of control down the vertical drop into New Quay, slamming on my brakes just before I plopped over the edge into the charming little harbour. New Quay, or Ceinewydd in Welsh, was named after the sturdy, two-tier, long stone pier that had been built to form a harbour in 1835. It provided one of the most sheltered anchorages in Cardigan Bay and by the 1860s there were at least six smithies and about 300 shipwrights in the town. Lists of nineteenth century dues on a noticeboard on the quayside hark back to a time when New Quay was a bustling port of brisk and lively coastal trade. It cost 4d for every calf, sheep, pig or fox; 2s per hundredweight of feathers; 1s 6d for a marble tombstone; a shilling for a ton of gunpowder, or five to land a billiard table or a barrel organ.

It all suddenly felt very Cornish, struggling up cliff faces only to fall down the other side into idyllic little fishing villages. What wasn't so idyllic was the weather – it was turning wetter and colder by the day. Camping was hard, but I was determined not to give in to the warmth of a bed-and-breakfast. Not just yet.

One night I camped on a farm up high on a headland over the bay. On one of the farm's outbuildings there was a short length of hosepipe sprouting off the end of a head-high tap. Although I was already wet and cold, I was suddenly struck by the unfathomable need to get even wetter and colder by stripping off all my clothes under cover of dusk to have the most agonising 'shower' I've ever had in my life. It's bad enough putting your body under a flow of frigid water but quite another to stick your head beneath it (I was set on washing my hair). Especially when standing in your altogether in a farmyard in a stiff, wintry wind. I never thought my head could achingly hurt so much. Before I crawled back into a dripping wind-raked tent, I first had to run up and down the dark muddy lane for half an hour before any semblance of non-numbness returned. Later on, still trembling uncontrollably down my sleeping bag and wearing every item of clothing I carried, I had a strange sense of satisfaction. I had put myself through a test, and survived. This felt good, because I now knew that if I ever had the need to hide from the enemy behind the curtain of an arctic waterfall (as one does from time to time), I might just live to tell the tale.

CHAPTER 58

Troubled clouds occupied most of the sky as I crossed the River Teifi at Cardigan and rode up the estuary in a tussling wind to the broad beach at Poppit Sands. The rain caught me just as I was getting nicely settled at a picnic table to chomp my way through a big bag-load of food. Huge, heavy rain. Panic pack-up. Snap down pannier lids. Pull on more wet-weather togs. Mad scramble for cover in sandy toilets across the road. What a way to be welcomed by Pembrokeshire!

There comes a point in one's life when you realise you can't stand around in public toilets all day, no matter what the weather. So I tally-ho'ed and onward went, splashing around up the deserted, muddy-flooded lanes and viciously steep inclines. Slopping and flapping in a great flushing fuss across the road, the autumnal leaf pulp storm-blasted against my wheels and legs and the sludgy banks of the hedge. I passed a few more 'pants' – Pantirion, Pantsaeson, and Pantygroes – plus a Cat Rock and a Pig y Baw to boot, before I came to rest in a watery glimmer of sun on a caravan site perched on a cliff over Fishguard Bay. Here I hunkered my flimsy abode down behind a thick whorl of blackberry bush, which I ransacked in the name of a hearty potful of fruity porridge.

It was also here that I was invited into the luxurious static caravan of Pete and Audrey Williams for a big bowl of stewed plums and to meet Amy, Pete's ninety-nine-year-old mother. Pete was a line controller on the Central Line of the London Underground, performing a job that was as stressful as any air traffic controller's. But he only had another year of making sure no trains collided before he retired at fifty-five. Then he was going to do more of what he loved – cycling and hiking, the latter with his wife and two German Shepherds, big gleaming-coated dogs that could carry their own made-to-measure packs with enough food and water for six days.

With only nine months to go before she hit 100, Amy was a picture of indomitable, century-old perfection. She had only just moved out of her own home in Ruislip, where she had fed and looked after herself without any help, and into Pete and Audrey's in Uxbridge. This wasn't because of her mind, which was still spot on the ball, but her legs.

'They're not so good,' she said, referring to her painful arthritis. 'And me eyes are going.'

But she could still crochet and had made a magnificent bedspread for Audrey.

'Unfortunately I put it in the washing machine,' said Audrey, laughing, 'and now it's big enough to cover Kosovo!'

Later, when I was lying in my sleeping bag, I thought what a funny country to choose to cover with a stretched mat of crochet. I mean Kosovo, like Uzbekistan or Burkina Faso, isn't the usual country to spring to mind on the size comparison front. Things are more as 'big as Birmingham', or, if you must get exotic, as 'vast as France'. But covering Kosovo in crochet? It wasn't the run-of-the-mill simile. Though I rather liked it.

It was a terrible night. Torrential rain and ripping wind tearing at my tent. Sleep was impossible as it sounded like I was caught in a gibing spinnaker at the height of an Atlantic storm. The forecast was for things to worsen. Radio Wales told me of ferry cancellations from Fishguard to Rosslare, but I didn't need the radio to tell me that. Peering through a slit of unzipped tent door, I could see the Irish Sea throwing a wobbly – ravingly rough and angrily slapping and slopping in a huge ruffled mass of spuming whitecaps. Way down in the toy-town sized harbour, semi-protected by the 2000-foot breakwater (constructed before the First World War to create a deep-water harbour in the vain hope of wooing the trans-Atlantic liners), the Stena Line Superferry was tethered tight to the dockside, lights blazing, but going nowhere.

At dawn I decided to act. The storm – the first proper storm of the season – was strengthening by the hour. Before the forecasted 70–90 mph gusts tore me to shreds, I had to 'get the hell out', as I believe they say in 'Nam movies. I really needed two of us to get the tent down, but as I was only one of me I struggled in sheeting rain and howling wind, hurling panniers on to flysheets and groundsheets to prevent them being blown to Bagshot – or even Baghdad. It was that strong. And that silly.

It was only three miles to Fishguard but I had to walk most of the way. The way the sopping wind slammed and banged into my side was most inconsiderate. One moment I was dragging a concrete girder, and the next I was being sent for a burton. I tell you, who needs to go to the ends-of-the-earth Patagonia for a spot of wind when you can go to the ends of Pembrokeshire simply by sticking to the A40?

I made it into KwikSave, where I met a kweer kween with a kwiff who was trying to kwench his thirst by kwaffing a squashed kwince for a kwid. Actually I didn't. But what was wrong with a 'Q' for a 'Quick', I wonder? Then I made it down the road to Londis, where I bought even more batten-down-the-hatches, sitting-out-the-storm food, which I sat out and ate up in a shoebox room down at Seaview Hotel on the seafront. There was room for a soggy single bed and a tall thin wardrobe, and little else. The only place for the television was on the lofty heights of this tall thin cupboard, which for any low-rise being such as myself was the height (ha!) of all impracticability. Ironically, with the TV positioned in the most remote location possible, there was no remote control to control it. As there was no chair upon which to stand, the only way I could switch the bloody thing on without flailing around with my bike pump was to open my door and stride purposefully out into the corridor. I then took a few deep breaths, did a quick pre-sprint limber-up for my run-up before turning to eye up the on–off knob of my target.

Ready . . . steady . . . bang! And she's off – tearing across the threshold with a hop, skip and a jump and . . . an outstretched arm . . . and . . . lo! *I'm a Celebrity – Get Me Out of Here!* bursts into life and I see Christine Hamilton looking a bit rough without her face on and Tony Blackburn trying to look all Indiana Jones but sounding just as much a corny wise-cracking deejay as ever he did.

I set off the next morning still in rain but a slightly less windy wind. The hill out of Goodwick, Fishguard's near neighbour, past a place on my map called Stop-and-Call, was so steep that it was all I could do to stop and not call my porridge from resurfacing. But the wild rocky promontory of Strumble Head rewarded me for my efforts and I stood on the prow of this lonely promontory, looking out into the face of the wind and the climbing seas of St George's Channel.

On the way back I stopped by at Tre-Howel farmhouse to say hello to Aunty

May. Aunty May was not my aunt (I haven't got any useful relatives like that – my parents were both only children) but the nearly ninety-year-old aunt of Mary Turton. Mary, whose maiden name is Morris, is Welsh and very lovely and has lived in my village for 21 years. When her children were small my mum used to give them piano lessons at home, so I've known Mary virtually as long as I can remember. She's what I think the term 'village stalwart' was made for – the sort of person to do anything for anyone. Whenever there are things to be done – village halls decorated, cakes baked for Christmas fairs, ovens borrowed – Mary is the ever-eager one who is always willing to help. When she heard I was cycling round the coast of Wales, she rang me up and gave me a list as long as my leg of the addresses of her Welsh relatives to visit. And these were just her coastal-dwelling 'rellies'. There were hundreds more inland. Clearly, the better part of the population of southwest Wales is related to Mary in some second-cousin-half-removed form or other.

Dating from the 1600s, Aunty May's farm is one of the oldest in the area and has played a notable historical role. If you walk out of the farmhouse, and cross a few fields, you will soon come to Carregwastad Point, a headland set at the western end of a small, rock-bound bay. This was the site of the last landing by a foreign army on the soil of mainland Britain. The great day was 22nd February 1797 when, during the Napoleonic Wars, three enemy ships, unable to get ashore at Bristol, landed a rabble of some 1400 Frenchmen, half of them soldiers, half ex-convicts released from jail on condition they joined the force, all under the command of an elderly Irish-American named Colonel Tate. Their intention was to march north through Wales to Chester, living off the country, and finally to take and burn the port of Liverpool.

Instead they took the opportunity to get thoroughly drunk, probably to try to blot out the fact that they had landed on one of the most exposed parts of the Pembrokeshire coast in mid-February without any tents or protection. Before they had a chance to set out on their long march, they were attacked by an equally mixed force of yeomanry and villagers who reacted vigorously to the affront of having their land invaded by a bunch of drunken Frenchmen. The story goes that the bemused troops mistook the traditional stove-pipe hats and the red cloaks of the Welsh womenfolk for the scarlet uniforms of British infantry and so surrendered a mere two days after they first set foot on Strumble. One redoubtable local heroine, Jemima Nicholas, was a woman of such formidable physique and alarming aspect that she led the local resistance, capturing no fewer than fourteen of the enemy single-handed, wielding only a pitchfork.

As she sat me down to coffee and cake served from the gleaming silverware and the best Dalton china, Aunty May, who emitted a comforting aroma of freshly ironed tea-towels, told me how her parlour had acted temporarily as the headquarters for Colonel Tate. Now it contains a piano and shelves and dressers bearing scores of framed family photographs. There were pictures of her handsome husband, a farmer, who had recently died, and her sisters, Bessie and Mabel and brother John, all of whom were dead. Aunty May's father had died when he was forty-five and she was brought up by 'mama'.

'You understand now?' she kept saying to me in her soft, lilting Welsh accent, making sure I was keeping up with the names and family history.

As we were talking, Aunty May's builders were putting the finishing touches to a stone garage they were making that would harbour her brand new Mercedes, currently housed in the cowshed.

'Jonathan,' (one of her younger relations who now farms her land) 'has to park it for me because the shed's too narrow to drive into for an old thing like me!' Then she said, 'The car's an automatic, the first I've had. When you get a car, you must get an automatic. They're marvellous!'

From Aunty May's, I followed a network of steep and narrow lanes, deserted save for one tractor and two escaped sheep. The next of Mary's relatives to visit was Rosalind Williams, who lives in Abereiddy overlooking a cove in a house evocatively called Llais-y-Tonnau ('Voice of the Waves'). I met her outside Berea church and followed her car a couple of hundred yards down the road to meet her brother Dave and his wife Judy. Once again I was fed and watered, plied with photographs of the extensive family, and given the run-down of local family happenings. The farmhouse they lived in had been in the family for 200 years, though Dave and Judy rented it out when they lived in Narbeth where Dave worked as a vet. As soon as he retired (due to a heart problem) they moved straight back. Apparently the farm across the lane used to be in the family, too, but rumour had it that it was gambled away one night.

Rosalind had only just retired herself. For years she owned the flower shop in Fishguard, but then the supermarkets came in and took most of the business away.

An old black-and-white photograph was pulled out, showing a small, frail woman surrounded by twelve strapping great men. The woman was Dave and Rosalind's grandmother and the men were all her boys. She'd had seventeen children altogether, but five had died when they were still very small. Another relation used to deliver butter and cream from one side of Milford Haven to the other, but she ended up drowned after the little passenger ferry she was on went down in the Haven.

The Williamses were keen for me to stay the night but, as it had stopped raining while we had been indoors, I wanted to press on to St David's Head (the westernmost point of Wales) and beyond. In the event, I spent so long wandering around 'Dewisland', as the region is known – St David, or Dewi Sant, is the patron saint of Wales – gazing out over the numerous rocks and islets known as the Bishops and Clerks that stud the big swelling seas west of the Head, and watching a clutch of hardy surfers skimming on the long, white-capped rollers thundering on to the crisp, clean sands of Whitesands Bay, that I never made it any further before the dim-lit October day fizzled to nothing. I thought about cycling back to Dave and Judy's, but the minute I thought that, the heavens opened. So as I didn't want to arrive on their doorstep all muddy and dripping and looking thoroughly unpleasant, I scarpered down a skinny road and up a long and very puddled and potholed lane to the isolated youth hostel. I threw up my tent on the bumpy patch of ground beside the dustbins (for some reason, I preferred the choice of sleeping outside in the wet and the cold rather than in the warm and the dry in a bunk) and then trotted over to the kitchen block to make my tea.

The only other person staying in the hostel was a triathlete called Rob. As I was making steady progress through the various foods I had found lurking in my panniers, he walked into the kitchen and sat down at a table opposite to eat a tin of baked beans with a bag of crisps finished off with a bowl of tinned pears (or peaches – it was a bit dark in there). The lot was washed down with a can of Fanta.

Rob was lithe and hugely fit (he had completed the Iron Man – swim 3.8 km, cycle 180 km and run a 42 km marathon, all on the trot – in 10 hours, 50 minutes) and was in his early to mid forties. He used to be a geologist, working for four years on oil rigs in the North Sea. Then he decided he wanted to get married and have a family. So he did, and had two daughters who both blossomed into fine teenage orchestral musicians. Rob now worked for an insurance company as a computer wizard, or, as his fancy job title had it, a 'Solutions Architect', which in layman's speak obviously means Computer Cock-up Solver with a Touch of Sir Norman Foster on the Side.

His wife had granted him leave to take a short break and he had driven to Pembrokeshire from his home in Swindon. That's Swindon as in Swine Down, or, to give it its literal meaning, 'Pig Hill' – if you ever have the misfortune to find yourself driving past Swindon on the M4, you might notice the older central part of this industrial town is set on a noticeable hill, and if you're still swivelling your head and haven't crashed by now, well, that hill used to be a pasture for swine. Now it's a prairie for Microsoft.

Rob had just spent his second day walking a portion of the 186-mile

Pembrokeshire Coast Path. Strangely he found walking far more exhausting than running marathons so he kept breaking into a run to conserve his energy.

After we had talked a while about the addictiveness of exercise, pain barriers, happy hormones and all sorts, Rob suddenly said, 'You remind me of someone who writes books . . . You're not Dervla Murphy, are you?'

Well, what an honour! To be mistaken for the hallowed doyenne of women's travel writing, even if she was in her seventies. It was good to think that all this struggling with life on the road, ravaged by wind and rain, had at last aged me enough to break free from my eternal gap year.

I sped on and out through Merry Vale to Carn ar Wig, from where I looked out over Ramsey Sound to Ramsey Island. Guarded by sheer cliffs and treacherous seas, this hilly island became a religious sanctuary in the sixth century. Legend has it that in those days Ramsey (Old Norse for Wild-garlic Island) was joined to the mainland by a natural bridge of rock. Craving solitude, the Breton saint Justinian built a retreat there, took an axe to the land bridge and hacked away until only the rocks now called The Bitches remained.

I rode back through St David's, dropping down the hill to the twelfth-century cathedral which lies in a grassy hollow, its big square purple-hued stone tower below the roof level of nearby cottages. Although St David's is the size of a small town, its cathedral status qualifies it as being the smallest city in Britain. It was incredible to come merrily rolling out of the fields on my wheels only to find this massive cathedral sitting pretty in a very big pothole. It's all so magnificently out of proportion with its surrounding smallness – like suddenly finding Notre-Dame decamped on to Nether Wallop's village green.

After all my Dewisland dawdlings, things then went quite fast. I powered past the rocky outcrops and sheltered anchorages of Half Tide Rock, The Cradle, The Mare, Rickets Head, Haroldston Chins, Settling Nose, The Rain, Huntsman's Leap, Jack Sound, Skomer Island with its Basin, Pig Stone and Pain and Shag Rocks and Skokholm Island with its Long Nose, Mad and Hog Bays. Next came Deadman's Bay, Rainy Rock, Runwayskiln, The Hookses, Welshman's Bay, Frenchman's Bay (was he pitchforked?), Watwick Bay, Musselwick and Sandyhaven Pill to Milford Haven, with its seventy-mile coastline of fine natural harbour.

Suddenly, no matter in which direction I looked, oil refineries and petrochemical plants filled the horizon. It had been raining hard on me for most of the morning, but by the time I pulled up at an official picnic site overlooking the toll bridge into Pembroke, the sun burst into brilliance. *Quick! Food! Now!* I thought, because I knew I didn't have long – a fresh bank of filthy black cloud was piling towards me off St Brides Bay. It's at premium *quick-food-now-before-I-get-rained-on* times like this that you really don't want anyone wandering up to you looking for a bit of light conversation. My maximum priority is to read my book while frenetically shovelling enough food to fill me up before my body temperature drops to teeth-chattering and/or the rain arrives.

So when a Mitsubishi Space Runner swung into the picnic table area and a large man with a round head and short bristly haircut heaved himself out of his Space vehicle to stretch and shake a leg, I thought: *Please don't come and talk to me*, and kept my head down to avoid all possibilities of eye contact.

But I knew I was doomed.

'Turned nice now!' he said, ambling in my direction.

'About time too!' I replied, thinking: *Stop there! Don't encourage him.*

'We've had some rain all right!'

'Yes.'

'Looks like we're in for some more.'

'Oh no!'

'That a motorbike you got there?'

'No, a bicycle.'

'What, to carry all that gear?'

'Yes.'

'Travelled far?'

'A little way.'

And then, miraculously, he must have got my monosyllabic message, because he gave a little shrug and walked back to his Runner, no doubt thinking: *Cyclists, ha! Bloody unsociable lot!*

Admittedly, I did feel pangs of uncongenial guilt. But it worked. I got to read six pages of my book and my last mouthful coincided perfectly with the first few drops of a fresh new cloud-burst. I jumped up from the picnic table, hurriedly closed up Anne Tyler's *The Accidental Tourist*, unable to decide whether Macon would stay with his floozy Muriel from the Meow-Bow dog clinic or return home to floss his teeth between love-making, placed it in a plastic bag and placed that bag into another plastic bag in my bag, and then made haste across the bridge to Pembroke where a last fiery fork of sunshine ignited the Great Keep of the castle to flame against a solid sky of ink.

CHAPTER 59

Somewhere between the end of October and the beginning of November I lost two weeks. I think this might have something to do with the fact that I went home. Catering duties were calling. Val was throwing her big sixtieth sit-down birthday bash in the village hall so I returned to my pots-and-pans post to cook for it, recruiting my motley assortment of waitering staff on the way – namely my mother and my builder and a late arrival, Clare, she of cow-in-the-pannier fame.

There were other duties calling too. I had to remember how to string words together again in phrases other than: 'I hear they've had a lot of rain in Vlissengen,' as Guildford Book Festival had invited me to give them a bit of cycling spiel. Then my own fair mother, who could add to her skills of waitressing, intermittent-to-non-existent participant of bicycling support crew, and maker of supreme steamed treacle sponge pudding, that of pianist. In the other village hall she was putting on a musical bonanza and was featuring on keyboards with her friend Bridget on fiddle. So the builder and I cycled over to cheer her on from the sidelines.

By the time I made it back to Tenby it was November 7th and tremblingly cold. As I cycled past a solid puddle near Waterwynch that withstood the weight of two waterfowl, I thought it didn't bode well, for in country folklore:

> If there's ice in November that will bear a duck,
> There'll be nothing later but sludge and muck.

And, true enough, the snap and crackle of amber leaves and the brittle crispiness of the south Carmarthenshire countryside soon turned to slop and sludge and mires of mud. After that first frosty day the cold rains came and it rained and it rained and it rained. At Carmarthen the River Tywi burst its banks, forcing me to overnight in a dubious back-street pub in a room the size of a horse trough furnished with a stained shagpile carpet that clearly had lived up to its name.

I bow-waved through Ferryside on lanes a-gurgle with water, wallowed through Kidwelly and found the Ship Aground Inn at Burry Port more awash than ashore. Down the road I dived for shelter into the church porch of St Mary's, its solid doors most definitely bolted against any slovenly behaviour from loitering clutches of bored blokes with their ladettes and yobettes. As I stood shivering, cramming food into my mouth at twice the speed of lightning, the organist turned up to practise for Remembrance Sunday.

'Come and warm up inside,' he said, unlocking the doors. 'You'll just have to ignore me I'm afraid!'

But ignore him I didn't. And though I never warmed up, I sat and listened to him demonstrating his thunderous prowess to an appreciative frozen-boned audience.

Late that fog-bound evening, I followed the blurry beam of my dynamo in a persistent heavy drizzle along the northerly shores of the Gower peninsula. Cycling in the furry darkness along a road you don't know to a sleeping location as yet unrevealed generates an apprehensive hyper-alertness of the senses. All systems are turned to super-perceptive. Ears are cocked, eyes are peeled, nose is rodently twitching. The body radar is bleeping, all defensive systems switched to go. It's a raw intensity, which by its very nature is almost tantalisingly primal and animal-like. A far cry, I imagine from the sensations experienced by the motorists who, on Amazon.co.uk, had voted as their 'most valued in-car features':

1. Air conditioning
2. Cupholder
3. Audio system
4. Adjustable/reclining seats
5. Satellite navigation
6. Controls for audio system on steering wheel
7. Central locking
8. 'Lights-on' buzzer

9. Trafficmaster
10. Automatic dipping mirror

Apart from my little interlude with my personal organist, it had been a bad day; rain, floods, cars, mud. And now, nowhere to sleep. Everywhere the ground was too saturated to put up my tent and all the bed-and-breakfasts were either shut for winter or untenanted when I called. It all felt really off-season – everything shuttered up, leaving me closed out in the dark and the driving rain. I glanced in windows and saw warm dry people slumped in floral armchairs either lost behind forests of weekend newspapers or lit blue and shivery by the flickering light of their televisions. In another house I saw a mother and son hanging streamers of paperchains across the ceiling. In an upstairs window a waving Santa sat ho-ho-hoing at my homeless predicament. *Oh please, not Christmas already!* And I thought of Tom Lehrer, the American satirical songwriter, and his rather splendid jaundiced view of this day of excess frivolity:

> Kill the turkeys, ducks and chickens,
> Mix the punch, drag out the Dickens,
> Even though the prospect sickens,
> Brother, here we go again.

Finally, at Llanmadoc, way down on the end of the Gower, I found a bed at Bremmel Cottage. Albert led me round the side to put my muddy, oil-splashed dripping bike in the workshop. Jean, who had been married to Albert for fifty years, showed me up the staircase to my attic-type room, for which she charged me only £10. It came cluttered with trinkets and clothes-horses and wardrobe doors that refused to shut and books with titles like *Blessing and Cursing* and *On the Road with Jesus*.

Jean, who had worked in all manner of places from betting shops and restaurants to pools offices and a factory for Philips' electrical equipment, lived in constant pain from her arthritis. Albert was in even less good shape: he'd had cancer and part of his lung removed, and had various other ailments. One of their daughters had died when she was only forty-one from a cancer that had riddled her body within six weeks.

Bremmel Cottage wasn't their house. They had driven to Wales from their home in Carshalton in Surrey and were only here to look after the bed-and-breakfast and numerous animals for their friends, David and

419

Robyn, who were on holiday for five weeks. David had an unusual profession: downstairs in his workshop he made metal plates to fit people's skulls. I was sorry not to meet him as I can't say I've met many metal skull-makers before.

The next day I continued cycling around the rest of the Gower in thick drizzly mist. Occasionally it thinned enough to allow me glimpses of sheep-studded green hillsides. But it stubbornly refused to lift. Even so, as it was low tide, I stopped to walk out past Tears Point, Kitchen Corner, Low Neck, Devil's Bridge and Blow Hole on the projecting limestone islet of Worms Head (actually *wyrm* means a more cut-throat 'dragon'). Visibility was so mushy I had no hope of seeing the wide sandy sweep of Rhossili Bay, a three-mile-long breezy yomp of sculptured sand that stretches all the way to Spaniard Rocks. But I didn't mind, I'd seen it (and yomped it) in all its glamorous glory when cycling out this way one astonishingly hot February.

Still enclosed in a dense commuter-man grey, I stumbled upon The Mumbles and the cycle path that links a half-moon loop around Swansea Bay. From now on it was going to be a mostly messy sprawl of big and busy roads all the way along Wales's industrial south coast to the Severn. I can't say the prospect of cycling among a mad jungle of motorway bedlam, truck-trundling trunk roads, flyovers, ride-unders, steelworks, motorworks, chemical plants, flaring chimneys, piles of pylons, wastelands, docklands, scrublands, graffitilands, rolling mills, strip mills and blast furnaces filled me with the joys of a gambolling spring, but it had to be done so I donned high-visibility battledress, looked the drivers in the eye and got on with it.

I hammered down the highway that beetled beneath Neath, passed small through Port Talbot with its cloud-scraping forest of chimneys breathing fire like the great dragon of Worms Head, and crawled into Porthcawl where I slung up my tent in a spongy field of mud off the Nottage-to-Newton bypass for another cold wet night dressed up to the nines. Something had clearly gone wrong with the Gulf Stream somewhere along the line – I thought the whole purpose of us lying in its tropical-sounding wash meant that the warm thermals should be coming off the Atlantic, rather than out of my meagre crumpled wardrobe.

The next morning I narrowly missed being flattened by a red BMW, which tried to surge past me at the very stupidest moment by overtaking me on a blind corner. But lo! What do you know? It met a skip lorry thundering down the road in the opposite direction. A bone-chilling squeal of skidding tyres filled my head as a sickening split-second sense of an imminent death-crash impact of buckled metal and warm blood shot through my veins. But I survived, by the good fortune of a centimetre.

At Bridgend I spun off for Ogmore and Monknash where I suddenly cycled into the unexpected splendour of farm-flanked lanes towards Llantwit Major. Across the wide, tousled disquiet of the Bristol Channel, silvered with light amid the thick thunderhead cloud-bursts, lay Minehead and Watchet and the sea-staring ramparts of Exmoor. Further over, the high hills of the brooding Brendons and Quantocks rose dark and menacing. It all looked so remote and far-off, like another land away. Which I suppose it was. It was England.

At St Athan, which backs on to Beggars Pound and fronts on to the dominating chimneys and beefy blocks of Aberthaw Power Station, I sheltered from the driving rain in a bus shelter to down some energy- and morale-boosting fodder. The dirty cream concrete shelter, completely open to the sloshing whoosh of the road on one side, was covered in adolescent graffiti. As I stood with my back to the wind, eating handfuls of food, I learnt more about Luke's rectum and his 'three-and-a-half inch floppy' than ever was tasteful for this time of day.

Barry docks, Sully Sound, Penarth Head and then the scary Scalextrix of Cardiff's artery of fat red roads. I thought I would skirt south of the city centre and barrel down the dual carriageway closest to the sea. But the big self-important roundabout I careered on to at truck-racing speed (Self-Preservation Note 1: when tackling major trunk-road rushing roundabouts it's important to leave all nerves at home and fly headlong into them at motoring speed) was having none of it. There I was, spinning round the traffic-racing circle, keeping to a no-messing middle of my lane (Self-Preservation Note 2: cycle tucked tentatively into the side and no one sees you), all ready to veer off on to my intended route, when, entering the gaping mouth of my flyover-type exit on a compass course for the docks, I suddenly caught sight of a sign that barred all bikes from using this road. *Who the sweet Fanny Craddock put that there?* I thought. But there was no time to wait for an answer. Fast glance over blind-spot shoulder, quick swerve and alter course and then I'm back in circular circulation, careering round the roundabout, panickingly scanning the house-size signposts of each exit hoping they will offer me a helping hand to get me the dithering Dickens out of here.

I cycled round the roundabout a dizzy three times in all, in various stages of fretful despair. Then I caught sight of Asda and sheered off down a slipway in that retail park direction.

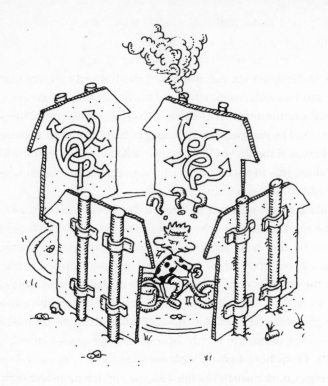

When I emerged a pannierful of produce later, I was in no less a predicament than before. But at least I had a booty of bananas to see me through the strain. Feeling my way, I rode off across the concrete savannah of retail parks, and on through the residential streets of Grangetown to the Cardiff city centre where the Millennium Stadium squatted like an enormous spacecraft, its UFO dome bristling with aliens' antennae.

Directions were sought from a mechanic with his head in an engine. Knowing what place to ask for proved tricky, because if I said, 'Can you point me in the direction of Newport?' (which is where I wanted to go), he would most likely send me off on to the A48 that fed inland on to the M4. So I had to do it in small stages and ask to be pointed in the direction of the docks and the steel works and the industrial park on the coast.

'Where're you ultimately trying to get to, love?' asked the mechanic, emerging from his lorry's viscera of pistons, cylinder heads and crank shafts to reveal heavily forested forearms and oil-slick hands.

'Well, ultimately, Land's End,' I said.

'Jesus Christ!' he replied. 'You're in the wrong bloody country!'

I made it to Newport via the reclaimed flat fertile fields, drainage ditches, channels and fancy electronically gated houses of the Wentlooge Level, all of which cowers behind, and is protected from, the huge flooding tides of the Bristol Channel by the long low ramparts of Peterstone Great Wharf. Once in Newport I crossed the River Usk in similar style as I did when crossing the Tees at Middlesbrough – in a swinging platform dangling on a cat's cradle of cables from one of Britain's two Transporter Bridges.

Pye Corner, Nash and Undy took me sailing along more ankle-revelling flatness on the Caldicot Levels – these ones saved from the overflowing mouth of the Severn by the great banks of the Porton Grounds. Up the road lay Caerwent where, 2000 years ago, the Romans founded Venta Silurum. Although the Romans conquered the whole of Wales, they failed to romanise anything more than the southern plain and the fringes of the mountains.

In the gloomy village of Sudbrook, I headed down a cul-de-sac until I reached a point where the Welsh shore swung out towards the Avon bank of the Severn. From here I could look out over the two stretched spans of the Severn bridges, under which the tide can rise and fall more than fifty feet. Only the Bay of Fundy in Nova Scotia can boast something better. Ahead of me spread the flat rocks of Lady Bench and Gruggy, leading to The Shoots of Crabs Bay. Beyond lay Goblin Ledge, English Stones and the giant cotton-reel fuel depots of Avonmouth. Directly below my feet passed the 130-year-old, three-and-a-half-mile Severn railway tunnel.

Once upon a time a train I was on broke down in this tunnel. In the seat opposite sat a bearded man in his sixties with a big box-hedge of hair that only a topiarist could ever have a hope of taming. When he saw me leaning against the glass, peering anxiously out into the black through cupped hands, he said, 'Don't open any windows or else the River Severn will come pouring in.'

CHAPTER 60

I could feel the wind pawing the ground, gearing itself up to charge as I shot down the slipway to the suspension bridge of the magnificent Severn. Halfway across I stopped on the bipedular path to peer down into the thick chocolate eddies of the river. Somewhere out there, the funnel shape of the estuary constricts the incoming tide and produces the Severn Bore, a steep wall of wave which during spring tides can be anywhere from three to nine feet high. Unlike a tsunami, which is a devastating ocean wave generated by an earthquake, landslide or submarine slide, growing in height as the water piles up, the Bore is a genuine tidal wave. For something so phenomenal, surely we could have named it something more exciting than a Bore.

Unfortunately I couldn't honour my predilection for cycling back and forth over long and glorious bridges because the weather was just too wild. High-sided vehicles were shuddering and shaking from the slamming jams of wind. I hadn't been back in England long when the violent storminess forced the bridge to be closed. And it stayed that way for a day. I'd fought my way in and out of Bristol by then but got caught in a scolding tempest that turned afternoon to night as I pounded through Portishead. Up until that moment I had only known Portishead as the band of that name – Beth Gibbons's haunting vocals on the Wandering Sweet Glory Box Biscuit et cetera Dummy CD, flowing through my head as the rain hammered down.

I took refuge from the rain on Clevedon seafront in a public toilet block distastefully wallpapered with *Smash Hits* posters of pretty boys Will Young and

Gareth Gates. When I got fed up of them watching me I made a break for a bed-and-breakfast and found a Victorian pile on the hill where the landlady gave me a dark, dingy basement shoebox that smelt of boiled cabbage and gerbils.

Though my box had no bog, it did come complete with a prehistoric kick-to-switch-on TV with a snowstorm two-of-everything picture. The good news was that it wasn't situated upon the craggy heights of a lofty wardrobe, but squatted in the foothills of a corner table. The bad news was that it told me nearly 200 people, most of them backpackers, were thought to have died in a bomb-blasted Bali nightclub and that tonight, at six o'clock, the firemen of Britain were going on strike for forty-eight hours. Three more strikes, lasting for eight days each, were planned in the run-up to Christmas. Set to take their place, a Dad's Army of geriatric Green Goddesses were brushing off the cobwebs and filling a token bucket or two with water. Later on, the camera panned in on one such Goddess – broken down the minute it had started out on its mercy dash. How very reassuring.

The best news of the night was how a fridge had been blown apart when a bottle of Marks and Spencer coconut and lemongrass salad dressing turned into a 'bomb'. Fifty-four-year-old Ann Britton, who lived in Bridport, Dorset, returned from a weekend break to find her kitchen in ruins. No traces of Osama bin Laden's al Qaeda network were found in the shattered fragments of the salad drawer. M&S said that the dressing, a discontinued line (I should hope so too – it sounds horrible) was long past its use-by date. Forensic experts said fermentation was to blame.

The morning forecast was not good; there were more gales on the way and overnight the flood warnings had jumped from fifty to seventy-one – most of them in the West Country. At least the firemen had timed their strike to let the weather help play an extinguishing role.

I continued battling southwards, togged up in my dripping and flapping waterproofs, past Weston-super-Mare's The Wonky Donkey gift shop, over the sluggish River Parrett at Bridgwater and on to East Quantoxhead and Watchet. One of the unsettling things I had found about cycling around England was the changing face of the villages and how so much of the land seemed to be over-populated by strangers in a hurry. Which I suppose wasn't really any wonder seeing as in 2002 some 300 people a day were moving out of the cities into the countryside, turning the villages into dormitory towns for commuters who, by demanding road signs and 'street' lighting everywhere, wanted to live in a tamed and quaint tea-cosy quasi-countryside that blocked out the worrying barking of the deer, the screeching of the owls and the blood-curdling screams of the vixens. So many villages were turning into nothing more than isolated lumps of suburbs with their low wooden fences and tidy front gardens containing either palmy plants studded among yin and yang gravel, or perfect petunias and poinsettias sprayed to ladybird extinction.

Village shops and pubs were closing down and getting turned into 'executive' homes. Agricultural labourers' hovels were transmogrified into suburban gents' des. res. Narrow country lanes built for slow, lumbering travel were getting the white-line treatment to make them safer for faster speed. Rough potholed tracks were turned into tarmac driveways with electric gates and entry phones. Old oak-beamed barns were now homes for Kensington migrants, and where once a cheery Fred Turnip might have stood with a straw in his mouth, milking his small herd of Daisy and Buttercups, now there was nothing more than a sweeping crunchy gravel parking lot for the latest must-have four-wheel-drive.

In the small port of Watchet I walked past a house in Market Street called Yankee Jack's Cottage. A small plaque explained that the long-lived Master Mariner John Short (1837–1933) once dwelt there. John Short, nicknamed Yankee Jack, was the town's most famous sailor, later to become Town Crier. He sailed the world, running the blockade during the American Civil War and, with his powerful voice, led the sailors in the singing of sea shanties as they worked.

Under an archway, opposite The Clipper Inn, stood another ancient abode. The house name said it was Sammy Hake's Cottage. I have no idea who Sammy Hake was, or is, but, like Yankee Jack, he sounded like an old salt of the sea with big, black gumboots, bushy foam-white beard and hands like a hide of halibut.

I made my way past a warehouse on the harbour side, its wall bearing in big letters the seafaring ditty:

THE FAIR BREEZE BLEW
THE WILD FOAM FLEW
THE FURROW FOLLOWED FREE

Hearing a patter of footsteps behind me, I turned to see a little five- or six-year-old girl running along the quayside towards her parents, her arms struggling to hold the full clutch of the *Mail on Sunday* with all its additional supplements and inserts. But it was all too much for her and they slipped out of her grasp and fanned all over the ground. A proper little drama queen, she put her hands on her hips and emitted a big sigh of exasperation.

'Oh, this drives me round the bend!' she said, with such dramatic emphasis that I laughed, because it sounded more the sort of thing that her granny would say.

I was stomping along the A39 when I came to a roundabout on the outskirts of Minehead. It was a quiet roundabout. The only car in sight was a stationary one, parked off to the left on a slip road leading to a residential lane. There were two people in the car. Both of them women. Both of them smiling and waving. At me.

I cycled up to them in case I could be of some help. Maybe they wanted to know what the weather was like in Vlissingen.

'Oh, it's a motorbike!' exclaimed the woman behind the wheel scanning her eyes over my mount.

'No it's not!' I laughed. 'It's a bicycle!'

'Ohh, but it's got such fat tyres!'

The woman was called Pat Gurnett and she was with her sister, Barbara Bacon. 'We're always interested in cyclists,' said Pat. 'We can't drive past one without having a good look. We passed you steaming along up the road and I said to Barbara, "That cyclist's pumping some iron!"'

'And I said, "Oh, and it's a girl!"' added Babs.

'Yes, because what struck us as unusual, apart from the amount of gear you're carrying, was that you're not a man!'

Pat was clearly of an excitable, not to mention observational nature.

'I only live up the road – why don't you come and have a cup of coffee? I know my husband Len would love to meet you. He's a keen Audax cyclist, rode Land's End to John O' Groats in four days. And he's done the Paris–Brest–Paris. But he's on crutches at the moment. He was hit by a lorry when out on his bike.'

I thanked her, but said I ought to get going to make the most of this dry interlude before it started raining again. They both asked me where I was going so I told them.

'You know, you remind me of someone who writes cycling books,' said Pat.

'Not Dervla Murphy?' I said.

'No,' she laughed. 'More your age.'

'Anne Mustoe? Bettina Selby?'

'It's Sophie someone,' chipped in Barbara.

'No, I'm sure it's a Rosie . . .'

'I can't think of any Sophies or Rosies,' I said. 'I know a Josie.'

'That's it! Josie Dew!'

'That's me!'

'Ohh my God! I didn't recognise you with a helmet on!'

'I don't usually wear one,' I said. 'But it keeps my head warmer and drier in all this lovely weather.'

'Right, that's it!' said Pat. 'You've just got to come and meet our Len. You'll make his day. We only live round the corner up the hill.'

'Oh no! Not another hill!'

'It's not far. Follow us!'

And off they went, with me puffing and panting in their slipstream. Opposite their drive, a neighbour was up a ladder cutting the hedge. Pat and Babs said something to him through the car window. *That's Josie Dew!* I could hear them saying. He turned to look at me salivating up the hill. Then he climbed down the ladder and walked across the road to Pat's. *Oh no!* I thought. *They're recruiting a reception committee!*

By the time I arrived fighting for breath, Len had hobbled out on his crutches. He was beaming from cheek to cheek. Len told me he was seventy and loved cycling.

'I've always been sporty,' he said, 'but I can honestly say I've had the most fun since I took up cycling at fifty.'

Three months ago, on a beautiful hot summer's day, Len was returning home after an eighty-mile ride across the hills and moors when a lorry drove straight out of a side turning and ran right over him. Though he was lucky not to have died, he was left with a lot of damage – handfuls of broken bones, a punctured lung and a crushed knee.

Laden down with a big bagful of Pat and Len's windfall apples, I rode on past Minehead's Mad Brain Sands before climbing Porlock's mad strain 1:4 hill, whose severe knee-buckling gradient and acute dog-legs were feared and respected by pioneering motorists. When I first struggled up this nigh-on sheer vertical climb on my three-speed Raleigh Misty when I was thirteen, my grand-father Frank told me how in the 1930s he used to go on hill-climbing races up here, road-testing his Lea Francis and Alvis Tourer. But the verticality of the climb was too much for many motors – they would stop, stall, conk out or drop off backwards down to Porlock.

I didn't *have* to explode my lungs and burst my knees up this hill because there was a gentler alternative on the toll road that ran just to the north through Birchanger. But as there's a perverse pleasure in pedalling pain, up I went.

Once at the top, I rode back down to Porlock via the toll road. And then I rode back up it again. It was a fantastic winding and weaving hairpin road, passing first through beautiful rocky-outcrop woodland before opening up to grassy sheep-cropped moorland with huge views out across Porlock Bay to Hurlstone Point and Bossington Hill, while to the west the hill fell away into a deep, dusk-darkening valley to Porlock Weir and Yearnor Wood.

There's a Devon saying:

> Vust 'er rained then 'er blawed,
> then 'er 'ailed then 'er snawed,
> then 'er comed a shower of rain,
> then 'er vruz an' blawed again.

Exmoor gave it to me like this. As the dramatic yellowy light drained from a stormy November sky, I rode across the scalp of the sandstone cliff-edged moor first in slashing rain and then in slanting hail that clattered like pinball wizards against my helmeted head. Icy wind-devils dared to capsize my equilibrium, tossing me this way, slamming me that.

Over the previous two weeks, as the rising flood waters played havoc with my sleeping bag, body and bottom bracket, I had on occasion come to the conclusion that November was perhaps not the best month to go cycle-camping around the ragged edges of the Welsh and South West coasts. But such despondent thoughts never lasted long because something always happened that suddenly made it seem so good.

And so it did on Exmoor. The weather may have been cruel and painful and penetratingly cold, but it all combined to add to the acute intensity and elation of the ride. The sky was a madhouse of colliding storm clouds crashing into the eclipsing obscurity of the hills and the sea. This was lonely Doone country, the area of Exmoor which R.D. Blackmore immortalised in his novel *Lorna Doone* as the stronghold of the murderous outlaws, the Doones. His story was based on the true exploits of a gang of desperadoes who settled on the moor in the seventeenth century, and the road past Deddy Combe and Desolate was . . .

well, Doone-like desolate. Had I not been riding this way at this time of day, at this time of year, in this type of weather, Desolate could well have been humming with humankind. As it was, it was mine and I didn't want the moment to end.

But it did, in spectacular style. I shot past Trilly and the wild moorland of Countisbury Common and Wind Hill before free-falling over my handlebars for what felt like for ever down the hilarious precipice of Countisbury Hill – a one-in-four road, cut into the side of the highest hog's-back cliffs in England – into the deep dark ravine of Lynmouth. By the time I screeched to a halt, I was wild-eyed and ecstatic. A woman wrapped in waterproofs stopped and stared at me as if I had just fallen out of the dripping, black-cloaked sky. Which I suppose I had.

It took a long time for me to regain full possession of my faculties – my frozen face refused to function for even the simplest procedure of saying thank you to a man who stooped to pick up my dropped glove. But what I had just endured was nothing compared with what happened in 1899 during a savage northwesterly gale. A ship was sending up distress signals off Porlock Weir, but the heavy seas at Lynmouth made it impossible to launch the lifeboat there. So a dozen horses and a hundred men dragged the lifeboat from Lynmouth thirteen miles across the ravaged bleakness of Countisbury moor and over the 991-foot-high Countisbury Hill to Porlock. For mile after gruelling mile the boat was hauled on a cart, up the one-in-four lane and on to the moor. When the cart lost a wheel the men dragged the boat bodily over skids. Ten hours later, after the long, back-breaking journey, the lifeboat was launched from Porlock Weir, and the ship's crew was rescued.

Lynmouth seems to have had more than its fair share of derring-do and disaster. In August 1952 the town, whose cliffsides are so steep that the houses stand on each other's shoulders, was devastated by a flood when, after weeks of rain, over nine inches of rain fell in twenty-four hours on the higher parts of Exmoor and unleashed a torrent of water in the East and West Lyn Rivers that swept 40,000 tons of boulders down the gorge-like valleys into Lynmouth. Buildings, like the hotel that used to straddle the road and where fishermen fished from the bedroom windows in the River Lyn, were washed clean into the sea and thirty-four people drowned.

In Lynmouth I was told the cheaper guest houses were up in Lynton. This was leg-deflating news. Lynton is poised on a cliff 600 feet above Lynmouth and the only way to reach it, apart from the Victorian, water ballast-operated cliff railway that hauls itself up and down the near-vertical 862-foot-long track, was by a hernia-inducing wall of hill. But if I didn't tackle it now, it would still be there in the morning. So, in pelting rain, I heaved and hurt my way up, eternally grateful to collapse finally on to a pink candlewick bedspread in a £15 room.

That night I learnt how Tony Blair was advising the public to be vigilant on the London Underground following evidence that the UK had been identified by al Qaeda as a target. 'TERROR ON THE TUBE' was the headline doing the rounds of the papers and there was talk of a terror onslaught using chemical and biological weapons that could wipe out hundreds of lives in a jiffy.

'Be alert, but not alarmed' were the reassuring words issuing forth from Whitehall. But what the sweet, macerated onions is that supposed to mean? Picture the scene: I'm waiting on the platform of Leicester Square station and I see a man with an Osama bin Laden beard remove a Snappy bag from his pocket and sprinkle what appears to be icing sugar over the tracks. So full marks there for the fact that I'm being alert. Now, what about the 'be not alarmed'? Oh no, I'm not alarmed at all! Heavens, Mr bin Beard was most likely only going to add a little water to his powdered sugar in order to form a nice concoction of glossy glacé icing with which to decorate the next train to come hurtling out of the tunnel.

I later read a piece in the paper by Tom Mangold, the author of *Plague Wars*, a book on biological warfare. In the event of a chemical or biological attack on the London Underground (which is designed not to be airtight), he wrote:

> The British Military do, in fact, have standby plans for such an attack, rehearsed in great secrecy. They divide the living into three rather brutally named groups, 'walkers, floppers and goners'. In the chaos, little could be done for the last two groups.

Well that's nice to know. As I digested this information, I thought it was worth making a mental note that if I did ever happen to find myself in the wrong Tube at the wrong time, I must remember not to look like a flopper or a goner. It could be more than my life was worth.

CHAPTER 61

More mad hills had me half-dying to Woody Bay and Hunter's Inn via the Valley of Rocks, a curious, twisting, streamless and steep-sided gorge surrounded by weather-eroded pillars, stony tors and massive castellated slab piles of rock with names like Castle Rock, Ragged Jack and Devil's Cheesewring, which on the seaward side fell as cliffs into the Bristol Channel. All along this stretch of isolated high-cliff coast, from Lynton to Combe Martin, there are names to make you wonder: Ruddy Ball, Hollerday Hill, Wringapeak, The Cow & Calf, Highveer Point, Heddon's Mouth, The Mare & Colt, Great and Little Hangman.

It was raining so hard along the lanes that the run-off was teeming in torrents, sending leaves and twigs and the odd wheel-crunched can surfing over the road. By midday the murky gloom had become oppressive. Dropping down past Hele Bay into Ilfracombe, cars (with their headlights on) swished by in waves of spray. But the names of the boats in the harbour cheered me up: *Our Josie Grace, Lone Shark, Hat Trick* and *Dab Chick*. So too did a blackboard outside The Pier pub advertising alongside its fare of roast beef and Yorkshire pudding, 'FRESH THICK GRAVY'. Presumably complete with lumps and skin on the side.

When the rain finally petered out and there was a winking blink of sun, I climbed up Hillsborough Hill, which overlooked the whole of Ifracombe or, as it was recorded in the Domesday Book of 1086, *Alfreincombe*, meaning Alfred's wooded valley.

Before our invading French friends turned up at Aunty May's on that fateful 22nd February 1797, they had come storming up the Bristol Channel in their men-of-war after scuttling several ships off the Devon coast. Since few men remained to defend the town, the good womenfolk of Alfred's Combe are said to have paraded high on a hill over the town with their scarlet petticoats draped fetchingly, if not a little provocatively, around their shoulders, so that from a distance those hot-blooded Frenchmen thought they looked like an army of Redcoats and scarpered off in the direction of Wales with their tails between their legs, never realising what a good thing they were missing. Alfred's Combe had the doughty hock of Betsy Gammon to thank, for it was she who banged the drum (on fine exhibit in Ilfracombe Museum) to rally the local women together to peel off their petticoats up high on yonder hilltop. I presume it was also our brazen Betsy who sent an e-mail to her Welsh counterpart, Jemima Nicholas, to rally her girls to start waving their undergarments from a prominent peak the moment they saw Johnny Foreigner bearing down on them.

Bearing down on me as I stood on the hillside was a sixty-five-year-old man with a rolled up copy of the *Sun* poking out of his back pocket. Originally from Darlington, he now lived in Littlehampton. I knew he was sixty-five because he told me that in 1952, when he was fifteen, he went to work on a farm on Exmoor owned by a Polish family. This was his second visit back this way since then, and that morning he had gone to the library to go through the telephone directories to look, without success, for the Polish family. I asked him what he did after leaving the farm.

'I had a choice of either joining the army or working down the mine, so I chose the pay. I worked sixteen years down them pits till I had an accident. Hit on the head, I were, by a girder.'

He was sent to Littlehampton to convalesce where he fell in love with a nurse. He never returned to the pits. From what could I gather in my gathering way, the nurse was no longer around. It was his niece who booked up his trip, sending him off on a £100 package deal to spend a week at a hotel in Ilfracombe. It was Wednesday 20th November and yesterday the hotel had served him and the rest of his coach party Christmas dinner 'with all the trimmings'. Today was Boxing Day.

'Another big spread,' he said. 'But it was too much. I needed to get away from it all. So I've come up here, like, to sit in the shelter up top and do the *Sun* crossword.'

Before we parted, he dug into the pocket of his jacket and pulled out a mince pie wrapped up in a red, peaked-too-early festive napkin.

'Merry Christmas, me darlin'!' he said, handing me the squashed but body-warmed mince pie. 'I'm sick of them bloody things already!'

Brandy Cove Point, Shag Point, Bull Point, Grunta Beach, and then it was headlong into the Bosom of the Family at Woolacombe Bay Hotel where I met up with mum and dad. The Billabong, Animal, Rip Curl and Quiksilver-clad surfing village of Woolacombe clamps itself to the hillside overlooking its grand scalloped strand – a luxurious infinity of pale honey sand, sugar-fine in places, crushed shells in others, caught between two grassy, sheep-nibbling headlands. Woolacombe, with its Victorian gabled villas and private hotels, faces the full force of the thunderous Atlantic rollers. At any time of year and in almost any type of weather, a flotsam of surfers in black body suits can be seen bobbing about in and out of the spray-blown breakers like a convention of empty-bottling seals.

With tent, clothes and feet dried out for the first time in three weeks, it was straight back to get them all wet again as I propelled myself onwards in tumultuous downpours past Baggy Point (no baggy bits, just lots of hard sandstone) and Horsey Island (no horses but spotted distant cow) until I joined the River Taw-hugging Tarka Trail (car-free heaven but dog-turd hell) all the way through Barnstaple (Old English for 'bearded post' – yes, yes, I know, doesn't make sense to me either), Saltpill Duck Pond and East-the-Water. In the white-washed rain-lashed River Torridge-side town of Bideford, I was going to catch the MS *Oldenburg* to Lundy (Old Norse for Puffin Island) but lo! 'Vust 'er rained then 'er blawed, then 'er 'ailed then 'er snawed', so the sailing was cancelled. And then . . . oh no! . . . Westward Ho!, which claims its fame as being the only place in the country to be named after a novel (*Water Babies*, Charles Kingsley's adventure story about Elizabethan seafarers, is to blame) and to have an exclamation mark after it!

But with warnings of a severe storm on the way I was in no mood for exclamation marks being thrown willy-nilly into the procedure, so pressed on to Knotty Corner where a mere wand's wave away at Fairy Cross I joined the A39(T) – oh, sweet Westward Ho! – not another Terrible Trunk? In county council terminology, major tourist attractions are unappealingly promoted and referred to as 'brands'. Hadrian's Wall is a brand, '1066 Country' is a brand, and now, judging from the signs fringing the roadside, the plain old A39 has borrowed a fancy feather out of California's sunhat and been branded as the 'Atlantic Highway'. But instead of the Santa Cruz, Monterey, Big Sur exotica of the Pacific Highway, we get to pass through places with rainy names like Minehead and Wadebridge, which doesn't exactly get the pulse palpitating with visions of on-the-road romanticism.

At Horn's Cross I looped a loop through Sloo and Hoops, aquaplaned through Watershute, didn't Bight a Doubleyou (because I didn't feel like it, thanks), cobbled my way through Clovelly, snacked near Snaxland, needed wellies at Velly, and felt tall at Titchberry (big cliff high-spot). Then, once past Cow & Calf (Mach 2 – another heap of Atlantic ruminant-pounded rocks), Speke's Mill Mouth and Welcombe, I was welcomed into Cornwall with a wall of water and a wall of hill and a wall of damp Friesians standing in line with their backs to the wind, which I assure you is no way to greet a fair maiden in pre-storm distress.

News of the week for Cornwallians, or 'Promontory People', as I believe they are more correctly called (at least, this is the literal translation of the old Cornovii tribe from whence they originate), was that '*Kernewek re be grontys dewhelans*'. Ha! You may think my brain has sprung a leaky puncture, but unless you are a Promontory Person of the very finest linguistic order, you won't know that this rabble-babble can be translated as, 'Cornish has been granted a comeback'.

Yes, it was indeed a monumental time for the ancient Celtic language (a tongue related to Welsh and Breton) spoken fluently by a hundred people (all of them of a Promontory nature), as it was suddenly granted official protection under the provisions of a European Union charter on 'minority languages', paving the way for schoolchildren to learn it. The Government, which likes to waver and backpedal on all things eco-friendly, decided it would commit itself to ensuring that Cornish lessons be available 'at all appropriate stages'. And a good thing too, because for a language that talks of '*grontys*' and '*dewhelans*', it's got to have something pretty good going for it. Though be warned, when conversing with locals it is advised that visitors (emmets) avoid the phrase, '*Ass yw an penty mai! A allaf vy y brena rag chy haf?*' – which means 'What a delightful cottage! Can I buy it for a second home?'

Talking of second homes (look away now if you're a Promontory Person) I stayed in a first-and-only-home of a woman who lived with her retired-butcher husband in Polzeath, a small resort which sits in a nook just down from Rumps Point and yet more bovine-flavoured Cow & Calf rocky outcrops. After several very wet and windy nights wallowing in the muddy water of saturated fields – the last on a sodden farm near the Beeny Sisters (not soft-cuddly toys but a wave-lashed reef lying off Fire Beacon Point) – I treated myself to a bed and hot water and rekindled toes in the butcher's B&B. Mrs Butcher told me that Polzeath is known as 'Kensington-on-Sea' with seventy-five to eighty per cent of houses being second homes – most of them to city-dwelling four-wheel-drive owners with born-to-rule voices.

'We're one of the few remaining families who live here year round,' she said, walking me over to the big front window with a view over the sands of Hayle Bay, where westerly winds provide perfect lip-curling rollers for surfers. 'See that house there?' she said, pointing up the hill. 'Empty. The house next to it? Empty. That little cluster down the bottom? Empty. There's still an old couple living in that one perched up there, but they haven't got any neighbours any-more.'

In the summer, she said, you can't move for cars and strangers, while in the winter it's like a ghost town.

'Our electricity man who reads the meter told me that Polzeath, Port Isaac and Treyarnon are the three places in Cornwall with the highest proportion of second homes.'

Three what were once humming fishing villages, all lying within ten miles of each other. That's a lot of ghost towns in a very small area.

'And another thing,' said Mrs Butcher on a letting-off-steam roll, 'our local shop must be the most expensive Spar in the country. They sell the fanciest bottles of wine, lemon grass and sun-dried tomatoes. All I want is a bag of sugar and a pint of milk!'

The next morning I rode past houses with names like Middle Hobby and Tiggywinkles, then rolled through Rock (where 'tis said the Princely Wills has holidayed with his Etonesque chums), following the River Camel inland to Wadebridge where I picked up The Camel Trail, the most popular Sustrans tourist cycle route in the country with getting on for 400,000 visitors a year, many of whom ironically arrive for their cycle-ride by car. But it pays to be cycling on a wildly squally day at the end of November because, apart from a couple of ramblers and two twitchers on the look-out for wintering wildfowl like wigeon, long-tailed duck and goldeneye, there was no one else around as I followed the abandoned railway line (the section from Wadebridge to Poley's Bridge being one of the oldest in the world, opened in 1834). Unlike other rail-way cycle paths that offer you views of nothing but dark overgrown embankments with the odd flasher thrown in for excitement value, here I cycled bang on the banks of the Camel estuary (really a ria, but I've been down that geography-lesson road before in Kingsbridge) and was rewarded for my wet-riding efforts by sweeping views across the water to Dinham, Trevelver, Cant Cove, Gentle Jane, Porthilly and Stoptide. Incidentally, if you're wondering what camels are doing in Cornwall, *cam* is Cornish for 'crooked' and 'bent', while the *el* comes from *pol* meaning 'pool' or 'stream'. Which is a bit disappointing really, as I was quite hoping to sail into a cushion-footed ship-of-the-desert somewhere along the trail.

The Camel led me straight into Padstow, now more famous for being the home of Rick Stein's Seafood Restaurant than for once being one of the largest medieval towns in Cornwall. They say Rick's joint is *the* place to eat in Padstow, but don't believe a word of it – I can highly recommend a bus shelter down near the dockside that offers a degree of protection from the westerly-steering rain and where pannier-squashed sarnies can be devoured at leisure while catching up on the latest squalid things that teenagers do to each other, thanks to the modern-day hieroglyphics scrawled all over the walls. But if what Tammy puts in her mouth or what Ben fancies doing to two girls all at the same time is of no interest to you (shame on you), then avert your gaze to the upper corner of the shelter where an interesting family of abseiling spiders can be observed. Failing that, you can always turn the other cheek and look out over the very lumpy humpy Camel to the rain-shrouded shores of Rock.

On mile 4976, Puncture No. 3 struck in a swift deflatory whoosh. Up until this point, all had been going swimmingly badly – swimming being the operative word. After weighing anchor in Padstow, I rode the waves of flooded lanes past Butter Hole, Cat's Cove, Stinking Bay, Booby's Bay, and . . . what's this? . . . not another Cow & Calf (must be something to do with that vast-bollocked bull who resided in the next-door field the other night when I was camping up near Foxhole Point). The socking headwind was so strong it felt like I stood a better chance of being blown 800 miles to John O' Groats faster than ever I would cycle the eighty-odd miles to Land's End.

And then . . . ker-*bang*! Shrapnel from a broken bottle causing the maritime equivalent of running on to the rocks. I'm as good as grounded. With steed dangerously listing to starboard, I drag it into the gateway of a boggy field. Rain hammers down. Tool bag fills with water. Pannier-dwelling replacement tube extracted. Quick release loosened. Rear wheel removed, releasing mini oil slick over clothing. Tussle with filthy grimy tyre. Wind gusts knock me sideways. Late November rain waterfalls down neck. Hands freeze to death.

Pull out flaccid tube. Run fingers round inside of tyre. *Ow!* Locate sabre-like glass fragment. Extract with mini tweezers. Semi-inflate new tube. Shove it into tyre. Feed tyre back on to rim. Hands too cold to flip in last tight bit of tyre. Filthy language escapes from lips. Wind whisks words away over cliff-face. Still struggling. I'm soaked, I'm freezing, I'm filthy and I'm wondering why I just don't jack it all in and go and buy a nice, big, warm and safe four-wheel-drive and give birth to 2.4 children and live crappily ever after. Because . . . because . . . because . . . this is my life – flailing around in the grime of the roadside . . . loving moments . . . hating moments. Pain. Anxiety. Exhaustion. Elation. Delight and despair. It's all fun in the long run. People driving past in fat-tyred vehicles send bow waves of water crashing over me. They stare at me like I'm mad. *What's she doing out in this weather?* I can hear them saying. *That girl's certainly picked the wrong time of year to go cycling! Look at her! Must be mad, being out in this!*

But I'm not mad. This is normal behaviour for a self-propelled person out travelling the highways and byways, just as much as reading the *Daily Telegraph* might be normal behaviour for a home-counties, train-travelling, London-bound commuter forced to travel in conditions illegal for sheep. You do what you know. And you do what you're used to. And, in my case, I do what I like. On a bike.

CHAPTER 62

One of the benefits of being out on the road on your own is that you know you're going to get that bloody sodding stubborn tyre back on whatever happens, because there's no one else who's going to help you. So with gnashing teeth I strained my frigid fingers to fight it back under the rim. Ten minutes later I was on my way, hoping for as many uphills as possible to rekindle my icy circulation.

The Met Office's severe weather warning finally hit as I was entering Newquay by way of Whipsiderry and Lusty Glaze, tossing the top of a wind-snapped pine tree across my flooding guttered path. I dived into the first budget accommodation I could find – a seedy workers' haunt on Henver Road where the previous 'guest' had obviously used the curtains in my room as giant handkerchiefs. The whole place stank of stale smoke and gravy. I shared a bathroom with the heavy-booted workers on my floor. One of the men left the most remarkable offering in the toilet which beggared belief.

Unfortunately I was forced to spend two nights storm-bound in this hovel. With westerly winds gusting up to 90 mph, the weather was just too wild to venture off along the coast. It rained so hard that Peter Gibbs, the weatherman on the Radio 4 forecast, began his morning bulletin by announcing that, following the previous day's rainfall, St Mawgan, which is four miles northeast of Newquay as the gale-hurled palm tree flies, had recorded its wettest November on record. Yes, well, as Dylan sang in his *Subterranean Homesick Blues*, you don't need a weatherman to know which way the wind blows.

In sheets of rain I walked, togged up in my rain kit, along the beaches and cliff-tops of Newquay, passing Pipers Hole, Dollar Rock, Blowing Hole, Great Cupboard, Wine Cove, Lusty Glaze, Pigeon Cove, Old Dane, Seal Hole, Spy Cove, Harbour of Refuge, Nun Cove and Sunny Corner. Up on top of one of the cliffs overlooking Newquay Bay, I came across a fence wearing a school tie, a pair of socks and a bedraggled bunch of flowers. Opposite the fence I sat on a new memorial bench. The engraved plaque told me that this spot was:

DOM'S PLACE

1983–2000

Who came into our lives

And quickly went

Moving our souls to dance and

Leaving footprints in our hearts

On the cliff edge beside the fence with the tie smacking hard in the wind, a low-legged wooden tablet sprouted from the ground. Carved upon its face was the explanation:

From this cliff fell Dominic Swanson – he led a full 16 yrs too short.

Despite the weather, I spent a long time hanging on to the fence in the buffeting wind and drowning rain, feeling incredibly sad for a boy and his family I never knew. I looked at the wind-frayed school tie, no doubt his tie, slapping this way and that in the gale. Finally I walked round to the other side of the bluff from where I could peer down to the beach, crinkle-cut into the granite cliff. From this spot I could look back to Dom's Place to see how far he had fallen. It was a sickeningly long way. And there were rocks at the bottom.

Newquay, once just a small fishing village, later to become, with the coming of the railway, a china-clay port for the nearby pits, is now Surf City. Hanging 10 in the barrel with your toes on the nose, then getting pitched off the lip and losing your sponge. That means surfing, man. All year round there are lean, wet-suited types, trotting out across the sands of the long parade of beaches, surfboard tucked under arm. It's not that surfing is new to Newquay – ever since a coffin-maker in nearby Perranporth started to make the first boards in

the 1920s, lithe and not so lithe forms have been riding the fast, hollow breakers of Fistral beach, Britain's most celebrated surfing hot spot, on their
metamorphosed coffin lids. There is even talk of building Europe's first artificial reef here, to guarantee optimum conditions. Now all the shops in Fore
Street are stuffed full of swanky surf gear and there are surfers' hangouts and
surf lodges everywhere: The Spot, The Tube, The Zone, Matt's Surf, Base Surf,
Home Surf, Wave Surf, Wave Board, Over Board, Super Surf, SURFs R US –
well, maybe not the last four, but give it a week and I'm sure as surf is surf
they'll appear.

In a heavy squall, I did quite a good job of surfing myself as I skimmed
through the overflowing lanes out past The Goose, The Chick and Gull Rocks
to Perranporth. Then it was on by the fenced-off and long-abandoned shaft
mines at Shag Rock, Cligga Head and Wheal Kitty where in the past the area
around has been ripped apart in the search for metals. 'Man & his man rocks'
guard the entrance to Trevaunance Cove, a rock-girt hideaway beneath St
Agnes Head where 150 years ago busied a harbour from which tin and copper
were exported. It's a quiet place now, the quays having long since been swept
away by the sea.

To add to the already dramatic geology, the whole region round here has
skylines dominated by the ruins of Cornwall's castles of industry. The stark
structures of engine-houses and chimney stacks are striking monuments to an
age when men burrowed beneath the granite cliffs and moors in search of tin,
copper, lead and zinc.

In the mid nineteenth century there were 600 active mines in Cornwall. As
I cycled round the cliffs past Tubby's Head, climbing up to the fine scenic

grandstand of St Agnes's 630-foot Beacon, the ghostly grey granite remains of mines appeared like tall keeps with tapering towers. When I rounded a bend or topped the brow of a hill, they showed themselves suddenly, sometimes standing austere and desolate against the grubby sky or merging into the background of a boulder-strewn moor. But always they were a reminder of the grim and brutal life where naked men stood up to their knees in water in the bowels of the mine for about twelve shillings a week (women and children received far less). To reach the surface after a crippling day's work, the miners had to clamber up hundreds of feet of ladders out of the 'zawns', or shafts, their only light underground coming from the candles fixed with clay to their hard felt hats, before walking home, wet and cold and hungry. Further along the coast in St Just, the funeral register shows the average age of 600 people buried there in the mid-nineteenth century was under twenty-six. James Watt, the engineer whose development of the steam engine (used to pump water away from the workings) contributed to the industrial revolution, is said to have found it stomach-turning to see starving men scraping the grease off his engines and eating it. Many miners died in steam boiler explosions, trying to warm themselves beside the boiler when it blew up.

There were more rocks to look down upon as I closed in on St Ives Bay, these ones being Tobban Horse, Sheep, Diamond, Horse and Gull. There were Cupboards belonging to Ralph, Islands of Samphire, Coves for a Deadman and Mouths of Hell. As I climbed up out of Portreath and rode across the springy turf and heathland of Reskajeage Downs along a shining road that almost ran clean off the cliff, the sun burst into brilliance, blinding me in its searchlight. All around me in a vast sky of huge horizons, stonking black rain clouds regrouped, their murderous wet ammo at the ready.

Things turned even more glorious as I shuddered around Hudder Down because along with the sparkling charge of sustained sunshine that rained down on me as I hit the 5000-mile mark, I had the whole road to myself. Not one soul to be seen. Not one vehicle to ruin the singing wind in my wheels. This could have quite a lot to do with the yellow sandwich sign straddling the road at the turning for Coombe and Menadarva. I shot by it with scarcely a blink. It said: ROAD AHEAD CLOSED. Another sign indicated a DIVERSION along a route inland that I had no intention of following. I stood my ground. I cycled my ground. And I said 'NO!' to DIVERSION. Because one mustn't let the dictatorial authorities divert one off one's chosen path in life. So I cycled on, revelling in the sudden limitless loveliness of the loneliness.

I had decided to run the risk of the road closure. While a car can become impotent in the face of a fallen tree or a landslide or verge-spanning three-foot-deep road trench, there's not a lot that a bicycle can't be squeezed by or dragged over. A bike is versatile. A car mostly futile.

I was about level with Castle Giver Cove, preparing my descent into Gwithian, when a canary yellow flat-bed truck came into view, rumbling up the hill towards me. It slowed as it approached. Then it stopped. 'CORMAC' was written in big letters along the lorry's flanks. Shovels, tar and a pile of grit half-filled the back. Two men sat in the cab. Two men in fluorescent yellow safety vests with 'CORMAC' spanning their backs. Two men looked at me. I looked at the two men. I cycled up to the two men's cab. One man wound down his window.

'You're not going to tell me I can't get through, are you?' I asked in a sort of double-negative hopeful-faced way.

'Not unless you're any good at cycling under four feet of water!' said Chief Cormac Man.

'Oh, is it really that bad?'

'Well, maybe three-and-a-half foot.'

'That's still up to my neck!' I looked at my handlebar bag-planted map. 'Is the only alternative to go out towards the A30 at Camborne and then round through Connor Down?'

'That's right, love. It's about a ten-mile diversion.'

I looked up. Although the sun was still shining on me, the sky was filled with enormous dollops of tormented cloud. The wind was still bleating and blowing hard from the west. And it was in that direction – the direction I was heading – that a menacing frontier of inky stormcloud spanning the snake-head of Cornwall was fast marching towards me. Given the time of day, it was obvious that if I went cavorting off on an inland diversion, I would get caught out in a very dank twilight.

'Can small lorries get through the flood?' I asked. 'Not that I'm hinting at anything, of course!'

Cormac Man regarded me with a don't-you-try-and-work-no-charm-on-me look.

'Go on, then,' he said. 'We'll meet you at the bottom of the hill.'

Without so much as a shilly-shally, I shot off downwards with a cheery heart. At the bottom I found the Red River had burst its banks. The fields were seas.

The road was a river ruffled with wavelets. In the middle of this river was a man-made island, which on closer inspection was a reddy-brown Jag doing a very poor impression of a boat. The Cormac men climbed out of the cab. They hauled my bike up into the back of the truck.

'Bloody hell!' they wheezed. 'Are you smuggling half the cliffs of Cornwall or something in here?'

'No,' I said. 'Just spare body parts.'

Cormac Man Copilot looked at me as if I was serious.

I thought they were just going to lean my bike down against a pile of road grit and then we'd all clamber into the cab together, but Cormac Man told Cormac Copilot to stand in the back and hold my bike.

'She won't want her bags to get all covered in tar – girls don't like dirt!' he said with a wink in my direction.

'Oh? We don't?' I said, covered in enough road gunk and bicycle chain oil that you could have got fifty miles per gallon out of me if you were a little light-weight run-around. But unless you're a 'ROAD CLOSED' sign, I'm not one to argue with authority when that authority is doing something that I want to do.

'Is that all right with you?' I asked Cormac Copilot.

'I just do what I'm told,' he said.

So I climbed into his seat, leaving him to stand in the cold, bone-slicing wind to hold on to my bike looking like a comical theatrical prop.

'Is he really all right out there, do you think?' I asked Cormac Man.

'It's good for him,' he replied. 'He hasn't done a bloody bit of work all day!'

In the time it took us to bow-wave slowly in high revs through the flood, looking down superciliously upon the drowned Jag, I learnt that Cormac Man was in the Cornish version of a Welsh male choir. He travelled all over the country with his group. He'd just got back from singing in a hall in Portsmouth.

Once back on terra firma, I climbed out to reclaim my bike.

'Thank God for that!' said Cormac Copilot, clearly not happy with his lot. 'I'm freezing my bloody nuts off up here!'

We all shook hands, they wished me luck, and I went on my way.

By the time I arrived in St Ives a deep-darkening dusk had fallen, even though it was only four o'clock in the afternoon. As I was heading down Lifeboat Hill, the heavens opened so I ran into the public toilets to take cover. The graffiti in here were not so much bawdy as bitchy. Judging from the insulting scrawl, the Penzance ladettes had been in town:

St Ives girls are so thick they get locked in supermarkets and starve.
St Ives girls are so dumb they get hit by parked cars.
St Ives girls are so stupid they sit on the TV to watch the sofa.

All the St Ives girls could manage in rivalry retaliation was:

Penzance girls are slappers.

I couldn't find a bed in St Ives. All the guesthouses were closed or full or too expensive. So I rode back up the hill to Carbis Bay in the dark of the raining rush hour. I was told there was quite a nice little B&B at the bottom of Boskerris Road, but when I got there after plunging down a precariously steep residential road, it was closed. As I was making my way at about 4 mph back up the hill, I heard a thudding crack from my back wheel. A split second later something jammed into my wheel and I came to an abrupt standstill. At first I thought my mudguard stay had broken, but when I pulled out my torch I saw that the rear rack chainstay braze-on (the part of the frame with a little threaded nodule to bolt the bottom strut of the rack on to the bike) had completely sheared off, pushing the rack into the wheel. I said something colourful and then took stock of the situation. It was dark, it was pissing down, it was freezing, I had nowhere to sleep and I had a bike that refused to move. Oh, halleluja!

No one was out on the street. Who would want to be in the rain and the dark and the cold? They were all cosily tucked up behind closed curtains. Using some fat plastic zip-ties I tried to yank the rack back out of the wheel to keep it out of my spokes just long enough for me to push my bike as far as a B&B that would have me. But the rack was having none of that and sprang back into my wheel. I couldn't remove the rack because it was loaded with my worldly possessions. And I didn't fancy bailing out and leaving them at the roadside. I thought about locking up my bike while I went to look for somewhere to stay. But then I decided I didn't fancy leaving it alone in the dark even though it wasn't very close to my heart at the moment.

In the end, using super-human peed-off-with-everything strength, I lifted up some eighty-odd pounds of bike and baggage and staggered, rolling it on the front wheel up the hill.

445

Then I came to Lamorna 'Christian Guest House'.

Hmm. Do I have to be a Christian to enter these hallowed walls? Or can I just say: *Please God, shine on me now in my sticky predicament, and I shall be eternally grateful and will make sure my braze-ons are brazed on better in future.*

I knocked on the door, hoping God would open it. But a man called Tony did instead.

I felt a luxurious wind of warmth escape from the house as Tony stood in the doorway. I asked him if I could stay there for the night, but he said that God was in the Seychelles on His winter break and wouldn't be back to open up until spring.

Or words to that effect.

I put on my downcast look and said I wouldn't need a bed or any food – just a little floor space to put my sleeping bag. I also told him about my bike.

'Sorry,' he said, 'but we're closed for winter.'

Then God's House closed the door on me and I was left in the dark and the rain to carry a bloody heavy broken bike out of the palm tree-fronted driveway, the palms' fronds dripping and blowing havoc in the wind.

Back on the road I suddenly felt almost eye-wateringly despondent. Where was the Christian spirit of this Christian House? People who weren't Christians had been far more hospitable and helpful and heart-warming to me in the past. So I turned round and dragged my bike back to God's Holiday Home and knocked on the door again, hoping that maybe Mary might open it this time. I could see her through the window, sitting in a sumptuously snug front room having afternoon tea and biscuits.

Tony opened the door. I apologised for disturbing him again, but asked if I could shelter in his open-fronted garage while I tried to mend my bike. He said yes, and then closed the door.

The garage was round the side of the house at the back. It wasn't much good for shelter because it had a broken roof through which a waterfall of rain was running, landing on the concrete floor with drenching splashes. Never mind, my feet couldn't be more wet if they tried. The garage was full of junk and old paint pots and soaking wet mouldy dustsheets. There was no electricity, so I was as good as outside. Still, it was something, so I removed all my panniers from the bike, put on my headtorch and rummaged in my tool bag for my 4 mm allen key. My plan was to try and shunt the rack on to the mudguard braze-on. Luckily I had a longer allen-headed bolt in my film canister of spare bolts and nuts and washers, to compensate for the extra width of mudguard stay. As I was crouched grovelling on the ground in the wind looking for screws, it suddenly dawned on me that had Cormac Man not come to my rescue, forcing me to take the diversion, my bike could have collapsed on me as I was careering along at 30 mph down the A30, which might well have spelt curtains.

I was in mid-tinker when Mary emerged out of the gloom – not with a halo but with a mug of tea and a Penguin.

'Are you all right out here?' asked Mary, whose name was really Sandra.

'Yes, thank you,' I replied, soaked, filthily oily and shivering uncontrollably. Then she turned round and disappeared back inside.

My hands were so cold that they weren't doing what I wanted them to do. They had turned so doo-lalley I couldn't even undo a clip on my pannier. The tea was a saviour. I wrapped my hands around the mug trying to resurrect a semblance of life. But really I needed a lot more than a mug of tea to feel my fingers again or to stop my teeth chattering.

For nearly an hour I struggled to force my rack into a place it didn't want to go while simultaneously trying with frozen hands to screw the allen bolt through the mudguard stay's eye and the mudguard braze-on without ruining the thread. I got close on several occasions, but couldn't quite manage it. I needed another set of hands. So resignedly, I went in search of a pair.

The pair I found belonged to Tony. By this stage we had my bike in the light of his lobby. He pushed down on the rack while I levelled up the allen bolt with the braze-on thread. At last, with target sighted, I hit success. *Ahh, praise be!* I thought that as Tony and Sandra had by now discovered what I was doing and where I was going, they might be a little more forthcoming in my plight for a bed. They allowed me to use the toilet, and offered the use of their phone should I want it – but who was I going to ring? The builder? (*ME, said with a tone of distress:* 'My bike's just broken and I can't find anywhere to sleep even though there is plenty of room at the Inn!' *BUILDER:* '. . . yes, the serpular lacryman content of the wood is looking good so I'll be putting a tension joint in to resist extension for the king post repairs using through splayed and tabled scarf abutments with through tennoned tabling using two-edge pegs and four-face pegs . . .')

I don't think so.

And then God and Mary shut the door on me again and I went back out into the night. A night of continuous wind-screaming and persistent cold rain.

But at least I could cycle.

Up on the main road I had several more attempts at trying to find a place to stay.

I ring on bell. Knock on door. I stand back, with a weary thrill of anticipation as I wait to see who will answer it. The feeling is always the same – a peculiar mixture of fear and hope and voyeuristic curiosity. The door opens. A woman with straggly long hair and a fag hanging from the corner of her lips stands listlessly looking at me. Behind her is a long narrow hallway with a grimy carpeted staircase off to the side.

'Hello!' I say. 'Have you got a room for tonight?'

'For how many people?' says the woman.

'Just me,' I reply.

'Sorry, love. We're full.'

Door bangs shut. Back out into the street. Into the rain.

I try more doors down the street. Some doors remain unanswered. Others open, to release a mauling of excitable dog. At another a man stands with his flies undone. Elsewhere I'm hit in the face by a powerful smell of curry on the cooker, reminding me just how hungry I am. But always the answer is the same – they either don't want one person, or they're closed for winter.

And I watch yet another door swing shut, closing me out in the cold.

CHAPTER 63

Eventually I found a place to stay. A horrible place where the carpet hadn't been vacuumed for at least five years, and the bog brush bore the remnants of a previous user's offerings, including chewed-up paper. I escaped early the next morning into brilliant sunshine. As I climbed up and over the bleakly beautiful heather moors of the Penwith peninsula my spirits were soaring, my speed was good. I've cycled this road to Land's End by way of Zennor, Boswednack, Botallack and Kelynack many times before and it's melodramatic and awesome in whatever weather I ride.

And this morning was no different. Savage cliffs of slate and granite fell away into the Atlantic where the wave-trains of rollers sent a lacework of foam and spray against the jagged rocks at their base. I passed through a radiant moorland of browns and greens and purples and golds interspersed with surrounding patterns of small and irregular stone-walled fields going back to the Stone Age. The whole area is strewn with carns, commons, downs, hills, hut circles, stone circles, abandoned mine shafts with gaunt ruins of engine-houses pointing fingers of chimneys skywards, Iron Age hill forts, ancient settlements, prehistoric cemeteries, quoits, coves, capes, rocks and tumuli bearing fanciful names: Kenidjack, Wheal Buller, Wheal Bal, Gloose, Conquer, Beagletodn, Wicca Pool, Great Zawn, Trewellard Zawn, Zawn a Bal, Hannibal, Avarack, Noongallas, Bodrifty, Nine Maidens, Tor Noon, Three Stone Oar, Woon Gumpus.

On up the hill to St Just, past Tom Thumb Rock, Cot Valley and the aerodrome with its flat-out flapping windsock telling me what I already knew – flippin' frisky headwind. But come hell, come hail, come a gale, come a flood without Cormac

Man in sight, it wasn't going to stop me now. As a black-veiled curtain of rain cloud, spanning from horizon to horizon, stormed on the war-path towards me, I emerged on to the deserted A30 and, with the excitement of the End of the Land in sight, barrelled down through Sennen, tearing into the Trevescan corner before levelling up for the final straight across Treve Common. Compared with my last lame-kneed visit at the height of summer, there were so few people this time around (I counted five in all) that I sailed straight through the horrors of the Theme Park and past The Last Post Box in England without even dismounting.

Heritage Experience, anyone? No thank you. It's an experience enough to stand on top of the cliffs at the tip of the land and look out upon the troubled meeting place of the three seas – the Irish one, the Channelled one and the almighty Atlantic, throwing their seething surf sucking and grumbling against the rocky bottom of the beetle-browed precipices.

After leaving Land's End I rode back to St Ives. When I arrived there it was still only early afternoon, so I turned round and rode back to Land's End – not because 'it's there' or I'd had a brainstorm, but because the road through the bleak, rock-tossed moorland of Zennor, Carn Galver and Woon Gumpus provides a perfect setting for unpredictable behaviour. And it's just too good to resist.

On the final lap, with the gloomy edges of twilight clawing in around me and the air expectant with yet more heavy winter rain, I slipped off on to a side road to Zennor Head. Here, 300 feet above the heaped slop and chop of the Atlantic, protrudes one of the wildest headlands in Cornwall, with a narrow gorge known as the Horseback Zawn, cutting deep into the granite.

As I stood on the Horse's bare back, the wind ripping and raw one moment before dropping to muffled skirls the next, I looked westwards out over the blackening sea and saw a 'green flash' – a phenomenon that occasionally occurs while the sun is sinking or rising. Its eerie, bilious, green light flooded the sky.

That was to be the last light of the day, for it was quickly swallowed by a skirmish of wrathful black cloud, riling with rain.

APPENDIX

Equipment Department

Bicycle

Frame	Custom-made 16″ Roberts (Roughstuff) with custom Columbus Nivacrom tubing
Rims	Mavic D521 (36 H)
Hubs	Shimano Deore XT (36 H)
Spokes	DT double-butted stainless steel
Rim tape	Velox
Tyres	Continental Top Touring 26 × 1.75
Tubes	Specialised 26 × 1.5–2.2 (schrader)
Headset	Stronglight Headlight 1⅛
Stem	Alloy A-Head Uplift
Handlebars	Forma (TTT)
Handlebar tape	Cinelli cork with Marsas foam padding
Chainset	TA Zephyr 150 mm (with TA 6 mm self-extracting bolts)
Chainrings	TA 20/34/40 (started with 25/4/12)
Chain	Sachs PC68
Bottom bracket	Shimano XT UN72
Front mech	Shimano RX 100
Rear mech	Shimano XT
Cassette	Shimano XT (11–34)
Gear levers	Shimano Dura Ace (downtube)

Brake levers	Campagnolo Super Record (with Campag white hoods)
Brakes	Shimano Deore XT Cantilever
Brake blocks	Shimano Deore XT
Pedals	TA Road Pedal (Campag copy)
Seat Post	Tranz X (alloy micro-adjust)
Saddle	Selle Italia trans am ldy
Racks	Tubus (seamless cromoly tubing). Front: Tara lowrider. Rear: Cargo
Water bottle cages	3 × Elite
Mudguards	SKS Chromo Plastics
Toe clips	Christophe, steel with leather toe protection
Toe straps	Mt Christophe
Computer	Speedmaster 7000
Bike lights	Front: Busch & Muller Lumotec Plus dynamo. Rear: Vistalite and Cateye (LED)
Bike stand	Esge Pletscher (double leg kick stand)
Mirrors	2 × Mirrycles

Panniers

Rear	Ortlieb Bike-Packer Plus (with additional outer pockets)
Front	Ortlieb Sport-Packer Plus (with additional outer pockets)
Handlebar bag	Ortlieb Ultimate 3 L Plus (with map case and inner pocket)
Rack packs	2 × Ortlieb roll-closure (size small)

Sleeping Arrangements

Tent	The North Face Tadpole (old style)
Pegs	10 × The North Face Super Tent Peg plus a small aluminium sleeve (in case of pole breakage)
Groundsheet	The North Face Tadpole Footprint plus a cheap plastic sheet cut to fit tent bell-end

Bivi bag	Mountain Range Goretex
Tent	The North Face Roadrunner 2 (used when joined by mother or builder)
Sleeping bag	The North Face Blue Igloo
Silk sleeping bag	Sea to Summit (Traveller)
Sleeping mat	Karrimor Karrimat Expedition, ¾-length
Sitting mat	Small square Karrimat (for sitting on in cold wet places)

Kitchen Department

Stove: MSR Superfly (canister mount)

Gas canisters: mixture of Coleman, Camping Gas and Go-Gas

Saucepan: MSR Alpine 2 -litre pot with detachable MSR pan handle

1.5-litre Addis round plastic pot with lid

Mini chopping board

Big plastic mug

2 × plastic screw top containers for decanting honey etc.

Plastic spout pot for decanting soy sauce

2 × small pots for decanting tins of beans etc.

Small serrated Kitchen Devil knife with homemade protective sheath

Kuhn Rikon vegetable peeler

Lightweight stainless steel spoon

Permaware plastic teaspoon

Lighter

Small box of matches

A few plastic-bag ties

Old pair of rubber gloves, cut up to make spectacular Blue Peter-style rubber
bands for sealing food bags etc.

Mini pot scourer

Mini tea-towel

3 × water bottles (to fit bicycle frame-mounted water cages – Specialised and
Nalgene)

4-litre Ortlieb water bag

Small Flexi Flask

Plastic bags – lots

Food – have always got porridge oats, honey, raisins and rice cakes on board

Clothing

(I didn't take all of the following all of the time, but I took most of it most of the time)

Specialised cycling helmet (started ride with an Allez and finished it with an S1)

Freestyle Goretex helmet cover

Karrimor O2 Stretch Jacket

Pair of Karrimor O2 Overtrousers

Mountain Hardware Ascent Parka

The North Face Ama Damlam jacket

Marmot lightweight jacket

Gore Bike Wear Goretex jacket

Gore Bike Wear windproof gillet

Pearlizumi Zephyr jacket

Rohan Backpacker Top

North Cape Thermolite Plus

The North Face Expedition fleece

The North Face El Cap shirt

Pair of Lowe Alpine zip-off trousers

Pair of Pearlizumi Women's Journey Shorts

Two pairs Corinne Dennis cycling shorts

Two pairs Pearlizumi cycling leggings

Two sleeveless T-shirts

The North Face T-shirt

Pair of Pearlizumi thermal leggings

Pearlizumi thermal long-sleeved shirt

Pair of Specialised Pro cycling mitts

Pair of The North Face Windstopper gloves

Pair of Mountain Hardware Ascent gloves

Pair of Extremities Goretex overmitts

Fleece hat

Fila baseball cap (found in road)

Pair of Porelle waterproof socks

Pair of Eager Clothing Overshoes

Buff neck gaiter

Trekmates Windstopper Face Mask

Light cotton scarf

454

Pair of Salomon hill-walking shoes
Pair of flip-flops
Pair of Madison short liners
Three pairs knickers
Two sports bras
Two pairs Pearlizumi white ankle socks
Pair of Pearlizumi black ankle socks
Speedo swimming costume
Pair of Speedo swimming goggles

Washbag/First Aid and Other Paraphernalia

Mini fast-drying travel towel
Lightweight stuffsack washbag filled with toothbrush, toothpaste, dental floss, shampoo, soap, razor, bodily unguents etc.
Mini flannel
Stash of toilet paper, Tampax and other such lovelies
Lip-salve
Sun-block cream (which blocked the sun a little too effectively – I only saw rain)
Tiger Balm (good for aching muscles and making your eyes water)
Arnica (pills and potion)
10 ml bottle tea tree essential oil (good antiseptic)
10 ml bottle lavender oil (good for anything from burns and insect bites to soporific pillow aromas)
Pot of Higher Nature Glucosamine Hydrochloride tablets for knee manoeuvrability
Pair of washable foam earplugs
Eyeshade (for blocking out light of glaring streetlights etc.)
Small selection of plasters, safety pins, needles and extra strong 100% polyester thread
Knee support bandage
Mini Swiss Army tweezers
Mini mirror, mini nail clippers and clothes pegs
Biro; pencil; half a rubber; permanent black marker pen; mini Pritt Stick; mini Sellotape; writing paper and envelopes; stamps; 'business' cards
Small notebook

Dictaphone (Sony M-530V)

Casio solar-powered credit card-size calculator

Oxford Minidictionary

Mini address book

Books – usually have at least three on board

Michelin map of the British Isles

Ordnance Survey Road Atlas of Britain 1:190000 (3 miles to 1 inch)

YHA map of hostels

Mini compass

Mini Field and Trek thermometer

Mini Maglite Solitaire torch on keyring

Inova Microlight

Leatherman Wave pocket knife

Wallet with cash, credit card (unused), service till card, YHA membership
    card, CTC membership card, organ donor card

Passport

Driving licence

Nokia 5210 mobile phone (bought it halfway through journey – spoke on it
    twice; used it for texting rest of the time)

Mobile phone charger

Dog Dazer (for dazing good-for-nuttin' dawgs – more info on 01733 315888 or
    www.dazer.com)

Petzl Micro headtorch

Petzl LED Tikka headtorch

Pair of Oakley Eye Jacket sunglasses with padded pouch

Mini Sony shortwave radio

Casio digital watch (which rarely saw the light of day)

Cannon Sureshot camera

Cannon AE1 Programme (SLR) with Tamron 70-210 lens (started out with this
    but later changed it for Pentax Espio 160)

Mini Minox tripod

Jessops Atlantic Alfa 3 tripod (didn't carry this with me the whole time)

10 × Fujicrome Sensia 200 ASA film (36 exps)

Spare batteries for cameras, torches, radio and LED rear bike light

Leica 8 × 20 BCA mini binoculars

The North Face Borealis daypack

The North Face bumbag

Bicycle Tools and Bicycle Bits

Two spare inner tubes
Three plastic tyre levers; puncture repair kit
Emergency tyre patch
Spare spokes, brake and gear cables
Allen keys – to fit all allen bolts on bike
Park cone spanner (for pedals)
Mini adjustable spanner
Chainlink tool (plus few spare links)
Shimano cassette remover
Spoke key
Few spare nuts, bolts, washers, zip ties, webbing, pannier clips
Gaffer tape, insulating tape, short length 4 mm rock-climbing cord
Karabiner
Mini pot of Finish Line Cross Country oil; rag; rubber gloves
Topeak Road Morph bicycle pump
Four bungees
Cable lock and padlock
Cheap bike cover
Reflective vest

*For the latest news about Josie's travels and
information on all her books,
please visit her website at:*

www.josiedew.co.uk